OXFORD STUDIES IN EUROPEAN LAW

The Governance of Migration in the European Union

OXFORD STUDIES IN EUROPEAN LAW

Series Editors:
Paul Craig, Professor of English Law at St John's College, Oxford and
Gráinne de Búrca, Professor of Law at the European University Institute, and
Florence Ellinwood Allen Professor of Law at New York University

The aim of this series is to publish important and original research on EU law. The focus is on scholarly monographs, with a particular emphasis on those which are interdisciplinary in nature. Edited collections of essays will also be included where they are appropriate. The series is wide in scope and aims to cover studies of particular areas of substantive and of institutional law, historical works, theoretical studies, and analyses of current debates, as well as questions of perennial interest such as the relationship between national and EU law and the novel forms of governance emerging in and beyond Europe. The fact that many of the works are interdisciplinary will make the series of interest to all those concerned with the governance and operation of the EU.

OTHER TITLES IN THIS SERIES

The Eurosceptic Mobilization of Constitutional Law
Pablo Castillo-Ortiz and Giuseppe Martinico

The Law of EU Border Controls
Constitutional Compliance and Conditions for an Area without Internal Frontiers
Leandro Mancano

The Competence Question in the (Con) Federal European Union
Sacha Garben

Protecting EU Consumers in Internet of Things Ecosystems
The Intersection between Consumer, Competition, and Data
Christof Koolen

When Deportation Fails
Non-Removable Migrants in the European Union
Diego Ginés Martín

EU Values in Investment Law and Policy
Promises of Democracy and Rule of Law?
Maria Laura Marceddu

Legal Mobilization for Migrant Rights
Opportunities and Barriers at the European Court of Justice
Virginia Passalacqua

Saving the European Union from its Illiberal Member States
András Jakab and Lando Kirchmair

Constitutional Disintegration and Disruption
Withdrawal and Opt-Outs from the European Union
Oliver Garner

Business Freedoms and Fundamental Rights in European Union Law
Niall O'Connor

Compliance with European Consumer Law
The Case of E-Commerce
Felix Pflücke

Legislative Authority and Interpretation in the European Union
Martijn van den Brink

Secession and European Union Law
The Deferential Attitude
Núria González Campañá

Fiscal State Aid Law and Harmful Tax Competition in the European Union
Dimitrios Kyriazis

The Abuse of Constitutional Identity in the European Union
Julian Scholtes

Judging European Democracy
The Role and Legitimacy of National Constitutional Courts in the EU
Nik de Boer

EU Values Before the Court of Justice
Foundations, Potential, Risks
Luke Dimitrios Spieker

Postnational Constitutionalism
Europe and the Time of Law
Paul Linden-Retek

The Legislative Priority Rule and the EU Internal Market for Goods
A Constitutional Approach
Eadaoin Ní Chaoimh

The Jurisprudence of Constitutional Conflict in the European Union
Ana Bobić

Reflexive Governance in EU Equality Law
Emma Lantschner

The Governance of Migration in the European Union

Law, Politics, and the Emergence of 'Formal Informality'

PAUL JAMES CARDWELL, *FAcSS, PFHEA, PHD*
Professor of Law and Vice Dean (Education), King's College London, UK

OXFORD
UNIVERSITY PRESS

OXFORD
UNIVERSITY PRESS

Great Clarendon Street, Oxford, OX2 6DP,
United Kingdom

Oxford University Press is a department of the University of Oxford.
It furthers the University's objective of excellence in research, scholarship,
and education by publishing worldwide. Oxford is a registered trade mark of
Oxford University Press in the UK and in certain other countries.

Published in the United States of America by Oxford University Press
546 Fifth Avenue, New York, NY 10036, United States of America.

British Library Cataloguing in Publication Data
Data available

Library of Congress Control Number: 2026946378

ISBN 9780192856227

DOI: 10.1093/9780191946592.001.0001

Printed and bound by
CPI Group (UK) Ltd., Croydon, CR0 4YY

The manufacturer's authorized representative in the EU for product safety is
Oxford University Press España S.A. of Parque Empresarial San Fernando de Henares,
Avenida de Castilla, 2 – 28830 Madrid (www.oup.es/en or product.safety@oup.com).
OUP España S.A. also acts as importer into Spain of products made by the manufacturer.

MIX
Paper | Supporting
responsible forestry
FSC
www.fsc.org
FSC® C013604

For my mother, Carol Cardwell
3 February 1949–31 December 2025

Series Editors' Preface

There are significant challenges posed by external migration, connoting those seeking entry to the EU from outside its borders. The difficulties are to some extent endemic, but have become more especially marked in the period since 2015. It is unsurprising that measures to meet the challenges posed by such migration have become a standard feature on the agendas of the EU institutions as well as those of the Member States. This study is therefore timely. It explores EU migration against the backdrop of four principal themes.

The first is the place of migration within the EU as an integration project. While the subject is a relative latecomer to the EU's institutional set of competences, it has nonetheless had significant influence over EU policy, as the EU strives to demonstrate that something is being done to address the problem. The second theme is the way in which migration straddles the internal and the external spheres of EU competence. The third theme concerns the ways in which EU legislation in this area reflects two tensions at the heart of EU migration governance, in particular in relation to asylum-seekers and refugees. There is the tension between the commitment to international protection, with the implication of individual rights and accountability for EU and Member State actions, and the desire to ensure that individuals are contained in third countries and prevented from reaching the territory of the EU. There is also the tension between the removal of internal borders within the EU and retaining the immobility of asylum-seekers and refugees under EU law. The fourth theme explores the idea of 'crisis' that besets discourse in this area.

These four themes structure the analysis in the book concerning the EU's contemporary governance of migration into the Union from outside its borders. The book explores migration governance through the prism of the distinction, or lack thereof, between the formal and the informal. There is discussion of the governance turn in EU studies, and how the identification and study of governance and new modes of governance in the 1990s and 2000s enriched our understanding of law and policymaking. This is followed by the framework of EU migration law and policy, and the ways in which legislative developments reflect the principal policy documents that give direction to the development of measures on the basis of Treaty competences. The focus then shifts to analysis of the numerous strategic documents devoted to migration and tracks how and why the emphasis on legislation as a key part of the integration or cooperation process has gone in waves. There is then discussion of the internal and external spheres of governance, and the inter-institutional competences that prevail in this area, followed by chapters that consider in greater detail the instruments that have emerged in migration governance.

This book explores a topic that is important in itself, with broader implications for the future of the European project. It will be of interest to all those who study EU law.

Paul Craig and Gráinne de Búrca

Preface

This book is the product of more than a decade of reflection on migration governance in the EU. My interest was sparked by a single reference to 'tools and instruments' in an EU strategic document that suggested to me that there was a rich category of law-like phenomena in this externally focused sphere that had not been systematically analysed. Having presented my ideas at various law, political science, and interdisciplinary conferences and workshops over the years that followed, I published some initial research findings, before deciding that the subject could only be done justice via a full-length monograph.

So, I embarked on the process of putting together the 'difficult second album'. Writing a full-length monograph is always a challenging process, and especially in such a dynamic and fast-moving area of law and policy. But the past decade has been especially difficult for European Studies academics based in the UK, for whom the future prospects of research, writing, and teaching about Europe and the EU were suddenly thrown into doubt. As a good friend once aptly characterized, most academics have a 'blended life', where the professional and the personal are often intertwined. This is certainly the case for me, where the impact of Brexit was more than just concern for my professional and research career, but also about my family, friends, and communities—both local and scholarly. Adding into the mix the birth of our son, a pandemic, and several changes of institution before arriving at King's College London as Professor of Law and taking on the demanding roles of Vice Dean (Education) and the co-editorship of the *JCMS: Journal of Common Market Studies*, it has been a busy few years, which has at times slowed progress on this book.

During the same period of the late 2010s, the EU's use of informality and avoidance of familiar legal processes became more widespread and prominent in the public domain. In the midst of a migration 'crisis'—which most commentators agree was a crisis of how to respond to migration pressures rather than an unprecedented situation in terms of numbers involved—the EU institutions and Member States sought out new ways forward. The rapid production of the EU–Türkiye Statement 2016 was a watershed moment in putting the spotlight on innovative ways to confront migration challenges in the midst of a 'crisis'. The Statement did not appear out of thin air, but rather as a product of longer-term institutional developments and interactions that this book seeks to uncover and explain. Since 2016, the institutional energy devoted to migration has increased exponentially, with a constant stream of strategic documents under a variety of guises and names, legislative proposals, cases before the Courts, and other initiatives constantly appearing. Such is the volume of the content in migration governance that I must apologize in advance for any omissions. The law is stated as at February 2026, and any remaining errors are my own.

One result of the heightened attention to migration and the EU's responses to it has been the impressive growth of a vibrant, interdisciplinary research community of scholars. The volume of literature looking at EU and Member State laws, policies, and practices relating to all the many different types and facets of migration is considerable, and I hope to have done justice to it here. It is no exaggeration to say that such is the depth and quality of such scholarship, including on informality, that it is now common practice to look beyond legal instruments to understand what the EU is doing and how. This is a major change in the way in which we understand EU law from when I began my career in the early 2000s. What I hope this book achieves is to continue this trajectory and offer a way of analysing instances of 'formal informality' that have arisen through the succession of EU strategies and institutional interactions in the EU's maturing system of governance.

This book would not have been possible without the support of many wonderful colleagues over the past decade at Sheffield, Strathclyde, City University of London, and my present institution, King's College London, including the Deans and Heads whom it has been a pleasure to work with: Claire McDiarmid, Andrew Stockley, Richard Ashcroft, Alex Türk (much missed), and Dan Hunter. I am very grateful to my student research assistants at King's, Louis Smith and Mariana Traykova, for their help, and for the funding provided by the Dickson Poon School of Law and King's Undergraduate Research Fellowship (KURF) scheme.

At King's, there are too many people to thank individually, but in the School of Law I am particularly grateful to Vigjilenca Abazi, Tanya Aplin, Yasmin Begum, Andrea Biondi, Mike Butler, Stephen Daly, James Dixon, Emma Eglington, Caitlin English, Alvaro Fernandez, Lloyd Gash, Polly Goodfellow, Grace Harkin, Darren Harvey, Andi Hoxhaj, Lesley Hulmes, Michelle Johnson, Phillip Johnson, Alison Jones, Satvinder Juss, Dionysia Katelouzou, Greta Kleen Gonzalez, Michelle Johnson, Anat Keller, Christoph Kletzer, Susanne Krieg, James Lee, Yael Lifshitz, Lerong Lu, Mark Lunney, Catharine MacMillan, Isidora Maletic, Nathan Marshall, Colm McGrath, Jamal Miah, Ivy Miller, Ann Mumford, Chris Norton, Federico Ortino, Shaila Pal, Gemma Pountney, Hannah Quirk, Massimo Renzo, Niccolò Ridi, Solène Rowan, Djakhongir Saidov, Irit Samet, Michael Schillig, Chloe Sheppick, Oana Stefan, Takis Tridimas, Joe Tomlinson, Caroline van Hensbergen, Vilija Vėlyvytė, Elin Weston, Lorenzo Zucca, plus the entire team of Vice Deans (Education), and many others, all of whom have helped me navigate the challenges of joining a new institution in a senior role, and supported the writing process in different ways. Working with my *JCMS* co-editors, Roberta Guerrina and Gabriel Siles-Brügge, and supportive colleagues in the Judicial Appointments Commission, Law Schools Global League, and Council for At-Risk Academics (CARA) has been a joy.

Special thanks are also due to fellow EU and Migration Studies and other travellers who have been an invaluable source of inspiration and in different ways (and with apologies to anyone I have missed): Jo Shaw, Helen Drake, Steven Vaughan, Paul Copeland, Nando Sigona, Kenneth Armstrong, Fabricio Fortese, Federico Casolari, Michela Ceccorulli, Marie-Pierre Granger, Ariadna Ripoll Servant, Fabien Terpan, Juan Santos Vara, Eleftheria Markozani, Foteini Asderaki, Hila Zahavi, Sharon Pardo, Ariadna Ripoll Servent, Toni Haastrup, Stéphane Beaulac, Owen Parker, Tamara Ćapeta, Richard Kirkham, Archil Chochia, Florian Trauner, Richard Collins, Veronica Ruiz Abou-Nigm, Ian Manners, Annika Bergman Rosamond, Ben Rosamond, Ramses Wessel, Balkissa Diallo, Simon Lightfoot, Damir Banović, Dimitry Kochenov, Sarah Ganty, Ester Herlin-Karnell, Jacob Öberg, Marja-Liisa Öberg, Tamara Perišin, Lilian Tsourdi, Eraj Haidari, Andrew Geddes, Saeed Bagheri, Dimitris Bouris, Will Daniel, Rebecca Zahn, Emma Nesbit (RIP), and the Newton family (Dan, Kerry, Paddy and Sam). Tamara Hervey has been an exceptional help in talking through the ideas behind this project and fine-tuning them as the book took shape. I am also grateful to the series editors, Gráinne de Búrca and Paul Craig, and colleagues at Oxford University Press, particularly Kezia Johnson, Alexander Hardie-Forsyth, and Paulina Dos Santos Major. I would also like to thank the anonymous peer reviewers of the proposal and the manuscript text for their helpful comments.

The final thanks are to those closest to me, for whom words cannot express my gratitude. To Carol and Alan Cardwell, my parents; Ian, Gayle, and Oliver Cardwell; Cathy and Jean-Eudes Dunant; Jérôme Dunant, Paola Ruiz, and Antoine Dunant; Stephanie, Robin, and Axel Killip; Anna Williams; and Tania Sydorenko. And finally, to my husband Etienne Dunant and our son, Thomas, with my eternal thanks for putting up with the long process of me writing a book—and yet another book which manages to have no pictures at all in it.

Sheffield and London, March 2026

Contents

Table of Cases

COURT OF JUSTICE OF THE EUROPEAN UNION

GENERAL COURT

EUROPEAN COURT OF HUMAN RIGHTS

Table of Legislation

DIRECTIVES

REGULATIONS

DECISIONS

OTHER EUROPEAN UNION INSTRUMENTS

INTERNATIONAL INSTRUMENTS

Abbreviations

ACP	African Caribbean and Pacific States
ALDE	Alliance of Liberals and Democrats for Europe Party
AMMR	Asylum and Migration Management Regulation
CAMM	Common Agendas on Migration and Mobility
CEAS	Common European Asylum System
CETA	EU–Canada Comprehensive Economic and Trade Agreement
CFSP	Common Foreign and Security Policy
CJEU	Court of Justice of the European Union
CSDP	Common Security and Defence Policy
DCI	Development Cooperation Instrument
DG	Directorate General (of the European Commission)
EASO	European Asylum Support Office
ECHR	European Convention on Human Rights
ECOWAS	Economic Community of West African States
ECtHR	European Court of Human Rights
EDF	European Development Fund
EEA	European Economic Area
EEAS	European External Action Service
ENI	European Neighbourhood Instrument
ENP	European Neighbourhood Policy
EPA	Economic Partnership Agreement
ERF	European Refugee Fund
EU	European Union
EUAA	European Union Agency for Asylum
EUCAP	EU Capacity Building Mission (in Mali, Sahel, Niger, and Somalia)
EURODAC	EU Fingerprint Database (European Dactyloscopy)
EUROMED	Euro-Mediterranean Partnership
EUROPOL	European Union Agency for Law Enforcement Cooperation
EUROSUR	European Border Surveillance system
EUTF	EU Trust Fund for Africa
FRiT	Facility for Refugees in Turkey
FRONTEX	European Border and Coast Guard Agency
FSJ	(Area of) Freedom, Security and Justice
GAM	Global Approach to Migration
GAMM	Global Approach to Migration and Mobility
IMMA	Irregular Migration Management Application
ICMPD	International Centre for Migration Policy Development
ILO	Immigration Liaison Officers
IOM	International Office for Migration

JHA	Justice and Home Affairs
MEP	Member of the European Parliament
MLG	Multi-level Governance
MOC	ADEM Operational coordination mechanism for the external dimension of migration
MOU	Memorandum of Understanding
MPF	Migration Partnership Framework
NGO	Non-Governmental Organization
OECD	Organisation for Economic Cooperation and Development
OLAF	European Anti-Fraud Office
OMC	Open Method of Coordination
PES	Party of European Socialists
QMV	Qualified Majority Voting
RABIT	Rapid Border Intervention Team
SIS	Schengen Information System
TCN	Third Country National
TEU	Treaty on European Union
TFEU	Treaty on the Functioning of the European Union
TTIP	EU–US Transatlantic Trade and Investment Partnership
UN	United Nations
UNHCR	United National High Commissioner for Refugees
VFA	Visa Facilitation Agreement

Introduction

> Migration is a fact of life and a force for good. It promotes the exchange of knowledge and ideas and contributes to economic growth. It enables millions of people to pursue opportunities and improve their lives. At the same time, poorly governed migration is a cause of great suffering.
>
> António Guterres, United Nations Secretary-General[1]

> Migration challenges need a European response with a fair and firm approach based on our values.
>
> Ursula Von der Leyen, President of the European Commission[2]

> The best migrant is the migrant who does not come. The best number is zero.
>
> Victor Orbán, former Prime Minister of Hungary[3]

Is migration the defining topic of the day in twenty-first-century Europe? At least arguably so. Barely a day goes by without migration dominating news headlines across the continent. Electoral battles focus ever more on migration as the issue which distinguishes political parties from each other, even as discourse from political actors across the spectrum increasingly hardens against incoming migrants. The work of the courts, including both national courts and the Court of Justice of the European Union (CJEU), deals with a constant flow of migration-related questions in what has become a complex and ever-changing legal and political landscape. Migration, according to the President of the Commission, 'is a common European challenge, that requires a common European solution'.[4] Other European

[1] António Guterres, 'Migration is a fact of life and a "force for good"' (UN, 18 December 2023) https://news.un.org/en/story/2023/12/1144897, accessed 9 June 2025.

[2] Ursula Von der Leyen, Statement at the European Parliament Plenary by President Ursula von der Leyen, candidate for a second mandate 2024–2029 (18 July 2024), https://enlargement.ec.europa.eu/news/statement-european-parliament-plenary-president-ursula-von-der-leyen-candidate-second-mandate-2024-2024-07-18_en, accessed 9 June 2025.

[3] Victor Orbán (22 January 2016). In Hungarian, 'a legjobb bevándorló a nem jövő bevándorló, tehát a legjobb szám a nulla', available in Hungarian at https://2015-2022.miniszterelnok.hu/orban-viktor-a-kossuth-radio-180-perc-cimu-musoraban-20160122/, as reported in English, available at https://www.dw.com/en/hungary-to-block-passage-for-migrants-calls-for-fences/a-18999604, accessed 9 June 2025. I am grateful to Viktor Szép for help locating the original Hungarian source.

[4] Ursula Von der Leyen, Statement by President von der Leyen with Friedrich Merz, Federal Chancellor of the Federal Republic of Germany (9 May 2025) https://ec.europa.eu/commission/presscorner/detail/ov/statement_25_1173, accessed 9 June 2025.

The Governance of Migration in the European Union. Paul James Cardwell, Oxford University Press.
 DOI: 10.1093/9780191946592.003.0001

politicians go further and reflect the position of the second Trump administration in the US, claiming that there is no more urgent challenge facing Europe than mass migration.[5] The characterization of migration as a challenge and a crisis cuts across many parts of the political spectrum across the continent and beyond.

For at least the period since 2015, the prioritization of measures to meet the 'challenges' of migration, as they are often termed, has thus become a standard fixture on the agendas of the EU institutions as well as those of the Member States. The challenges brought by inward migration intersect with many other challenges facing the contemporary EU, of which migration is only one. But migration deserves particular attention, not least because it is an area where the responses are found across the EU's internal and external spheres of governance, in different policy areas and institutional logics.[6]

There is little doubt that, in such a fast-moving area, where legal and political solutions are constantly sought for a perceived migration 'crisis', there is a strong emphasis on short-term measures and solutions, and finding new ways to do things, often as a means to show something is being 'done'.[7] But short-term measures can, of course, have longer-term effects which go beyond a period of 'crisis' and contribute to a shifting idea about what the EU is and does, particularly with regard to law-making. Some of these measures have the appearance of law in that they employ names and forms which appear like law, but not as we know it. An 'agreement' between the EU and a third state follows an established procedure—a 'statement' or Memorandum of Understanding (MOU) does not, but may nevertheless have similar effects. This is the essence of 'formal informality' in law-making, the use of which carries particular risks for the protection of rights and undermining of transparency and accountability associated with 'formal' legal instruments. These underlying questions guide the inquiry in this book.

Exploring EU migration governance therefore reveals four key themes. First is the place migration occupies within the EU as an integration project. Migration is a relative latecomer to the EU's institutional set of competences and, although legislation has emerged on the basis of the competences introduced by the Treaty of Amsterdam, it cannot be categorized as an area where the Member States have committed to harmonization. Yet harmonization is still understood—at the very least in legal scholarship—as the dominant mode of European integration. If migration is a common and important European challenge, what does it mean to say that the dominant mode of European integration is not fit for purpose to rise to

[5] JD Vance, Vice President of the United States, Speech at the Munich Security Conference 14 February 2025, https://securityconference.org/assets/02_Dokumente/01_Publikationen/2025/Selected_Key_Speeches_Vol._II/MSC_Speeches_2025_Vol2_Ansicht_gekürzt.pdf, accessed 9 June 2025.

[6] Graham Butler, 'Legal Responses to the EU's Migration Crisis' (2018) 19 San Diego International Law Journal 282.

[7] Giuseppe Campesi, 'Defining "Crisis" in Migration Governance: A Critical Legal Mapping of EU Crisis Response Mechanisms' (2024) 26(1) European Journal of Migration and Law 26.

this challenge? Over time, as migration has come to dominate national debates across the EU (and beyond), it has thus become bound up with powerful forces rejecting the nature of EU integration entirely, or pushing the EU institutions to act in ways which have not traditionally fit with the institutions' normative power projection of peaceful cooperation. Externalization of borders and the promotion of 'fortress Europe' (a term originally used to denote economic protectionism) are part of a continent-wide shift to impose 'tough' policies on inward migration and show that external borders are 'under control'.[8] Law, both national and EU, has become a key tool in proving to sceptical publics that something is 'being done'. The nature of that law—and what it tells us about the contemporary EU and its system of governance—is the focus of this book.

Second, migration straddles the internal and the external spheres of EU competences. Here, we find the nature of the EU as distinct from a nation state raising some of the familiar challenges for the EU's role in an international relations arena that struggles to handle the status of non-state actors. The EU as a global actor has made important contributions to international law on migration, despite its lack of statehood.[9] But here the familiar arguments about national sovereignty also come to the fore. The conclusion of the intergovernmental conference on the Global Compact for Migration[10] revealed sharp differences between the Member States, resulting in several of the (then) twenty-eight Member States not signing it, though for different reasons.[11] The consequent lack of a negotiating mandate for an externally facing instrument of 'soft law' binding the EU in international relations with third states exposed the limited ability of the EU institutions to forge consensus and enforce the principle of sincere cooperation.[12]

For an EU facing thus a common challenge, the obstacles in forging a consensus both in the global political arena and in the context of EU law-making are considerable. A third theme takes up discussion of these obstacles and how they are reflected in EU migration legislation. Legislation reflects two tensions at the heart of EU migration governance, and in particular towards asylum seekers and refugees, where the weight of the legislation has fallen. As identified by Tsourdi and Costello, the first is between the commitment or obligation of international protection—implying corresponding individual rights and accountability for

[8] James Hampshire, 'Speaking with One Voice? The European Union's Global Approach to Migration and Mobility and the Limits of International Migration Cooperation' (2016) 42(4) Journal of Ethnic and Migration Studies 571, 573.

[9] Tamás Molnár, 'The EU Shaping the Global Compact for Safe, Orderly and Regular Migration: The Glass Half Full or Half Empty?' (2020) 16(3) International Journal of Law in Context 321.

[10] On the Global Compact, see Antoine Pécoud, 'Narrating an Ideal Migration World? An Analysis of the Global Compact for Safe, Orderly and Regular Migration' (2021) 42(1) Third World Quarterly 16.

[11] Those declining to sign included Austria, which held the Council Presidency at the time. See further, Diego Badell, 'The EU, Migration and Contestation: The UN Global Compact for Migration, from Consensus to Dissensus' (2020) 6(4–5) Global Affairs 347.

[12] Pauline Melin, 'The Global Compact for Migration: Lessons for the Unity of EU Representation' (2019) 21(2) European Journal of Migration and Law 194.

EU and/or Member State actions—and the desire to ensure that individuals are contained in third countries and prevented from reaching the territory of the EU. The second tension is in the removal of internal borders (both physical and legal) within the EU while retaining the immobility of asylum seekers and refugees under EU law.[13] In the absence of harmonization, there are considerable disparities between Member States on the national legal regimes and resources made available, leading to unequal access to protection for asylum-seeking migrants and refugees depending on their physical location within the EU. This is the opposite of the collective, harmonized, and shared EU-level approach that the Treaty sets out. Similarly, the EU's legislative institutions have been slow and the oft-repeated need to 'do something' about migration to meet public expectations sits uneasily with an institutional law-making framework which is complex and time-consuming. As a result, there is widespread recognition that the legislative framework is insufficient and fails to meet the stated aims originally introduced in the Treaty of Amsterdam.

While this insufficiency was already evident during the two phases of legislative reforms and recasting processes of EU migration law in the 2000s, it has become even more evident during the period since the migration 'crisis'. The idea of 'crisis' is a fourth theme taken up in the book. Despite a widespread sharing of the idea that all migration is a challenge leading to a permanent state of crisis, the differences between the Member States on what to do—and how this affects other policy areas, such as internal movement in the Schengen area—have exacerbated existing tensions and revealed problems which are not merely procedural but structural. More than that, the tensions between the Member States revealed deep unease with the principles that underpin the Common European Asylum System (CEAS), or even the basis for EU legislation more generally, namely solidarity.[14] Hence, short-term solutions, implied by the language of 'crisis', have taken the place of longer-term processes and there has been an increased use of informal tools and instruments which depart from traditional (or 'formal') means of law-making in the EU. Yet short-term 'crisis' 'solutions' become reified as feasible modes of (EU) governance, and take on much longer-term significance.

Using this context as a background, the contribution of this book is two-fold. First, the book provides a deep analysis of migration governance through the prism of a distinction between the formal and the informal (or the lack thereof) in legal dynamics. The book does so by taking into account an analytical

[13] Evangelina (Lilian) Tsourdi and Cathryn Costello, 'The Evolution of EU Law on Refugees and Asylum' in Paul Craig and Gráinne De Búrca (eds), *The Evolution of EU Law* (3rd edn, Oxford University Press 2021) 793, p 794. On the latter, see also Violeta Moreno-Lax, *Accessing Asylum in Europe: Extraterritorial Border Controls and Refugee Rights under EU Law* (Oxford University Press 2017).

[14] For example, the temporary solution was to pass measures to alleviate problems associated with the Dublin system and benefit Italy and Greece (Council Decisions 2015/1523 and 2015/1601). See Evangelina (Lilian) Tsourdi and Cathryn Costello, 'The Evolution of EU Law on Refugees and Asylum' in Paul Craig and Gráinne De Búrca, The Evolution of EU Law (3rd edn, Oxford University Press 2021) 793, p 806.

distinction—between the formal and informal—that might otherwise be missed by a focus either on the fully 'legal' or 'policy' or 'practice'. Legal scholarship in the field has not fully explored the dynamics of the relationship between different governance tools and how they interact with more familiar types of EU legislation or formal agreements as an emerging field of enquiry. The increase in and emphasis on the use of newer tools as a means to meet Treaty-based goals in migration has not been accompanied by a deeper understanding of their properties, potential effects, and relationship with legislative tools. Furthermore, the relationships between the formal and informal are an integral part of governance, capable of having effects on individuals and their rights, and shedding light on the dynamics of decision-making and accountability for decisions made.

Second, although the focus is on 'external' migration and hence relations with third countries, much of this book is about the approach of the EU to migration, its internal workings, and its projection as a foreign policy actor. The book gives an insight into what the EU is and stands for. Although much work has been undertaken on the EU and governance, less attention has been paid to the internal–external crossover. Migration differs fundamentally from many of the policy areas under the governance microscope. Since the values of the Union in its external relations are anchored on the protection of human rights and 'the strict observance and the development of international law',[15] these are naturally the focal point for consideration of the implications of the EU's migration governance.

The rationale for bringing the 'formal' and the 'informal' together under the banner of governance is as follows. It has long been recognized that a doctrinal approach to (EU) legal scholarship goes only part of the way towards understanding the dynamics between enforceable law and non-enforceable measures such as guidelines, which nevertheless can have legal (or, at the very least, law-like) effects. Familiar legal tools including regulations and directives and their counterparts in the external field, such as association agreements with third countries, are central to migration governance. But they do not provide the full picture. Over time, we have witnessed growing use of measures which are not within the category of formal law, in that they are neither enforceable nor—in many cases—justiciable. The EU institutions themselves have placed emphasis on the advantages in terms of their flexibility to changing circumstances and their avoidance of the use of lengthy processes of enactment. Multi-annual programmes have featured fewer proposals for legislation but rather emphasized the use of all available 'tools'.[16] Such a shift is common in areas where legislation is not always seen as desirable in meeting goals, such as social policy. Social policy, environmental policy, aspects of health, and education policies are among those which have been under the governance

[15] Article 3(5) TEU.

[16] European Council, 'The Stockholm Programme: An Open and Secure Europe Serving and Protecting Citizens' [2010] C115/01, 7.

microscope for at least the past twenty years.[17] But it is still relatively uncommon to apply the same frame of analysis to migration as an externally facing sphere. In doing so, and bringing into focus the panoply of measures, policies, tools, instruments, and practices that play a role in shaping the governance of migration, we can more fully appreciate what this means for the EU, its own system of governance, and its values—and, at least as importantly, for individuals and respect for their rights. As noted above, particular attention is paid to 'formal informality' via the study of tools and instruments which share some characteristics of familiar law but, crucially, do not have the procedural safeguards in place to protect rights or ensure scrutiny.

The language of governance is thus appropriate for contemporary migration as the object of study. Although 'governance' is used so widely and in so many different contexts that it risks becoming meaningless through overuse, here the use is deliberate: the language of governance is capable of catching the legal, political, and institutional complexities of dealing with migration while at the same time allowing for emphasis on the (potential) effects of phenomena on individuals and what they tell us about the state of the EU today. As such, the definition adopted in this book is that provided by Rhodes, in which governance signifies 'a change in the meaning of government, referring to a new process of governing; or a changed condition of ordered rule; or the new method by which society is governed'.[18] Here, the latter part of the definition applies to European society insofar as migration law- and policymaking is undertaken by the EU and its Member States in conjunction, though the importance of the EU as an actor and the impact of its actions in migration can reasonably stretch the notion of 'society' much wider. In other words, migration governance is frequently framed in terms of the protection of European society but actually contributes to our understanding of global society too, due to the EU's weight as an international actor and agenda-setter.[19]

'Migration' and 'migrant' are used as the primary terms in this book to refer to the object of governance. Neither come with a precise definition in law, whether in the Member States, EU law, or international law. The interchangeability of categories of migration and the often deliberate blurring of categories in law and policymaking mean that terms which do come with a precise legal definition (such as 'refugee') are used when appropriate. It is recognized that reducing an individual's identity to that of their act of having crossed a border or being treated as an 'other' in the state they find themselves in is unsatisfactory. One of the themes of the book

[17] See, inter alia, Gráinne de Búrca and Joanne Scott, 'Introduction' in Gráinne de Búrca and Joanne Scott (eds), *Law and New Governance in the EU and the US* (Hart Publishing 2006); Kenneth A Armstrong, *Governing Social Inclusion: Europeanization Through Policy Coordination* (Oxford University Press 2010).

[18] RAW Rhodes, 'The New Governance: Governing Without Government' (1996) 44(4) Political Studies 654.

[19] Elaine Fahey, *The Global Reach of EU Law* (Routledge 2017).

is to examine the extent to which transparency in law and policymaking—and thus accountability for Union actions—might be sidestepped by the emergence of different modes—and the purpose therefore of using 'migrant' here is to ensure the focus remains on those who are most at risk of being deprived of rights, wherever these might be found. 'Regular' and 'irregular' are the preferred terms to distinguish types of migration, rather than 'legal' and 'illegal', but it is important to recognize that their use implies a derogatory 'norm' of regularity against which a human being is being implicitly judged. 'Irregular' migration is used here in the generally accepted sense, that is to say, to refer to migration that takes place outside the laws, regulations, or international agreements governing the entry into or exit from a state of origin, transit, or destination.

In terms of the time period explored in this book, as noted above, the major start date for competence in external migration law and policymaking was the Treaty of Amsterdam in 1998, which absorbed into the former first pillar the migration aspects of the intergovernmental third pillar of Justice and Home Affairs. Following Amsterdam, the European Council's Tampere Conclusions 1999 led to a proposed raft of legislative measures adopted pursuant to the Treaty which were (mostly) in place by 2004. Subsequent pieces of legislation have followed, but unevenly.[20] These measures are examined in more detail in Chapter 3. The successors to Tampere, the Hague and Stockholm Programmes, were launched in 2004 and 2009 and heralded the official emphasis on informal tools in migration governance. These were more explicitly recognized in the first iteration of the Global Approach to Migration (2005), later the Global Approach to Migration and Mobility (2011), which promoted the use of all available tools in migration governance. The European Neighbourhood Policy (ENP), which comprehensively covers all of the EU's neighbouring states (with the exception of the Russian Federation and Türkiye),[21] was launched in 2004 and provided the basis for and development of association and other bilateral agreements. As a result, Mobility Partnerships and other informal tools and practices began to appear in 2008.

The 'crisis' period in EU migration governance was initially regarded to be from 2015 until approximately 2019, with the focus on the increase in crossings from Türkiye to Greece and across the Mediterranean. The increasing use of 'crisis' in discourse since then, and the legal and political responses that it prompts, mean that this can also be applied to localized contexts which nevertheless maintain migration in its place high up on the agenda of the EU institutions.[22] The language of

[20] Steve Peers, 'The Rise and Fall of EU Justice and Home Affairs Law' in Maria Fletcher, Ester Herlin-Karnell, and Claudio Matera (eds), *The European Union as an Area of Freedom, Security and Justice* (Routledge 2017) 11–33.

[21] In this book, names of countries follow official, current usage. In particular, Cabo Verde, Côte d'Ivoire, Czechia, North Macedonia, and Türkiye are used throughout, except when quoting the official title of documents at the time they were issued (such as the EU–Turkey Statement) or when otherwise necessary.

[22] For example, Lampedusa (Italy) in 2011 and on the Finnish/Russian border in 2023.

crisis has in fact permeated the agenda since the early 2000s but was rather more localized—for example, relating to arrivals in Malta and the island of Lampedusa (Italy)[23]—but did prompt discussion about the appropriateness of legal instruments including the Dublin Regulations. The migration crisis since 2015 has, however, had a noticeable impact on the politics of many, if not all, Member States and the EU itself. Populist parties for whom migration has been a rallying call have experienced success across the continent, with other mainstream political parties internalizing positions that were previously regarded as the domains of extremists. While some measures to solve crises have been deliberately and loudly trumpeted, others were made more quietly. This book, therefore, adopts a longer-term perspective than the crisis since 2015.

As benefits a governance approach to migration, the sources used in this book are drawn from a variety of disciplines—primarily law, political science, and international relations, but also geography, social policy, and other disciplines that contribute to the broad landscape of interdisciplinary migration and EU studies. Alongside the academic literature from various fields, identifying the new processes of governing and considering a changed condition of ordered rule, as this book does, relies on analysing empirical material from official documentation from the institutions and agencies of the EU, the governments of Member States and third states, international organizations and non-governmental organizations (NGOs).[24]

The four main themes that are identified above provide the structure for the exploration in the rest of the book of the EU's contemporary governance of migration into the Union from outside its borders. The remaining chapters explore in greater detail the ways in which migration governance is subject to the emergence of new forms of governance, how we recognize them, and how to understand the effects they (might) have. Chapter 2 considers the governance turn in EU studies, and how the identification and study of governance and new modes of governance in the 1990s and 2000s enriched our understanding of law and policymaking. The chapter considers some of the policy areas in which new governance flourished, and reflects on why new governance appeared to be largely absent from both external relations and migration. In making the case that governance and new governance can be identified in contemporary migration law and policy, the chapter develops a theoretical governance framework drawing on institutional theory and constructivism. It argues that migration should be seen as a regular, and

[23] Elif Cetin, 'Migration in the Euro-Mediterranean Area' in Laure-Anne Bernes, Caroline Zickgraf, and Hassan Bousetta (eds), *Migration in the Western Mediterranean: Space, Mobility and Borders* (Routledge 2019).

[24] Andrew Geddes and Luca Lixi, 'New Actors and New Understandings in European Union External Migration Governance? The Case of EU–Tunisian Migration Relations' in Sergio Carrera, Leonhard Den Hertog, Marion Panizzon, and Dora Kostakopoulou (eds), *EU External Migration Policies in an Era of Global Mobilities: Intersecting Policy Universes* (Brill Nijhoff 2018) 60.

mainstream, part of European governance, despite its external focus. Therefore, the exploration of legal, policy, and institutional dimensions to migration governance and their formal and informal aspects should be seen in this light.

Chapter 3 set outs the framework of EU migration law and policy, tracking the legislative developments alongside the main policy documents that give direction to the development of measures on the basis of Treaty competences, in both regular and irregular migration. The chapter makes the case that, although legislation has been more limited than might be expected given its political salience on a long-term basis, the Treaty competences have allowed the institutions and the Member States to explore newer forms of governance over a significant period of time.

Chapter 4 connects the exploration of the law in Chapter 3 with the numerous strategic documents devoted to migration and tracks how and why the emphasis on legislation as a key part of the integration or cooperation process has gone in waves. Over time, the emphasis placed on formal legislation to meet goals in migration has largely declined, although with a more recent uptick in the New Migration Pact agreed in 2024.

Chapter 5 considers in more detail the internal and external spheres of governance, to dissect the inter-institutional competences, where the balances of power lie, and how frameworks for cooperation between Member States can give rise to informal governance. This is a significant aspect of the core argument, given the shared competences over migration, the emergence of measures that do not rely on formal legislative frames, and the creation of bodies (especially Frontex) that are both familiar within frames of governance and uncertain in terms of their formal role and responsibility.

Chapters 6 and 7 consider the degrees of formality in migration governance. Building on the previous two chapters, where the legal and policy frameworks and institutional dimensions were brought out, these two chapters consider in further detail the instruments that have emerged in migration governance. Chapter 6 analyses the extent to which the field is occupied by agreements or other 'formal' instruments that are provided for directly by Treaty competences, such as readmission agreements and multilateral agreements (such as with African, Caribbean, and Pacific (ACP) states) where migration is featured. Chapter 7 explores the instruments that have come to the fore in migration governance but lack formal definition, including Mobility Partnerships, and which do not follow a fixed template nor rely on Treaty competences. Special attention is devoted to the EU–Türkiye 'deal' of 2016 and the extent to which this innovation has proved resistant to legal definition or challenge but typifies the 'informal' approach in contemporary EU migration governance.

Finally, the concluding chapter brings together the findings and explains how the dynamism between the formal and the informal permits a better understanding of migration governance. In particular, it draws out how the Article 2 TEU values, including respect for human dignity, freedom, democracy, equality, the rule of law, and the rights of individuals, and also commitments to accountability, transparency, and good governance, are at stake. The chapter critiques the use of 'formal informality', where tools and instruments appear to have—but, crucially, lack—the procedural safeguards provided by law and legal processes. In doing so, the final chapter reflects on what contemporary migration governance in the EU tells us about the contemporary nature of the EU itself.

1
Defining the Scope of EU Migration Governance

Before taking office in November 2019, the incoming President of the European Commission, Ursula von der Leyen, sparked controversy by terming the portfolio of her appointee to the Commission for Migration as 'protecting the European way of life'. Condemnation, particularly by Members of the European Parliament, was swift.[1] The post was rapidly changed to '*Promoting* our European way of life', but the debacle was telling. Migration from outside the European Union has quickly risen to the top of the EU agenda and, in its characterization directly or indirectly in terms of a 'threat', has become intrinsically linked to the success of the European project as well as the future of Europe as we know it.

The advent of what has become characterized as a migration 'crisis' facing the EU has dominated policymaking since the mid-2010s. However, this book takes a longer-term look at the governance of migration. It analyses the extent to which law and policy towards managing migration to the EU has developed via the use of innovative tools and attempting to find solutions alongside established means. 'Platforms', 'pacts', 'statements', 'compacts', 'profiles', and 'arrangements' have come to be—at the very least—as widespread as familiar and formal legal instruments including directives, regulations, and agreements with third countries. Prominent examples such as the 2016 EU–Türkiye Statement[2] use similar language and are presented as law-like agreements, but in general lack the procedural and substantive safeguards associated with law. Crucially, these instruments bypass the Treaty-based processes that could—or perhaps should—have been used. Their legal effects, including the effects on individuals and rights, are thus often uncertain, along with their legitimacy, transparency, and accountability. As a result, informality tells us much about the contemporary state of EU law and governance and the Treaty-based values it is supposed to uphold.

Yet, much of what is happening in migration governance echoes other policy areas. Informality has been a common feature of governance within the EU over

[1] 'MEPs damn "protecting European way of life" job title' (*The Guardian*, 2019) https://www.theguardian.com/world/2019/sep/11/meps-damn-insulting-protecting-our-european-way-of-life-job-title, accessed 2 June 2025.

[2] European Council Press Releases, 'EU–Turkey statement, 18 March 2016' (European Council-Council of the European Union, 18 March 2016) https://www.consilium.europa.eu/en/press/press-releases/2016/03/18/eu-turkey-statement/, accessed 2 June 2025.

The Governance of Migration in the European Union. Paul James Cardwell, Oxford University Press.
 DOI: 10.1093/9780191946592.003.0002

the past twenty years and a recognized means to meet the EU's Treaty-based goals, especially in situations where legislation is neither viable nor desirable. This informality is often referred to as 'soft law', though there are important differences. Whilst often criticized on the grounds of lacking effectiveness or clarity, examples of 'new' governance, as it came to be known, have been extensively used in areas such as social policy. They have opened up opportunities to involve civil society or other actors in meeting goals without jeopardizing existing (legal) processes. Instead of top-down regulation by the institutions, instruments and mechanisms which promote sharing of good practice and building trust between a wide variety of actors can

Citizenship and EU Immigration: ACitizenship and EU Immigration: Apose questions as to the required standards of legitimacy, transparency, and accountability. But they are by no means the antithesis to effective governance.[3] Indeed, new governance has often been characterized as complementary to law, rather than replacing it and potentially beneficial for democratic governance.

Migration as an *externally* focused area has, in general, remained immune from this analysis, largely because external-facing areas are seen as part of, or akin to, foreign policy. In foreign policy, the place of law and regulation has traditionally been understood as limited. As a result, migration has usually been regarded as substantially different from many other areas where governance has been analysed.[4] Nevertheless, migration appears to have 'caught up' in scholarship on the EU, with a burgeoning interest in the actors, processes, and consequences of this important area on which the future existence of the EU as a polity has been linked.

This book considers the way in which governance has developed and what this means both for migration law and policy and for the EU itself, its internal governance, and its values. In making the case that a renewed understanding of governance can help uncover and explain contemporary developments in migration, we can also better understand the EU, its workings, and what its Treaty-based values mean in practice.

This chapter explores four of the main themes that are dealt with in detail in subsequent chapters. First, the parameters of 'external migration' and the EU are set out, noting the complexity of migration as a phenomenon and how adopting a wide scope of analysis permits a fuller understanding of the different types and forms of migration. After setting out in more detail the contribution of this book to the debate on migration, discussion turns to the EU itself, its role and competences in migration, and what makes this particular dimension of the integration process distinctive. The rationale for adopting the language of governance in this book is explored in the subsequent section, noting the ways in which this language is used

[3] This is explored more fully in the following chapter.

[4] Paul James Cardwell, 'Rethinking Law and New Governance in the European Union: The Case of Migration Management' (2016) 41(3) European Law Review 362–78.

(including in different disciplines) and exploring the challenges in applying it to the case of external migration. Finally, given that the focus of the book is on the external aspects of migration, the international, legal, and policy relationship between migration and foreign policy is discussed.

1.1 External migration and the European Union

The title of this book refers to migration but the emphasis is placed on what is often called external migration. External migration refers principally to the movement of individuals who enter, or attempt to enter, the territory of the EU and who are not citizens on an EU Member State. This definition is well-established in the literature,[5] but comes with significant caveats. External migration is not limited to the act of crossing an external border, but rather takes into account the legal status that accompanies an individual and the legal regime(s) that hence apply. External migration therefore brings within its scope the movement within the EU of individuals who are not EU citizens, and includes those who may never have crossed a border (such as children born to people who have migrated who do not have the citizenship of a Member State). This makes external migration distinct from 'immigration', which is usually referred to in the context of a nation state.

The most straightforward way to identify external migration in the EU is thus to discount what it does *not* cover as its main focus; that is to say, the movement or status of EU citizens using Treaty-based free movement rights. Here this is generally referred to as 'internal' migration, and provides a rationale for avoiding the use of 'immigration'/'emigration' in the context of the EU (as distinct from the Member States). Neither does it apply to EU citizens who leave the EU or re-enter in the future.

Governance of external migration is thus the range of law and policy measures that apply in full or in part to managing the way in which the different forms of migration—or potential migration—to the EU occur.[6] The scope of external migration covers a wide variety of individuals who migrate or have migrated, and may have done so via a variety of means, both regular and irregular, with their legal status fluctuating or uncertain.

[5] See, inter alia, Daniel Thym, 'European Migration Law Between "Rescuing" and "Taming" the Nation State: A History of Half-Hearted Commitment to Human Rights and Refugee Protection' (2024) 8(3) European Papers 1663–78; Philip Stutz, 'Political Opportunities, Not Migration Flows: Why the EU Cooperates More Broadly on Migration with Some Neighbouring States' (2023) 49(12) Journal of Ethnic and Migration Studies 3101–20; Mathias Czaika, Marta Bivand Erdal, and Cathrine Talleraas, 'Exploring Europe's External Migration Policy Mix: On the Interactions of Visa, Readmission, and Resettlement Policies' (2023) 49(12) Journal of Ethnic and Migration Studies 3140–61; and Georg Menz, 'The Promise of the Principal-Agent Approach for Studying EU Migration Policy: The Case of External Migration Control' (2015) 13(3) Comparative European Politics 307–24.

[6] See the further discussion in Chapter 2.

Migration occupies such a prominent place at the top of the EU's agenda that it is sometimes difficult to recall that it is a relatively late addition to the EU's competences. Furthermore, the rationale for giving the EU institutions competences in this field was at the outset part of the internally focused 'pillar' of Justice and Home Affairs in the Treaty of Maastricht,[7] which eventually became the external dimension of the (internal) Area of Freedom, Security and Justice, alongside the development of the (internal) Schengen area.[8] The current tendency is for official discourse to appear to almost exclusively focus on migration in terms of a 'crisis' or 'challenge' or as a result of 'waves' caused by events elsewhere in the world. Consequently, a strong emphasis emerges on preventing migration, often via the shifting of borders outwards, as if irregular migration is the only way in which people move to the EU. Yet, beyond this language of characterizing migration as a problem, migration is also part of the potential solution to many other problems faced by European states, not least the ageing society and declining population numbers, particularly in Eastern Europe (partly through free movement rights to elsewhere in the EU).

However, the idea and language of 'crisis' since 2015 has been strongly associated with the idea that the EU and its Member States are unable to cope with the influx of people, rather than unable to agree what the appropriate response(s) should be. Europe's ageing population, climate change, and uncertainty over the global economic and political order are intrinsically linked to migration.[9] In this respect, migration is often presented as a challenge in itself rather than as providing solutions, for example, to demographic changes. But longer-term challenges facing Europe are often not discussed within the same frames as political and legal responses to migration when characterized as a crisis or threat. The 'threat' has often been presented as one relating to Europe's security as well as its 'way of life'. As Scholten has argued, responding to migration as a complex problem via rapid changes does not allow for a fuller appreciation of the complexity of migration as a phenomenon

[7] Paul Craig and Gráinne de Búrca, *EU Law* (6th edn, Oxford University Press 2015) 965; Andrew Convey and Marek Kupiszewski, 'Keeping Up with Schengen: Migration and Policy in the European Union' (1995) 29(4) The International Migration Review 939–63.

[8] José Martín y Pérez de Nanclares, 'The External Dimension of the Area of Freedom, Security and Justice: An Essential Part of the European Union's External Action' in P Eeckhout and M Lopez-Escudero (eds), *The European Union's External Action in Times of Crisis* (Bloomsbury 2016).

[9] See, inter alia, Susan Martin, 'Climate Change, Migration, and Governance' (2010) 6(3) Global Governance 397–414; Gregory White, *Climate Change and Migration: Security and Borders in a Warming World* (Oxford University Press 2011); Kate Burrows and Patrick L Kinney, 'Exploring the Climate Change, Migration and Conflict Nexus' (2016) 13(4) International Journal of Environmental Research and Public Health 443–60; and specifically on Europe: Maria Julia Trombetta, 'Linking Climate-Induced Migration and Security within the EU: Insights from the Securitization Debate' (2014) 2(2) Critical Studies on Security 131–47; Leo Goff, Hilary Zarin, and Sherri Goodman, 'Climate-Induced Migration from Northern Africa to Europe: Security Challenges and Opportunities' (2012) 18(2) The Brown Journal of World Affairs 195–213; Giovanni Bettini, 'Where Next? Climate Change, Migration, and the (Bio)politics of Adaptation' (2017) 8 Global Policy 33–39; Elizabeth Ferris, 'Research on Climate Change and Migration: Where Are We and Where Are We Going?' (2020) 8(4) Migration Studies 612–25.

and its role in solving other complex challenges.[10] The 'crisification' of EU policy-making has only exacerbated this trend.[11]

Furthermore, the common characterization of the migration crisis as a *refugee* crisis points to only one singular aspect of migration to be 'solved'. Though often receiving less public attention, forms of regular migration to the EU and its Member States remain encouraged, and it is here competition between Member States and other developed economies for prized 'high-skilled' migration can be most obviously seen. Investor citizenship schemes operated by Member States are common and are a potential form of migration, since obtaining national citizenship of a Member State automatically confers EU citizenship, potentially with few obligations other than the financial. Until the Court of Justice recently found the Maltese scheme to be in breach of EU law,[12] investor citizenship as a form of migration had received much less attention in the public domain than the highly politicized focus on irregular crossing of borders.[13]

There is often an assumed and seemingly inescapable link between migration and 'borders', a link which connects directly to the securitization of EU migration.[14] Partly this is due to the emphasis placed on managing 'hotspots' where the visible arrival of migrants via irregular migration provides a visible representation of the challenges posed by migration, even if not representative of the whole.[15] The creation of Frontex, the EU external border agency, has focused attention on the shift in how management of migration works on the ground (or in the sea). But

[10] Peter Scholten, 'Mainstreaming versus Alienation: Conceptualising the Role of Complexity in Migration and Diversity Policymaking' (2020) 46 Journal of Ethnic and Migration Studies 108–26.

[11] Mark Rhinard, 'The Crisisification of Policy-Making in the European Union' (2019) 57(3) JCMS: Journal of Common Market Studies 616–33.

[12] C-181/23 *Commission v Malta (Investor Citizenship)* ECLI:EU:C:2025:283. See comment by Eric Fripp, 'EU Court of Justice finds Malta "golden passports" scheme incompatible with EU law' (EJIL: Talk!, 9 May 2025) https://www.ejiltalk.org/eu-court-of-justice-finds-malta-golden-passports-scheme-incompatible-with-eu-law/#:~:text = In%20an%20interesting%20and%20 important,with%20the%20principle%20of%20sincere; Dimitry Kochenov, 'Never Mind the Law, Again: Commission v Malta (C-181/23)' (Social Science Research Network, 29 April 2025) https://ssrn.com/abstract = 5250707, accessed 9 June 2025.

[13] Owen Parker, 'Commercializing Citizenship in Crisis EU: The Case of Immigrant Investor Programmes' (2017) 55(2) JCMS: Journal of Common Market Studies 332–48; Jelena Džankić, *The Global Market for Investor Citizenship* (Palgrave Macmillan 2019).

[14] See Gwendolyn Sasse, 'Securitization or Securing Rights? Exploring the Conceptual Foundations of Policies towards Minorities and Migrants in Europe' (2005) 43(3) JCMS: Journal of Common Market Studies 673–93; Andrew W Neal, 'Securitization and Risk at The EU Border: The Origins of FRONTEX' (2009) 47(2) JCMS: Journal of Common Market Studies, 333–56; Sarah Léonard, 'EU Border Security and Migration into the European Union: FRONTEX and Securitisation through Practices' (2010) 19(2) European Security 231–54.

[15] See further, Federico Casolari, 'The EU's Hotspot Approach to Managing the Migration Crisis: A Blind Spot for International Responsibility?' (2016) 25(1) The Italian Yearbook of International Law Online 109; Martina Tazzioli, 'Containment through Mobility: Migrants' Spatial Disobediences and the Reshaping of Control through the Hotspot System' (2016) 44 (16) Journal of Ethnic and Migration Studies 2764; Chiara Loschi and Peter Slominski, 'The EU Hotspot Approach in Italy: Strengthening Agency Governance in the Wake of the Migration Crisis?' (2022) 44(6) Journal of European Integration 769; Anna Papoutsi, Joe Painter, Evie Papada, and Antonis Vradis, 'The EC Hotspot Approach in Greece: Creating Liminal EU Territory' (2019) 45(12) Journal of Ethnic and Migration Studies 2200.

while borders are a clear site of activity in migration governance, this focus reveals only partly the many ways and legal regimes under which people migrate to, remain in, and leave a specific territory. In the EU context, the blurring of internal and external migration occurs most obviously within the Schengen area, since the lack of border checks applies to EU and non-EU citizens alike. Unlike states, where borders are generally fixed, the EU's borders shift via enlargement (and now, Brexit). And even while borders might appear to be fixed physical spaces, they occupy a less certain presence in legal and policy terms, hence the phenomenon of pushing borders and migration control 'out'.[16] The legal responsibility of Frontex for human rights violations has only recently been established by the Court of Justice.[17]

But the complexity of migration insofar as it relates to citizens of third countries in the EU (who may not have ever crossed a border) can be seen in the caselaw of the Court of Justice, where this area has become one of the most dynamic areas of interpretation of rights.[18] In addition, the intersection of human rights law, international law, and EU law is most obvious in the case of refugees and principles such as *non-refoulement*[19] and returns,[20] but occurs across the spectrum of the different forms of migration.[21] Furthermore, the rubbing together of EU law and national law joins migration law with another dynamic and evolving area, namely that of citizenship.[22]

Past and present migration to, from, and within Europe is a fact of life and part of what makes Europe what it is. A focus on the law and policy surrounding border security, the Common European Asylum System (CEAS), or even the enforcement of rights allows only a partial insight into this complex phenomenon. Part of the challenge in analysing migration governance is therefore defining the scope of enquiry. A binary separation of the 'internal' and 'external' spheres goes only some way in separating the movement and legal regimes applicable within the territory

[16] Sandra Lavenex, 'Shifting Up and Out: The Foreign Policy of European Immigration Control' (2006) 29(2) West European Politics 329–50.

[17] C-679/23 P *WS and others v Frontex* ECLI:EU:C:2025:976 and Case C-136/24 P *Hamoudi v Frontex* ECLI:EU:C:2025:977.

[18] Some of the major cases include Case 34/09 *Zambrano v Office national de l'emploi* ECLI:EU:C:2011:124. For summary and discussion of the law in this area, see Francesca Strumia, 'European Citizenship and EU Immigration: A Demoi-cratic Bridge between the Third Country Nationals' Right to Belong and the Member States' Power to Exclude' (2016) 22(4) European Law Journal 417–47; Daniel Thym, '"Citizens" and "Foreigners" in EU Law: Migration Law and Its Cosmopolitan Outlook' (2016) 22(3) European Law Journal 296–316.

[19] Roberta Mungianu, *Frontex and Non-Refoulement: The International Responsibility of the European Union* (Cambridge University Press 2016).

[20] Tamás Molnár, *The Interplay Between the EU's Return Acquis and International Law* (Edward Elgar Publishing 2021).

[21] Cathryn Costello, *The Human Rights of Migrants and Refugees in European Law* (Oxford University Press 2016). For a recent thorough exploration of EU citizenship law, see Niamh Nic Shuibhne, *EU Citizenship Law* (Oxford University Press 2023).

[22] Jo Shaw and Nina Miler, 'When Legal Worlds Collide: An Exploration of What Happens when EU Free Movement Law Meets UK Immigration Law' (2013) 38 European Law Review 137–66.

of the EU and its Member States. For this reason, this book focuses on external migration, but attempts to avoid the risk of defining what migration governance means with references to only one type. Instead, the aim is to take a wider view and consider how the different forms are linked. That being said, the weight of legislative and policy activity on migration and the shift to 'formal informality' point heavily to irregular forms of migration as a key focus.

While free movement rights within the EU are primarily for the benefit of EU citizens, some rights are attached for, inter alia, family members from third countries who enter and move with the EU. Some of the legislative measures dealing with external migration, such as the Dublin Regulation,[23] have a strong internal dimension since the premise of the regulation is the movement (back) from one Member State to the first Member State entered by the individual. As a result, the distinction between the internal and external is blurred, and also makes quantifying the scope of who is covered by the governance of migration even more difficult. As of 2024, the number of people residing in an EU Member State with citizenship of a non-member country was 29 million (up from 21.8 million in 2019), equating to 6.4 per cent of the EU population (up from 4.9% in 2019), with a further 3.3 million persons living in one of the EU Member States with the citizenship of another Member State.[24] But these figures do not tell us very much about the *ways* in which people migrated to the EU—if indeed they did migrate, since this total will also include people born in the EU but without the nationality of that state. Those in an irregular migration situation are, evidently, even more difficult to quantify. Dual citizenship, statelessness, and temporary movements across borders complicate the quantification process. And little academic attention is devoted to those—whether EU citizens or third country nationals—who leave the EU on a temporary or permanent basis.[25]

But even if we were able to more accurately quantify who is affected by EU migration governance, the limits of this sphere of governance do not lie there. Family members, employers who seek ways to engage workers from outside the EU or face sanctions for engaging irregular migrants in work without the proper checks, 'street-level' checking with public and private organizations, and of course any

[23] Regulation (EU) No 604/2013 of the European Parliament and of the Council of 26 June 2013 establishing the criteria and mechanisms for determining the Member State responsible for examining an application for international protection lodged in one of the Member States by a third-country national or a stateless person [2013] OJ L180/31.

[24] The increase can partly be explained by the use of the Temporary Protection Directive for people leaving Ukraine since 2022. Eurostat, 'EU population diversity by citizenship and country of birth' (Eurostat 2025) https://ec.europa.eu/eurostat/statistics-explained/index.php?title = EU_population_diversity_by_citizenship_and_country_of_birth>; Eurostat, 'People in the EU—statistics on origin of residents—statistics explained' (Eurostat 2020) https://ec.europa.eu/eurostat/statistics-explained/index.php?title = Archive:People_in_the_EU_-_statistics_on_origin_of_residents&oldid = 374953>, accessed 2 June 2025.

[25] For an exception, see Agnieszka Weinar, *European Citizenship and Identity Outside of the European Union* (Routledge 2019).

individual who might consider migrating are all covered by aspects of EU migration governance. In other words, migration governance most obviously concerns an individual who has migrated at some point or the facilitation or prevention of their ability to do so. The actual scope of migration governance is much, much wider. Here, the focus is on external migration and the way in which it is governed by the EU institutions and associated actors (such as agencies), Member States, third states, and other actors involved in the process. Thus, it is in some ways closer to the realm of external relations and foreign policy (discussed below), but also strongly associated with the other aspects of the Justice and Home Affairs 'pillar' in which it originated.

As well as the large scope of migration governance in terms of who it might impact, the complexity of rule-making, rule enforcement, and formal and informal practices is a strong feature of migration governance. It is also subject to rapid changes and, particularly in the informal domain, it is difficult to understand exactly what is happening or appreciate its effects. Greenhill has referred to 'policy schizophrenia' as a result of the migration crisis, suggesting that both the approach to and the pace of reforms to EU migration governance have been frenetic and confused.[26] But it is important not to be overly focused on the most recent changes and innovations only. Indeed, in the light of the structuring of migration governance in the EU in the 1990s and 2000s around the prioritization of measures to combat or restrict certain types of (irregular) migration,[27] we can see something of a continuity.[28] The emergence of 'formal informality' can be understood as a feature of the EU's maturing system of governance.

1.2 'Europe', 'the EU', and 'Europeanization'

The main focus of this book is the role of the European Union and its institutions in migration governance. Within Europe, membership of the EU is both extensive and geographically expansive. The countries in Europe that are not part of the EU do, for the most part, have extensive ties with the EU in migration law and policy. Thus, contemporary migration governance in Europe extends beyond the EU to include, inter alia, non-Member States, other international organizations (such as the Council of Europe), and transnational actors. They are often, however, involved with EU migration governance—for states, this might be via involvement in

[26] Kelly M Greenhill, 'Open Arms Behind Barred Doors: Fear, Hypocrisy and Policy Schizophrenia in the European Migration Crisis' (2016) 22(3) European Law Journal 317–32.

[27] Virginie Guiraudon, 'The 2015 Refugee Crisis Was Not a Turning Point: Explaining Policy Inertia in EU Border Control' (2017) 17(1) European Political Science 151–60.

[28] See, for example, the most recent initiative, the New Pact on Migration and Asylum: European Commission, 'Pact on Migration and Asylum: A common EU system to manage migration' (European Commission 21 May 2024) https://home-affairs.ec.europa.eu/policies/migration-and-asylum/pact-migration-and-asylum_en, accessed 2 June 2025.

Mediterranean operations, contributing to funding mechanisms, or technical cooperation. Non-Member States whose cooperation is sought in EU migration governance are found not only among the immediate neighbourhood but also much further afield in Africa, Asia, or the Americas. Much of the focus of this book is the engagement of third states in managing migration, which is in itself has become a strong feature of consecutive official strategies, including the Global Approach to Migration and Mobility. As such, while the focus is the legal, political, and institutional aspects of the EU's approach to migration governance, the role of non-Member States and other actors is crucial.

The EU hence operates a central role in migration governance in Europe. But it would be erroneous to treat the EU as a singular actor. The EU is not a state and has a complex institutional set-up in which the constituent parts have their own roles, values, powers, and interests. As per the second aim of this book, noted above, much of the story of how migration is governed in Europe is how the different institutions within the EU have evolved. Formal law-making generally follows an established and fixed path, but the institutional arrangements for other aspects of governance are not static. That is to say, the search for innovations beyond the Treaty structure, the emergence of institutional actors (such as agencies), and the possibility for activities to take place under the banner of 'the EU' while in fact only engaging some Member States muddies the waters. As noted above, this phenomena is particularly acute when the language of 'crisis' is deployed by the institutions. The complexity of migration governance—conceptually, institutionally, and practically—means that the scope must be narrowed. Here, the focus is on the EU and its institutions rather than the individual actions or approaches of the Member States, except where the latter helps explain activities and innovations co-opted by the EU more widely.[29]

The shared competence between the EU and the Member States in migration[30] is by no means unique in the legal order of the EU. Neither is the existence of competences which have hardly been used, nor that of language in the Treaty that suggests integration is far more complete than is the case. However, migration does have some important differences with other areas, which make it both an interesting case study of European integration as a mature stage in the EU's history and a demonstration of where the limits of integration lie. Some crises, such as

[29] Prominent examples here include bilateral deals and Memoranda of Understanding, such as those between Italy and Albania and Italy and Libya and the 'one in one out' agreement between France and the UK. See Matilde Rosina and Iole Fontana, 'The External Dimension of Italian Migration Policy in the Wider Mediterranean' (2024) Mediterranean Politics 1–32; Martino Reviglio, 'Externalizing Migration Management through Soft Law: The Case of the Memorandum of Understanding between Libya and Italy' (2020) 20(1) Global Jurist 18; Marianna Griffini and Matilde Rosina, 'An Ideological Divide? Political Parties' Discourse in Italy's Migration Cooperation with Libya and Albania' (2024) The International Spectator 1–20; Anne Daguerre, 'Macron's returns agreement gamble: checkmate or misstep?' UK in a Changing Europe (25 July 2025) https://ukandeu.ac.uk/macrons-returns-agreement-gamble-checkmate-or-misstep/, accessed 30 March 2026.

[30] Articles 67–80 TFEU.

economic or public health, can generally be attributed to a specific time period of several years. Migration, however, is the standout area where frenetic policy and decision-making has taken place under the guise of a crisis for at least a decade. The climate crisis is another example, though the use of crisis here is less common amongst political leaders in Europe than in migration. The template for 'formal informality' as explored later in this book was set out in the migration or refugee 'crisis', which began in 2015 but which, for policy-makers, has not ended.

But migration does not readily follow the script of 'integration' as there is no *finalité* of the process or 'end product' of migration as part of the 'Area' (rather than 'Single' or even 'Common') of Freedom, Security and Justice.[31] Unlike, for example, the single market programme, there is no agreement as to what the governance of EU migration *should* look like beyond certain discrete areas set out in the Treaty (such as the CEAS). And although the Treaty language suggests that integration of migration law across the EU *should* happen, the recent history of the EU suggests that on this issue at least, the possibility of agreeing a holistic common approach across all different types of migration is low.

Using integration as a means to confront common challenges does not operate in the same way as has historically been the case in other areas. While EU institutions have suggested that integration is the means by which migration 'crises' can be avoided via solidarity and burden-sharing, the sharp divisions in public rhetoric by heads of government are in stark difference to other areas of EU law and policy. Taken to its logical conclusion, the 'integration through law' approach that has been at the forefront of understand the process of European integration is not fully applicable here. Mention should also be made of migration as a flashpoint between national interests and the imposition of EU values. Although not limited to a North/South or East/West divide, it is significant to note that the staunchest opposition to liberalizing any migration regimes has generally come from some of the newer Member States.[32] Migration has even been weaponized as a means to assert national identity and reject collective values, particularly in Hungary, where the Orbán government expressly invited citizens to vent their frustration with the EU's 'interference' in migration as part of its 'Stop Brussels' campaign'.[33]

[31] Neil Walker, 'In Search of the Area of Freedom, Security and Justice: A Constitutional Odyssey' in Neil Walker (ed), *Europe's Area of Freedom, Security and Justice* (Oxford University Press 2004).

[32] See, inter alia, Péter Stepper, 'The Visegrad Group and the EU Agenda on Migration: A Coalition of the Unwilling?' (2016) 1(1) Corvinus Journal of International Affairs 62–82; Natascha Zaun, 'Fence-Sitters No More: Southern and Central Eastern European Member States' Role in the Deadlock of the CEAS Reform' (2022) 29(2) Journal of European Public Policy 96–217; Jan Kovář, 'Politicisation of Immigration in Central and Eastern Europe: Evidence from Plenary Debates in Two Countries' (2023) 70(6) Problems of Post-Communism 667–78.

[33] See Dermot Hodson and Uwe Puetter, 'The European Union in Disequilibrium: New Intergovernmentalism, Postfunctionalism and Integration Theory in the Post-Maastricht Period' (2019) 26(8) Journal of European Public Policy 1153–71; and Theodore Baird, 'Non-State Actors and the New Intergovernmentalism' (2017) 55(6) JCMS: Journal of Common Market Studies 1192–1202.

If the stipulation in the Treaty that the purpose of the EU is 'ever closer union' (Article 1 TEU) remains accurate, then we might question what this means in the context of migration. It is futile to suggest that this simply does not apply to migration since the amount of activity in this field makes it one of the most dynamic areas of policymaking, even if 'cooperation' rather than integration might be more appropriate. But as a contemporary area of focus which does not follow the same script as other areas, it should be seen in the context of the increased recognition of differentiated integration[34] and new intergovernmentalism.[35] Both of these approaches to understanding the EU downplay the one-way direction of travel that integration is supposed to follow. The distinctiveness of migration—even without the focus on crisis—is also an area where there are sharp differences in shared experiences, ranging from former colonial powers to countries more familiar with emigration than immigration or with painful recent experiences of forced migration. These differences can come to the fore when the language of 'crisis' is deployed, and the perceived success or failure of the EU to resolve the crisis is strongly linked to other policy areas where 'crisis' is also a familiar characterization. The answer does not appear to be integration as experienced in other areas. Rather, the common theme that emerges is securitization and the need for the EU and its Member States to protect a 'way of life', as the anecdote at the start of this chapter shows. Thus, migration is a means to discuss where the limits of integration lie and what this means for the future of the EU.

Accounts of integration among the Member States have often crystallized around 'Europeanization', which originally implied a pooling of sovereignty and 'becoming European' via a 'process by which domestic policy areas become increasingly subject to European policymaking'.[36] Radaelli placed emphasis on change in logics in political decision-making, including the institutionalization of formal and informal rules.[37] Much work has been undertaken on how this applies in the related contexts of enlargement (particularly in Central and Eastern Europe)[38] and to the EU's neighbours via the ENP.[39] In the migration context, this can mean the

[34] See Stefan Gänzle, Benjamin Leruth, and Jarle Trondal (eds), *Differentiated Integration and Disintegration in a Post-Brexit Era* (Routledge 2019); Frank Schimmelfennig and Thomas Winzen, 'Grand Theories, Differentiated Integration' (2019) 26(8) Journal of European Public Policy 1172–92.

[35] Hodson and Puetter, 'The European Union in Disequilibrium' (n 33).

[36] Tanja A. Börzel, 'Towards Convergence in Europe? Institutional Adaptation to Europeanization in Germany and Spain' (1999) 39(4) JCMS: Journal of Common Market Studies 573–96.

[37] Claudio M. Radaelli, 'Whither Europeanization? Concept Stretching and Substantive Change' (2000) European Integration Online Papers.

[38] See Frank Schimmelfennig and Ulrich Sedelmeier (eds), *The Europeanization of Central and Eastern Europe* (Cornell University Press 2005); Florian Trauner, 'From Membership Conditionality to Policy Conditionality: EU External Governance in South Eastern Europe' (2009) 16(5) Journal of European Public Policy 774–90; and Ulrich Sedelmeier, 'Europeanisation in New Member and Candidate States' (2011) 6(1) Living Reviews in European Governance 1–52.

[39] See, for example, Andrea Gawrich, Inna Melnykovska, and Rainer Schweickert, 'Neighbourhood Europeanization through ENP: The Case of Ukraine' (2010) 48(5) JCMS: Journal of Common Market Studies 1209–35; Tanja A Börzel, 'When Europe Hits . . . Beyond Its Borders: Europeanization and the Near Abroad' (2011) 9(4) Comparative European Politics 394–413.

adoption of (EU) rules and norms by third countries—and much of the analysis of the EU's relations with third countries in this book focuses on the EU's neighbours. The problem here is identifying what 'counts' as Europeanization: in the past, this suggested a process of becoming closer, or adaptation—whether this was part of integration or merely adopting norms belonging to one or more Member States. This might be the case here, if we accept that the language of securitization dominates efforts to confront irregular migration and tie in non-Member States to the EU's system of governance. But it also implies that Europeanization is not an unstoppable process—see for example the decision to quietly push back visa liberalization for Georgia and Ukraine in 2016 at the height of the migration crisis.[40]

What therefore might we mean by the 'Europeanization' of migration law and policy? Here it is likely that we would find a divergence in the official discourse and the practice, especially insofar as values are concerned. Officially, it might be that the EU and its Member States uphold the provisions of international law (for example, on refugees) and human rights, but we know from accounts of current practices around the EU's borders already that this is not necessarily the case. Increasingly, as the language of security and migration as a 'threat' permeates national and EU-level discourse, Europeanization might represent something different from the type of values contained in the Treaty.[41] Commitment to the (international) rights enshrined in EU's own legal order are treated as secondary to securing borders.[42] Therefore, Olsen's view that Europeanization represents a 'more unified and stronger political entity'[43] is not necessarily the case unless it refers to a different kind of EU than is reflected in the values contained in the Treaty. We should also refer to the difficulties identified above in terms of the lack of vision of what migration governance should look like—the Treaty suggests a (gradual) process of integration towards common policies, but the limits to doing so in a wider and more divided EU are challenges that the EU (and the literature on Europeanization) has not previously faced.

'Externalization' is a commonly applied phenomenon to explain contemporary trends in EU migration governance.[44] Externalization refers to the search for

[40] Richard Youngs, *Europe's Eastern Crisis: The Geopolitics of Asymmetry* (Cambridge University Press 2017) 101.

[41] Saskia Bonjour and Maarten Vink, 'When Europeanization Backfires: The Normalization of European Migration Politics' (2013) 48(4) Acta Politica 389–407.

[42] Marie-Laure Basilien-Gainche, 'Leave and Let Die: The EU Banopticon Approach to Migrants at Sea' in Violeta Moreno-Lax and Eftymios Papastavridis (eds), *Boat Refugees and Migrants at Sea: A Comprehensive Approach Integrating Maritime Security in Human Rights* (Brill 2016) 327–50.

[43] Johan P Olsen, 'The Many Faces of Europeanization' (2002) 40(5) JCMS: Journal of Common Market Studies 921–52.

[44] See, inter alia, Georgia Papagianni, 'Forging an External EU Migration Policy: From Externalisation of Border Management to a Comprehensive Policy?' (2013) 15(3) European Journal of Migration and Law 283–99; Michael Strange and Bruno Oliveira Martins, 'Claiming Parity between Unequal Partners: How African Counterparts Are Framed in the Externalisation of EU Migration Governance' (2019) 5(3) Global Affairs 235–46; Agnese Pacciardi and Joakim Berndtsson, 'EU Border Externalisation and Security Outsourcing: Exploring the Migration Industry in Libya' (2022) 48(17) Journal of Ethnic and Migration Studies 4010–28; Juan Santos Vara and Laura Pascual Matellán, 'The

solutions to irregular migration and involvement of third states, primarily around the EU's borders, which then become the de facto frontiers or 'buffers'. The pursuit of closer relations has—with mixed success—exported or pushed out the borders of Europe via a multitude of means. The oft-cited 'fortress Europe' and the securitization of borders are closely related to these processes. But, in attempting to influence neighbouring states, 'externalization' appears closer in definition to Europeanization when applied to migration. 'Securitization' or 'fortress Europe' are generally used to refer to resistance on the part of the Member States to permit migration and at the same time to insist that non-Member States reinforce their own migration law and policies. The rationale for the latter, as identified by Kostakopoulou, is that Member States via cooperation within the EU are able 'to construct new forms of power which do not only increase their regulatory capacity within a geographically contained structure, but also enable them to impose their security agenda beyond the confines of the Union'.[45]

As noted in the previous section, much of the time frame covered by the scope of analysis in this book begins from 2004. This is an appropriate start date for the analysis since it marked the beginning of a new chapter in the EU and for migration governance. The 'big bang' enlargement with ten new Member States occurred in 2004. The first-wave legislation passed on the basis of the changes brought about by the Treaties of Amsterdam (1998) and Nice (1999) was mostly in place and the Hague Programme on JHA set out the priorities for the following years. 2004 also marked the launch of the ENP, which itself built on bilateral frameworks with countries in Eastern Europe (who joined the EU in 2004, 2004, and 2013) and the Mediterranean countries via the Barcelona Process from 1994.[46] The ENP has provided the impetus (and funding) for enhanced relationships with countries around the EU's borders which include both formal and informal arrangements and practical cooperation. The first iteration of the EU's Global Approach to Migration was set out in 2005, which gave official recognition to some the types of less formal tools and instruments under analysis in this book and, in this way, marked a new approach in treating migration via legal and other means. The relatively long period of analysis also means that attention is not merely focused on law and policymaking during times of crisis but consideration is given to longer-term

Externalisation of EU Migration Policies: The Implications Arising from the Transfer of Responsibilities to Third Countries' in Wybe Th Douma and others (eds) *The Evolving Nature of EU External Relations Law* (TMC Asser Press 2021) 315–31; Tineke Strik and Ruben Robbesom, 'Compliance or Complicity? An Analysis of the EU–Tunisia Deal in the Context of the Externalisation of Migration Control' (2024) 71(1) Netherlands International Law Review 199–225.

[45] Theodora Kostakopoulou, 'The "Protective Union": Change and Continuity in Migration Law and Policy in Post-Amsterdam Europe' (2000) 38(3) JCMS: Journal of Common Market Studies 497–518.

[46] Paul James Cardwell, 'EuroMed, European Neighbourhood Policy and the Union for the Mediterranean: Overlapping Policy Frames in the EU's Governance of the Mediterranean' (2011) 49(2) JCMS: Journal of Common Market Studies 219–41.

strategies in migration governance. Therefore, initiatives taken as a response to different types of migration can be seen in their proper context.

1.3 Migration, foreign policy, and externalization

The comparative lack of the language of governance in relation to the external sphere was noted in the previous sections. External migration occupies a curious space, in legal terms, between what can be seen as two opposites. We expect migration in its different forms to be the subject of strong regulation by the state, since it goes to the core of what a state is. Regulating who can come and go, under what criteria, in which categories, who can settle, the penalties for not respecting rules, and where challenges can be made goes hand in hand with individual discretion in decision-making. We expect migration law to be extensive and though simplicity would be welcome in terms of legal certainty, in most cases it is anything but. The transfer of competences to the EU should not, in this sense, make a difference to our expectation that law and rules provide such certainty.

Foreign policy, on the other hand, is generally speaking an area where 'law' gives way to politics and policymaking. Foreign policy is often the domain of the executive, and where formal law or regulation is needed this is often done via a secondary process. An obvious example is where restrictive measures (sanctions) are placed by one state or entity or another: a political decision followed up by legal measures restricting private entities, such as companies, from exporting goods to the third state in question. Foreign policy and the language of 'governance' are not easy bedfellows. In the EU context, 'foreign policy' and its close association with state-ness does not adequately capture the complexity or depth of the EU's engagement with the outside world. For this reason, 'external relations' has generally been the preferred term. It incorporates the EU's powers to make international agreements with other states. But here too, there has been a recent preference for 'soft' international agreements.[47]

The hallmark of migration law is therefore its strongly internal dimension. But formal law has long since emerged too in the form of agreements (Treaties) between states or entities. In the EU migration context, the more prominent examples are readmission agreements, whereby the EU and the third state agree to take back their respective citizens who are found to have an irregular status. These are based on the specific competence for international agreements in the Treaty.[48]

[47] Ramses A Wessel, 'Normative Transformations in EU External Relations: the Phenomenon of "Soft" International Agreements' (2021) 44(1) West European Politics 72–92.

[48] Now found in Article 79(3) TFEU: The Union may conclude agreements with third countries for the readmission to their countries of origin or provenance of third-country nationals who do not or who no longer fulfil the conditions for entry, presence or residence in the territory of one of the Member States. For further discussion, see Marion Panizzon, "Readmission Agreements of EU Member States: A

Migration has, however, come to occupy a prominent position as a foreign policy issue for the EU as well as on national agendas, and not merely in times of crisis. The conceptualization of migration as a foreign policy[49] makes it subject to an uneasy combination of internal law-making and foreign policy tools. The reasons why this is 'uneasy' are largely internal to the EU: as a multi-layered polity, its institutional competences are restrained by the Treaty and subject to different dynamics across the Commission, Council, Parliament, and Court of Justice. The search for coherence in foreign policy across both institutions and externally facing policies (development, common commercial policy, and so on) has been a consistent theme in commentary on the EU and the subject of numerous studies[50] and Treaty-based innovations.[51] The institutions themselves are not static and subject to change. The Commission, for example, was explicitly positioned as a 'geopolitical' actor under President Ursula von der Leyen in 2019,[52] which has particular consequences for the way in which it works and interacts with other institutions and Member States.[53]

Furthermore, the placing of migration within a foreign policy context highlights its particular sensitivity as regards national sovereignty. The Treaty of Lisbon attempted to ensure that the CFSP was 'ring-fenced' away from the (assumed) 'integrationist' Court of Justice.[54] When coupled with the sensitivity among many

Case for EU Subsidiarity or Dualism?" (2012) 31(4) Refugee Survey Quarterly 101–33 and Chapter 6 of this book.

[49] Andrew Geddes, 'Migration as Foreign Policy? The External Dimension of EU Action on Migration and Asylum' (2009) Swedish Institute for European Policy Studies, Paper 2009:2.

[50] Christian Tietje, 'The Concept of Coherence in the Treaty on European Union and the Common Foreign and Security Policy' (1997) 2(2) European Foreign Affairs Review 211–33; Pascal Gauttier, 'Horizontal Coherence and the External Competences of the European Union' (2004) 10(1) European Law Journal 23–41; Daniel C Thomas, 'Still Punching Below Its Weight? Coherence and Effectiveness in European Union Foreign Policy' (2012) 50(3) JCMS: Journal of Common Market Studies 457–74; Hartmut Mayer, 'The Challenge of Coherence and Consistency in EU Foreign Policy' in Mario Telò and Frederik Ponjaert (eds), *The EU's Foreign Policy* (Routledge 2016) 123–36; Ramses A Wessel, 'The Inside Looking Out: Consistency and Delimitation in EU External Relations' (2000) 37(5) Common Market Law Review 1135–71; Peter Van Elsuwege, 'EU External Action after the Collapse of the Pillar Structure: In Search of a New Balance Between Delimitation and Consistency' (2010) 47(4) Common Market Law Review, 987–1019; and Andrea Ott, 'Between Pillars and Policies: The Quest for Consistency in EU External Relations' in M de Visser and AP van der Mei (eds), *The Treaty on European Union 1993–2013: Reflections from Maastricht* (Intersentia 2013) 243–68.

[51] Graham Butler, 'Legal Responses to the European Union's Migration Crisis' (2018) 19 San Diego Journal of International Law 277–310.

[52] Ursula von der Leyen, 'Speech by President-elect von der Leyen in the European Parliament Plenary on the occasion of the presentation of her College of Commissioners and their programme' (Strasbourg, 27 November 2019) https://ec.europa.eu/commission/presscorner/detail/es/speech_19_6408, accessed 30 March 2026.

[53] See, inter alia, Steven Blockmans, 'The Birth of a Geopolitical EU' (2022) 27(2) European Foreign Affairs Review 155–60; Pierre Haroche, 'A "Geopolitical Commission": Supranationalism Meets Global Power Competition' (2023) 61(4) JCMS: Journal of Common Market Studies 970–87; Elena Baracani and Hussein Kassim, 'The "Geopolitical Commission": An End of Term Review' (2024) 62(S1) JCMS: Journal of Common Market Studies 41–51.

[54] Paul James Cardwell, 'On Ring-Fencing the Common Foreign and Security Policy in the Legal Order of the European Union' (2013) 64(4) Northern Ireland Legal Quarterly 443–63.

Member States across the Union about migration and EU integration, it is not difficult to imagine how external migration is one of the most contested law and policy-making areas, no matter how high up the agenda for discussion. EU Member States have actively engaged in bilateral cooperation on migration with third states,[55] which suggests a lack of solidarity and even competition to 'solve' issues at the national level. Once again, this is the case not merely when confronted with issues of irregular migration but also when seeking common approaches to regular migration (such as attracting high-skilled migrants), which has been less conceived as a foreign policy issue, but where national competences are jealously guarded—and used.[56] Yet, legal spill over into foreign policy due to the supranational dynamics at play.[57] And, as Sjursen and Bicchi remind us, 'the procedural, and not only the substantive, norms of EU foreign policy have been constitutive of EU foreign policy'.[58] A wide body of literature has examined the interplay or 'nexus' between different aspects of foreign/external policy: on the migration–development nexus,[59] the migration–trade nexus,[60] and—increasingly—the migration–environment nexus.[61] The external dimension of migration law and policy has been a constant in EU governance, reflecting its late arrival as part of EU law and policy, where external relations had itself become a feature of governance.[62]

The externalization of EU migration law and policy refers to the practice of shifting border control and migration responsibilities beyond the territory of the EU and its Member States. As such, it fits between—or better still, straddles—foreign policy/external relations and internal law-making. This has particular consequences for the institutional mechanisms used, such as Treaty-based competences, budgets, and oversight, and generally does not permit clarity.

[55] Michael Collyer, 'Geopolitics as a Migration Governance Strategy: European Union Bilateral Relations with Southern Mediterranean Countries' (2016) 42(4) Journal of Ethnic and Migration Studies 606–24; Rosina and Fontana, 'The External Dimension of Italian Migration Policy in the Wider Mediterranean' (n 29) 1–32.

[56] Sami Mahroum, 'Europe and the Immigration of Highly Skilled Labour' (2001) 39(5) International Migration 27–43; Lucie Cerna, 'The EU Blue Card: Preferences, Policies, and Negotiations Between Member States' (2014) 2(1) Migration Studies 73–96.

[57] Peter Slominski, 'The Power of Legal Norms in the EU's External Border Control' (2013) 51(6) International Migration 41–53.

[58] Helene Sjursen, Federica Bicchi, and Marianna Lovato, 'Keep on Talking! The Resilience of Multilateral Communications in EU Foreign Policy' (2024) JCMS: Journal of Common Market Studies (early view) https://doi.org/10.1111/jcms.13691, accessed 7 June 2025.

[59] Sandra Lavenex and Rahel Kunz, 'The Migration–Development Nexus in EU External Relations' (2008) 30(3) European Integration 439–57.

[60] Fabienne Bossuyt, Jan Orbie, and Lotte Drieghe, 'EU External Policy Coherence in the Trade–Foreign Policy Nexus: Foreign Policy through Trade or Strictly Business?' (2020) 23(1) Journal of International Relations and Development 45–66.

[61] Andrew Geddes and William Somerville, 'Migration and Environmental Change in International Governance: The Case of the European Union' (2012) 30(6) Environment and Planning C: Government and Policy 1015–28; Maria Julia Trombetta, 'Linking Climate-Induced Migration and Security within the EU: Insights from the Securitization Debate' (2014) 2(2) Critical Studies on Security 131–47.

[62] Christina Boswell, 'The "External Dimension" of EU Immigration and Asylum Policy' (2003) 79(3) International Affairs 619–38.

Externalization has been strongly linked to an EU 'border regime', though the emphasis is very much on ensuring that migrants (or would-be migrants) do not physically reach the EU's border.[63]

Externalization manifests itself in a variety of forms, of which the informality identified in this book is very much a part. Cooperation with non-EU states, often through financial and technical means, may or may not rely on agreements which have followed Treaty-based processes to effectively transfer responsibilities.[64] Key examples include the EU–Türkiye Statement of 2016, which aimed to secure Turkish efforts to prevent irregular migration to Europe, and the various partnerships with North African countries to enhance border surveillance and detention capacities.[65] This process of outsourcing migration control, seeking to manage migration flows and address security concerns, is almost wholly focused on irregular migration, even where some of the incentives for cooperation with third countries relate to regular migration (e.g. visa facilitation)[66] or development.[67]

Unsurprisingly, the externalization of migration policy has raised significant ethical and legal concerns. These practices often compromise the human rights of migrants and asylum seekers by placing them in countries with poor protection systems and inadequate safeguards. For instance, migrants intercepted or returned to countries such as Libya frequently face detention in inhumane conditions and exposure to violence.[68] Additionally, such policies risk undermining the EU's commitment to international law and its own values of solidarity and human dignity. Scholars have also pointed to the practices of externalization being rooted in (neo)colonialism,[69] with a strong gendered dimension,[70] and thus requiring a decolonially centred approach to fully understand it.[71]

The externalization strategy and the practices it involves have also been criticized for fostering dependency on authoritarian regimes and prioritizing

[63] Lisa Marie Borrelli and Annika Lindberg, 'Making (In)formality Work in a Multi-Scalar European Border Regime' (2025) 51(2) Journal of Ethnic and Migration Studies 445–63.

[64] Vara and Matellán, 'The Externalisation of EU Migration Policies' (n 44) 315–31.

[65] See, for example, Gerda Heck and Elena Habersky, 'Externalising Migration Controls through Development Programs in Egypt' (2024) 30(1) Geopolitics 120–43.

[66] See, for example, Nora El Qadim, 'The Symbolic Meaning of International Mobility: EU–Morocco Negotiations on Visa Facilitation' (2018) 6(2) Migration Studies 279–305.

[67] Sandra Lavenex and Rahel Kunz, 'The Migration–Development Nexus in EU External Relations' (2008) 30(3) European Integration 439–57; Niels Keijzer, Julie Héraud, and Malin Frankenhaeuser, 'Theory and Practice? A Comparative Analysis of Migration and Development Policies in Eleven European Countries and the European Commission' (2016) 54(2) *International Migration* 69–81.

[68] Agnese Pacciardi and Joakim Berndtsson, 'EU Border Externalisation and Security Outsourcing: Exploring the Migration Industry in Libya' (2022) 48(17) Journal of Ethnic and Migration Studies 4010–28.

[69] Teresa Cappiali and Agnese Pacciardi, 'Reorienting EU Border Externalization Studies: A Decolonial Intersection Approach' (2024) 30(1) Geopolitics 300–24.

[70] Mary Bosworth, Andriani Fili, and Sharon Pickering, 'Women and Border Policing at the Edges of Europe' (2017) 44(13) Journal of Ethnic and Migration Studies 2182–96.

[71] Nora Fisher Onar and Kalypso Nicolaïdis, 'The Decentring Agenda: Europe as a Post Colonial Power' (2013) 48(2) Cooperation and Conflict 283–303; Veronica Corcodel, 'A Decolonial Agenda for EU Migration and Asylum Law' (2024) 24 European Journal of Migration and Law 474.

short-term deterrence over long-term solutions to the root causes of migration.[72] Consequently, externalization—which is ever more prominent in the EU's strategic goals, discourse, and practices—has been the focus of much of the criticism of contemporary EU migration governance.[73] As noted above, while new governance generally includes the involvement of other actors, including those from civil society, externalization of migration has prompted a significant counter-movement from NGOs and civil society actors explicitly acting against this type of governance.[74]

Finally, the EU's attempts to find its role in foreign policy have long been centred on its difference from nation states as a new type of actor, and one which is guided by values. The Treaty explicitly states the values the EU is obliged to promote in the wider world. And yet, because foreign policy is assumed to be at the level of the state, it is one step removed from individual rights. Certainly, the ways in which the EU expresses itself on global affairs are strongly related to its stated values.[75] But the purpose of migration law and policy is centred on humans, and therefore one does not need a human rights approach to appreciate that rights should figure, even if migration law separates out the rights between 'citizens' (who benefit from equal treatment) and 'others' (who do not).[76] The framing, therefore, of migration with a foreign policy domain is thus a significant aspect in undercovering the extent to which policy instruments and tools can directly or indirectly affect individuals.

1.4 Conclusion

Beyond its status as one of the causes of an existential crisis for the EU in the twenty-first century, migration sits at the crossroads of a number of competing ways to understand contemporary governance. The Treaty competences only tell part of the story in terms of what the EU does, and much of the current criticism of both the EU and the Member States can be assigned to either the institutions not

[72] Michael Strange and Bruno Martins, 'Claiming Parity Between Unequal Partners: How African Counterparts Are Framed in the Externalisation of EU Migration Governance' (2019) 5(3) Global Affairs 235–46.

[73] See, inter alia, Polly Pallister-Wilkins, 'Alter-Geographies of Everyday Externalisation: Shattering European Attempts at Policing Mobility?' in Ida Marie Savio Vammen, Signe Cold-Rannkilde, and Hans Lucht (eds), *The Long Shadow of the Border: Migrants, Brokers and European Border Governance in Africa* (1st edn, Routledge 2023).

[74] Paolo Cuttia, 'Over Land and Sea: NGOs/CSOs and EU Border Externalisation Along the Central Mediterranean Route' (2022) 30(1) Geopolitics 19–45.

[75] Paul James Cardwell, 'Values in the European Union's Foreign Policy: An Analysis and Assessment of CFSP Declarations' (2016) 21(4) European Foreign Affairs Review 601–21.

[76] Thym, '"Citizens" and "Foreigners" in EU Law: Migration Law and its Cosmopolitan Outlook' (n 18) 296–316; Daniel Thym, 'Ungleichheit als Markenzeichen des Migrationsrechts' (2019) 74(4) Zeitschrift für öffentliches Recht 905–28.

doing enough to 'solve' migration as a problem or the argument that the measures the EU is taking and the strategies it is pursuing run counter to its stated values.

Migration helps us to understand governance in a number of different ways, and the themes outlined in this chapter speak to the way in which migration helps us to adapt long-standing ways of understanding the EU, such as Europeanization; what governance during a period of crisis (or dealing with multiple crises) tells us; and how European integration can be seen not only through the lens of peaceful co-operation between Member States via shared values, but also that of the exclusion of those values to others.

2
The Language of Governance in Migration

Few terms have come more to the fore in explaining contemporary phenomena of law and politics than governance. The language and use(s) of governance have become pervasive in discourse in local, national, international, and transnational settings. The EU has been at the forefront of areas where the language of governance has been most readily applied, seemingly because it itself represents a new way of legal and political decision-making as distinct from both national settings and the 'classic' post-war international institutions. In this respect, the EU represents a different *form* of government, which has brought into question the nature of contemporary legal–political authority, bargaining, and institutional creation and development.

This book uses the language of governance to explore contemporary external migration law, policy, and practice in Europe. Since governance has become a commonplace term, referring to both a description of the changes in which how society in governed take place and an approach to understanding the phenomena, greater clarification is necessary. Since the 'governance turn' in EU studies[1] in the late 1990s and early 2000s, a large amount of literature has considered the changes in the way in which the EU is governed—though external relations and migration have generally escaped the attention of much of the scholarship.[2] The case is made here that governance warrants fresh examination and application to the governance of migration in the EU.

'Governance' in this book is used both for its descriptive qualities and as an approach to understanding the phenomenon. Governance's descriptive qualities capture the changes which have taken place in the shift away from 'government'.[3] While we might arguably say that migration is 'governed', given the core competences retained by the governments of the Member States, the fact that the EU has gained both competences in the strict sense and influence over the procedures

[1] Beate Kohler-Koch and Berthold Rittberger, 'The "Governance Turn" in EU Studies' (2006) 44(1) JCMS: Journal of Common Market Studies 27.

[2] Paul James Cardwell, 'Rethinking Law and New Governance in the European Union: The Case of Migration Management' (2016) 41(3) European Law Review 362.

[3] As per Rhodes, 'in which governance signifies "a change in the meaning of government, referring to a new process of governing; or a changed condition of ordered rule; or the new method by which society is governed": RAW Rhodes, 'The New Governance: Governing with Government' (1996) 44(4) Political Studies 654.

The Governance of Migration in the European Union. Paul James Cardwell, Oxford University Press.
 DOI: 10.1093/9780191946592.003.0003

means that governance is appropriate in the EU context too. For much of the period of development of the EU acquis, the dominant frame for understanding migration has been intergovernmental, given that a competence-based analysis of EU law does not reveal external migration—as distinct from internal migration—to be subject to high levels of integration.[4] But here, the use of governance speaks to the EU being at an advanced stage of integration in terms of its institutional familiarity, 'eurospeak', and ways of doing things. While migration, alongside defence and foreign policy, was a later addition to the EU range of competences, the different institutions have developed and adapted their ways of working and elaborated their own views on what the EU should be doing and how.

This advanced stage of the EU's *system* of governance means that the institutions are also empowered to seek the type of innovative solutions and ways of working that this book aims to uncover. This explains why this book uses earlier generations of scholarship on EU governance to understand how we got to where we are now. The institutional formats have become more complex via the creation of agencies such as Frontex, which, although not fully sharing characteristics with counterpart agencies, nevertheless have significant powers and open questions as to their transparency, accountability, and obligations vis-à-vis fundamental rights.[5] Frontex, as the largest and most visible agency in the public sphere, is also a good illustration of why migration governance is different. The emphasis on governance in the past has been about the organic emergence of practices which promise to do things differently, such as involving social partners and thus making governance processes less 'top down', and mainstreaming objectives such as gender equality.[6] More recent analysis of governance tells us that it is as much about power relations as anything else.[7] This is crucial to understanding how such a politically charged domain as the governance of migration works.

This chapter begins by navigating through the different uses of governance, including the emergence of 'new governance'. As an academic field of enquiry in EU studies, its rise and (apparent) fall makes the case for a reconceptualization of how

[4] Saskia Bonjour, Ariadna Ripoll Servent, and Eiko Thielemann, 'Beyond Venue Shopping and Liberal Constraint: A New Research Agenda for EU Migration Policies and Politics' (2017) 25(3) Journal of European Public Policy 409.

[5] See Roberta Mungianu, *Frontex and Non-Refoulement: The International Responsibility of the EU* (Cambridge University Press 2016) 32–33 and the discussion in Chapter 5. The CJEU has ruled in principle that Frontex can be held responsible for fundamental rights violations: C-679/23 P *WS and others v Frontex* ECLI:EU:C:2025:976 and Case C-136/24 P *Hamoudi v Frontex* ECLI:EU:C:2025:977.

[6] See, inter alia, Christine Booth and Cinnamon Bennett, 'Gender Mainstreaming in the European Union: Towards a New Conception and Practice of Equal Opportunities?' (2002) 9(4) European Journal of Women's Studies 430; Mieke Verloo, 'Displacement and Empowerment: Reflections on the Concept and Practice of the Council of Europe Approach to Gender Mainstreaming and Gender Equality' (2005) 12(3) Social Politics 344; Petra Debusscher, 'Mainstreaming Gender in European Commission Development Policy: Conservative Europeanness?' (2011) 34(1) Women's Studies International Forum 39.

[7] Paul Copeland, *Governance and the European Social Dimension: Politics, Power and the Social Deficit in a Post-2010 EU* (Routledge 2020).

we think about governance via the prism of migration. This fluctuation serves as a means to highlight how the debate about migration governance is structured. What follows is a contextualization of migration within the sphere of EU external relations and how this helps us see both the limitations of the way in which governance is understood and the opportunities for innovation that exist in an external framework free of some of the 'internal' constraints. Finally, the chapter refines the governance approach adopted in this book by setting out the theoretical framework, drawing on institutionalism and constructivism in combination with socio-legal analysis.

2.1 Exploring the different uses of 'governance'

Though widespread, 'governance' is a relative newcomer to the legal–political lexicon, having only become prominent in English-language discourse since the 1980s and at later points in other languages.[8] If all the different ways in which governance as a term is employed have one point in common, then it is likely to be that the use of 'government' has limitations in its ability to characterize the complexities of how societies are governed.[9] Governance has retained a certain 'newness' despite its familiarity, insofar as it is seemingly less concerned with traditional concepts of power and organization of state or government institutions but rather reflective of changing relationships, structures, and locations of power. Governance is not the same as 'big government', although the inclusion of other actors in processes that do not fit into traditional boxes is a key part of its core tenets.[10] One of the most frequent uses of governance, corporate governance, encapsulates this well. This encompasses the regulation of private interests via public-facing bodies combined with a system of self-regulation to a greater or lesser extent. As Rhodes succinctly put it, governance points to a changed condition of ordered rule; or the new method by which society is governed.[11]

Consequently, governance indicates an open-textured category of actors, processes, and means by which public, private, and individual interests interact. It points to the participation in governing society beyond the constraints of local or national 'government' and suggests that the public–private relationship is more layered and complex than our traditional understandings. But with this flexibility there is some uncertainty over its limits, with the location of power and the constituent relationships becoming more blurred—perhaps overwhelmingly so.

[8] Claus Offe, 'Governance: An "Empty Signifier"?' (2009) 16(4) Constellations 550.
[9] Rhodes, 'The New Governance: Governing with Government' (n 3) 652.
[10] David Levi-Faur, 'From "Big Government" to "Big Governance"?' in David Levi-Faur (ed), *The Oxford Handbook of Governance* (Oxford Academic, 18 September 2012), <https://doi.org/10.1093/oxfordhb/9780199560530.013.0001>, accessed 1 June 2025.
[11] Rhodes, 'The New Governance: Governing with Government' (n 3) 652.

There is a risk, therefore, that the use of governance can be taken to mean almost anything, including where 'government' might itself be most appropriate. In other words, if governance is used in situations where we might mean government, or simply as an indication of where there is uncertainty over the separation of the public from the private, then the term might become devoid of its indication of something different or transformative.

The use of governance in this way speaks to its descriptive qualities. Many uses of governance emerge from observations that the traditional nation state and its role was in decline, in an era of globalization, regional integration (not only in Europe), and the dismantling of economic and trade barriers. In its place, the growing importance of private actors and privatization, globalization, and the rising importance of international and regional bodies—of which the EU is the leading example—are cited as the main drivers of the shift. The recognition that the growth of public activity was incompatible with traditional ideas of government, especially in cross-national settings, prompted reflection on what takes its place. In some ways, governance identifies the emergence of new structures, which might be multi-level within a state or incorporate international or regional structures with decision-making processes.

But the use of governance has generally also conveyed a sense of better government—or the search for it with existing and newer structures. Herein lies the shift from a description of a state of affairs to a normative dimension on governance and its use. 'Good governance' is now frequently used in national and international contexts, including in constitutional texts,[12] and was first used in official EU documentation in 1991.[13] It has found a way into the EU's Treaty arrangements, both with regard to the internal and external spheres. Article 15(1) TFEU contains the following provision: 'In order to promote good governance and ensure the participation of civil society, the Union's institutions, bodies, offices and agencies shall conduct their work as openly as possible.' Further, Article 21(h) TEU requires the Union to 'promote an international system based on stronger multilateral cooperation and good global governance'. No further definition of 'good governance' is provided in the Treaties, but it is assumed to relate to a common set of practices and principles including the respect for human rights, transparency, and both fair and efficient administration. These are commonly found in the descriptions provided elsewhere by the EU institutions, and by international organizations including the

[12] See, for example, Constitution of Finland of 11 June 1999, s 124: 'A public administrative task may be delegated to others than public authorities ... if this is necessary for the appropriate performance of the task and if basic rights and liberties, legal remedies and other requirements of good governance are not endangered.'

[13] Resolution of the Council and of the Member States meeting in the Council on human rights, democracy and development, adopted on 28 November 1991, para 2. Cited in Jan Wouters and Cedric Ryngaert, 'Good Governance: Lessons from International Organisations' in Deirdre M Curtin and Ramses A Wessel (eds) *Good Governance and the European Union; Reflections on Concepts, Institutions and Substance* (Intersentia 2005) 74.

Council of Europe,[14] Organisation for Economic Cooperation and Development (OECD),[15] and World Bank.[16] 'Good governance' is taken to be a goal, a strategy, or even a process alongside longer-standing concepts of democracy and human rights (and their promotion) in external relations.[17]

'Bad governance' is much less widespread as a term, though there is no logical reason why it could not be applied to instances of institutional set-ups where processes do not work, or where there are more serious failings such as a lack of human rights protection, transparency, or openness, or widespread corruption.[18] As a result, the frequent use of 'governance' as allied with the 'good' means that even without this indicator, the nature of the 'governance' carries positive connotations. This is also the case for variations on governance, such as 'technocratic governance',[19] and implied by the use of 'better governance' as an outcome in national or international contexts.[20]

The general enthusiasm with which 'new governance' was welcomed in EU scholarship during the 2000s is demonstrated by the wealth of literature dealing with its contours. Much of the debate was on the possibilities for connecting

[14] See the 12 Principles enshrined in the Strategy on Innovation and Good Governance at local level, endorsed by the 15th session of the Conference of European Ministers responsible for local and regional government (Valencia, 15–16 October 2007) <https://search.coe.int/cm/Pages/result_details.aspx?ObjectID=09000016805d3dc8>, accessed 1 June 2025.

[15] Good governance 'encompasses the role of public authorities in establishing the environment in which economic operators function and in determining the distribution of benefits as well as the relationship between the ruler and the ruled': OECD, Participatory Development and Good Governance (1995) OECD, Paris: <https://www.oecd.org/dac/accountable-effective-institutions/31857685.pdf>, accessed 1 June 2025.

[16] '[E]pitomized by predictable, open and enlightened policy making; a bureaucracy imbued with a professional ethos; an executive arm of government accountable for its actions; and a strong civil society participating in public affairs; and all behaving under the rule of law.' 'Development in Practice: Governance' (*World Bank*, 1994) [Online] <http://www-wds.worldbank.org/servlet/WDSContentServer/WDSP/IB/1994/05/01/000009265_3970716142854/Rendered/PDF/multi0page.pdf>, accessed 1 June 2025.

[17] See Tanja A Börzel, Yasemin Pamuk, and Andreas Stahn, 'Good Governance in the European Union' (2008) Berliner Arbeitspapier zur Europäischen Integration Nr. 7/Berlin Working Paper on European Integration No. 7, <https://refubium.fu-berlin.de/bitstream/handle/fub188/19026/2008-7_Boerzel_Pamuk_Stahn.pdf?sequence=1>, accessed 1 June 2025.

[18] There are recent examples exploring 'bad governance' and these are generally used to point to trends including corruption, or sometimes even the negative features associated with good governance (such as the involvement of private actors or privatizations), especially in the Global South. See, for instance, Mick Moore, 'Political Underdevelopment: What Causes "Bad Governance"' (2001) 3(3) Public Management Review 385; Richard Rose and Caryn Peiffer, *Bad Governance and Corruption* (Palgrave Macmillan 2019); Bernhard Reinsberg and others, 'Bad Governance: How Privatization Increases Corruption in the Developing World'(2020) 14(4) Regulation & Governance 698. Of the rare examples of the use of 'bad governance' as a term applied to the EU and migration, see Deniz Sert and Şevval Alparslan, 'Externalising Externalisation and Bad Governance of Migration in the EU: Turkey Learning from Europe' in Digdem Soyaltin-Colella (eds), *EU Good Governance Promotion in the Age of Democratic Decline* (Palgrave Macmillan 2022).

[19] David Kosař, Jiří Baroš, and Pavel Dufek, 'The Twin Challenges to Separation of Powers in Central Europe: Technocratic Governance and Populism' (2019) 15(3) European Constitutional Law Review 427.

[20] See, for example, Christopher Hood and David Heald (eds), *Transparency: The Key to Better Governance?* (Oxford University Press 2006).

Europe with its citizens, reducing the democratic deficit, and, as such, adapting the integration process for the new millennium. In this way, it placed 'new' governance within the same bracket as 'good' governance. Inherent in these debates is the idea that governance means something more than government or governing, but is intrinsically linked with democracy, legitimacy, and accountability.[21] Governance also allows for the possibility that new institutional actors, new processes and informal means of working, and the emergence of ideas and innovations can be accounted for. This is often referred to as 'new' governance to distinguish from established 'old' patterns. At this stage of the integration process, we can suggest that the EU's governance of migration does not rely fully on the 'integration through law' paradigm but rather leaves open the possibility that a much wider variety of methods, tools and processes might be used to meet goals—and that those goals might not be the ones listed in the Treaty. Such questioning is fully in line with the way in which governance has been used, in particular since the early 2000s.

The Commission's White Paper on Governance (2001) abstractly examined the suitability of existing integration methods, particularly in areas of EU activity with varying degrees of legislation.[22] The White Paper generated extensive commentary, much of it critical of the prominent role the Commission assigned itself in both the traditional 'Community Method' and new governance modes.[23] Consequently, the foundation of new governance has emphasized successful integration and coordination in citizen-focused areas, promoting 'good' or 'better' governance. Even without the debated prefix 'new',[24] the term 'governance' carries overwhelmingly positive connotations in Europe and beyond.[25] The Commission's use of 'European governance' in its documentation suggests an open and inclusive structure.[26]

[21] Jonas Tallberg, Karin Bäckstrand, and Jan Aart Scholte (eds), *Legitimacy in Global Governance: Sources, Processes, and Consequences* (Oxford University Press 2018). This is explored further in the following section.

[22] European Commission, 'White Paper on Governance' COM (2001) 428. Despite being light on the role to be played by new modes of governance in the EU architecture, the paper generated a huge amount of interest and critique, in particular over its treatment of new governance as essentially a variant on the traditional 'Community' method.

[23] Daniel Wincott, 'Looking Forward or Harking Back? The Commission and the Reform of Governance in the European Union' (2001) 39(5) JCMS: Journal of Common Market Studies 897.

[24] Treib and colleagues avoid the use of 'new' and 'old' because of the differences in temporal perspective, and also because what is 'new' in one policy area in the EU might not be so in others: Oliver Treib, Holger Bähr, and Gerda Falkner, 'Modes of Governance: Towards a Conceptual Clarification' (2007) 14(1) Journal of European Public Policy 1.

[25] See, for example, on the US experience, Orly Lobel, 'The Renew Deal: The Fall of Regulation and the Rise of Governance in Contemporary Legal Thought' (2004) 89 Minnesota Law Review 324; Bradley Karkkainen, '"New Governance" in Legal Thought and in the World: Some Splitting as Antidote to Overzealous Lumping' (2004) Minnesota Law Review 471; Douglas NeJaime, 'When New Governance Fails' (2009) 70(2) Ohio State Law Journal 323; and contributors to G De Búrca and J Scott (eds), *Law and New Governance in the EU and the US* (Hart Publishing 2006).

[26] Cris Shore, '"European Governance" or Governmentality? The European Commission and the Future of Democratic Government' (2011) 17(3) European Law Journal 287, 301.

'New' governance has been enormously helpful in understanding the shifts that have occurred in the EU, even though there were debates at the high point of academic interest in new governance as to whether many of the examples were really 'new'. Here, 'new governance' and 'new modes of governance' are generally not used in favour of merely 'governance', except when referring to the body of literature that facilitated these insights. A 'system' of governance captures the way in which different actors are capable of producing and promoting instruments and policies, and do so taking into account that these might also be outside established frames. For example, some of the EU tools that are not legislative measures per se may allow for or even promote different correlations of Member States to work on common initiatives, projects, or missions. The system of governance also relies on the involvement of other actors, which might be NGOs or private actors, or the participation of non-Member States in tools.

The rise in EU agencies as autonomous actors is an example of this institutional dimension of change,[27] and migration has been at the forefront of the establishment and dynamism of agencies on the EU governance horizon. The rapid 'agencification' of EU governance in the 2000s prompted the Commission to call for greater clarity in the vision for and role of agencies.[28] The multiplication of agencies as examples of new institutional actors with varied roles, legal standing, and relationships with other institutions (including via networks and their own interest groups)[29] provides fertile soil for analysis but also a complex, or even confused, picture of governance.[30] The growth in agencies is not limited to the EU,[31] but there are particular issues in the concurrent centralization and decentralization processes within a supranational polity. The institutional diversity is also reflected in the increasingly diverse set of instruments at the disposal of the institutions. Even before considering new modes of governance, the Treaty on European Union introduced instruments such as common actions in the second and third 'pillars' of the Common Foreign and Security Policy (CFSP) and Justice and Home Affairs (JHA). These were not mere equivalents to the Regulations and Directives familiar to the 'core' of EU law-making in the first pillar, but measures whose legal

[27] Giandomenico Majone, 'The New European Agencies: Regulation by Information' (1997) 4(2) Journal of European Public Policy 262; M Groenleer, *The Autonomy of European Union Agencies* (Eburon 2009); Morton Egeberg and Jarle Trondal, 'Researching European Union Agencies: What Have We Learnt (And Where Do We Go from Here)?' (2017) 55(4) JCMS: Journal of Common Market Studies 675.

[28] European Commission, 'European Agencies—The Way Forward' COM (2008) 135 final, 9.

[29] Renaud Dehousse, 'Regulation by Networks in the European Community: The Role of European Agencies' (1997) 4(2) Journal of European Public Policy 246; Ixchel Durán, 'Interest Group Representation in the Formal Design of European Union Agencies' (2018) 12(2) Regulation & Governance 238.

[30] Morten Egeberg, Jarle Trondal, and Nina Vestlund, 'The Quest for Order: Unravelling the Relationship between the European Commission and European Union Agencies' (2015) 22(5) Journal of European Public Policy 609.

[31] See, inter alia, Martin Shapiro, 'The Problems of Independent Agencies in the United States and the European Union' (1997) 4(2) Journal of European Public Policy 276.

effects were undefined and untested. 'Governance' (and consequently describing the EU as a 'system of governance')[32] has thus encapsulated the description of a rich variety of measures without being overly concerned with the precise legal effects of each of the methods.

What is important here is that this advanced stage of governance permits innovation. There is enough familiarity around the legal processes to know what the pitfalls are—when, for example, a certain proposal is likely to meet opposition in the European Parliament, or unlikely to find favour with Member States in the Council. With such familiarity, even though the Treaty equips the institutions to act in a certain way, there are ways around—especially when there is a desire for some Member States to coordinate efforts. Responses to the Eurozone crisis are one such example.[33] Going back further, the Prüm Treaty[34] and the Schengen Agreement are examples of initiatives that started outside the EU institutional framework but were eventually co-opted within it. In migration, the main aim of the book is to try to capture what innovative tools have been emerging and what the relationship is between them in the EU's system of governance.

2.2 Explaining the lack of 'governance' in EU migration management

New governance typically emerges in newer areas of EU activity—especially where Member States are highly protective of their sovereignty, making deep integration and cooperation more challenging. In these contexts, legislation is often viewed as an unsuitable tool for coordination or integration, and achieving goals requires the involvement of multiple players beyond the traditional EU institutions and national governments, including specialized agencies[35] and civil society actors. External migration management shares some, though not all, of these traits.

External migration management is a relatively recent field within EU competence, evolving gradually since the 1990s. While the free movement of workers—as

[32] Paul James Cardwell, *EU External Relations and Systems of Governance: The CFSP, Euro-Mediterranean Partnership and Migration* (Routledge 2009) 36.

[33] See Kaarlo Tuori and Klaus Tuori, *The Eurozone Crisis: A Constitutional Analysis* (Cambridge University Press 2014); Paul Statham and Hans-Jörg Trenz, 'Understanding the Mechanisms of EU Politicization: Lessons from the Eurozone Crisis' (2015) 13(3) *Comparative European Politics* 287–306; James A Caporaso and Martin Rhodes (eds) *Political and Economic Dynamics of the Eurozone Crisis* (Oxford University Press 2016).

[34] Jacques Ziller, 'Le traité de Prüm Une vraie-fausse coopération renforcée dans l'Espace de sécurité de liberté et de justice' (2006) EUILaw Working Papers No. 2006/32, https://hdl.handle.net/1814/6401, accessed 30 March 2026.

[35] Ellen Vos, 'Reforming the European Commission: What Role for EU Agencies?' (2000) 37 *Common Market Law Review* 1113–34; Michelle Everson and others, *The Role of Specialised Agencies in Decentralising EU Governance* (EIPA 1999).

one of the 'four freedoms' of the Single Market—has always been a central element of European integration, attention to external migration became necessary following the removal of internal borders and a significant rise in the number of migrants entering the EU during the early 1990s.[36] Although external agreements addressing the rights of third country nationals date back to the 1970s,[37] it was only with the Treaty of Amsterdam that EU institutions were granted broader powers in this area.

Migration remains at the very core of contemporary debates about national sovereignty.[38] It occupies a prominent place on the domestic agendas of many Member States, reflecting how issues—especially those related to irregular migration—are increasingly portrayed as urgent challenges that Europe must collectively address. This prominence underscores the tension between national interests and the need for a coordinated, EU-wide response, in the absence of harmonization.

At the heart of the EU's efforts in this realm is the creation of an Area of Freedom, Security and Justice (AFSJ). Unlike the more straightforward, unified objectives of projects such as the 'Europe 1992' Single Market programme—which benefited from a clear, cohesive policy goal and robust institutional backing—the AFSJ is marked by a lack of both policy coherence and institutional unity.[39] The dismantling of the previous pillar structure meant that Treaty provisions on AFSJ were absorbed into the broader framework that once governed the Community pillar. However, even as the Treaty envisions an 'ever closer Union', Title V consistently uses terms such as 'cooperation' and 'common policies' rather than invoking full integration. This careful choice of language reflects a persistent sensitivity to national sovereignty.

The complexity deepens with the presence of opt-outs. Denmark, Ireland, and the United Kingdom negotiated specific exemptions from parts of the Treaty,[40] which underscores the clear delineation of competences in this domain. The Treaty itself is notably explicit about the powers that Member States retain over migration and justice, setting it apart from other policy areas where the transfer of authority

[36] This book concerns only the management of migration from outside the EU. Migration within the EU—ie free movement of EU citizens—is not considered, since the legal dispositions are fundamentally different. See further in Chapter 1.

[37] For example, the Association Agreement between the EEC and Turkey, Additional Protocol [1970] OJ L361/59 Arts 36–40.

[38] Jörg Monar, 'Experimental Governance in Justice and Home Affairs' in Charles F Sabel and Jonathan Zeitlin (eds), *Experimentalist Governance in the European Union: Towards a New Architecture* (Oxford University Press 2010) 239; Sandra Lavenex and William Wallace, 'Justice and Home Affairs' in Helen Wallace, William Wallace, and Mark A Pollack (Eds) *Policy-Making in the European Union* (5th edn, Oxford University Press 2005).

[39] Neil Walker, 'In Search of the Area of Freedom, Security and Justice: A Constitutional Odyssey' in N Walker (ed), *Europe's Area of Freedom, Security and Justice* (Oxford University Press 2004) 5.

[40] Protocols 21 and 22 attached to the TFEU. See Steve Peers, 'In a World of Their Own? Justice and Home Affairs Opt-Outs and the Treaty of Lisbon' (2008–09) 10 Cambridge Yearbook of European Legal Studies 383–412.

to the EU is more pronounced.[41] This arrangement creates a paradox: migration management is a top priority on the EU's agenda, yet it does not occupy the central core of European integration.

While external migration management shares several features with areas where new governance models have emerged, it does not neatly fit into these established paradigms. To understand this incongruity, four reasons are identified here. First is the dominance of regular (or 'hard') law. There is a prevailing expectation that migration should be governed primarily by strict, legally binding regulations—leaving limited space for the more flexible, network-based approaches typical of new governance. This hard law framework is seen as essential for managing the complexities and sensitivities inherent in migration issues.

Second is the lack of explicit new governance mechanisms. In contrast to other policy fields where tools such as the Open Method of Coordination (OMC) have been widely adopted, migration policy has not seen a clear, deliberate shift towards these newer modes of governance. The absence of OMC in migration suggests that traditional regulatory approaches continue to dominate.

Third, the external orientation of migration policy marks it out as different, with different institutional logics in play. Migration policy is often seen as an issue of external relations rather than an internal social policy matter. Because it primarily deals with non-EU countries and international borders, it is usually framed within the context of foreign policy, where the language and practice of new governance are less common.

Fourth, and finally, there is a limited role for civil society and participatory engagement. Unlike other areas of social policy, where diverse stakeholder involvement and civil society participation are hallmarks of new governance, migration policy appears to lack a similar participatory dimension. The exception might be in post-migration integration, but the weight of these tools would be in social policy rather than migration policy.[42] This absence further reinforces its categorization as a domain governed by traditional legal and political structures.

In arguing that a governance-based approach is still relevant for understanding migration policy, it is essential to delve deeper into these hypotheses. Rather than catalogue every example of new governance in migration, the aim is to use targeted cases to challenge and refine our current understanding of what new governance can be and how it might operate within the context of migration. By critically engaging with these hypotheses, we can begin to bridge the gap between traditional

[41] Compare special provisions (Articles 23–41 TEU) for the Common Foreign and Security Policy (CFSP). See Paul James Cardwell, 'On Ring-Fencing the Common Foreign and Security Policy in the Legal Order of the European Union' (2013) 64(4) Northern Ireland Legal Quarterly 443.

[42] See, for example, Peter Scholten, Elizabeth Collet, and Milica Petrovic, 'Mainstreaming Migrant Integration? A Critical Analysis of a New Trend in Integration Governance' (2016) 83(2) International Review of Administrative Sciences 283–302.

regulatory frameworks and the emerging, more flexible modes of governance that have reshaped other areas of EU policy.

As explored later in Chapter 3, the initial emphasis on the gaining of competence over migration for the EU institutions was strongly placed on elevating the rights of migrants and third country nationals to those enjoyed by EU citizens. As such, 'migration governance', as described by Thym, seems to be following the same lineage of governance as positively infused with rights protection and therefore 'good' governance. Thym states that the use of 'migration governance' is 'a choice of terminology that recognises that the migration control perspective of state authorities must be accommodated with legitimate interests of migrants, including human rights, and which emphasises that rules on migration are bound to have limited factual impact in practice, especially with regard to cross-border movements'. The choice of 'governance' is closely related to the practicalities of rules and their effects, but also incorporates the recognition of rights.[43]

Similar points can be made in relation to global governance of migration. For Pécoud, global migration governance is associated with the normative quest for 'better' governance. This characterization of migration contrasts with other phenomena of transnational flows, such as trade in goods or capital movements, where international cooperation mechanisms are extensive. In migration, the comparative lack of mechanisms for global migration governance leads to 'suboptimal results, both in socio-economic terms (concerning the benefits of migration for growth and development) and legal/moral terms (with the abuses and tragedies stemming from irregular migration)'.[44] This characterization applies to the EU perspective too: the way in which internal migration governance within the EU (especially vis-à-vis EU citizens, and to a more limited extent third country nationals too) contrasts with external governance is striking, and is at odds with the initial emphasis on EU migration governance being concerned with rights as much as repression.

And yet, much of the argument made in this book is that governance, while benefiting from positive connotations, can and should be used in a way which highlights the potential for the 'bad'. In other words, the way in which innovation applies is rather different to other law and policy areas where governance is more readily applied. In turn, migration helps understand the contemporary nature of the EU in a way which sheds light on its distinctive system of governance.

[43] Daniel Thym, '"Citizens" and "Foreigners" in EU Law: Migration Law and Its Cosmopolitan Outlook' (2016) 22(3) European Law Journal 296, 304.

[44] Antoine Pécoud, 'Narrating an Ideal Migration World? An Analysis of the Global Compact for Safe, Orderly and Regular Migration' (2021) 42(1) Third World Quarterly 16, 17.

2.3 Academic approaches to governance

The language of governance has long been associated with the study of the EU. Though often employed within English-language scholarship in political science and management scholarship, the use of governance in EU studies became increasingly prominent in the 1990s. Using governance as a means to approach and analyse the EU pre-empted the more widespread 'official' use of governance by the EU institutions, characterized in particular by the White Paper on Governance in 2001.[45] The use of 'governance' in EU studies fulfilled a distinct need in the context of an entity that defies the easy categorization of an emerging state, 'super-state', federation, or polity.

Disciplinary traditions that make up the more general canon of EU scholarship underwent governance 'turns' in the early to mid-1990s. Bulmer outlined the 'toolkit' that EU scholars had developed in relation to different areas of EU activity, drawing on the rich tradition of international relations (IR) scholarship.[46] Jachtenfuchs subsequently reflected on the extent to which governance could provide a theory of European integration, but concluded that such a thing would be neither feasible nor desirable.[47] Rather, the opportunity provided by governance was to incorporate the application of theories beyond IR to the EU, as the EU 'is the place where fundamental developments that are transforming the possibilities of effective and responsible governance are probably stronger than elsewhere'.[48] Common to these approaches is a move away from understanding the EU and its institutions, policies, and politics through the lens of centralized, formal procedures, including legislative processes.[49]

In the absence of a single theoretical or conceptual framework,[50] the governance *approach* to the study of the EU has been associated with where (institutional) power lies. It closely linked to the idea that governance can—or should—be *better* by prioritizing the role of democratic input into processes and institutional arrangements. The role of the European Parliament as a component in the legitimacy/oversight dimension of governance had long been highlighted, even before direct elections to the Parliament in 1979.[51] However, governance carries

[45] White Paper on Governance (n 22).

[46] Simon Bulmer, 'The New Governance of the European Union: A New Institutionalist Approach' (1994) 13(4) Journal of European Public Policy 351.

[47] Markus Jachtenfuchs, 'The Governance Approach to European Integration' (2001) 39(2) JCMS: Journal of Common Market Studies 245, 259.

[48] ibid 260.

[49] Kohler-Koch and Rittberger, 'The "Governance Turn" in EU Studies' (n 1) 42.

[50] Oliver Treib, Holger Bähr, and Gerda Falkner, 'Modes of Governance: Towards a Conceptual Clarification' (2007) 14(1) Journal of European Public Policy 1.

[51] See, inter alia, Desmond Dinan, 'Governance and Institutions: The Unrelenting Rise of the European Parliament' (2014) 52 JCMS: Journal of Common Market Studies 109; Berthold Rittberger, 'Institutionalizing Representative Democracy in the European Union: The Case of the European Parliament' (2012) 50(1) JCMS: Journal of Common Market Studies 18, 24–33; Cristina Fasone,

an implicit recognition that increasing the Parliament's powers would not alone combat democratic legitimacy concerns.[52] Within the unique institutional set-up of the EU, replacing national Parliamentary oversight with the European Parliament's oversight powers alone has generally been thought to be insufficient.[53]

For legal scholars, much of the discussion since the 1990s has centred on looking beyond the traditional lenses of integration through law. The increasing complexity of the EU horizon, and in particular the inclusion of new instruments in the second and third pillars of the TEU at Maastricht,[54] confronted the EU legal academy with a challenge of how to account for them (if at all). As Möllers noted, the adoption of the language of governance permitted scholars to gain new perspectives on old problems.[55] At the heart of this debate was the potential shift in paradigm from the centre of gravity of legal study of the EU's legal order, that is to say the integration process centred on the Community Method, to other phenomena either where the Community Method did not apply or where it was unable to account for everything happening. Legal accounts that were restricted to analysis of enforceable legal texts were increasingly unable to explain even in part some of the most dynamic areas of European integration, particularly around Social Europe.[56] This shift heralded an explosion of studies of 'new governance' across different disciplines, including law. Scott and Trubek's special issue of the *European Law Journal* in 2002 placed new governance in the mainstream of EU legal scholarship and demonstrated the diversity of the policy areas in which new governance could be observed and subject to analysis.[57]

Recognition of the diversity of tools of governance was then retrospectively applied to instruments and techniques, such as coordination mechanisms, stretching back through the EU integration process.[58] Economic integration has generally

'European Economic Governance and Parliamentary Representation: What Place for the European Parliament?' (2014) 20(2) European Law Journal 164.

[52] Gavin Barrett, 'European Economic Governance: Deficient in Democratic Legitimacy?' (2018) 40(3) Journal of European Integration 249.

[53] Ben Crum, 'Parliamentary Accountability in Multilevel Governance: What Role for Parliaments in Post-Crisis EU Economic Governance?' (2017) 25(2) Journal of European Public Policy 268; Johannes Pollak and Peter Slominski, 'The European Parliament' in Christopher J Bickerton, Dermot Hodson, and Uwe Puetter (eds), *The New Intergovernmentalism: States and Governmental Actors in the Post-Maastricht Era* (Oxford University Press 2015) 245.

[54] Bruno de Witte, 'An Undivided Union? Differentiated Integration in Post-Brexit Times' (2018) 55 Common Market Review 227, 239; see also Jo Shaw and Gillian More (eds), *The New Legal Dynamics of European Union* (Clarendon Press 1995).

[55] Christoph Möllers, 'European Governance: Meaning and Value of a Concept' (2006) 43(2) Common Market Law Review 313.

[56] David Trubek and James Mosher, 'New Governance, Employment Policy and the European Social Model' in David Trubek and Johathan Zeitlin (eds), *Governing Work and Welfare in a New Economy* (Oxford University Press 2004).

[57] Joanne Scott and David M Trubek, 'Mind the Gap: Law and New Approaches to Governance in the European Union' (2008) 8(1) European Law Journal 1.

[58] See Dermot Hodson and Imelda Maher, 'The Open Method as a New Mode of Governance: The Case of Soft Economic Policy Co-ordination' (2001) 39(4) JCMS: Journal of Common Market Studies 719.

been regarded as the starting point for many of the instruments and innovations of 'new governance' which have then been applied across numerous policy areas, though with less attention to migration.[59] The informality associated with governance equally became prominent in scholarship.[60]

Governance approaches thus incorporated the rise of specific instruments whose legal and political effects are not adequately defined in the Treaty or elsewhere. Some of these, such as the OMC,[61] have evolved into much more formal instruments becoming 'regularized', including via judicial review challenges in the Court.[62] The OMC was often written about in terms of its promise and ability to 'regulate' in newer areas of competence[63] (although with some exceptions).[64] The possibilities that OMC appeared to offer for Social Europe, and to move beyond long-standing barriers in integration, were at the forefront of the debate.[65] Over the course of the 2000s, greater attention focused on whether the OMC was capable of meeting its objectives[66] and whether it had a demonstrable impact on the policy areas that it was supposed to help pursue.[67]

Governance permitted scholarly accounts of the raft of instruments which sit somewhere between the formal and the informal and defy easy characterization. Tools and instruments that do not enjoy legal definitions but may well have law-like effects can be accounted for. This was recognized as a constitutional challenge to establish ways of making and enforcing law, but also to recognize when and where it occurs[68] and whether the presence or absence of 'traditional' legislation was a matter for concern or not.[69]

59 See the discussion that follows.

60 Mareike Kleine, 'Informal Governance in the European Union' (2014) 21(2) Journal of European Public Policy 303.

61 Kenneth Armstrong, 'The Open Method of Coordination: Obstinate or Obsolete?' in Robert Schütze and Takis Tridimas (eds), *Oxford Principles of European Union Law Volume I: The European Legal Order* (Oxford University Press 2018).

62 See Emilia Korkea-aho, *Adjudicating New Governance: Deliberative Democracy in the European Union* (Routledge 2015) 88.

63 Susana Borrás and Claudio Radaelli, 'Recalibrating the Open Method of Coordination: Towards Diverse and More Effective Usages' (2010) Swedish Institute for European Policy Studies No 7 55.

64 Vassilis Hatzopoulos, 'Why the Open Method of Coordination Is Bad For You: A Letter to the EU' (2007) 13(3) European Law Journal 309.

65 Kenneth Armstrong and Claire Kilpatrick, 'Law, Governance, or New Governance? The Changing Open Method of Coordination' (2007) 13 Columbia Journal of European Law 649.

66 Caroline de la Porte and Philippe Pochet, 'Why and How (Still) Study the Open Method of Co-ordination (OMC)?' (2012) 22(3) Journal of European Social Policy 336.

67 See, in particular, Kenneth Armstrong, *Governing Social Inclusion: Europeanization through Policy Coordination* (Oxford University Press 2010); Paul Copeland and Beryl ter Haar, 'A Toothless Bite? The Effectiveness of the European Employment Strategy as a Governance Tool' (2013) 23(1) Journal of European Social Policy 21.

68 Gráinne de Búrca, 'The Constitutional Challenge of New Governance in the European Union' (2003) 28(6) European Law Review 814; Vassilis Hatzopoulos, 'Hard to Soft: Governance in the EU Internal Market' (2012) 15 Cambridge Yearbook of European Legal Studies 101.

69 Renaud Dehousse (ed), *The 'Community Method': Obstinate or Obsolete?* (Palgrave Macmillan 2011); Adrienne Heritier, 'New Modes of Governance in Europe: Policy-Making Without Legislating?' in A Heritier (ed), *Common Goods: Reinventing European and International Governance* (Rowman and Littlefield 2002).

Questions of how to recognize, approach, and study such phenomena arose concurrently. As a meeting point between academic traditions of law and politics, the focus on governance permitted respective disciplines to take seriously the possibilities of hitherto underexplored dimensions and to recognize both the importance of legislation and its absence.[70] The extent to which the new modes of governance were considered to be significant resulted in their characterization as a constitutional 'challenge'[71] and as part of an overall transition of one type of governing by a set of institutions to another. The obsolescence or sidelining of the Community Method was extensively discussed, and along with it the assumptions about how to study and understand EU law, bringing in an emphasis on coordination as well as integration and harmonization.[72] As a result, deeper consideration was devoted to phenomena such as post-legislative guidance,[73] guidelines,[74] benchmarking,[75] and mainstreaming.[76] When looking across the wide horizon of policy areas and cross-cutting themes, these phenomena and our understandings of them contributed to a transformation of EU law to EU governance.[77] The oft-highlighted danger was that the 'fuzziness' associated with such measures risked the charge of their existence being ineffective window-dressing.

The issue of enforceability has been central to the debate over the significance of instruments or tools that lack substantive links to enforceability. This is particularly relevant as the Court of Justice has stated that soft law 'cannot be regarded as having no legal effect'.[78] Trubek and Trubek argued against dismissing new modes of governance due to their supposed unenforceability.[79] They suggested that these

[70] Scott and Trubek, 'Mind the Gap: Law and New Approaches to Governance in the European Union' (n 57).

[71] Gráinne de Búrca, 'The Constitutional Challenge of New Governance in the European Union' (2003) 56(1) Current Legal Problems 403.

[72] Stijn Smismans, 'From Harmonization to Co-ordination? EU Law in the Lisbon Governance Architecture' (2011) 18(4) Journal of European Public Policy 504.

[73] Joanne Scott, 'In Legal Limbo: Post-Legislative Guidance as a Challenge for European Administrative Law' (2011) 48(2) Common Market Law Review 329.

[74] Steven Vaughan, 'Differentiation and Dysfunction: An Exploration of Post-Legislative Guidance Practices in 14 EU Agencies' (2015) 17 Cambridge Yearbook of European Legal Studies 66.

[75] Graham Room, 'Policy Benchmarking in the European Union: Indicators and Ambiguities' (2005) 26(2) Policy Studies 117.

[76] Christine Booth and Cinnamon Bennett, 'Gender Mainstreaming in the European Union: Towards a New Conception and Practice of Equal Opportunities?' (2002) 9(4) European Journal of Women's Studies 430; Stijn Smismans and Rachel Minto, 'Are Integrated Impact Assessments the Way Forward for Mainstreaming in the European Union?' (2017) 11(3) Regulation & Governance 229, 231.

[77] Mark Dawson, *New Governance and the Transformation of European Law: Coordinating EU Social Law and Policy* (Cambridge University Press 2011).

[78] Case C-322/88 *Grimaldi v Fonds des maladies professionnelles* ECLI:EU:C:1989:646; for analysis of the line of case law starting with Grimaldi, see Oana Stefan, 'European Union Soft Law: New Developments Concerning the Divide Between Legally Binding Force and Legal Effects' (2012) 75(5) Modern Law Review 879; Emilia Korkea-aho, 'National Courts and European Soft Law: Is Grimaldi Still Good Law?' (2018) 37 Yearbook of European Law 470.

[79] David Trubek and Louise Trubek, 'Hard and Soft Law in the Construction of Social Europe: The Role of the Open Method of Coordination' (2005) 11(3) European Law Journal 343, 356.

new modes could 'bring about change' through processes such as shaming, diffusion through imitation or discourse, deliberation, learning, and networks.[80] Traditional legal instruments do not always necessarily change behaviour, and the relationship between the courts and new governance modes is now seen as closer than previously thought. These various means of effecting change demonstrate that new governance modes employ diverse methods to achieve their goals in less direct, more abstract ways, and through multiple, complex institutional frameworks. While the debate has primarily focused on internal governance, valuable insights have also been developed on how governance frameworks operate within the EU's neighbourhood through both formal and informal promotion of rules and persuasive forums.[81]

The language of governance has helped blur the lines between law and policy, or 'hard' and 'soft' EU law. However, this blending raises as many questions as it answers due to the flexible nature of 'governance' and its implications. As Armstrong has pointed out, focusing on classifying tools such as post-legislative guidance and guidelines as 'hard' or 'soft' can be overly simplistic and ignore the diverse forms of governance.[82] An instrument that is non-binding in the legal form can nevertheless contain enforcement measures which make it 'binding' on a different level.[83] Treating everything that is not legally binding as 'soft' law risks creating an overly broad category that fails to capture important distinctions.[84] Certain 'new' governance modes, such as benchmarking, peer review, and mainstreaming, challenge the hard/soft dichotomy because they can influence actors' behaviours without formal enforcement mechanisms.

Some of these modes appear in the governance of migration, alongside tools such as migration profiles, migration partnerships, compacts, and 'statements'. A reliance on 'hard' or 'soft' implies a categorization that, in turn, risks neglecting the processes that link them and their effects. For example, the EU–Türkiye Statement could be considered to be soft law (as a political agreement) but appears to produce hard law effects, albeit ones that cannot be challenged.[85] Moreno-Lax has convincingly argued that 'softification' in migration law has a strategic aim behind it, which not only bypasses frames of transparency and process (as is

[80] ibid 356.

[81] Frank Schimmelfennig and Wolfgang Wagner, 'External Governance in the European Union' (2004) 11(4) Journal of European Public Policy 657; Sandra Lavenex, 'EU External Governance in "Wider Europe"' (2004) 11 Journal of European Public Policy 680; S Lavenex and Frank Schimmelfennig, 'EU Rules beyond EU Borders: Theorizing External Governance in European Politics' (2009) 16(6) Journal of European Public Policy 791.

[82] Kenneth Armstrong, 'The Character of EU Law and Governance: From "Community Method" to New Modes of Governance' (2011) 64 Current Legal Problems 179, 206.

[83] Anne Ausfelder and others, 'EU Soft-Law: Non-Binding but Enforceable' (2024) 30(4) European Law Journal 668.

[84] ibid 208.

[85] See discussion in Chapter 7.

also argued here) but goes as far as the 'constitutional dismantling' of migration policy.[86] In this respect, the shift to soft law and informality is less of an organic process than one used in coordination with the response by the EU institutions to migration as a fundamental 'crisis' threatening the continent.

As a result, although many works find a satisfactory working definition between hard and soft law in different contexts, here there is a risk of obscuring the main thrust of the book, namely to explore where instruments in migration may take on the appearance of established legal tools but in fact are not. For this purpose, the distinction is made between formal and informal legal tools, and the term 'formal informality' is used to denote where the lines are blurred rather than 'hard' and 'soft'.

2.4 The maturing governance debate

The discussion of governance in the EU has evolved into various forms, with Multi-Level Governance (MLG) being the most established.[87] MLG emphasizes non-hierarchical decision-making and has generated extensive scholarship across different policy areas and institutional levels. This approach involves seeking the location of political authority, which has shifted focus to agencies and new actors such as the European Ombudsman and networks such as the European Judicial Network.[88] While legal scholars have utilized MLG frameworks and acknowledged the EU's layered structure, MLG has primarily been of interest to those studying policy and policy processes. MLG has proved to be resilient and has found its way into legal accounts.[89] But even here, it remains an under-developed concept. This is partly due to the fluidity in governance processes that it seeks to capture and investigate, but also 'points to the need for greater precision and rigour in the different types of MLG that combine in complex webs of modern governance'.[90]

[86] Violeta Moreno-Lax, 'EU Constitutional Dismantling through Strategic Informalisation: Soft Readmission Governance as Concerted Dis-integration' (2024) 30(1–2) European Law Journal 29.

[87] Liesbet Hooghe and Gary Marks, *Multi-Level Governance and European Integration* (Rowman and Littlefield 2001); Ian Bache and Matthew Flinders (eds), *Multi-Level Governance* (Oxford University Press 2004); Simona Piattoni, *The Theory of Multi-Level Governance: Conceptual, Empirical, and Normative Challenges* (Oxford University Press 2010); Paul Stephenson, 'Twenty Years of Multi-Level Governance: "Where Does It Come From? What Is It? Where Is It Going?"' (2013) 20(6) Journal of European Public Policy 817; Arjan Shackel, Liesbet Hooghe, and Gary Marks, 'Multilevel Governance and the State' in S Liebfried and others (eds), *The Oxford Handbook of Transformations of the State* (Oxford University Press 2015) 271.

[88] See, inter alia, Nikos Vogiatiz, *The European Ombudsman and Good Administration in the European Union* (Palgrave Macmillan 2018); Anne Weyembergh, Inés Armada, and Chloé Brière, 'Competition or Cooperation? State of Play and Future Perspectives on the Relations between Europol, Eurojust and the European Judicial Network' (2015) 6(2) New Journal of European Criminal Law 258–87.

[89] Firat Cengiz, 'Legitimacy and Multi-Level Governance in European Union Competition Law: A Deliberative Discursive Approach' (2016) 54(4) JCMS: Journal of Common Market Studies 826.

[90] Ian Bache, Ian Bartle, and Matthew Flinders, 'Multi-Level Governance' in C Ansell and J Torfing (eds), *Handbook on Theories of Governance* (Edward Elgar 2016) 486; see also Paul James Cardwell,

A more recent and influential strand of governance research is experimentalist governance. This approach integrates new modes of governance into a broader pattern of democratic problem-solving processes, extending beyond regulation by central authorities. By viewing these new modes as part of the established system rather than external to it, legal scholars were invited to explore the implications of this new architecture.[91] The approach retains some of the optimism of the new governance debates insofar as it is concerned with the better ways in which governance might function as a democratic process. However, some aspects of the approach in terms of its democratic potential might only be applicable to the kinds of policies where, for example, civil society actors or other non-state actors play a key role, such as in social policy or economic governance.[92] With the advent of crisis and crises-focused policymaking in areas beyond these areas, including in migration, experimental governance's democratizing aspect may be lost.[93]

By the late 2000s, the 'governance turn' increasingly focused on Europeanization and relationships among institutional actors.[94] The failed process of enacting a Treaty Establishing a Constitution for Europe in 2005 and the subsequent 'rescuing' of many of its provisions in the Treaty of Lisbon has spurred institutional questions, particularly in economic governance, external relations, and the AFSJ, which need adaptation to a larger EU with little prospect of further Treaty reform. As the new modes of governance became more familiar and regularized, they continued to attract academic interest. However, the prolonged economic crisis, along with other crises such as migration, Brexit, the Covid-19 pandemic, and rising populism and democratic backsliding in several Member States, has significantly impacted the EU and contemporary approaches to studying it. Against this background, some of the approaches to understanding the EU focus on the dynamics of cooperation and decision-making in ways which—at least partly—depart from our previous understandings. New intergovernmentalism[95] and differentiated

'Governance as the Meeting Place of EU Law and Politics' in Paul James Cardwell and Marie-Pierre Granger (eds), *Research Handbook on the Politics of EU Law* (Edward Elgar 2020) 10–30.

[91] Charles Sabel and Jonathan Zeitlin, 'Learning from Difference: The New Architecture of Experimentalist Governance in the EU' (2008) 14(1) European Law Journal 3; Charles F Sabel and Jonathan Zeitlin, *Experimentalist Governance in the European Union: Towards a New Architecture* (Oxford University Press 2010); Mark Dawson, 'New Modes of Governance' in D Patterson and A Södersten (eds), *A Companion to European Law and International Law* (Wiley 2016) 119.

[92] Tanja Börzel, 'Experimentalist Governance in the EU: The Emperor's New Clothes?' (2012) 6(3) Regulation & Governance 378.

[93] Jonathan Zeitlin, 'EU Experimentalist Governance in Times of Crisis: West European Politics' 39(5) West European Politics 1073. See, however, on the UN Global Compact, Sandra Lavenex, 'The UN Global Compacts on Migration and Refugees: A Case for Experimentalist Governance?' (2020) 26(4) Global Governance: A Review of Multilateralism and International Organizations 673.

[94] Rebecca Adler-Nissen, 'Towards a Practice Turn in EU Studies: The Everyday of European Integration' (2016) 54(1) JCMS: Journal of Common Market Studies 87, 89.

[95] Chris Bickerton, Dermot Hodson, and Uwe Puetter (eds), *The New Intergovernmentalism: States and Supranational Actors in the Post-Maastricht Era* (Oxford University Press 2015).

integration[96] are two such examples. Both emphasize the importance of mechanisms of features in the EU governance architecture which are not particularly new, but have moved from the periphery to the centre. The hallmark in the increasingly complex system of governance and institutional interactions at the EU level is the rise of consensus-seeking deliberation as well as contestation, including legal contestation through the CJEU.[97]

The interface between the legal–political authority of the state and regional, international, or transnational actors has led to the language of governance being used in particular areas, of which the governance of migration is one, alongside environment, health, trade, and so on. The association of migration with governance in the EU context has been a later development. This is partly because of the lack of EU competence in this area, but also because of the extent to which the EU has gained a role in the institutions and processes associated with migration to the EU over time. But by the time that there is sufficient interaction between the institutions, Member States, and other actors operating with the sphere of migration, the use of the language of governance has already become extremely familiar and widespread.

Crucially, the use of governance allows for the taking into account of the formal and the informal—and modes, measures, tools, policies, and instruments that fall somewhere in-between. This book is concerned with looking at the content and effects of the multitude of names that these phenomena go by, which are situated in what Scott has referred to as 'legal limbo'.[98] Tracking the vocabulary is a significant challenge, since there are no definitions (legal or otherwise) of the kind of instances that are capable of having an impact on the governance of migration. Looking behind this new language of 'pacts', 'ways forward', and 'hot spots'[99] suits both the language of governance and many of its tenets.

[96] Frank Schimmelfennig, Dirk Leuffen, and Berthold Rittberger, 'The European Union as a System of Differentiated Integration: Interdependence, Politicization and Differentiation' (2015) 22(6) Journal of European Public Policy 764; Benjamin Leruth and Christopher Lord, 'Differentiated Integration in the European Union: A Concept, a Process, a System or a Theory?' (2015) 22(6) Journal of European Public Policy 754; Frank Schimmelfennig, 'Good Governance and Differentiated Integration: Graded Membership in the European Union' (2016) 55(4) European Journal of Political Research 789; Paul James Cardwell, 'The End of Exceptionalism and a Strengthening of Coherence? Law and Legal Integration in the European Union Post-Brexit' (2019) 57(6) JCMS: Journal of Common Market Studies 1407.

[97] Vivian Schmidt, 'Rethinking EU Governance: From "Old" to "New" Approaches to Who Steers Integration' (2018) 56(7) JCMS: Journal of Common Market Studies 1544, 1557–58.

[98] Scott, 'In Legal Limbo: Post-Legislative Guidance as a Challenge for European Administrative Law' (n 73) 329.

[99] Alexandra Bousiou and Evie Papada, 'Introducing the EC Hotspot Approach: A Framing Analysis of EU's Most Authoritative Crisis Policy Response' (2020) 58(6) International Migration 139.

2.5 Governance in the context of migration

Since the aim of this book is to uncover and subject to analysis the increasingly rich horizon of the governance of migration, the book will use 'formal' and 'informal' as relatively open categories, placing the emphasis on tools and measures that follow established (and transparent) processes and those which have emerged in a less formal manner. But the relationships between the different measures are equally important: if the EU's legal–constitutional framework suggests that the goals will be achieved via legislation, then the emphasis on informal means to do so via policymaking is equally important to understand how and why this is so.

Such policy instruments, to use the term commonly applied in recent literature to these instances,[100] can be praised for their effectiveness—and this is certainly the case for the EU–Türkiye Statement, in the eyes of the Commission.[101] However, as Hartlapp has argued in a more general context, there is a question mark over the transparency of modes that appear in different contexts and institutional settings.[102] Involvement of other actors is an integral part of governance and, in areas such as employment and social policy, usually refers to civil society bodies, where concerns about transparency do not apply in the same way. For migration, the involvement of third states, organizations such as the International Office of Migration (IOM), and other NGOs raises questions of transparency, since migration is inherently connected to the exercise of rights.[103] Information-sharing with third countries is one such example.[104]

Raising transparency and openness brings into focus the normative aspects usually associated with governance. Much 'new governance' literature has focused on the potential for innovative instruments to promote good or better governance. This is especially the case where aims—including those stated as goals in the Treaty—such as gender equality or environmental protection cut across different law and policymaking areas as well as being the subject of instruments themselves.

[100] See for example Florian Trauner and Sarah Wolff, 'The Negotiation and Contestation of EU Migration Policy Instruments—A Research Framework' (2014) 16(1) European Journal of Migration and Law 1; Peter Slominski and Florian Trauner, 'Reforming Me Softly—How Soft Law Has Changed EU Return Policy since the Migration Crisis' (2020) 44(1) West European Politics 93.

[101] European Commission, 'EU–Turkey Statement: Four Years On', https://home-affairs.ec.europa.eu/system/files/2020-03/20200318_managing-migration-eu-turkey-statement-4-years-on_en.pdf accessed 2 June 2025. For a full analysis, see Gamze Ovacık, Meltem Ineli-Ciger, and Orçun Ulusoy, 'Taking Stock of the EU–Turkey Statement in 2024' (2024) 26(2) European Journal of Migration and Law 154.

[102] Miriam Hartlapp, 'Soft Law Implementation in the EU Multilevel System: Legitimacy and Governance Efficiency Revisited' in Nathalie Behnke, Jörg Broschek, and Jared Sonnicksen (eds), *Configurations, Dynamics and Mechanisms of Multilevel Governance* (Palgrave Macmillan 2019).

[103] Paolo Cuttitta, 'Repoliticization through Search and Rescue? Humanitarian NGOs and Migration Management in the Central Mediterranean' (2018) 23(3) Geopolitics 632.

[104] Hartmut Aden, 'Interoperability between EU Policing and Migration Databases: Risks for Privacy' (2020) 26(1) European Public Law 93; and Luisa Marin, 'The Cooperation Between Frontex and Third Countries in Information Sharing: Practices, Law and Challenges in Externalizing Border Control Functions' (2020) 26(1) European Public Law 157.

In this way, and echoing the widespread use of 'good governance' in national and international contexts, there is a sense imbued in the term that governance is somehow better—in terms of the inclusion of citizens in process and the respect for rights—than 'government' or 'management'.[105] The use of governance in this book questions this assumption, since the emphasis on the risk to the protection of rights in migration shows that governance can have just as much of a 'harder edge' and repressive character as 'government'.

In a governance-based account of EU integration, the emphasis is placed on the possibility that a more diverse set of tools opens the possibility for greater effectiveness in meeting goals. These goals are set out in the Treaty or in the various migration-related strategies, notably the Global Approach to Migration and Mobility. But the difficulties of measuring effectiveness are inherent the less tangible the various modes are. Instances of new governance as social interactions creating shared social understandings have been instructive here in terms of the emergence and operation of new modes.[106] As already noted, a common theme in recent years has been the development of ways of dealing with migration in the context of crisis, thus placing the emphasis on speed as well as effectiveness. Even without the crisis context, newer modes are more responsive to changing contexts and preferences than is provided by the regularity of law.[107] Further, modes rarely exist in isolation from familiar, traditional law in the form of Regulations and Directives, which also helps to explain the difficulties in delimiting them and subjecting them to analysis. In the migration context, this type of traditional law also includes the type of international agreements that follow the Treaty-based processes and are as such open to both debate and scrutiny. Variety, as Sabel and Zeitlin have argued, is an integral part of governance and thus over-categorization is not fruitful.[108]

The extent to which 'crisis' is an appropriate material characterization of what has occurred in patterns of migration to Europe in recent years based on actual numbers of people migrating does not tell the full story. Rather, there is little doubt that the reinforcing of the language of crisis in discourse and practice emerging from the EU institutions and the Member States has had an impact on governance. Significantly, as Fine and Thiollet tell us, this relationship is not one-way; rather, 'crisis is also produced through governance'.[109] The way in which a situation

[105] See further discussion later in this chapter.

[106] Gráinne de Búrca and Joanne Scott, 'Introduction' in de Búrca and Scott (eds), *Law and New Governance in the EU and the US* (n 25).

[107] Neil Walker and Gráinne de Búrca, 'Narrowing the Gap? Law and New Approaches to Governance in the European Union' (2007) 13 Columbia Journal of European Law 521.

[108] Sabel and Zeitlin, 'Learning from Difference: The New Architecture of Experimentalist Governance in the EU' (n 91) 305.

[109] Shoshana Fine and Hélène Thiollet, 'Does Crisis Matter for European Migration Governance? A Framework Paper' (2020) Migration Governance and Asylum Crises <https://www.magyc.uliege.be/upload/docs/application/pdf/2021-09/d3.1-v2-april-2020-1.pdf> accessed 2 June 2025.

is perceived as a crisis means that the search for what is an appropriate response is embedded as 'common sense'.[110]

Here, this insight into the implications of the language of 'crisis' can help explain innovation in governance as less the product of reflective practices seeking optimum ways to meet the goals, but rather normalizing departures from established practices and processes. That is to say, the language of crisis would justify a departure from transparent but slow or efficient law-making, to do something different. The result would be successful in terms of effecting change and doing so rapidly, but at the price of setting a precedent of alternatives and normalizing means that do not, for example, take into account obligations found in international law, human rights, or procedural fairness. 'Common sense' becomes normalized as a response.[111] Put even more starkly, the different modes in new governance cannot be dismissed as inexistent or irrelevant since the official discourse refers to the use of 'all available tools' and—unlike in areas where the promise of 'new' governance was most keenly stressed (such as employment and Social Europe)—migration is one area where the words and promises of 'action' have been backed up with a budget to match.

2.6 Migration governance versus migration management

This book adopts the terminology of governance, rather than the—oft competing—notion of management. Aside from the normative associations of governance with something positive, as explored above, the distinction between management and governance might appear to be slight. In management the focus is very much on the role of state actors, acting in coordination or conjunction with 'others' in a top-down manner to define the ways and means by which individuals may enter, stay in, or leave a territory. Management carries with it the notion that individuals themselves are to be managed. In both a legal and a practical sense, there is more limited scope for the place and role of the individual, although individuals may have rights associated with legal changes to decisions relating to them and management structures may need to pay regard to administrative or procedural standards. Certainly, the inability of individuals—particularly those caught up in some of the innovative forms of governance that have emerged—to assert any rights has been a growing theme.[112] In this respect, just as governance has the same root as government but indicates something different, the same can be said of governance as distinct from management.

[110] ibid.

[111] James Brassett and Nick Vaughan-Williams, 'Crisis Is Governance: Sub-Prime, the Traumatic Event, and Bare Life' (2012) 26(1) Global Society 19.

[112] Refer to General Court; see T-257/16 *NM v European Council* ECLI:EU:T:2017:130.

In the EU context, the transfer of decision-making has occurred in wide fields, though less so in migration. Nevertheless, the emergence of agencies, including Frontex, as well as the roles of the EU institutions[113] show that while a wholesale transfer of competences has not occurred, we see a picture building of interactions between public bodies in the pursuit of certain goals. It is therefore possible to identify EU—as opposed to national—migration governance since the 1990s and in particularly since the 2000s. By its very nature, governance of migration paints a complex picture which is asserted here to not be fully captured by management. Management does not preclude the involvement of other bodies and institutions, including international organizations, NGOs, and civil society, as a long line of literature on New Public Management as a governmental 'paradigm' stretching back to the 1980s tells us.[114] Even in (global) migration, the prominent role played by the IOM as a 'service body'[115] sitting outside the UN framework is often characterized as a management role.[116] In the EU context, the use of international organizations in migration has become commonplace.[117] Spijkerboer has written of the 'clientelism' associated with the outsourcing of EU migration policy to third states, international organizations, and corporations.[118]

Yet, management implies a top-down relationship between the manager (largely the state actor) and the recipient (i.e. the individual migrant) which is less easily identifiable in the EU context due to the only partial sharing of competence in this field. Moreover, the use of governance implies a much more complex relationship and, crucially, a blurring of the lines between these parties. First, this is implied by the complexity of the relationship between the Member States and the EU institutions. There is little denying that these actors are the main players in the

[113] See Chapters 3 and 4.

[114] Georg Menz, 'Neo-Liberalism, Privatization and the Outsourcing of Migration Management: A Five-Country Comparison' (2011) 15(2) Competition & Change 116; Anne McNevin, Antje Missbach, and Deddy Mulyana, 'The Rationalities of Migration Management: Control and Subversion in an Indonesia-Based Counter-Smuggling Campaign' (2016) 10(3) International Political Sociology 223. See also the contributions to Thomas Gammeltoft-Hansen and Ninna Nyberg Sørensen (eds), *The Migration Industry and the Commercialization of International Migration* (Routledge 2013).

[115] Sara Kalm, 'Liberalizing Movements? The Political Rationality of Global Migration Management' in Martin Geiger and Antoine Pécoud (eds), *The Politics of International Migration Management* (Palgrave Macmillan 2010).

[116] See, for example, Ishan Ashutosh and Alison Mountz, 'Migration Management for the Benefit of Whom? Interrogating the Work of the International Organization for Migration' (2011) 15(1) Citizenship Studies 21; Younes Ahouga, 'The Local Turn in Migration Management: The IOM and the Engagement of Local Authorities' (2018) 44(9) Journal of Ethnic and Migration Studies 1523; Fabian Georgi, 'For the Benefit of Some: The International Organization for Migration and Its Global Migration Management' in Martin B Geiger and Antonie Pécoud (eds), *The Politics of International Migration Management* (Palgrave Macmillan 2010); and case studies including Inken Bartels, '"We must do it gently": The Contested Implementation of the IOM's Migration Management in Morocco' (2017) 5(3) Migration Studies 315.

[117] Sandra Lavenex, 'Multilevelling EU External Governance: The Role of International Organizations in the Diffusion of EU Migration Policies' (2015) 42(4) Journal of Ethnic and Migration Studies 554.

[118] Thomas Spijkerboer, 'Migration Management Clientelism' (2012) 48(12) Journal of Ethnic and Migration Studies 2892.

governance of migration. However, and second, the way in which governance of migration works is not merely by the law-based rules relating to migration. Rather, the deliberate blossoming of tools and instruments which are at arm's length from the core of the 'state' suggests something more. In a similar vein, the substance of governance can include such phenomena as mainstreaming,[119] where considerations on, inter alia, human rights and gender[120] can be brought into scope. This sits less well with conceptions of management. Nevertheless, while governance points to often rights-based (or at the very least, rights-sensitive), collaborative approaches where the role of the state is less prominent, there are multiple examples where the reality does not match the rhetoric.[121]

It is particularly useful in the EU context to refer to the institutional set-up as a system of governance. Once again, this implies a number of actors working within a legal–political space, but also encapsulates the kind of diversity found among the outputs and workings of such a system. In other words, the system of governance does not merely produce laws in the forms of regulations, directives, and decisions, but gives rise to other forms of institutional phenomena via the iterative, regularized processes of cooperation. More concretely, the complexity inherent in a system of governance both permits innovation—as can be seen via the analysis later in this book—and obfuscates the transparency required in how these innovations affect rights. The informal dimensions of what emerge from a system of governance which involves not only the EU and its institutions, agencies, and Member States but others too, thus becoming as significant as the formal. 'Formal informality' thus comes into play as a particular type of tool or measure, which appears to share characteristics of both.

2.7 The theoretical framework of the book

The use of governance, as detailed above, allows for a wide scope of enquiry beyond what might be considered as 'law' in migration. Governance does not, however, denote a particular or specific conceptual framework to answer the questions posed by this book. The approach to uncovering and understanding the governance of migration adopted in this book uses in its framework the rich theoretical traditions of institutionalism in both political science and law, and incorporates insights from

[119] See François Crépeau and Idil Atak, 'Global Migration Governance: Avoiding Commitments on Human Rights, Yet Tracing a Course for Cooperation' (2016) 34(2) Netherlands Quarterly of Human Rights 113.

[120] Jane Freedman, 'Mainstreaming Gender in EU Immigration and Asylum Policy' in Heather MacRae and Elaine Weiner (eds), *Towards Gendering Institutionalism: Equality in Europe* (Rowman & Littlefield 2017).

[121] See later chapters in this book.

constructivism (largely familiar to scholars of IR theories), Europeanization, and New Intergovernmentalism.

2.7.1 Institutionalism

Institutionalism is the study of institutions. Such institutions are not only those which are formally constituted, visible, or have a physical presence, such as the Commission or the European Parliament. Institutions are also the set(s) of practices and rules that emerge from and between different actors. 'Institutions' therefore has a very wide scope. Although institutionalism has a very long scholarly tradition, the approach here is particularly aligned with the 'new institutionalism' developed by March and Olsen since the 1980s.[122] March and Olsen tell us that institutions are 'living'.[123] They are a 'relatively stable collection of practices and rules defining appropriate behaviour for specific groups of actors in specific situations'.[124]

Although relatively stable, institutions change via processes of learning and adaptation. In turn, this provides us with an indication or compass as to the possibilities for change and the elaboration of accepted standards within the institutional setting. A key component is thus the possibility for innovation and identifying how and where this occurs and the extent to which the practices and rules permit or prevent innovation. Alongside its descriptive qualities, governance is an approach to studying and understanding the EU, but is not equipped with its own theoretical or methodological framework of analysis. The governance 'turn' cuts across disciplines. The EU is ripe for this type of institutional-focused analysis because it is suited to the different ways of going about things as a supranational polity, and taking account of the multi-level, cross-border dimensions, including citizenship.

For example, a legal agreement might provide the basis for relations (either generally or specifically in migration) between the EU and a third state. The agreement might combine explicit obligations and responsibilities, but open the possibility for dialogue or cooperation in a regular or ad hoc fashion. The agreement might therefore have facilitated the establishment of an institution (as per March and Olsen's definition) between the EU, its Member States, and the third country. What happens subsequently to that agreement is thus important—that is to ask, what takes place operationally; what can be explored but not necessarily formalized? In this

[122] James March and Johan Olsen, 'The New Institutionalism: Organizational Factors in Political Life' (1984) 78(3) The American Political Science Review 734; James March and Johan Olsen, *Rediscovering Institutions: The Organizational Basis of Politics* (Free Press 1989).

[123] ibid 159.

[124] March and Olsen, *Rediscovering Institutions: The Organizational Basis of Politics* (n 122) 948; Cardwell, *EU External Relations and Systems of Governance* (n 32) 71.

respect, what is not written can be as significant as what is. The interface between these institutions and governance is provided by the replication of behaviours and what is deemed appropriate. The emergence of new actors, such as Frontex, which are themselves both *de novo* and without direct counterparts elsewhere, contributes to a rich horizon where interactions potentially create institutions and mould their evolution. March and Olsen refer to 'logics of appropriateness' and emphasize the adaptation of institutions to different environments which, via iterative processes, they change and shape.[125] Hence, practices that arise in other aspects of the European integration process—such as in the internal market, foreign policy, or Social Europe—find their way into migration. Similarly, if the institution created with a third state begins to produce practices, these can feed into relationships with other states. Innovation is thus followed by adaptation, particularly in the contexts where there is no formal, legal agreement as a springboard but rather a vague indication for cooperation using non-binding language.

The task therefore of this book is to uncover the links between the formal and the informal, the 'law' and the practice. Institutionalism recognizes and brings to the fore how regularized processes of coordination have in turn created common outlooks between the Member States and the EU institutions around rule-based norms. Although migration is a recent addition to the EU's set of competences, the intensity of interactions and the high importance of migration on the EU and national agendas have provided a strong catalyst for migration to both 'catch up' and to establish its own innovations and institutional practices. The specific context of migration is instructive in fostering creative solutions which go beyond existing templates and frameworks of law-making. The lack of harmonization; decision-making and policy-making in times of crisis; and the high political profile of migration are key in understanding how different solutions emerge. These factors do not prevent the Member States and EU institutions from seeking solutions, but rather provide the motivation for finding ways in which goals can be reached via informal means. The later part of this book examines the instances where these creative solutions appear to have the features of regular law, but do not have the necessary procedural safeguards and risk bypassing established rules and norms in national, EU, and international law, that is, 'formal informality'.

2.7.2 Governance as a legal institution

The Institutional Theory of Law, developed since the 1980s and most closely associated with MacCormick and Weinberger,[126] helps us understand how the

[125] Alexander Wendt, 'Driving with the Rearview Mirror: On the Rational Science of Institutional Design' (2001) 55(4) International Organization 1024.
[126] Neil MacCormick and Ota Weinberger, *An Institutional Theory of Law: New Approaches to Legal Positivism* (Springer 1986).

institutions can be regarded as *legal* institutions. Legal institutions are part of an institutional normative order which seeks to include principles and values as arising from practices.[127] Behaviours such as social practices lead to the emergence of legal facts which are given specific meanings through rules and conventions.[128] The Institutional Theory of Law finds a strong synergy with March and Olsen's new institutionalism, given the weight attached in the latter to the importance of rules as constitutive.[129] The formal procedural and substantive rules of law are thus important, but they are not the only ways in which (legal) institutions arise. Social practices and interactions between actors can lead to the emergence of norms, and their development or evolution can be understood as parallel to the emergence, development, and evolution of institutions.

No formal enforcement of such norms and institutions is required; it is simply that they are followed as an appropriate thing to do. Flexibility is thus a built-in quality within the Institutional Theory of Law and dependent on the social and political environment. Therefore, a relatively vague commitment between two sides—such as the EU and a third state—might, through interactions between the actors that become more regular and rely on shared understandings, lead to consolidation of practices into what we could perceive as rules. This might also be despite such norms and rules running counter to other, more formally expressed legal institutions such as instruments of international law. In other words, the Institutional Theory of Law helps us account for the possibility that the use of tools beyond those provided for in the Treaty creates set(s) of norms and institutions that allow us to comprehend the value and meaning of informality in EU migration law. Migration governance can thus be expressed though hard and soft norms working in parallel, with the possibility that the 'soft' can become 'hard' and vice versa.[130]

In a more concrete fashion, and returning to the hard versus soft law distinction that frames some of the discussion here, the latter was not originally thought to be within the scope of the Courts, but this has now been partly recognized.[131] Migration occupies a place between—or overlapping with—the internal and external spheres of governance. As such, as the scholarship on (EU) foreign policy

[127] Deirdre Curtin and Ige Dekker, 'Good Governance: The Concept and Its Application by the European Union' in DM Curtin and RA Wessel (eds), *Good Governance and the European Union; Reflections on Concepts, Institutions and Substance* (Intersentia 2005) 8.

[128] Neil MacCormick, *Institutions of Law: An Essay in Legal Theory* (Oxford University Press 2007) 18.

[129] March and Olsen, *Rediscovering Institutions: The Organizational Basis of Politics* (n 122) 22.

[130] Fabien Terpan and Sabine Saurugger, 'Normative Transformations in the European Union: On Hardening and Softening Law' (2021) 44(1) West European Politics 1.

[131] Korkea-aho, *Adjudicating New Governance: Deliberative Democracy in the European Union* (n 62); Stefan, 'European Union Soft Law' (n 78) 879. See also C-660/13 *Council v Commission* ECLI:EU:C:2016:616 and analysis in Anders Neergaard, 'Institutional Balance in the Conclusion of Non-Binding International Agreements Revisited: Council v Commission (Swiss MoU)' in Graham Butler and Ramses A Wessel (eds), *EU External Relations Law: The Cases in Context* (Hart 2022).

tells us, a gradual process of legalization via a broad understanding of law incorporates 'not only legally binding yet rather vague rules, but also the abundance of legally non-binding rules (soft law) and their interaction with one another'.[132] These insights draw on the inspiration provided by constructivist approaches to how rules and behaviours operate in social settings.[133]

The social setting is thus crucial for the types of instruments, tools, and practices that this book explores. As a polity at an advanced stage of integration, where competences on migration are relatively recent but part of a complex set of institutional structures, there is ample opportunity to engage in interactions producing norms and rules. This advanced stage of governance thus permits innovation. There is enough familiarity around the legal processes to know what the pitfalls are—when, for example, a certain proposal is likely to meet opposition in the European Parliament, or unlikely to find favour with Member States. Möllers refers to using governance as a means of transforming our understanding from 'questions of legality to questions of the optimal institutional arrangement'.[134] In migration, since there is a lack of harmonization, innovation to EU activity can be uploaded via practices provided by Member States, which in turn have a legitimizing effect. Bilateral, informal migration-focused 'deals' with third countries have been established by Member States, alongside other potential examples (such as the UK–Rwanda partnership).

Much of the focus on new governance highlights its potential effectiveness in achieving goals. However, measuring this effectiveness is challenging when the governance methods being examined are less tangible. New governance, in contrast to traditional law, is more adaptable to changing contexts and preferences. Moreover, as governance scholarship has recognized, these modes rarely exist independently of 'traditional' law, such as Regulations and Directives, which complicates their delineation and analysis.[135] Neither is it the case that there is a wholesale shift from one type of governance (i.e. by Regulation) to another; migration is one of many policy areas where the different types sit alongside each other.[136] Once

[132] Patrick Müller and Peter Slominski, 'The Role of Law in EU Foreign Policy-Making: Legal Integrity, Legal Spillover, and the EU Policy of Differentiation towards Israel' (2017) 55(4) JCMS: Journal of Common Market Studies 871.

[133] Christian Reus-Smit, 'Constructivism' in Scott Burchill, Andrew Linklater, and Richard Devetak (eds) Theories of International Relations (5th edn, Palgrave 2022); Sabine Saurugger, 'Constructivism and Public Policy Approaches in the EU: From Ideas to Power Games' (2013) 20(6) Journal of European Public Policy 888.

[134] Christoph Möllers, 'European Governance: Meaning and Value of a Concept' (n 55) 318.

[135] Walker and de Búrca, 'Narrowing the Gap' (n 106) 521; Adrienne Heritier, 'New Modes of Governance in Europe: Policy-Making Without Legislating?' (n 69) 5; Daniel Wincott, 'Beyond Social Regulation? New Instruments and/or a New Agenda for Social Policy at Lisbon?' (2003) 81(3) Public Administration 533, 535.

[136] See the exploration of the Global Approach to Migration and Mobility in Chapter 4. For further examples, see environmental regulation: Andrew Jordan, Rüdiger Wurzel, and Anthony Zito, 'The Rise of "New" Policy Instruments in Comparative Perspective: Has Governance Eclipsed Government?' (2005) 52(3) Political Studies 477; and Directives on parental leave and part-time work which combine

again, however, the impact of crisis-focused decision- and policymaking suggests that new norms are rapidly created in a shifting environment.

New governance embraces the idea that diversity is essential, and attempting to limit or 'concretize' its modes risks missing the holistic nature of governance.[137] For instance, mutual peer review is unlikely to be effective as a standalone measure but can be impactful when integrated into the 'architecture' of a governance system and used alongside learning strategies, possibly within a network. Constructivist approaches, which view new governance as a social interaction that creates shared social understandings and how 'law operates normatively as part of an interactional process over time', have been valuable here.[138] Soft law, as per de Búrca and Scott, is 'presented and understood less as a tool for directly constraining behaviour than as a transformative tool capable of changing behaviour'.[139] Taken together, the interdependent nature of law and governance could lead to a rethinking of the basic premises and normative assumptions of law, its forms, and its functions. The potential result is an interpretative evolution and a deeper understanding of law and European integration through the prism of informality.[140]

Therefore, what is required here is a focus on institutions and processes, and the way in which norms are created. Not only the formal nature of institutional creation, such as Frontex, is significant or 'counts'; so too do the iterative processes by which institutional norms can arise. Understanding the way in which the formal and the informal come together, and the emphasis laid on the latter, is illuminating. The norms themselves need to shift away from a reflexive association of 'governance' with 'good' governance, which tends to suggest that democratic processes and rights are both respected in full. While a focus on the Treaty goals might be met by the shift to informality, the justification of crisis should also return the focus to the values of the Treaty as goals. The 'crisisification' of governance is thus central,[141] as well as the changing nature of the EU, where differentiation and even

binding standards with recommendations: Gerda Falkner and others, *Complying with Europe: EU Harmonisation and Soft Law in the Member States* (Cambridge University Press 2005).

[137] Sabel and Zeitlin, 'Learning from Difference: The New Architecture of Experimentalist Governance in the EU' (n 91) 305; Burkard Eberlein and Dieter Kerwer, 'New Governance in the European Union: A Theoretical Perspective' (2004) 42(1) JCMS: Journal of Common Market Studies 121.

[138] Gregory Shaffer and Mark A Pollack, 'Hard and Soft Law' in Jeffrey L Dunoff and Mark A Pollack (eds), *Interdisciplinary Perspectives on International Law and International Relations: The State of the Art* (Cambridge University Press 2012) 199.

[139] De Búrca and Scott, *Law and New Governance in the EU and the US* (n 25) 6.

[140] Trubek and Trubek, 'Hard and Soft Law in the Construction of Social Europe' (n 79) 365; Louise Trubek, 'New Governance Practices in US Health Care' in de Búrca and Scott, *Law and New Governance in the EU and the US* (n 25) 267; Kenneth Armstrong, 'New Governance and the European Union: An Empirical and Conceptual Critique' in G de Búrca, C Kilpatrick, and J Scott (eds), *Critical Legal Perspectives on Global Governance* (Hart Publishing 2013) 261.

[141] Mark Rhinard, 'The Crisisification of Policy-Making in the European Union' (2019) 57(3) JCMS: Journal of Common Market Studies 616.

disintegration are emerging as more constant themes.[142] Since all institutions are in a state of flux, the framework here must pay attention to shifting priorities and ways of working. The shift to executive dominance as a challenge to liberal constitutionalism is one such theme, and Curtin's identification of the use of 'far reaching secrecy agreements' exemplifies this.[143] Similarly, the changing nature of the institutions, such as the increasing size and prominence of Eurosceptic and populist parties represented in the European Parliament and Council,[144] is an aspect of the successor to the governance turn: namely, the 'practice turn'.[145]

2.8 Conclusion

For this book, governance remains the most appropriate means for the study of where law and politics meet, and where different institutions are created and interact, creating norms. The technical nature of EU migration law is important, not only because of the link to 'high' politics and how political agreements are put into place through an established and familiar legal system, but also in relation to the allocation of resources (particularly financial).[146] Migration law scholarship benefits from not only the analysis of the text of Regulations and Directives and agreements such as Readmission Agreements with third countries, but also the succession of strategic documents which help understand the direction of travel and overcoming obstacles, including the passing of 'traditional' legislative tools. Examining the practices which have emerged via institutional interactions reveals what the possibilities and limitations of informality are, and the risks involved. In such a complex and fast-moving area as migration, the descriptive qualities of governance allow us to capture some of what is happening. The challenge remains to seek to identify what is less visible, since any shift away from traditional tools or established instruments and processes necessarily invites questions as to what is happening, where, and how.

While this book cannot capture all instances of informality, the aim is to identify how these can arise with a focus on the institutions of governance in migration law and policy. Understanding the politics of the EU via new or renewed institutional formats, bargaining, and positioning is becoming ever more important. Tracing

[142] Benjamin Leruth, Stefan Gänzle, and Jarle Trondal, 'Exploring Differentiated Disintegration in a Post-Brexit European Union' (2019) 57(5) JCMS: Journal of Common Market Studies 1013.

[143] Deirdre Curtin, 'Challenging Executive Dominance in European Democracy' (2014) 77(1) Modern Law Review 1, 16–17; Gráinne de Búrca, 'Is EU Supranational Governance a Challenge to Liberal Constitutionalism?' (2018) 85(2) University of Chicago Law Review 337, 361.

[144] Anna Grzymala-Busse, 'How Populists Rule: The Consequences for Democratic Governance' (2019) 51(4) Polity 707.

[145] Adler-Nissen, 'Towards a Practice Turn in EU Studies' (n 94).

[146] Andrew Geddes, 'The Politics of European Union Migration Governance' (2018) 56(1) JCMS: Journal of Common Market Studies 120, 125.

the ways in which such interactions shape our understandings is vital in linking the practice with the theory, and additionally the values that—as per the Treaty—are supposed to lie at the heart of all the EU does. Given the continued validity and relevance of the view that there is no singular means to understand the EU and the way it works, there is much to gain from the continued use of governance as a meeting place for law and political insights.

Growing scepticism about the unfulfilled promises of new governance reflects the evolving nature of the EU, which does not easily align with interpretations of governance that emphasize transparency and accountability. The renewed prominence of Member States in EU decision-making alongside the attempts of the Commission to cast itself as a 'geopolitical' actor, political bargaining, and a diminished focus on Social Europe have contributed to governance losing some of its appeal.[147] Prolonged economic crisis and the apparent decline of globalization, shared sovereignty across national lines, and the re-enacting of borders (for both trade and mobility) have cast doubt on the EU's foundational values and its relationship with citizens. But calls for 'stronger governance' in certain areas have placed the EU institutions in roles which they have hitherto not occupied.[148] Political bargaining has increasingly become a tool for addressing the EU's various crises—whether economic, migratory, or otherwise—raising concerns about what institutions and Member States are doing, and, more importantly, how they are doing it.[149] Governance remains a useful framework for analysing these developments, but only if we recognize that it now applies to a more pragmatic, power-driven EU, one that is at least partially removed from the idealistic notions that have shaped its discourse in the past.

[147] Desmond Dinan, 'Governance and Institutions: The Insidious Effect of Chronic Crisis' (2017) 55(S1) JCMS: Journal of Common Market Studies 73, 84.

[148] Nicolas Jabko, 'Contested Governance: The New Repertoire of the Eurozone Crisis' (2019) 32(3) *Governance* 493.

[149] See Philipp Genschel and Markus Jachtenfuchs, 'More Integration, Less Federation: The European Integration of Core State Powers' (2016) 23(1) Journal of European Public Policy 42.

3
The Framework of EU Migration Law and Policy
From Law to Governance

Legal analysis of EU integration generally starts with the premise of a Treaty-based set of competences and core legislation to kick start the process of integration. Then, added to this analysis can be the work of the Court of Justice in furthering integration or gap-filling (for example, on free movement of goods) or, in scholarship from the 1990s onwards, the emergence of new modes of governance (such as social inclusion). The development of migration governance tells a rather different story, although this is not merely because migration was a much later addition to the set of competences enjoyed by the institutions. Migration is not the only area where legislation has been limited, or where a legislative programme has stalled. However, it is one of the key areas where there is a huge amount of activity in the form of decision-making and policymaking against a background of high political salience and public scrutiny. Nevertheless, while the waves of legislation go some way to meeting the expectations set out in the Treaties, a comparison alongside the various programmes in Justice and Home Affairs and the Area of Freedom, Security and Justice and external relations (including the neighbourhood) reveals, at best, a shift in the emphasis placed on formal legislation to meet goals.

To understand the shift towards informality and its relationship with formal legislation, this chapter considers the development and scope of the legislative framework of EU migration law since its inception in the Treaty of Amsterdam. Defining this scope is a challenging task and this chapter does not purport to be exhaustive. Although Title V on the Area of Freedom, Security and Justice of the TFEU (Articles 67–80) provides a natural focal point for EU migration law, relevant pieces of legislation emerge via a wide variety of competences. Partly this stems from the late emergence of migration law as an autonomous law and policymaking area, which was only confirmed by the Treaty of Lisbon. This did not prevent the emergence of migration-related initiatives before the formal acquisition of competences, reflecting the emergence of 'soft' law in the EU's maturing system of governance in the 1980s and 1990s.[1]

[1] See, inter alia, Elspeth Guild, *Immigration Law in the European Community*, Vol 2 (Kluwer Law International 2001); Cathryn Costello and Minos Mouzourakis, 'The Common European Asylum

The Governance of Migration in the European Union. Paul James Cardwell, Oxford University Press.
 DOI: 10.1093/9780191946592.003.0004

Despite these complexities, the Treaty foresees legislation playing a key role in the formation of an acquis of EU migration law. Thus, what follows is not a detailed examination of every piece of legislation adopted under the relevant Treaty competences,[2] but rather an exploration of the horizon of the traditional methods of integration. In doing so, it allows for clarity in how informality has come to the fore.

Much of the focus of this chapter is on irregular migration, since this is where the bulk of legislation is found. Legislative proposals on regular migration have become notoriously slow to emerge and be adopted. The Blue Card Directive on High-Skilled Migrants is a case in point.[3] Even in situations where legislation exists, the vaguely defined notion of an Area of Freedom, Security and Justice and the relationship with other Treaty-based rights—for example the rights of family members of EU citizens—has left much of the work to be done by the Court of Justice. Though often presented as generous towards third country nationals, these rights have not followed the free movement rights of EU citizens.[4] Yet, there is evidence that gradual shifts to informality occur across the different types of migration and, as explored in subsequent chapters, the engagement of the EU institutions with third countries as a means to pursue migration-related goals blurs the distinction. Tracing the legislative developments is essential in revealing both the achievements and the sensitivities/institutional barriers but also the opportunities this has opened for institutional innovations.

The aim of this book is to demonstrate that informal policies and practices which may or may not be connected to formal legal instruments play an important role. To understand how the informal fits with the formal, an exploration of the legislative horizon is necessary. The legislation might appear less comprehensive than is suggested by both the Treaty text and the political attention paid to migration. However, the competences have been a springboard for different, emerging forms of governance and 'formal informality' explored in later chapters.

System: Where Did It All Go Wrong?' in Maria Fletcher, Ester Herlin-Karnell, and Claudio Matera (eds), *The European Union as an Area of Freedom, Security and Justice* (Routledge 2017) 266.

[2] For comprehensive analysis, see Steve Peers, *EU Justice and Home Affairs Law: Volume I; EU Immigration and Asylum Law* (5th edn, Oxford University Press 2023); Daniel Thym, *European Migration Law* (Oxford University Press 2023) 74.

[3] See, inter alia, Yasin Gümüş, 'EU Blue Card Scheme: The Right Step in the Right Direction?' (2010) 12(4) European Journal of Migration and Law 435; Lucie Cerna, 'The EU Blue Card: Preferences, Policies, and Negotiations Between Member States' (2014) 2(1) Migration Studies 73.

[4] Thym, *European Migration Law* (n 2) 82.

3.1 Towards the Treaty of Amsterdam and beyond: from the outside to the centre

The development of EU migration law is more than the sudden emergence of legal competences in the Treaty on European Union at Maastricht and subsequently in the Treaty of Amsterdam. While these Treaties mark important turning points, some of the groundwork for the development of migration governance was already under way as a consequence of the general integration process. Against the background of the operation of the Schengen area[5] and the completion of the 'Europe 1992' programme and Single Market, the introduction of a Justice and Home Affairs (JHA) 'pillar' was a priority for the Treaty on European Union 1992, marking the progression of the integration process from trade and the Single Market to other key areas. Migration was one aspect, albeit an important one, of the new JHA pillar. Concurrently, the impact of waves of migration from the Balkans in the early 1990s catapulted migration as a political issue up the EU agenda.

However, given that one of the four freedoms associated with the internal market was the free movement of persons, the issue of migration—even of those not possessing the nationality of a Member State—was already on the horizon. Initial moves on coordination were outside the scope of EU law but were viewed as a necessary counterpart to the completion of the Single Market and abolition of internal EU borders.

Discussions on 'clandestine' migration, the inclusion of TCNs in social action programmes, and an EC-wide policy on migration were put forward by the Commission in the 1970s and 1980s but amounted to little action and no substantive legislation. Even before the formal process towards drafting the TEU began, by the mid-1980s the Commission's 'Guidelines for a Community Policy on Migration' was the subject of consultation, experimentation and information. It did not result in any legislation and suffered from a lack of specific legal competence.[6]

The groundwork for migration as an EU competence was laid during the period 1992–98. The Treaty on European Union 1992 created two intergovernmental 'pillars', on Common Foreign and Security Policy and JHA. These pillars sat outside the regular law-making processes associated with the first, 'Community' pillar and relied on measures adopted by the Council.[7] The reticence of some Member States towards supranationalism in these pillars resulted in their intergovernmental character being a 'necessary evil'[8] for proponents of the first pillar, the Community

[5] Schengen Agreement 1985 and Convention 1990.

[6] Rachael Dickson, 'The Politics of EU Migration' in Paul James Cardwell and Marie-Pierre Granger, *Research Handbook on the Politics of EU Law* (Edward Elgar 2020) 357, 359.

[7] See Eileen Denza, *The Intergovernmental Pillars of the European Union* (Oxford University Press 2002).

[8] Bruno de Witte, 'The Pillar Structure and the Nature of the European Union' in Ton Heukels and others (eds), *The European Union after Amsterdam* (Kluwer Law International 1998) 51.

Method, or a form of 'diluted intergovernmentalism'.[9] The Commission called for a recognition of a common right of asylum as far back as 1991, which was resisted by the Member States.[10] Tsourdi and Costello have referred to the early initiatives as 'flanking measures to the completion of the internal market and the abolition of internal border controls'.[11] The Court of Justice also took the view that internal border checks could not be fully abolished without common external border checks.[12] Chetail goes further in suggesting that the motivation was linked to the political will to exclude asylum-seekers from free movement.[13] As a result, recalling the discussion in the previous chapter, migration finds itself between two competing modes of governance in which legislation has very different roles: one (internal) where legislation has been the main driver of integration, and another (external) where intergovernmentalism and a general lack of integration and favouring of cooperation logics apply. However, neither of these spheres can be hermetically sealed off from each other, and it has long been recognized that, despite its name, JHA has a strong external dimension.[14]

Beyond the JHA pillar which provided a home for the new competences on migration, the introduction of EU citizenship in the Treaty on European Union was an important innovation.[15] In establishing EU citizenship as a legal concept, a distinction was made between an 'in-group' who benefit from specific rights attached to their nationality of one of the Member States and an 'out-group' who fall within rules on third country nationals, even though they may or may not be migrants (i.e. individuals who have actually moved). Such a distinction between 'citizens'

[9] Theodora Kostakopoulou, 'The "Protective Union": Change and Continuity in Migration Law and Policy in Post-Amsterdam Europe' (2000) 38(3) JCMS: Journal of Common Market Studies 497.

[10] Commission, 'Communication from the Commission to the Council and the European Parliament on the right of asylum' (Communication) SEC (1991) 1857 final.

[11] Evangelia (Lilian) Tsourdi and Cathryn Costello, 'The Evolution of EU Law on Refugees and Asylum' in Paul Craig and Gráinne de Búrca (eds), *The Evolution of EU Law* (Oxford University Press 2021) 797.

[12] Case C-378/97 *Criminal proceedings against Florus Ariël Wijsenbeek* ECLI:EU:C:1999:439, para 42: 'as long as Community provisions on controls at the external borders of the Community, which also imply common or harmonised rules on, in particular, conditions of access, visas and asylum, have not been adopted, the exercise of those rights presupposes that the person concerned is able to establish that he or she has the nationality of a Member State.'

[13] Vincent Chetail, 'The Common European Asylum System: Bric-à-Brac or System?' in Vincent Chetail, Philippe De Bruycker, and Francesco Maiani (eds), *Reforming the Common European Asylum System: The New European Refugee Law* (Brill 2016) 11.

[14] See, for example, the contributors to Thierry Balzacq (ed), *The External Dimension of EU Justice and Home Affairs: Governance, Neighbours, Security* (Palgrave 2009).

[15] The literature on EU citizenship is voluminous. See, for instance, Jo Shaw, 'The Interpretation of European Union Citizenship' (1998) 61(3) Modern Law Review 293; Theodora Kostakopoulou, 'European Union Citizenship: Writing the Future' (2007) 13(5) European Law Journal 623; Henri De Waele, 'EU Citizenship: Revisiting Its Meaning, Place and Potential' (2010) 12(3) European Journal of Migration and Law 319; Francesca Strumia, *Supranational Citizenship and the Challenge of Diversity: Immigrants, Citizens and Member States in the EU* (Martinus Nijhoff Publishers 2013); Dimitry Kochenov, 'EU Citizenship Without Duties' (2014) 20(4) European Law Journal 482; Pavlos Eleftheriadis, 'The Content of European Citizenship' (2014) 15(5) German Law Journal 777.

and 'persons' is implied via Article 3 TEU.[16] Other pieces of legislation find their origins in free movement law; for example, for family reunification, Regulation 15/1961 stipulated the right of a spouse and children under 21 to join a worker in another Member State.

Looking more broadly at the TEU and the journey to the Treaty of Amsterdam, it is crucial not to underestimate the important role played by developments outside the legislative process, which did eventually provide a foundation for legislation. Member States were already developing and sharing 'safe country' concepts which became part of the—non-binding—acquis pre-Amsterdam.[17] As Costello and Mouzourakis have noted, many of the logics of the earlier period were incorporated into formal law-making competence on asylum.[18]

An exception to the rule that legal competence is the starting point was the Dublin Convention 1990. The Convention formed the template for successive Dublin Regulations within the EU's legal order.[19] The Convention, plus the 1992 resolutions, provided the 'soft' basis for what would eventually morph into the Dublin Regulations on determining the responsible Member State for assessing an asylum application.[20] The Schengen Agreement, agreed outside the framework of EU law but eventually brought within its scope, was a milestone on the route to the Treaty of Amsterdam.[21] In a sense, therefore, informal interactions between the institutions and Member States provided the groundwork for a transition from 'soft' to 'hard' measures, as noted in a Commission 'Action Plan' published in December 1998 which emphasized the need for the new legal competences to be fully realized and away from soft law.[22] A Commission communication of 14 July 1998[23] on how best to implement provisions of the Treaty of Amsterdam is notable for its critique of the limitation of soft measures explored so far: 'An impressive amount of work has already been carried out. However, the instruments adopted so far often suffer from two weaknesses: they are frequently based on "soft-law" such as resolutions

[16] Loïc Azoulai and Karin De Vries (eds), *EU Migration Law: Legal Complexities and Political Rationales* (Oxford University Press 2014).

[17] Cathryn Costello, 'The Asylum Procedures Directive and the Proliferation of Safe Country Practices: Deterrence, Deflection and the Dismantling of International Protection' (2005) 7 European Journal of Migration and Law 35—cited in Costello and Mouzourakis, 'The Common European Asylum System: Where Did It All Go Wrong?' (n 1).

[18] Costello and Mouzourakis, 'The Common European Asylum System: Where Did It All Go Wrong?' (n 1).

[19] See Tsourdi and Costello, 'The Evolution of EU Law on Refugees and Asylum' (n 11).

[20] ibid 808; Kay Hailbronner and Claus Thiery, 'Schengen II and Dublin: Responsibility for Asylum Applications in Europe' (1997) 34 (4) Common Market Law Review 957.

[21] Julian Schutte, 'Schengen: Its Meaning for the Free Movement of Persons in Europe' (1991) 28(3) Common Market Law Review 549; Daniel Thym, 'The Schengen Law: A Challenge for Legal Accountability in the European Union' (2002) 8(2) European Law Journal 218.

[22] Dickson, 'The Politics of EU Migration' (n 6) 358.

[23] Commission, 'Towards an area of freedom, security and justice' (Communication) COM (98) 459 final; see also, Council of the EU, Action Plan of the Council and the Commission on how best to implement the provisions of the Treaty of Amsterdam on an area of freedom, security and justice, Text adopted by the Justice and Home Affairs Council of 3 December 1998 [1999] OJ C 19/1, 1.

or recommendations that have no legally binding effect. And they do not have adequate monitoring arrangements. The commitment in the Amsterdam treaty to use European Community instruments in the future provides the opportunity to correct these weaknesses.'

The limits of intergovernmental cooperation in the third pillar became apparent during the 1992–97 period. Kostakopoulou's analysis identified numerous interconnected problems hampering the development of an EU migration acquis. These included the ineffectiveness of policymaking based on unanimity, an overly cumbersome five-tier decision-making structure; the absence of transparency via European or national Parliamentary involvement and judicial supervision; and the absence of binding legal instruments and the lack of enforcement mechanisms.[24] Similar problems were experienced in other third pillar dimensions including policing and criminal law, where only six of the eight agreed conventions entered into force, and even then took between four and eleven years to ratify.[25] A Commission proposal to bring the third pillar within the scope of the first was supported by the European Parliament and launched during the Irish and Dutch Council Presidencies in 1996 and 1997.[26] At the same time, the Common Foreign and Security Policy as the 'second pillar' did not experience the same level of enthusiasm for a role for the Commission, beginning a path of divergence or 'disparate integration'[27] between competences in these two areas that had, in 1992, been launched on a similar footing.

The argument for regularizing much of the JHA pillar into the 'Community Method' of the (former) first pillar's legislative process was won. What eventually became the current Articles 77–79 TFEU started in the Treaty of Amsterdam. As Peers noted at the time, 'the argument of competence is over; long live the argument over substance'.[28] This quote neatly encapsulates one of the themes of this book: there is little doubt that the EU institutions have the option to use legislation as the main tool of governance in migration management, but it is far from the case that legislation has emerged as the central core of contemporary migration governance. Nor is it the case that the early stages of the formation of EU migration law, particularly on refugees and asylum-seekers, had the same political resonance present today.[29] In this respect, migration governance does not entirely follow the

[24] Kostakopoulou, 'The "Protective Union"' (n 9).

[25] Steve Peers, 'The Rise and Fall of EU Justice and Home Affairs Law' in Maria Fletcher, Ester Herlin-Karnell, and Claudio Matera (eds) *The European Union as an Area of Freedom, Security and Justice* (Routledge 2017) 13.

[26] See European Council, *Presidency Conclusions* (Florence, 21 and 22 June 1996); European Council, *Presidency Conclusions* (Amsterdam, 16 and 17 June 1997).

[27] Tanja Börzel, 'Mind the Gap! European Integration Between Level and Scope' in Tanja Borzel (ed), *The Disparity of European Integration* (Routledge 2013).

[28] Steve Peers, 'Building Fortress Europe: The Development of EU Migration Law' (1998) 35(6) Common Market Law Review 1235.

[29] Maarten den Heijer, Jorrit Rijpma, and Thomas Spijkerboer, 'Coercion, Prohibition, and Great Expectations: The Continuing Failure of the Common European Asylum System' (2016) 53(3) Common Market Law Review 607, 614.

established path of European integration in other areas, and there is a considerable gap between what the Treaty (appears to) promise and the extent to which legalization has occupied the field. The limits to the legislative approach were already in evidence soon after the entry into force of the Treaty of Amsterdam.

3.2 Post-Amsterdam legislative activity to 2005

Upon the entry into force of the Treaty of Amsterdam and the shift of much of JHA competences into the first pillar, the pattern for furthering integration suggested following a more well-established path. There were some important caveats to this normalization, most notably the more limited role for the Court of Justice than in other areas of the first pillar.[30] The Commission quickly proposed legislative measures to further the Treaty aims, capitalizing on the new-found competences and perceived enthusiasm for migration and home affairs as the logical next step in European integration. Longer-term discussions between the Member States and the institutions meant that these proposals did not emerge from a vacuum, and the Treaty called for a number of specific measures on asylum and immigration within five years.[31] The prevailing logic was also that the dismantling of internal borders within the EU necessitated the harmonization, or at least the coordination, of the external border and status of third country nationals in the EU.[32] Although the CFSP remained intact in its second, intergovernmental pillar, external cooperation mechanisms in JHA were first introduced by the Treaty of Amsterdam. This allowed JHA to start to have its own external identity and opened the door to the EU institutions having a more proactive role in external cooperation.[33]

Much of the early focus on legislation was devoted to the growing disparity between the rights enjoyed by EU citizens and third country nationals (TCNs) in the EU, many of whom may have been long-standing residents but without the same access to the rights that emerged from the maturing EU integration process. Guided by the milestones envisaged by the Council's Tampere Conclusions,[34] the initial drive for legislation represented, for the EU institutions, a 'youthful enthusiasm echoing the optimistic outlook on globalisation after the end of the cold war'.[35] The 'fair treatment' principles in Tampere[36] could be characterized as an

[30] Albertina Albors-Llorens, 'Changes in the Jurisdiction of the European Court of Justice under the Treaty of Amsterdam' (1998) 35(6) Common Market Law Review 1273.

[31] See further below and Peers, 'Building Fortress Europe: The Development of EU Migration Law' (n 28).

[32] Paul James Cardwell, *EU External Relations and Systems of Governance: The CFSP, Euro-Mediterranean Partnership and Migration* (Routledge 2009) 145.

[33] This is considered further in the following chapters.

[34] See Chapter 4 for further analysis.

[35] Thym, *European Migration Law* (n 2) 75.

[36] Azoulai and De Vries, *EU Migration Law: Legal Complexities and Political Rationales* (n 16) 3.

attempt to 'catch up' with the mobility rights enjoyed by EU citizens.[37] Initial emphasis was placed squarely on the language of fairness, and for TCN on ensuring a uniform set of rights 'as near as possible to those enjoyed by EU citizens'.[38] This reflected a commonly held view that the supranational level is able to offer a higher level of protection of rights, reducing the room for manoeuvre of the Member States.[39]

The Treaty provisions themselves though reveal a sharp difference in the possibility for integration compared with, in particular, the provisions on the Single Market and four freedoms, and the Common Commercial Policy. For the latter, the Treaty language spoke of the lowering of barriers as a means of ensuring the realization of the goals of the Treaty and promoting international openness in trade[40] via a demonstration of its own achievement of a Customs Union.[41] For migration, the 'headline' goal of the Treaty provisions which pointed to harmonization of migration law was undermined by three factors. First, the provisions themselves and their substance did not require the same level of integration via harmonization. Second, although there was divergence with the CFSP, the role of the Council and thus the Member States was largely retained in the legislative process.[42] The Court's decision in *Pupino*[43] later clarified the 'read-across' of principles from the first to the third pillar.[44] Third, the opt-outs from JHA by Denmark, Ireland, and the UK clearly marked out migration as substantially different from other areas of integration and already suggested that further integration would only occur between some—rather than all—Member States. Alongside the advanced stages of Economic and Monetary Union, JHA seemed set to either contribute to a

[37] Cardwell, *EU External Relations and Systems of Governance* (n 32) 145.

[38] European Council, *Presidency Conclusions* (Tampere, 15 and 16 October 1999) A (2).

[39] Daniel Thym, 'European Migration Law Between "Rescuing" and "Taming" the Nation State: A History of Half-Hearted Commitment to Human Rights and Refugee Protection' (2023) 8(3) European Papers 1663.

[40] For example, Article 34 TEU, 'Quantitative restrictions on imports and all measures having equivalent effect shall be prohibited between Member States'.

[41] Article 206 TFEU: 'By establishing a customs union in accordance with Articles 28 to 32, the Union shall contribute, in the common interest, to the harmonious development of world trade, the progressive abolition of restrictions on international trade and on foreign direct investment, and the lowering of customs and other barriers.'

[42] See Kay Hailbronner, 'European Immigration and Asylum Law under the Amsterdam Treaty' (1998) 35(5) Common Market Law Review 1047, 1053.

[43] Case C-105/03 *Criminal proceedings against Maria Pupino* ECLI:EU:C:2005:386; see also Carl Lebeck, 'Sliding towards Supranationalism? The Constitutional Status of EU Framework Decisions after Pupino' (2007) 8(5) German Law Journal 501; Maria Fletcher, 'Extending "Indirect Effect" to the Third Pillar: The Significance of Pupino?' (2005) 30(6) European Law Review 862; Paul James Cardwell and Tamara Hervey, 'The Roles of Law in a New Intergovernmentalist European Union' in Christopher J Bickerton, Dermot Hodson. and Uwe Puetter (eds), *The New Intergovernmentalism: States and Supranational Actors in the Post-Maastricht Era* (Oxford University Press 2015).

[44] See Steve Peers, 'Salvation Outside the Church: Judicial Protection in the Third Pillar after the Pupino and Segi Judgments' (2007) 44 Common Market Law Review 883; Eleanor Spaventa, 'Opening Pandora's Box: Some Reflections on the Constitutional Effects of the Decision in Pupino' (2007) 3(1) European Constitutional Law Review 5.

two- or multi-speed Europe or result in a fractured decision-making and institutional picture.

Much of the initial emphasis on legislation following the entry into force of the Treaty of Amsterdam was put in place pursuant to (then) Article 62 EC, which required, within five years of entry into force of the Treaty, measures in 'asylum, refugee, entry and residence and immigration policy'. These were, as per Article 67 EC, proposals that would require unanimity between the Member States in the Council. The legislation proposed by the Commission did not result in rapid adoption in the Council, a pattern which has since become a hallmark of migration law. The progress of the initial legislation was slow. The relevant Directives were eventually passed after extensive negotiations between the institutions. On irregular migration, progress was 'piecemeal' in the 1999–2001 period but then a flurry of attempts by the Commission and Council to have a more coherent policy led to a series of proposals for Regulations, Directives, and Decisions.[45]

Of particular note is the Temporary Protection Directive.[46] This was the first measure adopted after the institutions gained competences in migration and was designed to be deployed in urgent situations where the Member States were facing a 'mass influx' of individuals.[47] The Directive outlines measures for EU Member States to take when faced with a sudden and large-scale arrival of displaced persons, particularly in cases of armed conflicts and situations that lead to a significant and temporary increase in the number of people seeking refuge. The Directive relies on solidarity between Member States, 'to promote a balance of effort between Member States in receiving and bearing the consequences of receiving such persons'. The Directive specifies the rights and benefits that individuals under temporary protection should receive, such as access to education, healthcare, and the labour market, as a short-term measure only.

Despite situations where the Directive might have been used, and calls to do so including during the 'migration crisis' in 2015–16,[48] it remained dormant, with

[45] See Steve Peers, 'The Rise and Fall of EU Justice and Home Affairs Law' (n 25). Included Commission, 'Common Policy on illegal immigration' (Communication) COM (2001) 672 final; Council, 'Proposal for a comprehensive plan to combat illegal immigration and trafficking of human beings in the European Union' (Action Plan) [2002] OJ C 142/23; Commission, 'Green Paper on Return Policy on Illegal Residents' COM (2002) 175 final; Council, 'Proposal for a Return Action Programme' (Action Plan) 14673/02. Regulations include Council Regulation (EC) 377/2004 on creating a network of immigration officers [2004] OJ L 64/1.

[46] Council Directive 2001/55/EC of 20 July 2001 on minimum standards for giving temporary protection in the event of a mass influx of displaced persons and on measures promoting a balance of efforts between Member States in receiving such persons and bearing the consequences thereof [2001] OJ L 212/12.

[47] The Directive specifies, in Article 5(1), that the existence of a 'mass influx' for the purposes of the Directive will be established via Decision, adopted via QMV on a proposal from the Commission.

[48] Meltem Ineli-Ciger, 'Time to Activate the Temporary Protection Directive: Why the Directive Can Play a Key Role in Solving the Migration Crisis in Europe' (2016) 18(1) European Journal of Migration and Law 1; Olga Mitrovic, 'Used during the Balkan crises, the EU's Temporary Protection Directive may now be a solution to Europe's refugee emergency' (*LSE European Politics and Policy (EUROPP)*, 22 December 2015) https://blogs.lse.ac.uk/europpblog/2015/12/22/the-eus-temporary-protection-directive-as-a-solution-to-europes-refugee-crisis/, accessed 2 June 2025; Danielle Gluns and Janna

no single, clear explanation as to why this was the case. As such, after its passing it largely remained a footnote in the story of the development of the acquis in migration.[49] However, the Directive was invoked after a unanimous agreement in the Council by the Member States on 3 March 2022 following Russia's full-scale invasion of Ukraine.[50] It is scheduled to remain in force until 2027. Nevertheless, the lack of use of the Directive over a twenty-year period, despite the opportunity to do so arising on numerous occasions, tells us both something about the willingness of the Member States to engage in burden-sharing and that the mere presence of legislation does not necessarily entail that it will be used to its full potential.

The initial legislation proposed during the transitional period under the Treaty of Amsterdam (until 1 May 2004)[51] focused on establishing a set of baselines across aspects of migration law. This was the first two major rounds of legislation to establish and consolidate the CEAS, supplemented by decisions of the CJEU, although the Court has been much less active on the rights of those in the asylum system than the ECHR, in spite of its numerous rulings on the CEAS.[52] The first phase, from 2000 to 2005, established the legal instruments which attempted to establish minimum standards in reception and treatment of asylum-seekers.[53]

Wessels, 'Waste of Paper or Useful Tool? The Potential of the Temporary Protection Directive in the Current "Refugee Crisis"' (2017) 36(2) Refugee Survey Quarterly 57; Deniz Genç and Nedime Öner, 'Why Not Activated? The Temporary Protection Directive and the Mystery of Temporary Protection in the European Union' (2019) 7(1) International Journal of Political Science and Urban Studies 1.

[49] Costello and Mouzourakis, 'The Common European Asylum System: Where Did It All Go Wrong?' (n 1). See also Karoline Kerber, 'The Temporary Protection Directive' (2002) 4 European Journal of Migration and Law 193.

[50] Daniela Vitiello, 'The Nansen Passport and the EU Temporary Protection Directive: Reflections on Solidarity, Mobility Rights and the Future of Asylum in Europe' (2022) 7(1) European Papers 15; Meltem Ineli-Ciger, 'Reasons for the Activation of the Temporary Protection Directive in 2022: A Tale of Double Standards' in Sergio Carrera and Meltem Ineli-Ciger (eds), *EU Responses to the Large-Scale Refugee Displacement* (European University Institute 2023); Tamara Kortukova and others, 'Peculiarities of the Legal Regulation of Temporary Protection in the European Union in the Context of the Aggressive War of the Russian Federation against Ukraine' (2023) 36(2) International Journal for the Semiotics of Law—Revue internationale de Sémiotique juridique 667; Florian Trauner and Gabriele Valodskaite, 'The EU's Temporary Protection Regime for Ukrainians: Understanding the Legal and Political Background and Its Implications' (2022) 23(4) CESifo Forum 17; Esin Küçük, 'Temporary Protection Directive: Testing New Frontiers?' (2023) 25(1) European Journal of Migration and Law 1; Jean-François Durieux, 'Temporary Protection: Hovering at the Edges of Refugee Law' (2014) 45 Netherlands Yearbook of International Law 221; Lucas Rasche, 'Implementing Temporary Protection in the EU' (Policy Brief) (Jacques Delors Centre, 23 March 2022) https://www.delorscentre.eu/en/publications/detail/publication/ukraine-a-paradigm-shift-for-the-eus-asylum-policy, accessed 2 June 2025; Julia Motte-Baumvol, Tarin Mont'Alverne, and Gabriel Guimarães, 'Extending Social Protection for Migrants Under the European Union's Temporary Protection Directive: Lessons from the War in Ukraine' (2022) Oxford University Comparative Law Forum 2 https://ouclf.law.ox.ac.uk/extending-social-protection-for-migrants-under-the-european-unions-temporary-protection-directive-lessons-from-the-war-in-ukraine/, accessed 2 June 2025; Ineli-Ciger, 'Time to Activate the Temporary Protection Directive' (n 46); Kerber, 'The Temporary Protection Directive' (n 47); Gluns and Wessels, 'Waste of Paper or Useful Tool?' (n 46).

[51] Peers, 'The Rise and Fall of EU Justice and Home Affairs Law' (n 25).

[52] Tsourdi and Costello, 'The Evolution of EU Law on Refugees and Asylum' (n 11).

[53] Nicola Rogers, 'Minimum Standards for Reception' (2002) 4 European Journal of Migration and Law 215.

This first phase included five pieces of legislation: the Dublin Regulation,[54] the Qualification Directive,[55] the Reception Conditions Directive,[56] the Asylum Procedures Directive,[57] and the Eurodac Regulations.[58]

In the context of European integration, adopting minimum standards rather than full harmonization as a starting point is far from unusual.[59] The common thread of these early measures was their relationship to irregular migration and asylum, and the early emphasis on raising standards for the reception and treatment of asylum-seekers was soon overtaken by a race to ensure that raising standards did not amount to a 'pull' factor. As such, the early characterization of 'Fortress Europe'—a term that had previously applied to the economic context of a perceived 'protectionist' EU—was set.[60]

The Commissioner for Justice and Home Affairs, António Vitorino, spoke of the legislation providing 'building blocks' for the migration acquis, with the aim being 'to level the asylum playing field' in laying the foundations for a Common European Asylum System.[61] In one sense, the emphasis on minimum standards continued the trend established in the post-Maastricht, pre-Amsterdam period, although 'maximalist' directives started to appear in the political domain of the Area of Freedom, Security and Justice.[62] Writing in the early 2000s, Peers noted that EU immigration and asylum law was yet further unbalanced towards migration

[54] Known as Dublin II. Council Regulation (EC) No 343/2003 of 18 February 2003 establishing the criteria and mechanisms for determining the Member State responsible for examining an asylum application lodged in one of the Member States by a third-country national [2003] OJ L50/1.

[55] Council Directive 2004/83/EC [2004] OJ L304/12; Directive 2011/95/EU of the European Parliament and of the Council of 13 December 2011 on standards for the qualification of third-country nationals or stateless persons as beneficiaries of international protection, for a uniform status for refugees or for persons eligible for subsidiary protection, and for the content of the protection granted (recast) [2011] OJ L337/9.

[56] Council Directive 2003/9/EC of 27 January 2003 laying down minimum standards for the reception of asylum seekers [2003] OJ L31/18.

[57] Council Directive 2005/85/EC of 1 December 2005 on minimum standards on procedures in Member States for granting and withdrawing refugee status [2005] OJ L326/13.

[58] Council Regulation (EC) No 2725/2000 of 11 December 2000 concerning the establishment of 'Eurodac' for the comparison of fingerprints for the effective application of the Dublin Convention [2000] OJ L316/1.

[59] Dougan cites environment, consumer, and employment protection as areas where this has traditionally applied: Michael Dougan, 'Minimum Harmonization and the Internal Market' (2000) 37(4) Common Market Law Review 853. See also, in the context of rights, Eleanor Spaventa, 'Should we "Harmonize" Fundamental Rights in the EU? Some Reflections about Minimum Standards and Fundamental Rights Protection in the EU Composite Constitutional System' (2018) 55(4) Common Market Law Review 997.

[60] The term was still used in an economic, non-migration sense in the 1990s, as its use in relation to migration and borders increased. See, for example, Kym Anderson and Hege Norheim, 'From Imperial to Regional Trade Preferences: Its Effect on Europe's Intra- and Extra-Regional Trade' (1993) 129(1) Review of World Economics 78; Brian Hanson, 'What Happened to Fortress Europe? External Trade Policy Liberalization in the European Union' (1998) 52(1) International Organization 55.

[61] Antonio Vitorino speech 4/435 (Brussels, 4 October 2024) https://www.temaasyl.se/Documents/EU-dokument/VitorinosTal.pdf, accessed 2 June 2025.

[62] Elaine Fahey, *The Global Reach of EU Law* (Routledge 2017) 72–73.

control principles[63] and the standards of protection were so low in many respects as to raise doubts about the legitimacy of the EU's policy.[64]

Given the importance migration now has on the EU's general agenda, it is important to recall that during the initial period after Amsterdam, the CEAS was essentially a 'sidekick'. The CEAS was cited in the Tampere Conclusions in terms of the European Council having 'agreed to work towards establishing a Common European Asylum System, based on the full and inclusive application of the Geneva Convention, thus ensuring that nobody is sent back to persecution, i.e. maintaining the principle of non-refoulement', with indicative short and longer-term goals, all to be met by legislation (or at the very least, 'rules').[65] Only in the Treaty of Lisbon was the CEAS upgraded to an objective in its own right, via Article 78 TFEU.[66]

As Tsourdi and Costello explain, 'the inclusion of asylum policy in the Amsterdam Treaty was ambivalent. Certain elements still conceived the asylum policy as a corollary to internal freedom of movement for others, predominantly EU citizens. In particular, measures related to responsibility allocation for the examination of asylum claims, as well as those related to the establishment of minimum standards for giving temporary protection to displaced persons, were explicitly formulated as "directly related flanking measures" that would support the aim of a common external border—and the abolition of internal borders—within the Schengen area.'[67] Thus, the central rationale for migration law as a 'normal' area of EU legislating was more because of its importance to the development of the concepts of free movement and citizenship (of EU citizens) rather than a full-fledged effort to occupy the terrain in migration law and policy. The legislation passed during this initial period has remained largely in force (albeit with several recasting efforts).

3.2.1 The Dublin Regulations

At the core of the CEAS lie the successive Dublin Regulations. The first Dublin Regulation was in force from 2003 to 2013.[68] The Regulation was the successor to the Dublin Convention 1990 and a set of 1992 Resolutions; it is hence referred to as 'Dublin II'. This Regulation determined which EU Member State had the

[63] Steve Peers, 'Key Legislative Developments on Migration in the European Union' (2004) 6 European Journal of Migration and Law 67.
[64] Steve Peers, 'Key Legislative Developments on Migration in the European Union' (2003) 5 European Journal of Migration and Law 387.
[65] Tampere Conclusions (n 38) points 13–15.
[66] Article 78(1) TFEU: 'The Union shall develop a common policy on asylum, subsidiary protection and temporary protection with a view to offering appropriate status to any third-country national requiring international protection and ensuring compliance with the principle of non-refoulement.'
[67] Tsourdi and Costello, 'The Evolution of EU Law on Refugees and Asylum' (n 11).
[68] Council Regulation (EC) No 343/2003 [2003] OJ L50/1.

responsibility for receiving and processing asylum applications. The general principle relies on the first EU Member State that the individual entered in an irregular manner having sole responsibility. The aim of the Regulation is to prevent 'asylum shopping' and ensure that one Member State takes responsibility for each asylum application, and individuals may be transferred to the first entry state (but this is not an obligation). The enduring fear of 'asylum shopping' does not have a strong basis in evidence[69] but the Dublin Regulations have become emblematic of the 'Fortress Europe' approach to migration.[70]

The spirit of solidarity underpins the wording of the Regulation.[71] The Regulation has proven to be the most politically contested and controversial of the CEAS.[72] For frontline states on the geographical periphery of the EU, their complaint is that the Regulation imposes a disproportionate burden on them, since they have the challenge of managing the reception of migrants who cross into their territory, but also the return of others who have travelled into one (or more) Member States. The nature of frontline states has also shifted, partly due to the enlargement of the EU and partly also due to the evolution of migration flows. It is hardly surprising, therefore, that fault lines between the Member States have opened up. Since each Member State remains largely competent to devise its own asylum policy, the danger of the Dublin system is the temptation for the Member States to provide lower levels of protection, the so-called race to the bottom.[73] This would be far from the spirit present in the wording from the launch of the competences in migration. Yet, as Tsourdi and Costello note,[74] the Dublin system has a 'puzzling longevity' given that the basic premise of the system has changed little since its original form in 1990 and survived several iterations and interventions by the Court of Justice, which 'has largely refused to innovate legally in the field of asylum, and its judicial passivity in this case is particularly striking'.[75] Differences in interpretation of the Regulation with EU and international human rights law, and particularly the principle of *non-refoulement*,[76] have long characterized the Dublin Regulation's legal regime.[77]

[69] Tsourdi and Costello, 'The Evolution of EU Law on Refugees and Asylum' (n 11) 809; Leila Abdou, '"Push or Pull?" Framing Immigration in Times of Crisis in the European Union and the United States' (2020) 42(5) Journal of European Integration 643.

[70] Ashley Binetti Armstrong, 'You Shall Not Pass! How the Dublin System Fueled Fortress Europe' (2020) 20(2) Chicago Journal of International Law 332.

[71] Article 80 TFEU; see also Hemme Battjes and Evelien Brouwer, 'The Dublin Regulation and Mutual Trust: Judicial Coherence in EU Asylum Law?' (2015) 8(2) Review of European Administrative Law 183.

[72] Steve Peers and others, 'The Dublin III Regulation' in Steve Peers and others (eds), *EU Immigration and Asylum Law (Text and Commentary)* (2nd rev edn, Brill 2015).

[73] Maarten Den Heijer, Jorrit Rijpma, and Thomas Spijkerboer, 'Coercion, Prohibition, and Great Expectations' (n 29) 612.

[74] Tsourdi and Costello, 'The Evolution of EU Law on Refugees and Asylum' (n 11) 807.

[75] ibid 804.

[76] Violeta Moreno-Lax, 'Dismantling the Dublin System: M.S.S. v. Belgium and Greece' (2012) 14(1) European Journal of Migration and Law 1.

[77] See Giulia Vicini, 'The Dublin Regulation between Strasbourg and Luxembourg: Reshaping Non-Refoulement in the Name of Mutual Trust' (2015) 8(2) European Journal of Legal Studies 50; Bernard

Much has been written on the way in which the Dublin Regulations fail to either uphold standards or undermine solidarity. In a sense, the Dublin Regulations encapsulate the gap between the expectations set out in the Treaty, which points—without explicitly setting out a route—to harmonization, and the ability of the EU institutions and Member States to agree on a legally robust framework. Echoing Christopher Hill's 'capability–expectations gap' in relation to the CFSP,[78] the Dublin Regulations have been stuck between a position where Member States expect solidarity in dealing with migration and a lack of ability to commit to positions doing so. Furthermore, the inclusion of the Charter of Fundamental Rights in the EU's legal order has led to inevitable clashes between the purpose of the Regulations and the upholding of rights at the Court of Justice.[79] Even more recently, the Court has been faced with situations where Member States have deliberately refused to accept their Dublin obligations to take back individuals.[80]

3.2.2 Other CEAS (non-Dublin) legislation

The Dublin Regulation was flanked by other directives initially passed during the same period, which remain in force, albeit in recast forms. The Qualification Directive[81] aims to set out common standards for recognizing and granting international protection to asylum-seekers. It defines the criteria for refugee status and subsidiary protection, with the stated aim of ensuring that asylum-seekers are treated fairly across the EU.[82] Given the complexities involved in seeking

McCloskey, 'Third-Country Refugees: The Dublin Regulation/Article 8 ECHR Interface and Judicial Remedies' (2017) 29(4) International Journal of Refugee Law 641.

[78] Christopher Hill, 'The Capability–Expectations Gap, or Conceptualizing Europe's International Role' (1993) 31(3) JCMS: Journal of Common Market Studies 305–28.

[79] See, for example, Case C-392/22 *X v Staatssecretaris van Justitie en Veiligheid* ECLI:EU:C:2024:195.

[80] Case C-458/24 *Daraa v Germany* ECLI:EU:C:2026:146. See comment by Jonas Bornemann, 'Op-Ed: "Reviving the Dublin System through intergovernmental pressure? The Italian refusal to accept Dublin Transfers and the Court's judgment in Daraa (C-458/24)"' (2026) EU Law Live, https://eulawlive.com/op-ed-reviving-the-dublin-system-through-intergovernmental-pressure-the-italian-refusal-to-accept-dublin-transfers-and-the-courts-judgment-in-daraa-c-458-24/, accessed 30 March 2026.

[81] Council Directive 2004/83/EC of 29 April 2004 on minimum standards for the qualification and status of third country nationals or stateless persons as refugees or as persons who otherwise need international protection and the content of the protection granted [2004] OJ L304/12; Directive 2011/95/EU [2011] OJ L337/9.

[82] Jane McAdam, 'The European Union Qualification Directive: The Creation of a Subsidiary Protection Regime' (2005) 17 (3) International Journal of Refugee Law 461; Jonah Eaton, 'The Internal Protection Alternative under European Union Law: Examining the Recast Qualification Directive' (2012) 24(4) International Journal of Refugee Law 765; Harald Dörig, Ingo Kraft, Hugo Storey and Hemme Battjes, 'Asylum Qualification Directive 2011/95/EU' in Kay Hailbronner and Daniel Thym (eds), *EU Immigration and Asylum Law* (Beck/Hart/Nomos 2016) 1109–1284; Boštjan Zalar, 'Legal Implications of the "Presumption of Innocence" and the Exclusion Clauses in International Protection

acceptable common standards across the Member States and groups and sub-groups of categories of migrants falling within the scope of the Directive, the CJEU has engaged in gap-filling[83] while also demonstrating the significance of judicial dialogue between the CJEU and national courts.[84]

The Reception Conditions Directive establishes common standards for the reception and living conditions of asylum-seekers in Member States. It outlines the rights and entitlements of asylum-seekers, including access to housing, healthcare, and education.[85] As a Directive, much of the criticism has been focused on the stark differences in transposition and, ultimately, the standards of reception across the Member States, including detention.[86]

The Asylum Procedures Directive[87] sets out common procedures for processing asylum applications in EU Member States. It establishes guidelines for conducting interviews and providing legal representation, with the aim of ensuring a fair and efficient process.[88] The Directive has, as with the other pieces of legislation in the package, attracted criticism for variations in the treatment of asylum-seekers, with some Member States offering better protection and procedural fairness than others and with overly bureaucratic procedures. This undermines the stated goal and results in an uneven distribution of responsibility. Furthermore, the Directive

Cases: The European Law Perspective' in Jaces C Simeon (ed), *Serious International Crimes, Human Rights, and Forced Migration* (Routledge 2022).

[83] See, for example, Case C-31/09 *Nawras Bolbol v Bevándorlási és Állampolgársági Hivatal* ECLI:EU:C:2010:351. See Paul James Cardwell, 'Determining Refugee Status under Directive 2004/83: Comment on Bolbol (C-31/09)' (2011) 36(1) European Law Review 135.

[84] See, for example, Koen Lenaerts, 'The Contribution of the European Court of Justice to the Area of Freedom, Security and Justice' (2010) 59 International and Comparative Law Quarterly 255, 291.

[85] Rogers, 'Minimum Standards for Reception' (n 51); Samantha Velluti, 'The Revised Reception Conditions Directive and Adequate and Dignified Material Reception Conditions for Those Seeking International Protection' (2016) 2(3) International Journal of Migration and Border Studies 203; Charles O'Sullivan and Delia Ferri, 'The Recast Reception Conditions Directive and the Rights of Asylum Seekers with Disabilities: Opportunities, Challenges and the Quest for Reform' (2020) 22(2) European Journal of Migration and Law 272; Markus Peek and Lilian Tsourdi, 'Asylum Reception Conditions Directive 2013/33/EU' in Kay Hailbronner and Daniel Thym (eds) *EU Immigration and Asylum Law* (Beck/Hart/Nomos 2016) 1382–1478 and contributions to Paul Minderhoud and Karin Zwaan (eds), *The Recast Reception Conditions Directive: Central Themes, Problem Issues, and Implementation in Selected Member States* (Wolf Legal Publishing 2016).

[86] See, for example, the Opinion by AG Sharpston in C-704/17 *DH v Ministerstvi vnitra* ECLI:EU:C:2019:85, paras 34–56 (the referring Czech court withdrew the reference before the Court could give its decision).

[87] Council Directive 2005/85/EC [2005] OJ L326/13; Recast as Directive 2013/32/EU of the European Parliament and of the Council of 26 June 2013 on common procedures for granting and withdrawing international protection (recast) [2013] OJ L 180/60.

[88] Cathryn Costello, 'The Asylum Procedures Directive and the Proliferation of Safe Country Practices: Deterrence, Deflection and the Dismantling of International Protection' (2005) 7(1) European Journal of Migration and Law 35; Doede Ackers, 'The Negotiations on the Asylum Procedures Directive' (2005) 7(1) European Journal of Migration and Law 1; Karin Schittenheim, 'Implementing and Rethinking the European Union's Asylum Legislation: The Asylum Procedures Directive' (2019) 57(1) International Migration 229; Jens Vedsted-Hansen, 'Asylum Procedures Directive 2013/32/EU' in Kay Hailbronner and Daniel Thym (eds), *EU Immigration and Asylum Law* (Beck/Hart/Nomos 2016).

permits Member States to reject asylum claims if the applicant has passed through a 'safe third country' en route to the EU. This term has been interpreted too broadly, sometimes labelling countries as 'safe' despite an inability to guarantee effective protection and thus resulting in a violation of non-refoulement.

The final legislative instrument completing the CEAS is the Eurodac Regulation.[89] The Eurodac system is a fingerprint database used to compile, identify, and track asylum-seekers within the EU. It is used to implement the Dublin Regulation and prevent multiple asylum claims in different Member States.[90]

Further, the institutional arrangements for managing migration were completed in this initial period by the creation of Frontex—the 'Agency for the Management of Operational Cooperation at the External Borders of the Member States of the European Union',[91] to give it its full title—and the European Border Surveillance System (EUROSUR).[92] Frontex is considered in more detail later in the book, but in its initial incarnation its role was rather limited to improving operational cooperation between the Member States and their external border management, and with third countries,[93] including joint return operations.[94] It has since grown and evolved into the most publicly visible agency, with a size and budget comparable to full-fledged EU institutions but with a lack of similar safeguards in terms of the protections of the Charter of Fundamental Rights and right to an effective remedy.[95]

3.2.3 Provisions on regular migration

The Tampere Conclusions did not explicitly refer to regular migration for the purposes of work, but only to 'the need for approximation of national legislations

[89] Council Regulation (EC) No 2725/2000 [2000] OJ L316/1.

[90] Somewhat surprisingly, given the importance of Eurodac, literature on the Regulations is relatively limited. See, inter alia, Evelien Brouwer, 'Eurodac: Its Limitations and Temptations' (2002) 4 European Journal of Migration and Law 231; Steve Peers and Nicola Rogers, 'Eurodac' in Steve Peers and Nicola Rogers (eds), *EU Immigration and Asylum Law* (Brill/Nijhoff 2006); Niovi Vavoula, 'The Recast Eurodac Regulation: Are Asylum Seekers Treated as Suspected Criminals?' in Céline Bauloz and others, *Seeking Asylum in the European Union* (Brill/Nijhoff 2015); Benedita Queiroz, 'The Impact of EURODAC in EU Migration Law: The Era of Crimmigration?' (2019) 3(1) Market and Competition Law Review 157; Ibrahim Soysüren and Mihaela Nedelcu, 'European Instruments for the Deportation of Foreigners and Their Uses by France and Switzerland: The Application of the Dublin III Regulation and Eurodac' (2022) 48(8) Journal of Ethnic and Migration Studies 1927.

[91] Council Regulation (EC) No 2007/2004 of 26 October 2004 establishing a European Agency for the Management of Operational Cooperation at the External Borders of the Member States of the European Union (no longer in force) [2004] OJ L349/136; see further in Chapter 5.

[92] Regulation (EU) No 1052/2013 of the European Parliament and of the Council of 22 October 2013 establishing the European Border Surveillance System (EUROSUR) (no longer in force).

[93] Article 14.

[94] Articles 1(f) and 9.

[95] However, see the decision of the Court of Justice in C-679/23 P *WS and others v Frontex* ECLI:EU:C:2025:976 and Case C-136/24 P *Hamoudi v Frontex* ECLI:EU:C:2025:977

on the conditions for admission and residence of third country nationals'.[96] A Directive to harmonize admission to the EU for paid and self-employed work was first proposed by the Commission in 2001.[97] However, a political consensus on the harmonization of migration legislation at EU level for workers was markedly different from that on the CEAS, even taking into account the shortcomings of the legislation explored above. Member States were reluctant to move towards any substantive role for the EU institutions or EU law on the admissions criteria for TCNs in their national labour markets or the numbers of individuals who might be permitted to enter and stay in the territory.[98] As a result, measures on what might be termed as economic or work-based migration only materialized some years later. Instead of a broad-brush approach, Directives on sector-specific forms of migration were concluded, where the overall categories would be smaller in volume and much less controversial in the public sphere since they would concern only high(er)-skilled individuals.[99] Such Directives included students and researchers.[100]

The most far-reaching legislation—in terms of the numbers affected—on 'regular' migration is that on long-term residents in the EU and family reunification. The Family Reunification Directive (2003/86) was the first major piece of legislation adopted under Article 63 EC. Member States to whom the Directive applied had two years for transposition.[101] The Directive had originally been proposed by the Commission in 1999 but, despite the positive opinion of the European Parliament,[102] failed to progress in the Council. The Commission responded to a request to put forwarded an amended proposal, which was eventually adopted in 2003, on the basis that harmonization would progress in stages, of which this Directive was intended to be the first.[103]

[96] Tampere Conclusions point 20.

[97] Commission, 'Proposal for a Council Directive on the conditions of entry and residence of third-country nationals for the purpose of paid employment and self-employed economic activities' COM(2001) 386 final.

[98] Herwig Verschueren, 'Employment and Social Security Rights of Third-Country Nationals under the EU Labour Migration Directives' (2018) 20(2) European Journal of Social Security 100.

[99] Lucie Cerna and Meng-Hsuan Chou, 'The Regional Dimension in the Global Competition for Talent: Lessons from Framing the European Scientific Visa and Blue Card' (2014) 21(1) Journal of European Public Policy 76.

[100] Council Directive 2004/114/EC of 13 December 2004 on the conditions of admission of third-country nationals for the purposes of studies, pupil exchange, unremunerated training or voluntary service [2004] OJ L375/12; Council Directive 2005/71/EC of 12 October 2005 on a specific procedure for admitting third-country nationals for the purposes of scientific research [2005] OJ L298/15; for a fuller analysis see Anja Wiesbrock, *Legal Migration to the European Union*, Vol 22 (Brill 2010).

[101] As per Protocols 18 and 21 attached to the TFEU, Denmark, Ireland, and the UK were not bound by the Directive.

[102] European Parliament, *Report on the Proposal for a Council Directive on the Right to Family Reunification* (European Parliament, A5-201/2000, 2000).

[103] Kees Groenendijk and others, 'The Family Reunification Directive in EU Member States: The First Year of Implementation' (2007) Nijmegen Migration Law Working Papers Series 2007/01, 6–7.

The Directive was significant because in numerical terms, family reunification is the main form of regular migration to the EU.[104] It drew on common legal principles of family reunification in the Member States. This is understood to be a right at national level, recognized as such in some Member States, including Germany, France, and Italy.[105] But sharp differences emerged in the legislative process as to whether family reunification should be regarded as a right and whether refugees should be included, who counts as a 'family member',[106] and in what circumstances applications can be rejected.[107] The original motivation of the Directive related to the situation of settled migrants bringing family members to join them; over time such family members may have entered the territory of an EU Member State in an irregular way but are nevertheless able to assert reunification rights. Melissourgos, Leerkes, and Klassen refer to a 'family reunification hierarchy' where different legal rights apply but where there are significant gaps, even for those for whom family reunification should be relatively straightforward (often pertaining to the long wait for administrative decision-making and necessary authorizations).[108]

Given the large scope for interpretation of the text, it has been subject to frequent instances of judicial interpretation. National bureaucratic authorities have also played a strong role in operationalizing the text.[109] The CJEU has pronounced on some aspects of the Directive where the text is silent, noticeably on same-sex marriage, since the Directive refers only to 'spouse'.[110] In some instances, the Directive used the case-law of the ECtHR to define the limits of 'family', such as the rejection of polygamous marriages.[111] In other areas which were unforeseen in the original legislative process, 'soft' guidance has been provided by the Commission. For example, the Commission issued guidelines in 2014 on sham marriages.[112] This is a

[104] European Commission, 'Green Paper on the right to family reunification of third-country nationals living in the European Union (Directive 2003/86/EC)' COM (2011) 735 final.

[105] Pieter Boeles, 'Directive on Family Reunification: Are the Dilemmas Resolved?' (2001) 3 European Journal of Migration and Law 61.

[106] Natalie Welfens and Saskia Bonjour, 'Families First? The Mobilization of Family Norms in Refugee Resettlement' (2021) 15(2) International Political Sociology 212.

[107] Proportionality is key. See Cases C-381/18 and C-382/18 *GS and VG v Staatssecretaris van Justitie en Veiligheid* ECLI:EU:C:2019:1072, para 64 and Boeles, 'Directive on Family Reunification: Are the Dilemmas Resolved?' (n 99) 65.

[108] Stamatis Melissourgos, Arjen Leerkes and Mark Klaassen, 'Stuck in Greece? Unaccompanied Minors' Stratified Access to Family Reunification on the Way to Other EU Member States' (2023) 25(3) European Journal of Migration and Law 301, 309–10.

[109] Carla Mascia, 'How Bureaucracies Shape Access to Rights: The Implementation of Family Reunification in Belgium' (2021) 47(9) Journal of Ethnic and Migration Studies 2127.

[110] Case C-673/16, *Coman and Others v Inspectoratul General pentru Imigrări and Ministerul Afacerilor Interne*, ECLI:EU:C:2018:385.

[111] From the ECtHR: *EA and AA v the Netherlands* (No. 14501/89), *M and OM v the Netherlands* (No 12139/86) and *Bibi v the United Kingdom* (No 19628/92). Further, see Nicole Stybnarova, 'Teleology behind the Prohibition of Recognition of Polygamous Marriages under the EU Family Reunification Directive: A Critique of Rule Effectiveness' (2020) 40(1) Journal of Muslim Minority Affairs 104.

[112] Stefano Montaldo, Francesco Costamagna, and Francesca Romanelli, *Family Reunification in EU Law* (Università Di Torino 2022) https://iris.unito.it/bitstream/2318/1880604/1/2022%20Book%20Essentials%20-%20Family%20reunification.pdf, 7, accessed 2 June 2025.

good example of the synergy between formal law, expressed via a Directive, and an informal tool, yet one where the purpose is clear and where the content and purpose would not be easily met by amending the text of the Directive.

Soon after, Directive 2004/38 on the rights of EU citizens to move and reside freely within the EU was passed. It establishes the principles of non-discrimination and equal treatment for EU citizens exercising their right of free movement. The Directive covers the right of entry and residence for up to three months without any conditions, as well as the conditions for longer stays, such as employment, self-employment, study, or family reunification. It also addresses the grounds for expulsion and the rights of permanent residents. Overall, Directive 2004/38 aims to facilitate the exercise of the right to free movement while balancing it with safeguards to protect public order, public security, and public health. While the focus of the Directive was squarely on the rights of EU citizens, it also covered their TCN family members.

The Long-term Residents Directive (2003/109)[113] was passed after a lengthy process of back-and-forth between the Commission and the Council. The Directive states that a Member State 'shall grant long-term resident status to third-country nationals who have resided legally and continuously within its territory for five years immediately prior to the submission of the relevant application'.[114] The Directive also requires migrants to show access to 'stable and regular resources'.[115]

The result was a Directive which contained so many derogations and exceptions that it is difficult to see how it meets the goal of rights 'as near as possible to those enjoyed by EU citizens'.[116] Some gap-filling has been undertaken by the CJEU by 'reading across' from—in this case—Member States' discretion over public policy requirements relating to a right against expulsion that EU citizens enjoy under Article 27 of Directive 2004/38.[117]

3.3 Legislation on migration after 2005

The response to the slow-moving nature of the legislative process was to further the 'normalization' process of migration law in the Treaty of Nice. Upon its entry into force on 1 February 2003, decision-making rules should have shifted to Qualified Majority Voting (QMV) and co-decision between the Council and the Parliament. This was on the condition of the Council first adopting measures 'defining the

[113] Council Directive 2003/109/EC of 25 November 2003 concerning the status of third-country nationals who are long-term residents [2003] OJ L16/44.
[114] Article 4(1).
[115] Article 5(1)(a).
[116] European Council, *Presidency Conclusions* (Tampere, 15 and 16 October 1999) A(2).
[117] For example, in *WT*. See commentary by Diego Acosta, 'Court of Justice of the European Union (Ninth Chamber), *WT v Subdelegación del Gobierno en Guadalajara*: Case C-448/19, Judgment of 11 June 2020, EU:C:2020:467' (2020) 22(3) European Journal of Migration and Law 457.

common rules and basic principles on asylum issues'.[118] Overall, the Treaty failed to make significant progress, as the unanimity rule remained.

In the same vein, the Treaty Establishing a Constitution for Europe proposed more substantial QMV and fully normalizing the use of the Community Method in JHA 'to a large extent'.[119] The rationale for doing so, according to the Commission, was to allow for a reinforcement of the Parliament's role as a means to increase democratic legitimacy.[120] The Constitutional Treaty also proposed a 'specific legal basis for policy areas such as the integration of third-country nationals and the Common European Asylum System'.[121] Meanwhile, what remained in the third pillar saw a gradual increase in activity in several areas, of which two (external frontiers and Schengen) were closely linked to migration.[122]

After the Constitutional Treaty was abandoned following its rejection in referendums in France and the Netherlands, the Treaty of Lisbon 'rescued' its provisions.[123] The changes in immigration and asylum contained in the Treaty of Lisbon was largely the same as in the Constitutional Treaty, except for some details on the opt-out rules of Denmark, Ireland, and the UK.[124] The achievement of the Common European Asylum System became an objective in itself[125] rather than its previous 'sidekick status'.[126] The Community method took the central place in migration law, with QMV and the ordinary legislative procedure (formerly the co-decision procedure) extended to legal migration.[127] Furthermore, the Court of Justice would enjoy full jurisdiction in all JHA areas, which, given the extensive revision of most competences in this area, including immigration, asylum, and criminal law, opened the door to a major role for the Court in the future.[128] As Thym has explained, the retention of migration in the Treaty of Lisbon was significant for the 'upgrading' of migration to a policy field in its own right:

> Besides the consolidation of Union competences, changes concentrate on the self-sufficiency of migration law. EU activity is no longer presented as spillover of the single market in line with the original assumption that the abolition of border

[118] Peers, 'The Rise and Fall of EU Justice and Home Affairs Law' (n 25).
[119] Antonio Vitorino speech 4/435 (n 59).
[120] ibid.
[121] ibid; Treaty Establishing a Constitution for Europe (Draft) [2004] OJ C 310/1, Article III-260.
[122] Börzel, 'Mind the Gap! European Integration Between Level and Scope' (n 27); Jörg Monar, 'Justice and Home Affairs in the Treaty of Amsterdam: Reform at the Price of Fragmentation' (1998) 23(4) European Law Review 320, 326.
[123] Article III 267(5) Treaty Establishing a Constitution for Europe; see Steve Peers, 'EU Immigration and Asylum Competence and Decision-Making in the Treaty of Lisbon' (2008) 10(2) European Journal of Migration and Law 219.
[124] Peers, 'EU Immigration and Asylum Competence and Decision-Making in the Treaty of Lisbon' (n 118) 220.
[125] Article 78(1)–(2) TFEU.
[126] Tsourdi and Costello, 'The Evolution of EU Law on Refugees and Asylum' (n 11).
[127] Articles 77–80 TFEU.
[128] Peers, 'The Rise and Fall of EU Justice and Home Affairs Law' (n 25).

> controls necessitated 'flanking measures' compensating Member States for the loss of control options at domestic borders, which had characterized Justice and Home Affairs cooperation since the 1980s. Instead, migration law emancipated itself from the single market, defining itself as an integral part of the Area of Freedom, Security and Justice.[129]

There is little doubt that Thym's characterization of post-Lisbon migration as an EU policy field in its own right has been borne out, given the place of migration as a constant on the agendas of the EU institutions. But this does not necessarily indicate that the legislative powers have been used in the fuller way that the Treaty of Lisbon and its 'upgrading' might have prompted. In particular, the ordinary legislative procedure in use since Lisbon needs to be understood in the light of Article 79(5) TFEU, in which it is stated that 'This Article shall not affect the right of Member States to determine volumes of admission of third-country nationals coming from third countries to their territory in order to seek work, whether employed or self-employed'. As a result, the weight of the measures passed since the Treaty changes in the 2000s, including the Treaty of Lisbon, largely again falls on advancing the CEAS, with only later attempts to address the gaps in EU legislation on facilitating regular migration.

3.3.1 CEAS phase two

The second phase of the CEAS ran from 2006 to 2013. On the institutional front, a Regulation created the European Asylum Support Office (EASO) with the stated aim 'to help to improve the implementation of the Common European Asylum System (the CEAS), to strengthen practical cooperation among Member States on asylum and to provide and/or coordinate the provision of operational support to Member States subject to particular pressure on their asylum and reception systems'.[130] The EASO, which eventually became the EU Agency for Asylum,[131] has witnessed an expansion in its role and powers, but not without questions over its accountability and relationship with the protection of fundamental rights,[132]

[129] Daniel Thym, 'EU Migration Policy and Its Constitutional Rationale: A Cosmopolitan Outlook' (2013) 50(3) Common Market Law Review 709.

[130] Regulation (EU) No 439/2010 of the European Parliament and of the Council of 19 May 2010 establishing a European Asylum Support Office (no longer in force), Article 1.

[131] Regulation (EU) 2021/2303 of the European Parliament and of the Council of 15 December 2021 on the European Union Agency for Asylum and repealing Regulation (EU) No 439/2010 [2021] OJ L468/1.

[132] See, inter alia, Françoise Comte, 'A New Agency Is Born in the European Union: The European Asylum Support Office' (2010) 12(4) European Journal of Migration and Law 373; Stephanie Schneider and Carolin Nieswandt, 'EASO—Support Office or Asylum Authority? Boundary Disputes in the European Field of Asylum Administration' (2018) 43(1) Österreichische Zeitschrift für Soziologie 13; Evangelia (Lilian) Tsourdi, 'Holding the European Asylum Support Office Accountable for Its Role

including the Eurodac information system.[133] A new proposal emerged in 2016, and another in 2020.[134]

During this period, the weight of legislative activity rested on the recasting of almost all of the legislative instruments in force. Recasting allowed for the taking account of some of their flaws, although the new versions largely retained the principles behind them while streamlining some of the practices. The overall purpose of the recast directives as a form of legislative harmonization to realize the CEAS relied on cross-references between the instruments and 'reading together' to promote and ensure a more holistic 'system' and confront some fundamental issues such as the disparate levels of procedural standards, reception conditions, and protection measures.[135]

However, the legal clarity of the instruments as initially provided by the Commission was undermined by the long-drawn-out negotiations. The harmonizing potential of the recast instruments was thus diluted,[136] and further hampered by the intrinsic links between the lack of harmonization in migration law and the intersecting areas of education, welfare, and healthcare, which are also not harmonized.[137]

in Asylum Decision-Making: Mission Impossible?' (2020) 21(3) German Law Journal 506; Salvatore Nicolosi and David Fernandez-Rojo, 'Out of Control? The Case of the European Asylum Support Office' in Miroslava Scholten and Alex Brenninkmeijer (eds), *Controlling EU Agencies* (Edward Elgar Publishing 2020).

[133] The Eurodac regulation was recast in this period as Regulation (EU) No 603/2013 of the European Parliament and of the Council of 26 June 2013 on the establishment of 'Eurodac' for the comparison of fingerprints for the effective application of Regulation (EU) No 604/2013 establishing the criteria and mechanisms for determining the Member State responsible for examining an application for international protection lodged in one of the Member States by a third-country national or a stateless person and on requests for the comparison with Eurodac data by Member States' law enforcement authorities and Europol for law enforcement purposes, and amending Regulation (EU) No 1077/2011 establishing a European Agency for the operational management of large-scale IT systems in the area of freedom, security and justice (recast) [2013] OJ L180/1. See also Niovi Vavoula, 'Transforming Eurodac from 2016 to the New Pact: From the Dublin System's Sidekick to a Database in Support of EU Policies on Asylum, Resettlement and Irregular Migration' (2020) ECRE Working Paper no 13, https://ecre.org/wp-content/uploads/2021/01/ECRE-Working-Paper-Transforming-Eurodac-from-2016-to-the-New-Pact-January-2021.pdf, accessed 2 June 2025.

[134] Commission, Amended proposal for a regulation of the European Council on the establishment of 'Eurodac' for the comparison of biometric data for the effective application of Regulation on Asylum and Migration Management and of Resettlement Regulation, for identifying an illegally staying third-country national or stateless person and on requests for the comparison with Eurodac data by Member States' law enforcement authorities and Europol for law enforcement purposes and amending Regulations (EU) 2018/1240 and (EU) 2019/818, COM(2020) 614 final.

[135] EASO, *Annual Report on the Situation of Asylum in the European Union 2013* (EASO 2014) https://euaa.europa.eu/publications/annual-report-situation-asylum-european-union-2013, accessed 9 June 2025.

[136] Tsourdi and Costello, 'The Evolution of EU Law on Refugees and Asylum' (n 11) 811.

[137] Den Heijer, Rijpma, and Spijkerboer, 'Coercion, Prohibition, and Great Expectations: The Continuing Failure of the Common European Asylum System' (n 29) 610.

The Returns Directive[138] was the first piece of legislation passed using co-decision post-Lisbon. The purpose of the Directive was to agree on common standards and procedures in Member States for returning TCNs in an irregular state. The negotiations challenging lasted more than three years, and a compromise text was only agreed after several informal 'trilogues' between the Commission, Parliament, and Council.[139]

Notably, the Returns Directive represented a shift in the European Parliament from a more liberal to a restrictive position, and accepted the lower level of protection for irregular migrants than was originally proposed by the Commission.[140] This is significant for the discussion here because the European Parliament had generally been counted on to be the 'defender' of rights.[141] In a sense, this greater alignment between the tendency of the European Parliament and many of the Member States in the Council might have suggested that the passage of legislation would be easier. However, it has not resulted in either a greater amount of legislation or speedier passage through the process.

3.3.2 Provisions on regular migration post-2005

For regular migration, on which there had been a notable lack of progress in the initial period following the Treaty of Amsterdam, the post-Lisbon period marked the appearance of a succession of directives.[142] These included the 'Blue Card' Directive for High-Skilled Workers in 2009[143] (recast in 2021),[144] the Single Work and Residence Permit Directive (2011,[145] recast in 2024),[146] the Seasonal

[138] Directive 2008/115/EC of the European Parliament and of the Council of 16 December 2008 on common standards and procedures in Member States for returning illegally staying third-country nationals [2008] OJ L348/98.

[139] Katharina Eisele (ed), *The Returns Directive 2008/115/EC: European Implementation Assessment* (European Parliamentary Research Service 2020) https://www.europarl.europa.eu/RegData/etudes/STUD/2020/642840/EPRS_STU(2020)642840_EN.pdf, accessed 2 June 2025.

[140] Diego Acosta, 'The Good, the Bad, and the Ugly in EU Migration Law: Is the European Parliament Becoming Bad and Ugly? (The Adoption of Directive 2008/15: The Returns Directive)' (2009) 11(1) European Journal of Migration and Law 19.

[141] This point is returned to in Chapter 4.

[142] See Peers, 'The Rise and Fall of EU Justice and Home Affairs Law' (n 25).

[143] Council Directive 2009/50/EC of 25 May 2009 on the conditions of entry and residence of third-country nationals for the purposes of highly qualified employment [2013] OJ L 155/17.

[144] Directive (EU) 2021/1883 of the European Parliament and of the Council of 20 October 2021 on the conditions of entry and residence of third-country nationals for the purpose of highly qualified employment, and repealing Council Directive 2009/50/EC [2021] OJ L382/1.

[145] Directive 2011/98/EU of the European Parliament and of the Council of 13 December 2011 on a single application procedure for a single permit for third-country nationals to reside and work in the territory of a Member State and on a common set of rights for third-country workers legally residing in a Member State [2011] OJ L343/1.

[146] Directive (EU) 2024/1233 of the European Parliament and of the Council of 24 April 2024 on a single application procedure for a single permit for third-country nationals to reside and work in the territory of a Member State and on a common set of rights for third-country workers legally residing in a Member State (recast) [2024] OJ L2024/1233.

Employment Directive (2014),[147] the Directive on Intra-corporate Transfers (2014),[148] and a Directive on Students, Researchers, and Au Pairs (2016).[149]

However, while the list might seem to show an impressive amount of legislative activity, the measures do not harmonize migration law and policy in any meaningful sense. The directives do not set out, on an EU-wide basis, how many individuals might be admitted or what conditions there might be for doing so in numerical terms. Rather, they establish common procedures and rights for those who are admitted.[150] During this period too, the theme evident in the Tampere Conclusions of enhancing rights of TCNs to levels approximating those of EU citizens was replaced by a widespread resistance to doing so by the Member States, pushing the former liberal approach beyond recognition.[151] By way of example, the Single Permit Directive 2011/98/EU[152] for social rights protection failed to take significant steps forward in facilitating the ability of TCNs to enjoy more enhanced—and similar—rights across the Member States.[153]

The first legislative instrument to specifically apply to regular migration for the purposes of word only appeared in 2009. The 'Blue Card' Directive[154] was modelled on the familiar 'Green Card' approach of the United States, as a means for high-skilled migrants to enter (and reside) for the purposes of work. Although there are important differences between the US and EU approaches,[155] the attempt by the EU—as distinct from the Member States—to enter the arena of competing for highly skilled individuals to migrate was enough to concern the US about a potential loss of talent to Europe.[156]

The legislative process began before the entry into force of the Treaty of Lisbon, and hence the principle of unanimity applied to the Council. The Commission

[147] Directive 2014/36/EU of the European Parliament and of the Council of 26 February 2014 on the conditions of entry and stay of third-country nationals for the purpose of employment as seasonal workers [2014] OJ L94/375.

[148] Directive 2014/66/EU of the European Parliament and of the Council of 15 May 2014 on the conditions of entry and residence of third-country nationals in the framework of an intra-corporate transfer [2014] OJ L157/1.

[149] Directive (EU) 2016/801 of the European Parliament and of the Council of 11 May 2016 on the conditions of entry and residence of third-country nationals for the purposes of research, studies, training, voluntary service, pupil exchange schemes or educational projects and au pairing [2016] OJ L132/21.

[150] James Hampshire, 'European Migration Governance since the Lisbon Treaty: Introduction to the Special Issue' (2016) 42(4) Journal of Ethnic and Migration Studies 537; Adam Luedtke, 'Uncovering European Union Immigration Legislation: Policy Dynamics and Outcomes' (2011) 49(2) International Migration 1.

[151] Galya Ruffer, 'Pushed Beyond Recognition? The Liberality of Family Reunification Policies in the EU' (2011) 37(6) Journal of Ethnic and Migration Studies 935.

[152] Directive 2011/98/EU [2011] OJ L343/1.

[153] Ana Beduschi, 'An Empty Shell? The Protection of Social Rights of Third-country Workers in the EU after the Single Permit Directive' (2015) 17(2–3) European Journal of Migration and Law 210.

[154] Council Directive 2009/50/EC [2005] OJ L155/17.

[155] Elspeth Guild, 'EU Policy on Labour Migration: A First Look at the Commission's Blue Card Initiative' (CEPS Policy Brief, No 145, 2007).

[156] Cerna, 'The EU Blue Card: Preferences, Policies, and Negotiations Between Member States' (n 4).

adopted a key role as a policy entrepreneur,[157] and the conditions for entry under the Blue Card scheme were relatively clear-cut.

The Directive required applicants to have a higher education qualification, such as a university degree, alongside a valid job offer or work contract with a duration of at least one year. A Blue Card would generally be issued for one year initially, with the possibility of renewal. The total duration varies depending on the Member State but is typically around four years. Furthermore, the Directive includes provisions for family members of Blue Card holders to join them in the EU and, after a certain period of legal residence in one Member State, Blue Card holders may move to another EU Member State for employment purposes.

Nevertheless, in terms of attracting—as opposed to regulating—entrance and stay, the Directive opted for a 'lowest common denominator' approach.[158] A Commission Report in 2014 noted that the impact had been modest at best in terms of the number of individuals it attracted and who continued to reside in the EU.[159] While there was potential to attract, for example from India,[160] the Directive seemed stuck on the 'potential' to attract, rather than actually doing so.

There are multiple reasons behind this lacklustre performance. Attracting highly skilled migrants in what is often called a race for global talent can be challenging in convincing individuals to move under favourable conditions. This is a shared experience among countries including the (post-Brexit) UK, Japan, and even Denmark, which, due to its JHA opt-out, chose its own 'Green Card' scheme.[161] Yet, some challenges are specific to the EU and the Blue Card Directive itself. First, the institutional framing of the Directive has been within the sphere of migration, which, as identified throughout this chapter, has overwhelmingly been defined by exclusionary logics beyond the initial stages, rather than the more economic/Lisbon Strategy-led frames of 'competitiveness' or 'excellence'.[162] This has affected the promotion of the Blue Card as a means to attract, but also crucially to retain, highly skilled migrants, who may have a number of different global options.

[157] Sidonie Paris, 'The European Commission and the Blue Card Directive: Supranational Policy Entrepreneurship in Troubled Waters' (2017) 13(2) Journal of Contemporary European Research 1025.

[158] Cerna, 'The EU Blue Card: Preferences, Policies, and Negotiations between Member States' (n 4).

[159] Commission, 'The implementation of Directive 2009/50/EC on the conditions of entry and residence of third-country nationals for the purpose of highly qualified employment ("EU Blue Card")' (Communication) COM(2014) 287 final.

[160] Anja Wiesbrock and Metka Hercog, 'Making Europe More Attractive to Indian Highly-Skilled Migrants? The Blue Card Directive and National Law in Germany and the Netherlands' (Migration Policy Centre, CARIM-India Research Report, 2012/09).

[161] See, inter alia, Schon Beechler and Ian Woodward, 'The Global "War for Talent"' (2009) 15(3) Journal of International Management 273; Nana Oishi, 'Redefining the "Highly Skilled": The Points-Based System for Highly Skilled Foreign Professionals in Japan' (2014) 23(4) Asian and Pacific Migration Journal 421; Daisuke Wakisaka and Paul James Cardwell, 'Exploring the Trajectories of Highly Skilled Migration Law and Policy in Japan and the UK' (2021) 9 Comparative Migration Studies 43; Marlene Wind and Silvia Adamo, 'Is Green Better than Blue? The Danish JHA Opt-Out and the Unilateral Attempt to Attract Highly Skilled Labour' (2015) 17(4) European Journal of Migration and Law 329.

[162] Cerna and Chou, 'The Regional Dimension in the Global Competition for Talent' (n 93).

Second, there have been vast differences in the number of Blue Cards granted in Member States, with differences in transposition and some opting for the minimum of standards only. Finally, as an area of shared competence, there is nothing to prevent Member States from enacting their own schemes to attract migrants in particular areas to contribute to their own needs and avoid the risk of would-be migrants going elsewhere. In this sense, Member States are not only competing with other states around the world, but also with each other. The latter point was recognized by the Commission in its evaluation of the (limited) impact of the Directive.[163]

3.4 Legislation in the 'crisis' period since 2015

The oft-cited migration or refugee 'crisis' said to be engulfing the EU and its Member States has led to a great deal of institutional activity. Although the narrative of crisis is often, and publicly, related to the numbers of individuals attempting to reach the EU and overwhelming national reception capacities, the term crisis can be appropriately applied to the legal design and structures of EU migration law, which were revealed to be deeply flawed.[164]

The crisis did not spur a major push for new or revised legislation. The major pieces of legislation passed in this period related to the expansion in size and mandate of Frontex via Regulations in 2016 and 2019.[165] The non-legislative EU–Türkiye Statement is considered more fully later in this book. Initially, the Commission's efforts were focused on enforcement actions against Member States and thus making the existing law more effective.[166] Two emergency decisions on the relocation of asylum-seekers based on Article 78(3) TFEU[167] were

[163] COM(2014) 287 final.

[164] Daniel Thym, 'The "Refugee Crisis" as a Challenge of Legal Design and Institutional Legitimacy' (2016) 53(6) Common Market Law Review 1545.

[165] Regulation (EU) 2016/1624 of the European Parliament and of the Council of 14 September 2016 on the European Border and Coast Guard and amending Regulation (EU) 2016/399 of the European Parliament and of the Council and repealing Regulation (EC) No 863/2007 of the European Parliament and of the Council, Council Regulation (EC) No 2007/2004 and Council Decision 2005/267/EC (no longer in force) [2016] OJ L251/1; Regulation (EU) 2019/1896 of the European Parliament and of the Council of 13 November 2019 on the European Border and Coast Guard and repealing Regulations (EU) No 1052/2013 and (EU) 2016/1624 [2019] OJ L295/1.

[166] European Commission, 'More responsibility in managing the refugee crisis: European Commission adopts 40 infringement decisions to make European Asylum System work' Press release of 23 Sept. 2015; 'Implementing the Common European Asylum System: Commission escalates 8 infringement proceedings' Press release of 10 Dec. 2015; 'Implementing the Common European Asylum System: Commission acts on 9 infringement proceedings' Press release of 10 Feb. 2016; from Den Heijer, Rijpma, and Spijkerboer, 'Coercion, Prohibition, and Great Expectations: The Continuing Failure of the Common European Asylum System' (n 29) 625.

[167] Article 78(3) TFEU: In the event of one or more Member States being confronted by an emergency situation characterized by a sudden inflow of nationals of third countries, the Council, on a proposal from the Commission, may adopt provisional measures for the benefit of the Member State(s) concerned. It shall act after consulting the European Parliament.

adopted,[168] and were unsuccessfully challenged by Hungary and Slovakia.[169] Legislative proposals in response to the crisis were eventually dropped.[170] Much of the legislation proposed has been the attempted recasting of existing Regulations and Directives, with a central focus on reforming the CEAS. Recasting Regulations and Directives in itself does not signify a lack of political will to use the legislative process as a means to confronting migration challenges, but much depends on the content of the recast legislation and whether it actually responds adequately to the critiques of its usefulness or operational ability.

For the CEAS, a total of seven proposals were made to reform or recast existing Regulations and Directives in 2016.[171] Revision to the Reception Conditions Directive was proposed by the Commission in 2016,[172] with the aim of ensuring greater consistency in reception conditions and the ability of the EU and the Member States to meet challenges of larger-scale inward movements. It aimed to improve access to housing, healthcare, education, and employment while reducing disparities in treatment that encouraged secondary movements. Although this was provisionally agreed by the Council and Parliament in 2018, the proposal lost momentum in the COREPER stage, where Member State representatives could not agree on the technical details of how the revision would work.[173] As

[168] Council Decision (EU) 2015/1523 establishing provisional measures in the area of international protection for the benefit of Italy and Greece [2015] OJ L239/146 and Council Decision (EU) 2015/1601 establishing provisional measures in the area of international protection for the benefit of Italy and Greece [2015] OJ L248/80.

[169] Cases C-643/15 *Slovakia v Council* and C-647/15 *Hungary v Council* ECLI:EU:C:2017:631.

[170] Steve Peers, 'The New EU Asylum Laws: Taking Rights Half-Seriously' (2024) 0 Yearbook of European Law 1, 3. The failed proposals were on adding relocation rules in the Dublin Regulation and on a common list of 'safe countries of origin': COM (2015) 450 and 452, 9 September 2015; withdrawn [2019] OJ C 210.

[171] On reception: Commission, 'Proposal for a Directive of the European Parliament and of the Council laying down standards for the reception of applicants for international protection (recast)' COM (2016) 465 final; on qualification for international protection: COM (2016) 466 final; on procedures: Commission, 'Proposal for a Regulation of the European Parliament and of the Council establishing a common procedure for international protection in the Union and repealing Directive 2013/32/EU' COM(2016) 467 final; on resettlement: Commission, 'Proposal for a Regulation of the European Parliament and of the Council establishing a Union Resettlement Framework and amending Regulation (EU) No 516/2014 of the European Parliament and the Council' COM(2016) 468 final; on Dublin: Commission, 'Proposal for a Regulation of the European Parliament and of the Council establishing the criteria and mechanisms for determining the Member State responsible for examining an application for international protection lodged in one of the Member States by a third-country national or a stateless person (recast)' COM(2016) 270 final; on EASO: Commission, 'Proposal for a Regulation of the European Parliament and of the Council on the European Union Agency for Asylum and repealing Regulation' (EU) No 439/2010 COM(2016) 271 final; on Eurodac: Commission, 'Proposal for a Regulation of the European Parliament and of the Council on the establishment of "Eurodac" for the comparison of fingerprints for the effective application of [Regulation (EU) No 604/2013 establishing the criteria and mechanisms for determining the Member State responsible for examining an application for international protection lodged in one of the Member States by a third-country national or a stateless person], for identifying an illegally staying third-country national or stateless person and on requests for the comparison with Eurodac data by Member States' law enforcement authorities and Europol for law enforcement purposes (recast)' COM(2016) 272 final.

[172] COM (2016) 465 final.

[173] Lieneke Slingenberg, 'Political Compromise on a Recast Asylum Reception Conditions Directive: Dignity Without Autonomy?' (*EU Immigration and Asylum Law and Policy*, 3 March

such, the Directive was later bound into the proposals for a New Pact on Migration and Asylum.[174]

A similar fate befell the proposals to recast the Return Directive and Qualification Directive. The Commission's 2018 Recast Return Directive proposal[175] put forward a new mandatory return border procedure, with the aim of reversing the decrease in return rates from the EU to third countries from 45.8 per cent in 2016 to 36.6 per cent in 2017. It linked return policies to asylum by requiring the issuing of a common administrative decision for both the rejection of an asylum claim and return decision.[176] Returns had been identified by the Commission and the Member States as a core aspect of EU migration governance and the CEAS, and the Commission had 'produced a cascade of policy documents on return policies'[177] in this period, including multiple recommendations,[178] a returns handbook,[179] and two Action Plans[180] as a means to better implement the existing Directive. Yet, the Commission then proposed to recast the Directive, although without undertaking an impact assessment, in a shift away from its previous insistence that the framework of the legislation was sufficient if adequately put in place to increase returns.[181] The proposed Directive bounced between the Parliament and the Council for several years, and was only eventually passed in 2021 as part of the New Pact.

For the Qualification Directive,[182] a revised Regulation was proposed in 2016,[183] with the aim of reducing the variations between the Member States and

2021) https://eumigrationlawblog.eu/political-compromise-on-a-recast-asylum-reception-conditions-directive-dignity-without-autonomy/, accessed 2 June 2025.

[174] See below and Chapter 4.

[175] Commission, 'Proposal for a Directive of the European Parliament and of the Council on common standards and procedures in Member States for returning illegally staying third-country nationals (recast)' COM (2018) 634 final.

[176] Madalina Moraru, 'The new design of the EU's Return System under the Pact on Asylum and Migration' (*EU Immigration and Asylum Law and Policy*, 14 January 2021) https://eumigrationlawblog.eu/the-new-design-of-the-eus-return-system-under-the-pact-on-asylum-and-migration/#:~:text=The%202018%20Recast%20Return%20Directive%20proposal%20put%20forward%20a%20new,asylum%20claim%20and%20return%20decision, accessed 2 June 2025.

[177] Izabella Majcher and Tineke Strik, 'Legislating Without Evidence: The Recast of the EU Return Directive' (2021) 23(2) European Journal of Migration and Law 103.

[178] Commission, 'Commission Recommendation (EU) 2017/432 of 7 March 2017 on Making Returns More Effective When Implementing the Directive 2008/115/EC of the European Parliament and of the Council' [2017] OJ L 66/15.

[179] Commission, 'Commission Recommendation (EU) 2017/2338 of 16 November 2017 Establishing a Common "Return Handbook" to Be Used by Member States' Competent Authorities When Carrying out Return-Related Tasks' [2017] OJ L 339/83).

[180] Commission, 'Communication from the Commission to the European Parliament and the Council: EU Action Plan on Return' COM (2015) 453 final; Commission, 'Communication from the Commission to the European Parliament and the Council on a More Effective Return Policy in the European Union: A Renewed Action Plan' COM (2017) 200 final.

[181] Majcher and Strik, 'Legislating Without Evidence' (n 177).

[182] Directive 2011/95/EU [2011] OJ L337/9.

[183] Commission, 'Proposal for a Regulation of the European Parliament and of the Council on standards for the qualification of third-country nationals or stateless persons as beneficiaries of international protection, for a uniform status for refugees or for persons eligible for subsidiary protection and for the

'a lack of convergence as regards decisions on the type of protection status granted by each Member State'.[184] In moving beyond the minimum standards approach, the Regulation proposed much greater clarity on treatment of those needing protection, while also maintaining discretion and exceptions for the Member States. The Qualification Regulation's progress also stalled, and after its inclusion in the New Pact, it was eventually passed in May 2024, to enter into force on 1 July 2026.[185] Finally, for Eurodac—which might be considered the least politically contentious—the recast Regulation 2013[186] was the subject of a new proposal in 2016, subsequently amended in 2020[187] and passed in May 2024[188] with an entry date of June 2026.[189]

For regular migration, the Blue Card Directive, originally passed in 2009 and explored above,[190] was widely seen as falling short of expectations. Recognizing the limitations of the Blue Card Directive,[191] the proposal in 2016 to replace the original Directive sought to increase intra-EU mobility and increase the attractiveness of the EU scheme. The adopted Directive[192] now includes an extension of eligibility to certain graduates and refugees, and it seeks to minimize the attractiveness of parallel national schemes by offering more favourable terms. Passed in 2021, the Directive had a transposition limit of November 2023. It remains to be seen whether the revised law may increase the number of Blue Card holders, especially as it depends on both the general attractiveness of the EU and rival schemes

content of the protection granted and amending Council Directive 2003/109/EC of 25 November 2003 concerning the status of third-country nationals who are long-term residents' COM(2016) 466 final.

[184] ibid.

[185] Regulation (EU) 2024/1347 of the European Parliament and of the Council of 14 May 2024 on standards for the qualification of third-country nationals or stateless persons as beneficiaries of international protection, for a uniform status for refugees or for persons eligible for subsidiary protection and for the content of the protection granted, amending Council Directive 2003/109/EC and repealing Directive 2011/95/EU of the European Parliament and of the Council [2024] OJ L2024/1347, Article 42.

[186] Regulation (EU) No 603/2013 (recast) [2013] OJ L180/1.

[187] COM(2020) 614 final.

[188] Regulation (EU) 2024/1358 of the European Parliament and of the Council of 14 May 2024 on the establishment of 'Eurodac' for the comparison of biometric data in order to effectively apply Regulations (EU) 2024/1351 and (EU) 2024/1350 of the European Parliament and of the Council and Council Directive 2001/55/EC and to identify illegally staying third-country nationals and stateless persons and on requests for the comparison with Eurodac data by Member States' law enforcement authorities and Europol for law enforcement purposes, amending Regulations (EU) 2018/1240 and (EU) 2019/818 of the European Parliament and of the Council and repealing Regulation (EU) No 603/2013 of the European Parliament and of the Council [2024] OJ L2024/1358.

[189] ibid Article 63(2). The exception is Article 26 in the direction, by which 'Each Member State shall promptly take the biometric data of every third-country national or stateless person of at least six years of age registered as a beneficiary of temporary protection in the territory of that Member State'. This article will enter into force, as per Article 63(2), in June 2029.

[190] Directive (EU) 2021/1883 OJ L382/1.

[191] COM(2014) 287 final.

[192] Directive (EU) 2021/1883 OJ L382/1.

from both Member States and third countries, which now includes the post-Brexit UK.[193]

The latest attempt to rethink the approach to attracting skilled migration to the EU is provided by a Commission proposal for a Regulation to develop a 'Talent Pool' as part of a Skills and Mobility package.[194] The proposed Regulation is based on Article 79(2)(a) TFEU on the entry and residence of TCNs. The Talent Pool would be voluntary for the Member States, but participating states would be required under the Regulation to apply the directly applicable rules, although they remain free to operate their own schemes. The Commission hopes that operating an EU Talent Pool to 'facilitate international recruitment'[195] would help match job-seekers with employers in participating Member States via an IT platform. However, since Member States are ultimately responsible for entry and residence conditions, it is difficult to see how the Talent Pool will add value to national schemes unless it creates a 'one-stop shop' for the whole EU, which seems unlikely. If participation from Member States, particularly larger states and employers, is low, and in the absence of firm assurances about entry conditions, 'the venture risks to boil down anyhow to an innocuous recruitment and information platform'.[196]

3.5 Conclusion

The account of EU legislative activity on the basis of competences granted in the Treaty of Amsterdam and since then is one where several themes emerge. The first is that despite the agreement by the Member States to introduce competences on migration in the Treaties and to eventually shift the legislative process towards the use of QMV, legislation has not emerged at either the quantity or speed that the text of the Treaty suggests. The political salience of migration on the EU's agenda appears to assert a strong influence on the (lack of) progress: on the one hand, the Commission has brought forward proposals to move towards greater cooperation or even harmonization, but the sharp divisions between the Council (and the Member States within it) and the Parliament has required proposals to languish and face extensive changes to allow a way forward. In this sense, migration does not entirely follow the script provided by—for example—the Single Market

193 Summary of Peers blog: Steve Peers, 'The revised Blue Card Directive: the EU's search for more highly skilled non-EU migrants' (*EU Law Analysis*, 20 May 2021).

194 Proposal for a Regulation of the European Parliament and of the Council establishing an EU Talent Pool COM(2023) 716 final. See the further discussion on the package in Chapter Four.

195 ibid para 5.2.

196 Tesseltje de Lange and Henri de Waele, 'The Constitutional Conundrums of Regulating Skilled Migration into the EU' (2024) 49(3) European Law Review 237–55. For an earlier discussion of these proposals, see Tesseltje De Lange and others, 'The EU Legal Migration Package. Towards a Rights-Based Approach to Attracting Skills and Talent to the EU' (December 2022) Study for the European Parliament, Brussels.

programme, since the European Council and Council of Ministers have continued to exercise strong control over the process.[197]

Regular migration for the purposes of work, often termed 'economic' migration, has been a much more tortuous process, with only scant legislative provisions emerging. One might expect that the Single Market and familiarity with free movement, coupled with employment shortages and an ageing population, might make the EU Member States more likely to agree a common approach and legislative framework on the basis of the Treaty competences. However, this has not occurred. In a sense, migration within the changing EU after the enlargements of 2004 and 2007 has fulfilled the need—at least for states in Western Europe—to resist any moves to place migration vis-à-vis TCNs on a common footing. The political discourse, particularly in the UK during the Brexit referendum, often characterized the movement of 'new' EU citizens in the same terms as non-EU 'economic' migration. While this might have been the most obvious example of hostility to free movement, the transitional controls placed on new members in 2004 and 2007 by most existing Member States feed into this view of a need to restrict migration, even for the purposes of work. This feeds into the 'categorization' of migrants into different groups, with differentiated rights attached.[198] With this being an area of shared competence, Member States of course retain the legal powers to act in areas which are not included within the EU's competences, in particular the use of the criminal law.[199]

Therefore, for regular or legal migration, the central plank of legislation that we might expect from the well-trodden path of many areas of EU law is absent. This might seem counter-intuitive, since the EU's traditional characterization as a polity based around an internal market would suggest that the economic drivers for migration would find a natural home in the integration process towards people (i.e. workers) from outside the bloc. However, this is not the case, due to the lack of an overall aim or political will. By contrast, the Member States—despite national political protestations—have more readily found common cause in preventing irregular migration, even if there are sharp differences in terms of the measures to be

[197] Christopher Bickerton, Dermot Hodson, and Uwe Puetter, 'Conclusions: The Post-Maastricht Period and Beyond' in Christopher J Bickerton, Dermot Hodson, and Uwe Puetter (eds), *The New Intergovernmentalism: States and Supranational Actors in the Post-Maastricht Era* (Oxford University Press 2015) 316–17.

[198] Julia Permoser, 'Redefining Membership: Restrictive Rights and Categorisation in European Union Migration Policy' (2017) 43(15) Journal of Ethnic and Migration Studies 2536.

[199] See, for example, Matilde Rosina, 'Criminalising Migration: The Vicious Cycle of Insecurity and Irregularity' (2024) 13(10) Social Sciences 529; Valsamis Mitsilegas, *The Criminalisation of Migration in Europe: Challenges for Human Rights and the Rule of Law* (Springer 2014); Luisa Marin and Alessandro Spena, 'Introduction: The Criminalization of Migration and European (Dis)integration' (2016) 18(2) European Journal of Migration and Law 147; Didier Bigo, 'Criminalisation of "Migrants": The Side Effect of the Will to Control the Frontiers and the Sovereign Illusion' in Barbara Bogusz and others (eds), *Irregular Migration and Human Rights: Theoretical, European and International Perspectives* (Brill Nijhoff 2004).

taken. The role of legislation in migration should thus not be discounted entirely. The following chapter traces the centrality, or otherwise, of the legislative process in fulfilling the terms of the Treaty. And while legislation appears to have been sidelined in the period following the Treaty of Lisbon, the latest iteration of migration policy via the Migration Pact (which was approved in 2024) once again appears to return legislation to a more central place in the governance of migration.[200]

[200] See the further analysis in Chapter 4.

4

Strategic Approaches to Migration Law and Governance

From Tampere to the New Pact on Migration and Asylum

The preceding chapter demonstrated that migration law has found its place at the heart of the Treaties, and that the institutional logics associated with it in the legislative sphere resemble many of the policy areas where harmonization has taken place in the EU. But it also shows that the legislative process has been slow to produce legislation, and the actual law is to a certain degree removed from what the comprehensiveness of the Treaty text suggests.

As detailed in earlier chapters, migration occupies a space which is the focus of both internal law and policymaking, insofar as it relies on Regulations and Directives applicable across the Member States but also external relations and foreign policy. The latter is a space where the formal aspect of legislation in the internal sphere is mirrored by a set of general and specific competences on agreements with third countries (such as Association Agreements and, on migration, Readmission Agreements).[1] Both legislation and external agreements follow a defined process as set out in the Treaties—not always without controversy or legal challenges, but which nevertheless results in visible instruments which can be enforced.

The core theme of this book is the move away from legislation to other forms of governance. To fully understand the governance of migration, and the place of both legislation and other instruments, the later stage of upgrading migration within the Treaty coincides with a more general search for strategy in EU policy. That is not to say that earlier stages of European integration occurred without a plan; rather, it is a feature of modern national, European, and international governance that strategic objectives are agreed and published. In the EU context, the growth in competences has made the need for strategic direction around the general Treaty aims more compelling, and thus programmes have appeared in relation to the Single Market, regional development, environment, and agriculture and in response to major shifts, such as the 'NextGenerationEU' economic recovery plan to the Covid-19 pandemic.[2] The fear that the integration process may grind to a

[1] See Chapter 6.

[2] See, inter alia, Caroline de la Porte and Mads Jensen, 'The Next Generation EU: An Analysis of the Dimensions of Conflict behind the Deal' (2021) 55(2) Social Policy & Administration 388; Amandine Crespy, Tom Massart, and Vivien Schmidt, 'How the Impossible Became Possible: Evolving Frames

The Governance of Migration in the European Union. Paul James Cardwell, Oxford University Press.
 DOI: 10.1093/9780191946592.003.0005

halt—or fall apart—provides an impetus for strategic planning.[3] These documents themselves play an important role in EU governance,[4] though not without raising questions about their place in the EU's legal and constitutional order.[5] Since the European Council's Tampere Conclusions in 1999, migration and European integration are increasingly part of a new dividing line in European politics with the capacity to shape both elections and governments.[6]

The development of EU legislation on migration can thus be understood alongside a succession of strategic documents on either migration specifically or Justice and Home Affairs and the Area of Freedom, Security and Justice more widely. Tracing the development of migration law and governance through these documents informs the way in which legislation plays a central or an ancillary role in the *means* for the pursuit of strategic objectives in migration. This includes instances where the need for legislation has been mooted or even proposed, but has not materialized, or where legislation exists but is recognized as falling short of goals and where the pursuit of objectives by alternate means emerges. Furthermore, given the importance placed on the analysis on informal governance here, the strategic programmes, approaches, or pacts are in themselves an indication of the variety of language employed in governance and the emergence of *de novo* bodies and agencies. In exploring the success of strategic documents relating to migration, the shifts to and from the use of legislation explored in the previous chapter can be more readily understood. This chapter traces how migration governance and the place of law within it has developed from the Tampere Conclusion to the current proposals under the New Pact on Migration and Asylum.

4.1 The Tampere Conclusions

The Presidency Conclusions of the European Council at Tampere (1999) launched the Roadmap to 'develop the Union as an area of freedom, security and justice'[7] on the basis of the new competences agreed in the Treaty of Amsterdam. The role of the European Council here is significant, insofar as it set the template for leadership in JHA and the focus on providing guidance to the Commission and the

and Narratives on Responsibility and Responsiveness from the Eurocrisis to NextGenerationEU' (2024) 31(4) Journal of European Public Policy 950.

[3] See, for instance, Kalypso Nicolaïdis, 'Sustainable Integration: Towards EU 2.0?' (2010) 48 JCMS: Journal of Common Market Studies 21.

[4] Fabien Terpan, 'Soft Law in the European Union—The Changing Nature of EU Law' (2015) 21(1) European Law Journal 68.

[5] Paul Dermine, 'The Planning Method: An Inquiry into the Constitutional Ramifications of a New EU Governance Technique' (2024) 61(4) Common Market Law Review 959.

[6] Swen Hutter and Hanspeter Kriesi, 'Politicising Immigration in Times of Crisis' (2021) 48(2) Journal of Ethnic and Migration Studies 341. doi:10.1080/1369183X.2020.1853902.

[7] European Council, 'Presidency Conclusions' (Tampere, 15 and 16 October 1999).

Council of Ministers, which continued even when the legislative process moved beyond the intergovernmental towards the 'Community method'.[8] The 'milestones' envisaged as part of the Common European Asylum System (CEAS), were to be completed in two phases. As a counterpart, the rights and obligations of third country nationals who are legally resident in the territories of the Member States would be set 'as near as possible to those enjoyed by EU citizens' via a 'vigorous integration policy'.[9]

It is significant that legislation appears as the main way in which the goals of the Tampere Conclusions were to be achieved: 'the need for approximation of national legislations on the conditions for admission and residence of third country nationals, based on a shared assessment of the economic and demographic developments within the Union, as well as the situation in the countries of origin. It requests to this end rapid decisions by the Council, on the basis of proposals by the Commission.' As explored in the previous chapter, several Regulations and Directives formed the first part of the move towards creating a comprehensive body of EU law on external migration. At the same time, Tampere explicitly recognized the external dimension of migration as integral to the 'substance' of the new competences.[10]

The emphasis on speed was, however, not realized. As explored in the previous chapter, the core legislation for CEAS was proposed in 2000 and 2001 and only adopted in the 2003–05 period after a difficult political process.[11] Although the legislation covered most of the subject-matter of asylum law envisaged in the Tampere Conclusions, it was criticized for setting low standards which went against the spirit of the area of freedom, security and justice for *all*, regardless of nationality and migration status or holding of EU citizenship.[12] The status of refugees remains dependent on individual Member States, with the idea of asylum valid throughout the Union—although appearing in Treaty Article 78(2)(a) TFEU—not yet realized.[13] In regular migration too, the Family Reunion Directive 2003/86 was unsuccessfully challenged by the European Parliament for setting standards below minimum levels and contrary to fundamental rights.[14] The results of the legislative

[8] Uwe Puetter, 'The European Council' in Christopher J Bickerton, Dermot Hodson, and Uwe Puetter (eds), *The New Intergovernmentalism: States and Supranational Actors in the Post-Maastricht Era* (Oxford University Press 2015) 170.

[9] Tampere Conclusions (n 7); Theodora Kostakopoulou, '"Integrating" Non-EU Migrants in the European Union: Ambivalent Legacies and Mutating Paradigms' (2002) 8 Columbia Journal of European Law 181, 183.

[10] Anna Liguori, *Migration Law and the Externalization of Border Controls* (Routledge 2019) 52.

[11] Steve Peers, 'The Rise and Fall of EU Justice and Home Affairs Law' in Maria Fletcher, Ester Herlin-Karnell, and Claudio Matera (eds), *The European Union as an Area of Freedom, Security and Justice* (Routledge 2017) 21.

[12] ibid 22.

[13] Cathryn Costello and Minos Mouzourakis, 'The Common European Asylum System: Where Did It All Go Wrong?' in Maria Fletcher, Ester Herlin-Karnell, and Claudio Matera (eds) *The European Union as an Area of Freedom, Security and Justice* (Routledge 2017) 268–69.

[14] C-540/03 *European Parliament v Council of the European Union* ECLI:EU:C:2006:429.

process are thus quite far from the discourse about rights being as close as possible to those of EU citizens and being achieved via legislative means.[15]

Elsewhere in the Tampere Conclusions, partnerships with third countries were highlighted as a priority, and one which has become a hallmark of post-Tampere policymaking.[16] The importance of partnerships was placed within the context of development priorities rather than on preventing migration as a headline goal. The Conclusions did not lay down the mechanisms for operationalizing development and migration, but made an explicit reference on returns to the competence of the institutions conferred by the Treaty of Amsterdam 'to conclude readmission agreements or to include standard clauses in other agreements between the European Community and relevant third countries or groups of countries'.[17] In short, these would use the formal powers of the institutions as found in the Treaties, with no reference to the use of mechanisms on (informal) instruments beyond them.

4.2 The Hague Programme

Five years later in 2004, the Hague Programme, 'Strengthening freedom, security and justice in the European Union', included the second phase of the common policy towards asylum, migration, and integrated borders.[18] Although the prevention and suppression of terrorism was highlighted in the introduction as a priority, the weight of the text of the Hague Programme fell squarely on migration. It stopped short of laying down a specific legislative programme as was created at Tampere. It did however foresee in the Treaty establishing a Constitution for Europe the advent of qualified majority voting in freedom, security, and justice matters.[19] The language in relation to legal measures shifted notably from the immediate aftermath of the conclusion of the Treaty of Amsterdam, which identified legislation as the starting point for further integration—along the same path. Rather, the emphasis here was placed on implementation and pursuing 'coordinated, strong and effective working relations between those responsible for migration and asylum policies and those responsible for other policy fields relevant to these areas'.[20]

[15] Peers, 'The Rise and Fall of EU Justice and Home Affairs Law' (n 11) 26.

[16] Virginie Guirandon, '20 Years after Tampere's Agenda on "Illegal Migration": Policy Continuity in Spite of Unintended Consequences' in Sergio Carrera, Deirdre Curtun, and Andrew Geddes (eds), *20 Years Anniversary of the Tampere Programme: Europeanisation Dynamics of the EU Area of Freedom, Security and Justice* (European University Institute 2020) https://cadmus.eui.eu/bitstream/handle/1814/66986/MPC-Tampere-Programme-final.pdf?sequence=1&isAllowed=y#page=54, accessed 9 June 2025, 150–51.

[17] European Council, 'Presidency Conclusions' (n 7) para 27.

[18] Council, 'The Hague Programme: strengthening freedom, security and justice in the European Union' [2005] OJ C 53/1 (The Hague Programme).

[19] Commission, 'The Hague Programme: Ten Priorities for the Next Five Years' COM(2005) 184 final.

[20] The Hague Programme [2005] OJ C 53/1 (n 18) para 1.2.

For the CEAS, the Hague Programme pointed to the need for the Asylum Procedures Directive to be adopted as soon as possible and the second phase of instruments to be submitted to the Council and Parliament for adoption by 2010.

From the lack of progress towards meeting the previous milestones, the Hague Programme can be taken as a reflection of the Member States' preferences for maintaining national migration regimes with only limited scope for a fully European system.[21] The implementation of the Hague Programme was successively described by the Commission in its annual reports as, at best, 'mixed',[22] with transposition and enforcement of EU law by the Member States identified as a particular concern.[23] The Commission cited the lack of impetus on many aspects of the AFSJ, though did note that migration and border management fared better than other AFSJ matters, such as organized crime and police and judicial cooperation. Progress was also limited on regular migration, with minimum harmonization and 'Member States free to maintain or introduce parallel regimes as regards the admission of highly skilled workers'.[24]

The conclusion of readmission agreements with six non-EU European countries and a proposal for a Directive on minimum standards on sanctions and measures against employers of illegally staying third country nationals[25] were the headline achievements. What this tells us is that the Hague Programme continued the emphasis on using the formal, Treaty-based competences to realize goals, with a lesser role given (yet) to informal tools or instruments. Where these do appear in either the Programme or the evaluation reports, such as the establishment of the European Migration Network,[26] they are characterized as additional measures rather than being at the core of integration or harmonization.

4.3 The Stockholm Programme

Following the abandonment of the Treaty establishing a Constitution for Europe and the 'rescuing' of certain provisions via the Treaty of Lisbon, the current

[21] Madeline Garlick, 'The EU Discussion on Extraterritorial Process: Solution or Conundrum' (2006) 18 (3–4) International Journal of Refugee Law 610.

[22] Commission, 'Communication from the Commission to the Council and the European Parliament—Report on the implementation of the Hague Programme for 2006' SEC(2007) 897; Commission, 'Communication from the Commission to the Council and the European Parliament—Report on the Implementation of the Hague Programme for 2006' COM(2008) 373 final.

[23] ibid 12.

[24] Peers, 'The Rise and Fall of EU Justice and Home Affairs Law' (n 11) 27; Council Directive 2009/50/EC of 25 May 2009 on the conditions of entry and residence of third-country nationals for the purposes of highly qualified employment [2009] OJ L 155, Article 3(4).

[25] Directive 2009/52/EC of the European Parliament and of the Council of 18 June 2009 providing for minimum standards on sanctions and measures against employers of illegally staying third-country nationals [2009] OJ L 168/24.

[26] COM(2008) 373 final.

Treaty provisions in force recognize the different legal systems and traditions of the Member States (Article 67(1) TFEU) but adopt an expansive scope of migration, requiring the Union to develop 'a common immigration policy aimed at ensuring, at all stages, the efficient management of migration flows' (Article 79(1) TFEU). Majority voting was extended to measures on legal migration which could go beyond minimum standards. Upon Lisbon's entry into force, the Stockholm Programme, entitled 'An Open and Secure European Serving and Protecting the Citizen', was the final multi-annual FSJ Programme, to run from 2010 to 2014.[27] The lengthy, eighty-page Programme adopted a more forthright security focus by attempting to satisfy the 'interests and needs' of citizens and respect for fundamental freedoms 'while guaranteeing security in Europe'. 'Security' discourse also applies to the protection of the internal market as being core to the EU project, which 'needs to be preserved at all costs in the face of new forms of crisis'. In this sense, AFSJ 'acquires a distinctive meaning, because security functions as the precondition for the existence of the internal market'.[28] The bringing of AFSJ into the main Treaty body would mean that the regular judicial review controls would apply, as well as the Charter of Fundamental Rights, thus opening the possibility for tests before the Court of Justice.[29]

Proposed legislation to further the completion of the CEAS in the 2011 to 2013 period aimed to increase uniformity, with Member States adhering to higher standards in reception and asylum via the creation of an asylum support agency, the European Asylum Support Office (EASO).[30] The overarching rationale, however, was still firmly anchored to movement between Member States, with emphasis on deterring and reducing external migration rather than facilitation.[31]

There was, in the Stockholm Programme, no longer a model of setting minimum standards as a means of recognizing the social benefit of doing so for migrants or third country nationals, but rather a great link with security and the protection of *Europe's* citizens in an area of freedom, security, and justice built for them, rather than the more universal theme present in earlier programmes. The securitization of the AFSJ preceded its increased use as a justification to restrict irregular migration after the onset of a 'crisis'.[32] This can be seen first in the EU's immigration

[27] Council, 'The Stockholm Programme—An open and secure Europe serving the citizen' (14449/09, 16 October 2009) https://data.consilium.europa.eu/doc/document/ST-14449-2009-INIT/en/pdf, accessed 9 June 2025.

[28] Massimo Fichera, 'Sketches of a Theory of Europe as an Area of Freedom, Security and Justice' in Maria Fletcher, Ester Herlin-Karnell, and Claudio Matera (eds), *The European Union as an Area of Freedom, Security and Justice* (Routledge 2017) 34–35.

[29] Sionaidh Douglas-Scott, 'The EU's Area of Freedom, Security and Justice: A Lack of Fundamental Rights, Mutual Trust and Democracy?' (2009) 11 Cambridge Yearbook of European Legal Studies 53.

[30] Peers, 'The Rise and Fall of EU Justice and Home Affairs Law' (n 11) 22.

[31] ibid 22.

[32] Valeria Bello, 'The Spiralling of the Securitisation of Migration in the EU: From the Management of a "Crisis" to a Governance of Human Mobility?' (2022) 48(6) Journal of Ethnic and Migration Studies 1327; Scarlett McArdle and Arantza Gomez Arana, 'The EU and the Migration Crisis: Reinforcing a Security-Based Approach to Migration?' in Sergio Carrera, Juan Santos Vara, and Tineke Strik (eds),

legislation increasingly having a free movement element, setting out specific rules governing the secondary movement of the relevant categories of third country nationals between Member States. Second, the more recent EU legislation frequently confines Member States' power to set higher standards to only specific provisions of immigration Directives.[33] While the Stockholm Programme was widely recognized for its ambition in forging EU consensus on decision-making, there were far fewer calls for specific pieces of legislation than had been the case at Tampere or the Hague, even though there were undoubtedly areas which *could* have been the focus of legislation.[34]

There was a notable omission of references to third country nationals within the context of reinforcing the aim of the Programme to protect rights,[35] though the Action Plan to put it in place does note that the prevention and reduction of irregular immigration should be 'in line with the Charter of Fundamental Rights (of the EU)'.[36]

In an indication of the incorporation of the AFSJ within mainstream processes of EU law-making, the Programme explicitly called for the strengthening of the external dimension to the AFSJ. Somewhat curiously, the justification for doing so was not security, but as a means of 'providing greater opportunities for EU citizens to work and do business with countries across the world'.[37] The twin drivers for more integrated border management are migration management and the fight against organized crime. Under the Stockholm Programme there were more proposals relating to migration than to other themes including victims' rights, fighting serious crime, or terrorism, leading to some criticisms of the AFSJ being overly focused on migration as a threat to the area.[38]

Comparing the Tampere Conclusions and the Hague and Stockholm programmes, the central place of legislation as the main driver of the migration law acquis appears to decline, with fewer references to the legislative competences enjoyed by the institutions. At the outset, Tampere set out the building blocks of legislation as the 'milestones', but the two subsequent programmes were more

Constitutionalising the External Dimensions of EU Migration Policies in Times of Crisis (Edward Elgar Publishing 2019) 272.

[33] ibid 28.

[34] Paul James Cardwell and Tamara Hervey, 'The Roles of Law in a New Intergovernmentalist European Union' in Christopher J Bickerton, Dermot Hodson, and Uwe Puetter (eds), *The New Intergovernmentalism: States and Supranational Actors in the Post-Maastricht Era* (Oxford University Press 2015) 73, 78.

[35] Dora Kostakopoulou, 'An Open and Secure Europe? Fixity and Fissures in the Area of Freedom, Security and Justice after Lisbon and Stockholm' (2010) 19(2) European Security 151, 159.

[36] Commission, 'Communication from the Commission to the European Parliament, the Council, the European Economic and Social Committee and the Committee of the Regions—Delivering an area of freedom, security and justice for Europe's citizens—Action Plan Implementing the Stockholm Programme' COM(2010) 171 final.

[37] (2010) 171 final.

[38] Elaine Fahey, *The Global Reach of EU Law* (Routledge 2018) 74–76.

restrained, despite the additional competences granted. Justice and Home Affairs, having begun as an intergovernmental pillar, retained the practices of recommendations, conclusions, resolutions, and guidelines that would eventually complement some of the legislative measures put in place once the competences have been extended. Many of these texts 'often resemble legislative texts in the density and nature of their provisions'.[39] Yet, by the advent of the Stockholm Programme, the start of the process of informalization and a more intense search for the use of measures outside the legislative framework were in evidence. Although the Stockholm Programme placed heavy reliance on legislation to meet Treaty goals, the weight of these measures was in non-migration aspects of the Programme, including criminal law.[40] This can partly be explained by the emphasis on externalization, as the Stockholm Programme referred to 'strategic, evidence-based and systematic use of all available instruments of the Global Approach to Migration' and 'existing cooperation instruments' with third countries.[41] The instruments to which this provision pointed were migration profiles, migration missions, cooperation platforms on migration and development, and Mobility Partnerships. Mobility Partnerships were further identified as 'the main strategic, comprehensive and long-term cooperation framework for migration management with third countries, adding value to existing bilateral frameworks',[42] although at the time of the Stockholm Programme only three had been put in place (with Georgia, Moldova, and Cabo Verde).[43]

4.4 The Global Approach to Migration (GAM)

In parallel with the three programmes on the AFSJ, which have an 'internal' focus on the *area* within the territorial space of EU, the institutions were also engaged in developing a Global Approach to Migration (GAM) (later the Global Approach to Migration and Mobility (GAMM)) and a strategy on external relations more

[39] Terpan, 'Soft Law in the European Union' (n 4) 85.

[40] Paul Craig, *The Lisbon Treaty: Law, Politics and Treaty Reform* (Oxford University Press 2010) 376–77.

[41] European Council, 'The Stockholm Programme—An Open and Secure Europe Serving and Protecting Citizens' [2010] OJ C 115/1, 6.1.1.

[42] Mobility Partnerships are considered in more detail in Chapter 7. But see Katharina Eisele and Anja Wiesbrock, 'Enhancing Mobility in the European Neighbourhood Policy? The Cases of Moldova and Georgia' (2011) 36(2) Review of Central and East European Law 127; Paul James Cardwell and Rachel Dickson, '"Formal Informality" in EU External Migration Governance: The Case of Mobility Partnerships' (2023) 49(12) Journal of Ethnic and Migration Studies 3121; Fanny Tittel-Mosser, 'Legal and Policy Relevance of EU Mobility Partnerships in Morocco and Cape Verde: The Role of Epistemic Communities' (2023) 49(12) Journal of Ethnic and Migration Studies 3043; Peter Seeberg and Federica Zardo, 'From Mobility Partnerships to Migration Compacts' (2022) 48(6) Journal of Ethnic and Migration Studies 1345.

[43] Fanny Tittel-Mosser, 'The Unintended Legal and Policy Relevance of EU Mobility Partnerships' (2018) 20(3) European Journal of Migration and Law 314.

generally. The growing impetus for engagement with third countries to meet migration goals, as per the programmes discussed above, could not be seen in isolation from other bilateral and multilateral engagements with third countries. These documents, which were seemingly concerned with the world beyond the EU's borders, were in fact heavily focused on internal institutional questions, such as coherence. They merit closer examination because of the light they shine on the framing of the governance of migration and the instruments to be used. In a document focused on external relations, we would not normally expect the same kind of use of legislation—in terms of Regulations and Directives—as in the programmes explored above. However, it is interesting to note the extent to which—in a somewhat parallel fashion—these external strategies rely on existing competences and instruments which are provided for in the Treaties.

The GAM was presented by the Commission to the Council in late 2005 and adopted in December 2005. It emphasized prioritizing the rights of migrants and addressing the root causes of migration, rather than the security-led discourse of many of the Member States.[44] This can be seen in the inclusion of legal migration opportunities and the facilitation of remittances. Yet, the Council's reception of the GAM itself starts its rationale with a reference to 'recent events in the Mediterranean region',[45] meaning the migration pressures experienced in the North African Spanish enclaves of Ceuta and Melilla.[46] As a result, despite its 'global' focus, the GAM itself is subtitled 'Priority actions focusing on Africa and the Mediterranean' and takes in the bilateral and multilateral engagement with African states, foreseen with conferences in Rabat and Tripoli in 2006.

There are two aspects of the initial version of the GAM to note here. With the priority placed squarely on relations with three large North African states bordering the Mediterranean, there was a strong differentiation in the nature of how cooperation should be pursued. Partly this was a result of the stark divergence in the nature and depth of bilateral relations with the EU. For Morocco, the priority was identified as the conclusion of the readmission agreement, for which there is a specific competence in the Treaty.[47] For Algeria, which had (and continues to have) a much weaker bilateral relationship with the EU, the emphasis was on migration aspects of the negotiation of the Association Agreement[48] and a future readmission agreement. For Libya, which had very limited relations with the EU, the GAM states that the priorities are 'to conclude the work to agree the EU–Libya

[44] Tineke Strik, 'The Global Approach to Migration and Mobility' (2017) 5(2) Groningen Journal of International Law 310, 316.

[45] Council, 'Global approach to migration: Priority actions focusing on Africa and the Mediterranean' (15744/05, 13 December 2005) https://data.consilium.europa.eu/doc/document/ST-15744-2005-INIT/en/pdf, accessed 9 June 2025, 3.

[46] Sandra Lavenex and Rahel Kunz, 'The Migration–Development Nexus in EU External Relations' (2008) 30(3) Journal of European Integration 439.

[47] Article 73(3) TFEU.

[48] Article 217 TFEU.

Action Plan on migration as early as possible in 2006, in accordance with the Council Conclusions of 3 June 2005 on initiating dialogue and cooperation with Libya on migration issues, and implement projects as soon as possible thereafter'. Here, we see the beginning of the explicit use of legally undefined 'Action Plans' with a country with whom the bilateral relationship was very weak.

Second, the kinds of tools noted elsewhere in the GAM are very familiar to those involved in studying (new) governance as outlined in the previous chapter: for instance, 'Establish regional networks of Immigration Liaison Officers (ILOs) involving priority countries', 'Make available experiences and best practices where appropriate from other regional cooperation structures', and 'build capacity to better manage migration, and explore how best to share information on legal migration and labour market opportunities'.[49]

The Commission's own evaluation of GAM revealed its limitations.[50] The formal aspects to be pursued—including the Readmission Agreement with Morocco and Association Agreement with Algeria—have yet to be concluded, and there appears to be no magic solution on the EU is capable of promoting to secure agreement.[51] This is indicative overall of the difficulties in implementation of a 'Global Approach'. The Commission's 'Global Approach one year on' communication (2006) emphasized the need to open the possibility for legal migration routes for third countries.[52] Even with an emphasis limited to the Eastern and South-Eastern regions neighbouring the EU (which are part of the European Neighbourhood Policy), which would therefore seem to undermine the concept of a 'Global Approach', 'the innovation potential of Commission proposals, such as the promotion of circular migration and mobility partnerships between the

[49] Global Approach to Migration (n 45).

[50] Commission, 'Communication from the Commission to the Council and the European Parliament—The global approach to migration one year on: towards a comprehensive European migration policy' COM(2006) 735 final.

[51] Tasnim Abderrahim, 'A Tale of Two Agreements: EU Migration Cooperation with Morocco and Tunisia' (2019) Papers Series no 41 EurMesCo 15, https://www.euromesco.net/wp-content/uploads/2019/04/EuroMeSCo-Paper_A-tale-of-two-agreements.pdf: 'These talks were eventually suspended in 2010 as they failed to reach results after fifteen rounds of negotiations despite joint progress on co-operation on migration in other issue areas like border surveillance'; Francois Barbieux and Dimitris Bouris, 'Decentring European Union Foreign Policy: Addressing Colonial Dynamics in EU–Algeria Relations' (2024) 63(4) JCMS: Journal of Common Market Studies 1138, 1151: 'Article 83 that refers to the movement of persons is 1 paragraph, 2 sentences and 79 words long. On the other hand, Article 84 that deals with co-operation in the prevention and control of illegal immigration/readmission is 3 paragraphs and 229 words long. This simple example displays how even the space allocated to text is telling of the focus on security in the EU's foreign policy. And this point is further amplified by the subsequent articles 86, 87, 89, 90 and 91, which, respectively, tackle organised crime, money laundering, drug trafficking, terrorism and corruption. In comparison to the pale 79 words mentioned about free movement of persons between the two territories, the negative emphasis of security issues is clearly predominant.'

[52] Commission, 'Communication from the Commission to the European Parliament, the Council, the European Economic and Social Committee and the Committee of the Regions on circular migration and mobility partnerships between the European Union and third countries' COM(2007) 248 final.

Union and third countries, is sometimes more rhetorical than practical'.[53] The relaunch of GAM as the Global Approach to Migration and Mobility (GAMM) is discussed below.

4.5 The European Pact on Immigration

The European Pact on Immigration (2008)[54] appeared as the result of efforts of the French EU Presidency to demonstrate that, in a period of heightened public scrutiny and criticism of responses to migration, EU governments were able to demonstrate a certain control of the narrative. As such, it was not a successor to either the Hague Programme (which was not yet completed) or the GAM. Rather, it formed part of a now common practice and trend for Member States to push for public agreements via the Council. Such documents would explicitly be non-legally binding but would 'help the positioning of the rotating presidency around operational and pragmatic goals'.

The European Pact on Immigration was one of a number of JHA pacts, which also include the subjects of international drug trafficking[55] and synthetic drugs.[56] However, the European Pact on Immigration agreed under the French Presidency reaffirmed the interests of Member States and thus has been criticized for undermining the goals of the Programme and the GAM (and the Treaty) for common policies.[57] The Pact referred to the likely need for 'changes to the legal framework, and in particular to the treaty bases' but did not specify what these might be. The remainder of the Pact does not, in fact, call for new legislation, but rather to 'speed up the deployment of the key tools of the Global Approach to Migration', including migration balances, cooperation platforms, and partnerships.[58]

[53] Lavenex and Kunz, 'The Migration–Development Nexus in EU External Relations' (n 46).

[54] Council, 'European Pact on Immigration and Asylum' (2008) 13440/08, https://data.consilium.europa.eu/doc/document/ST-13440-2008-INIT/en/pdf, accessed 9 June 2025.

[55] Council, 'European pact to combat international drug trafficking—disrupting cocaine and heroin routes, 3018th Justice and Home Affairs Council meeting, Luxembourg, 3 June 2010' (Justice and Home Affairs Council Meeting, Luxembourg, June 2010) https://www.consilium.europa.eu/uedocs/cms_data/docs/pressdata/en/jha/114889.pdf, accessed 9 June 2025.

[56] Council, 'European pact against synthetic drugs, 3121st Justice and Home Affairs Council meeting, Luxembourg, 27 and 28 October 2011' (Justice and Home Affairs Council Meeting, Luxembourg, October 2011) https://www.consilium.europa.eu/uedocs/cms_data/docs/pressdata/en/jha/125709.pdf, accessed 9 June 2025.

[57] Sarah Wolff, 'Integrating in Justice and Home Affairs: A Case of New Intergovernmentalism Par Excellence?' in Christopher J Bickerton, Dermot Hodson, and Uwe Puetter (eds), *The New Intergovernmentalism: States and Supranational Actors in the Post-Maastricht Era* (Oxford University Press 2015) 135.

[58] Council, 'European Pact on Immigration and Asylum' (n 56) 12.

4.6 The Global Approach to Migration and Mobility (GAMM)

In 2012 the GAM was repackaged and relaunched as the GAMM,[59] which attempted to balance the emphasis on irregular migration with regular migration ('mobility') and international protection and to tie migration more closely to development across four 'pillars'.[60] The GAMM recognized a 'migrant-centred' approach and there was some initial welcoming[61] of the emphasis placed on a policy about 'people' rather than 'flows' and the place of the EU Charter for Fundamental Rights in ensuring respect for migrants' fundamental rights under EU law.[62] Yet, the substance of the GAMM placed the emphasis squarely on preventing irregular migration, and on returns. The cornerstone of the relationships with third countries remained the conclusion of readmission agreements under Article 73(3) TFEU. Where GAMM did try to distinguish itself from its previous iteration as the GAM was in promoting legal/regular migration routes as a means of engaging third countries in cooperation. Here, however, the difficult political realities of securing adequate buy-in from Member States for visa facilitation led to strong criticism of the lack of progress on GAMM from the Commission and elsewhere, making it among the least developed of the GAMM's principles.[63]

For the purposes of this chapter, therefore, GAM and GAMM were notable for underlining the possibility of partnership and enhancing relationships with third countries, but with only limited references to Article 218 or the legal competences. In these documents we see both an increase in the reference to undefined instruments for seeking cooperation, including operational cooperation, with third states as tools of governance, and a stronger emphasis placed on more specific tools, such as Mobility Partnerships, which nevertheless all lack clear definitions and priorities.

The GAM and GAMM, despite not achieving many of the objectives set, did contribute strongly to the normalization of vaguely defined instruments for governing migration, including with non-EU states with whom the EU enjoyed a very limited institutional relationship, such as Libya. The advent of the 'migration crisis' from 2015–16 demonstrates both the incoherent response of the Member States with regard to preventing or allowing asylum entry, and thus the use of existing instruments including readmission agreements. The EU–Türkiye Statement

[59] Commission, 'Communication from the Commission to the European Parliament, the Council, the European Economic and Social Committee and the Committee of the Regions, The Global Approach to Migration and Mobility' COM(2011) 743 final (GAMM).

[60] James Hampshire, 'Speaking with One Voice? The European Union's Global Approach to Migration and Mobility and the Limits of International Migration Cooperation' (2016) 42(4) Journal of Ethnic and Migration Studies 571.

[61] Liguori, *Migration Law and the Externalization of Border Controls* (n 10) 71.

[62] See GAMM (n 59); also Liguori, *Migration Law and the Externalization of Border Controls* (n 10) 53.

[63] Paula Andrade, 'The Legal Feasibility of the EU's External Action on Legal Migration: The Internal and the External Intertwined' (2013) 15(3) European Journal of Migration and Law 263.

was forged as an 'alternative' plan as relocation via Decisions 'ineffective in practice'.[64] Where the Member States could agree, however, was on the importance of preventing migrants from entering EU territory and thus engaging the Member States in the difficult issues of solidarity and burden-sharing. As a result, from 2015–16 much greater focus was placed on finding a way to avoid refugees and irregular migrants crossing borders into the EU.[65]

4.7 The European Agenda on Migration 2015 and the EU–Türkiye Statement 2016

The European Agenda on Migration[66] was presented by the Commission on 13 May 2015 as a 'road map' to forge a 'new, European approach' to migration as a means to 'restore confidence in our ability to bring together European and national efforts to address migration'.[67] The Agenda attempted to focus on both the immediate response to a crisis in the Mediterranean, and especially multiple tragedies around the island of Lampedusa in which more than a thousand people died,[68] and structuring a longer-term policy around four 'pillars' of reducing the incentives for irregular migration, strengthening and securing external borders, full implementation of the CEAS, and a new policy on legal migration.

The European Agenda on Migration faced significant criticism from multiple quarters for its emphasis on burden-sharing, border security, and asylum policy reforms which had already been proposed.[69] Many argued that it placed an unfair load on frontline countries, including Greece and Italy, as the relocation quota system to redistribute asylum seekers across the EU faced strong resistance, especially from Member States in Central and Eastern Europe.[70] The emphasis on border security and the role of Frontex and 'hotspot' centres continued to draw concerns from NGOs and others about the potential for human rights abuses.[71]

[64] Peers, 'The Rise and Fall of EU Justice and Home Affairs Law' (n 11) 23.

[65] Strik, 'The Global Approach to Migration and Mobility' (n 42).

[66] Commission, 'Communication from the Commission to the European Parliament, the Council, the European Economic and Social Committee and the Committee of the Regions: A European Agenda on Migration' COM(2015) 240 final.

[67] COM(2015) 240 final 2.

[68] IOM, 'Two Years On from Lampedusa Tragedy, IOM Reflects on Mediterranean Deaths' *IOM UN Migration* (2 October 2015) https://www.iom.int/news/two-years-lampedusa-tragedy-iom-reflects-mediterranean-deaths, accessed 9 June 2025.

[69] Angeliki Dimitriadi, 'The European Agenda for Migration: A New Narrative for an Old Tale?' (2015) ELIAMEP Briefing Notes 35/201 5, Criminal Justice, Borders and Citizenship Research Paper No 2602707, https://ssrn.com/abstract=2602707 or http://dx.doi.org/10.2139/ssrn.2602707, accessed 9 June 2025.

[70] Marta Pachocka, 'Understanding the Visegrad Group States' Response to the Migrant and Refugee Crisis 2014 + in the European Union' (2016) 19 Yearbook of Polish European Studies 101; Vladislav Strnad, '*Les Enfants Terribles de l'Europe?* The "Sovereigntist" Role of the Visegrád Group in the Context of the Migration Crisis' (2021) 74(1) Europe–Asia Studies 72.

[71] See Judith Sunderland and Bill Frelick, 'EU's Approach to Migrants: Humanitarian Rhetoric, Inhumane Treatment', *Human Rights Watch* (15 April 2015), https://www.hrw.org/news/2015/04/

From an institutional perspective, the Agenda was an attempt by the Commission to forge consensus among the Member States but also to recentre the attempts to meet the challenges of migration around legislation, particularly via a reform of the Regulations and Directives making up the CEAS and attempting to use the proposed Blue Card Directive for legal migration routes. The problem, as Smeets and Beach describe, was that, 'It is fair to say that this was a case of self-mandating (what we call 'championship') by the Commission ... The idea was to embed mandatory relocation in a broader recast of the Dublin Regulation. The political level of the Commission anticipated (wrongly as it would turn out) that there was momentum for broader reform.'[72] The speed and lack of usual processes such as impact assessments meant that the supposed enthusiasm for revising legislation was not there.

In a 2017 review of its delivery,[73] the Commission continued to underline reformed legislation but also took in a number of 'softer' mechanisms including reporting and the Irregular Migration Management Application (IMMA) system.[74] The attempts by the Commission to position itself at the centre of migration governance are clear, even where the competence lies solely with the Member States; for example, in proposing a move away from ad hoc schemes of resettlement towards an EU Resettlement Framework which it proposed.[75]

One innovation in migration governance that arose after the European Agenda on Migration was the EU–Türkiye Statement of 2016. The statement is considered more fully later in this book,[76] but it represented a major shift in what both the EU and a third country found to be possible when pursuing an innovative solution outside the usual, legal framework. Having first been publicized as a means to confront the humanitarian aspect of crossings from Türkiye to Greece, the emphasis quickly shifted to the protection of the EU's borders. The Commission's 2017 review of the European Agenda on Migration praised the statement, noting

15/eus-approach-migrants-humanitarian-rhetoric-inhumane-treatment, accessed 9 June 2025. See, however, the decisions of the Court of Justice on the right to an effective remedy under the Charter of Fundamental Rights: C-679/23 P *WS and others v Frontex* ECLI:EU:C:2025:976 and Case C-136/24 P *Hamoudi v Frontex* ECLI:EU:C:2025:977.

[72] Sandrino Smeets and Derek Beach, '"It takes three to tango": New Inter-Institutional Dynamics in Managing Major Crisis Reform' (2021) 29(9) Journal of European Public Policy 1414, 1422.

[73] Commission, 'Communication from the Commission to the European Parliament, the Council, the European Economic and Social Committee and the Committee of the Regions on the Delivery of the European Agenda on Migration' COM(2017) 558 final.

[74] See further Commission, 'Irregular Migration Management Application (IRMA)' (*European Commission: Migration and Home Affairs*) https://ec.europa.eu/assets/home/emn-glossary/glossary.html?letters=&classification=13&detail=Irregular+Migration+Management+Application+(IRMA), accessed 9 June 2025.

[75] Commission, Communication from the Commission to the European Parliament, the Council, the European Economic and Social Committee and the Committee of the Regions on the Delivery of the European Agenda on Migration' COM(2017) 558 final 19.

[76] See Chapter 7.

that 'This joint effort of the EU and Turkey has created an alternative to the dangerous migratory flows with organised, safe and legal pathways to Europe for those entitled to international protection, while also facilitating the returns, in line with EU and international law, even if further efforts are still needed'.[77] The legality of the Statement was premised on the 'safe third country' designation of Türkiye, although the extent to which migrants are safe in Türkiye is contested.[78]

The EU–Türkiye Statement did not involve the European Parliament. The challenge at the General Court by three individuals in *NF* failed,[79] precisely because the Court stated that it fell outside the scope of EU law. The effect of the EU–Türkiye statement on the development of migration law is two-fold. First, it was hailed as a success insofar as it prevented lives being lost.[80] Second, and as a consequence, it rapidly formed the template for the Migration Partnership Framework with third countries in 2016,[81] where the statement was hailed as a model to follow.[82] Yet, it also needs to be considered in light of the changing bilateral relationship between the EU and Türkiye and stalled EU accession process.[83]

4.8 The EU Global Strategy

The previous chapters noted the unique place of migration as a space where legislation and regulation are expected, but it is also a foreign policy issue. As such, the EU's successive foreign policy strategies have increasingly included references to migration. Here, we can also detect a shift. Migration was mentioned only briefly in the 2003 European Security Strategy (ESS), 'A Secure Europe in a Better World',[84] in terms of 'illegal migration resulting from state failure and conflict' as presenting a 'challenge' to the EU but not as a security threat per se. The ESS's replacement,

[77] ibid 4. 'Turkey' is used in the original document, and has been retained in this quote.

[78] See, inter alia, Elif Demirbaş and Christina Miliou, 'Looking at the EU–Turkey Deal: The Implications for Migrants in Greece and Turkey' in Richard Zapata-Barrero and Ibrahim Awad (eds), *Migrations in the Mediterranean* (IMISCOE Research Series, Springer 2024) 17.

[79] Case C-208/17 P *NF v European Council* ECLI:EU:C:2018:705.

[80] Commission, 'Communication from the Commission to the European Parliament, the European Council and the Council: Second Report on the progress made in the implementation of the EU–Turkey Statement' COM(2016) 349 final 2.

[81] Daniela Vitiello, 'Legal Narratives of the EU External Action in the Field of Migration and Asylum: From the EU–Turkey Statement to the Migration Partnership Framework and Beyond' in Valsamis Mitsilegas, Violeta Moreno-Lax, and Niovi Vavoula (eds), *Securitising Asylum Flows* (Brill Nijhoff 2020).

[82] See Liguori, *Migration Law and the Externalization of Border Controls* (n 10) 66.

[83] Gamze Ovacık, Meltem Ineli-Ciger, and Orçun Ulusoy, 'Taking Stock of the EU–Turkey Statement in 2024' (2024) 26(2) European Journal of Migration and Law 154.

[84] Council and General Secretariat of the Council, *European Security Strategy—A Secure Europe in a Better World* (European Union Publications Office 2009), https://www.consilium.europa.eu/media/30823/qc7809568enc.pdf, accessed 9 June 2025; see also Asle Toje, 'The 2003 European Union Security Strategy: A Critical Appraisal' (2005) 10(1) European Foreign Affairs Review 117; Sven Biscop and Jan Joel Andersson (eds), *The EU and the European Security Strategy: Forging a Global Europe* (1st edn, Routledge 2007).

the EU Global Strategy (2016)—which aims to promote peace and guarantee the security of its citizens and territory—cites migration throughout and is discussed with reference to foreign policy objectives (including internal repercussions), geographical areas, and the purported values of the European Union.'[85]

The Global Strategy places great emphasis on resilience, but in terms of ensuring and enhancing solidarity between the Member States rather than with migrants (particularly refugees) as in the earlier days of migration competence. There was fierce debate between the Member States over the desire by some to remove any references to internal questions such as asylum, while others emphasized instead the link between internal and external policies in this field. Although the Member States did agree on a final text, it took, as Tocci notes, 'endless discussions to find the middle way in which all Member States were equally satisfied and equally dissatisfied'.[86]

In the end, the Global Strategy stated: 'Together with countries of origin and transit, we will develop common and tailor-made approaches to migration featuring development, diplomacy, mobility, legal migration, border management, readmission and return.'[87] Some question whether this represents a 'resilience' turn in the Global Strategy, marking a departure from normative power, where the values of the EU, including the importance of international law, take precedence.[88]

4.9 The New Pact on Migration and Asylum 2020

The problem remains—and has even increased—in terms of the difficulties of finding agreement or solidarity between the Member States in the case of asylum and migration since 2016.[89] Previous efforts by the Commission during the 2010s to launch a comprehensive reform of the CEAS were not realized.[90] In more recent years, therefore, the Commission has tried to find a means to enforce the requirement for solidarity, which is designed to be a fundamental underpinning of the EU as stated in the Treaties, while keeping the Member States on board and

[85] Michela Ceccorulli and Sonia Lucarelli, 'Migration and the EU Global Strategy: Narratives and Dilemmas' (2017) 52(3) The International Spectator 83.

[86] Nathalie Tocci, 'From the European Security Strategy to the EU Global Strategy: Explaining the Journey' (2017) 54(2) International Politics 487, 494.

[87] European External Action Service, 'Shared Vision, Common Action: A Stronger Europe: A Global Strategy for the European Union's Foreign and Security Policy (June 2016) https://www.eeas.europa.eu/sites/default/files/eugs_review_web_0.pdf, accessed 9 June 2025, 27.

[88] Regine Paul and Christof Roos, 'Towards a New Ontology of Crisis? Resilience in EU Migration Governance' (2019) 28(4) European Security 393.

[89] Natascha Zaun, 'States as Gatekeepers in EU Asylum Politics: Explaining the Non-adoption of a Refugee Quota System' (2018) 56(1) JCMS: Journal of Common Market Studies 44.

[90] Commission, 'Towards a sustainable and fair Common European Asylum System' *European Commission* (Brussels, 4 May 2016) https://ec.europa.eu/commission/presscorner/detail/en/ip_16_1620, accessed 9 June 2025.

simultaneously working on ways in which the EU's migration goals can be realized. These efforts failed in the European Agenda on Migration.[91]

The main issue is turning commitments made on paper into reality, especially in the context of sharp divisions between the Member States over, in particular, democratic backsliding, which has been closely linked in some domestic political scenes with the 'requirement' (whether or not this is the case in reality) to accept more migrants via burden-sharing.[92]

Five years after the European Agenda on Migration in 2015, a 'New Pact on Migration and Asylum' was proposed by the Commission in 2020.[93] Billed as a 'fresh start'[94] to 'build a system that manages and normalises migration for the long term and which is fully grounded in European values and international law',[95] the Migration Pact is both lengthy and, at first glance, reasonably comprehensive in terms of the different forms of migration it covers and their complexity, though not in equal detail. The Pact proposed to combine legislative measures, some new and others replacing existing Regulations and Directives, with other instruments, enhanced cooperation with third states, and—significantly—more intensive coordination efforts between the Member States themselves. As such, the Migration Pact was an attempt to restart progress in a more comprehensive rather than piecemeal fashion. Against the background of a fragmented EU dealing with open hostility to migration and the role of the EU institutions from some (newer) Member States,[96] the Commission's attempts to revise current legislation and address the structural weaknesses[97] were met with—at best—a lukewarm response.

The language of 'pact' has become more prominent in EU discourse, and appears to denote something more akin to an agreement than a strategy. Indeed, De

[91] Philippe De Bruycker, 'The New Pact on Migration and Asylum: What It Is Not and What It Could Have Been' in Daniel Thym (ed), *Reforming the Common European Asylum System* (Nomos Verlagsgesellschaft 2022).

[92] See, in the case of Hungary: Attila Melegh and others, 'Positional Insecurity and the Hungarian Migration Policy' in Michela Ceccorulli, Enrico Fassi, and Sonia Lucarelli (eds), *The EU Migration System of Governance* (Palgrave Macmillan 2021); Balazs Szent-Ivanyi and Patryk Kugiel, 'The Challenge from Within: EU Development Cooperation and the Rise of Illiberalism in Hungary and Poland' (2020) 16(2) Journal of Contemporary European 120; Florian Trauner and Philipp Stutz, 'Hungary's Renationalisation Strategies: How a Populist Radical Right Government May Seek Control over (EU) Migration Policy' (2021) 72(2) Politique Européenne 94.

[93] Commission, 'Communication from the Commission to the European Parliament, the Council, the European Economic and Social Committee and the Committee of the Regions on a New Pact on Migration and Asylum' COM(2020) 609 final.

[94] European Commission, 'A fresh start on migration: Building confidence and striking a new balance between responsibility and solidarity' (European Commission Press Release, 23 September 2020) https://ec.europa.eu/commission/presscorner/api/files/document/print/en/ip_20_1706/IP_20_1706_EN.pdf, accessed 9 June 2025.

[95] Council, 'Communication from the Commission to the European Parliament, the Council, the European Economic and Social Committee and the Committee of the Regions on a New Pact on Migration and Asylum' COM(2020) 609 final 1.

[96] Joint Cases C-643/15 and C-647/15, *Slovakia and Hungary v Council*, ECLI:EU:C:2017:631.

[97] See European Parliament, 'Reform of the asylum procedures directive: In promoting our European Way of Life' (*EP Legislative Train Schedule*, May 2025), https://www.europarl.europa.eu/legislative-train/spotlight-JD21/file-jd-reform-of-the-asylum-procedures-directive, accessed 9 June 2025.

Bruycker has questioned why the opportunity was not taken to launch a multi-annual programmatic document in the similar vein to the Tampere, Hague, and Stockholm Programmes or identify the policy guidelines in detail.[98] Neither does this represent a new-found consensus between the Member States on solidarity, since the concept of 'flexible solidarity' which it introduces 'is not a real pact made to reconcile different views, but a bad compromise made of contradictory elements'.[99]

The aims of the Pact remain similar to past strategies, that is to say, resisting irregular migration, strengthening borders, and ensuring more effective and rapid returns. The Pact raises rather more vague possibilities for legal migration routes—some new and recast legislation was placed at its heart as the key to reform and making EU migration governance work. On the legislative front, the Pact urged progress via a roadmap on some proposals which were already on the table and which had been cited in the European Agenda on Migration, but which had not yet gained common agreement. These included the recast Reception Conditions Directive, Asylum Procedures Regulation, Union Resettlement Framework, Qualification Regulation, and Eurodac Regulation and the recast of the Return Directive. Additional proposals launched in 2020 as part of the New Pact on Migration and Asylum included amendments to the Asylum Procedures Regulation, the Regulation on Asylum and Migration Management, the Screening Regulation, and the Regulation for Crisis and Force Majeure (the Crisis Regulation). Yet more proposals were launched in 2021, including a reform of the Schengen Border Code[100] and the Instrumentalisation Regulation.[101] Despite the lengthy period during which the Pact was considered before its eventual adoption, the process of the reform proposals is flawed, insofar as they have not been preceded by impact assessment reports or full consideration of evidence, often because of the need to quickly react to the 'crisis'.[102]

After years of deadlock, the 2016 proposal to transform the EASO into the EU Asylum Agency (EUAA) entered into force via a Regulation in 2021,[103] with the aim of improving the CEAS by increasing assistance to Member States and

[98] De Bruycker, 'The New Pact on Migration and Asylum' (n 91) 34.

[99] ibid 36.

[100] Eventually adopted as Regulation (EU) 2024/1717 of the European Parliament and of the Council of 13 June 2024 amending Regulation (EU) 2016/399 on a Union Code on the rules governing the movement of persons across borders.

[101] Proposal for a Regulation of the European Parliament and of the Council addressing situations of instrumentalisation in the field of migration and asylum COM/2021/890 final. In its 2025 work programme, the Commission announced the withdrawal of the instrumentalization proposal as obsolete as the content of the proposal was merged into Regulation (EU) 2024/1359 addressing situations of crisis and force majeure in the field of migration and asylum and amending Regulation (EU) 2021/1147. For comment, see Mariana Gkliati, 'Let's Call It What It Is: Hybrid Threats and Instrumentalisation as the Evolution of Securitisation in Migration Management' (2023) 8(2) European Papers 561.

[102] Marguerite Arnoux Bellavitis, '(De)politicising Migration Management Policymaking: Limiting Participation, Challenging Democratic Legitimacy and Undermining Migrants' Rights' (PhD thesis, Università Degli Studi Di Palermo/Paris-Lodron Universität Salzburg, 2025).

[103] Regulation (EU) 2021/2303 of the European Parliament and of the Council of 15 December 2021 on the European Union Agency for Asylum and repealing Regulation (EU) No 439/2010 [2021]

moving towards a more harmonized assessment of applications for international protection.

Yet, despite migration occupying the highest place on the EU's agenda since the Pact and the launch of a 'fresh start', there was an admission by Commission President Von der Leyen in the State of the Union address in September 2021 that little further had been achieved. The main stumbling block, according to the Commission President, is its reliance on the need to find consensus on a number of different fronts in this politically charged sphere:

> The New Pact on Migration and Asylum gives us everything we need to manage the different types of situations we face. All the elements are there. This is a balanced and humane system that works for all Member States—*in all circumstances.* We know that we can find common ground.[104]

One year later, Von der Leyen's State of the Union address in September 2022 noted that there had been movement on moving forward with the Pact. A roadmap[105] was agreed in early September 2022 between the European Parliament and five Member States holding the Council Presidencies,[106] itself a novel institutional means of trying to smooth both the policy and legislative process. For Von der Leyen, the institutional barriers were not with the EU institutions but rather with the Member States: 'We have progress on the Pact, we now have the Roadmap. And we now need the political will to match.'[107] The Council and Parliament finally

OJ L 468/1; Decision 2010/762/EU of the Representatives of the Governments of the Member States, meeting within the Council of 25 February 2010 determining the seat of the European Asylum Support Office [2010] OJ L 324/47. 2010/762/EU established the seat of the Agency as Valetta, Malta. For comment, see Mariana Gkliati and Salvatore Nicolosi, 'External Solidarity in Integrated Border Management: The Role of EU Migration Agencies' in Eva Kassoti and Narin Idriz (eds), *The Principle of Solidarity. Global Europe: Legal and Policy Issues of the EU's External Action*, vol 2 (TMC Asser Press 2023); David Fernández-Rojo, 'Transforming the European Asylum Support Office into the European Union Agency for Asylum' (2019) 23 Spanish Yearbook of International Law 285; Ariadna Ripoll Servent, 'A New Form of Delegation in EU Asylum: Agencies as Proxies of Strong Regulators' (2018) 56(1) JCMS: Journal of Common Market Studies 83.

[104] Ursula von der Leyen (President of the Commission), '2021 State of the Union address by President von der Leyen' (European Parliament, 15 September 2021) https://ec.europa.eu/commission/presscorner/detail/ov/SPEECH_21_4701, accessed 7 June 2025.

[105] European Parliament, 'Joint Roadmap of the European Parliament and Rotating Presidencies of the Council on the organisation, coordination, and implementation of the timeline for the negotiations between the co-legislators on the CEAS and the New European Pact on migration and asylum' (7 September 2022) https://www.europarl.europa.eu/resources/library/media/20220907RES39903/20220907RES39903.pdf, accessed 7 June 2025.

[106] Czechia, Sweden, Spain, Belgium, and France. See European Parliament, 'Migration and Asylum: Roadmap on the way forward agreed between European Parliament and rotating Presidencies' (*European Parliament*, 7 September 2022) https://www.europarl.europa.eu/news/en/press-room/20220905IPR39714/migration-and-asylum-roadmap-on-way-forward-agreed, accessed 7 June 2025. For critique, see Editorial, 'European Pact on Migration and Asylum—Latest Developments' (*ECRE: European Council on Refugees and Exiles*, 17 March 2023) https://ecre.org/editorial-european-pact-on-migration-and-asylum-latest-developments/, accessed 7 June 2025.

[107] Von der Leyen, '2021 State of the Union address' (n 104).

reached a political agreement on the Pact in December 2023, leading to the adoption of the legislative texts by the Parliament on 10 April 2024.[108] The Pact entered into force in June 2024, with most of the legislation due to come into effect in 2026.[109] Since the UK has left the EU, the number of states who are outliers in terms of participation in EU asylum law is two: Denmark and Ireland. However, in June 2024 the Irish government signalled its intention to participate in the New Pact.[110]

The final legislative package included the Asylum and Migration Management Regulation,[111] Asylum Procedure Regulation (including the Return Border Procedure Regulation),[112] Crisis and Force Majeure Regulation,[113] Eurodac Regulation,[114] Screening Regulation,[115] Qualification Regulation,[116] Reception Conditions Directive,[117] and Union Resettlement Framework Regulation.[118]

[108] European Parliament, 'MEPs approve the new Migration and Asylum Pact' (*European Parliament*, 10 April 2024) https://www.europarl.europa.eu/news/en/press-room/20240408IPR20290/meps-approve-the-new-migration-and-asylum-pact, accessed 7 June 2025.

[109] The exception is the Union Resettlement Framework Regulation, which entered into force immediately: Regulation (EU) 2024/1350 of the European Parliament and of the Council of 14 May 2024 establishing a Union Resettlement and Humanitarian Admission Framework, and amending Regulation (EU) 2021/1147 [2024] OJ L 2024/1350.

[110] See Commission, 'Ireland will participate in the EU Pact on Migration and Asylum (*European Commission: Migration and Home Affairs*, 31 July 2024) https://home-affairs.ec.europa.eu/news/ireland-will-participate-eu-pact-migration-and-asylum-2024-07-31_en, accessed 9 June 2025; Elspeth Guild, 'The EU's New Asylum Pact and Ireland's Opt-In' (2025) 27(1) European Journal of Migration and Law 41.

[111] Regulation (EU) 2024/1351 of the European Parliament and of the Council of 14 May 2024 on asylum and migration management, amending Regulations (EU) 2021/1147 and (EU) 2021/1060 and repealing Regulation (EU) No 604/2013 [2024] OJ L 2024/1351.

[112] Regulation (EU) 2024/1348 of the European Parliament and of the Council of 14 May 2024 establishing a common procedure for international protection in the Union and repealing Directive 2013/32/EU and Regulation (EU) 2024/1349 of the European Parliament and of the Council of 14 May 2024 establishing a return border procedure, and amending Regulation (EU) 2021/1148 [2024] OJ L 2024/1348.

[113] Regulation (EU) 2024/1359 of the European Parliament and of the Council of 14 May 2024 addressing situations of crisis and force majeure in the field of migration and asylum and amending Regulation (EU) 2021/1147 [2024] OJ L 2024/1359.

[114] Regulation (EU) 2024/1358 of the European Parliament and of the Council of 14 May 2024 on the establishment of 'Eurodac' for the comparison of biometric data in order to effectively apply Regulations (EU) 2024/1351 and (EU) 2024/1350 of the European Parliament and of the Council and Council Directive 2001/55/EC and to identify illegally staying third-country nationals and stateless persons and on requests for the comparison with Eurodac data by Member States' law enforcement authorities and Europol for law enforcement purposes, amending Regulations (EU) 2018/1240 and (EU) 2019/818 of the European Parliament and of the Council and repealing Regulation (EU) No 603/2013 of the European Parliament and of the Council [2024] OJ L 2024/1358.

[115] Regulation (EU) 2024/1356 of the European Parliament and of the Council of 14 May 2024 introducing the screening of third-country nationals at the external borders and amending Regulations (EC) No 767/2008, (EU) 2017/2226, (EU) 2018/1240 and (EU) 2019/817 [2024] OJ L 2024/1356.

[116] Regulation (EU) 2024/1347 of the European Parliament and of the Council of 14 May 2024 on standards for the qualification of third-country nationals or stateless persons as beneficiaries of international protection, for a uniform status for refugees or for persons eligible for subsidiary protection and for the content of the protection granted, amending Council Directive 2003/109/EC and repealing Directive 2011/95/EU of the European Parliament and of the Council [2024] OJ L 2024/1347.

[117] Directive (EU) 2024/1346 of the European Parliament and of the Council of 14 May 2024 laying down standards for the reception of applicants for international protection.

[118] Regulation (EU) 2024/1350 of the European Parliament and of the Council of 14 May 2024 establishing a Union Resettlement and Humanitarian Admission Framework, and amending Regulation (EU) 2021/1147 [2024] OJ L 2024/1346.

In addition, new 'non-legislative' files include a recommendation on Migration Preparedness and Crisis Blueprint,[119] a recommendation on Resettlement and Complementary pathways,[120] a recommendation on Search and Rescue Operations by Private Vessels,[121] and new guidance on the Facilitators Directive.[122]

The Commission has a Common Implementation Plan 'to translate the Pact from legislative acts into an operational reality'.[123] The Commission plan carefully tries to avoid picking and choosing, by stressing the interdependency of the legislative measures around the theme of 'building blocks'.[124] Member States were obliged to put together their national implementation plans by December 2024. Most have now done so, although not all are publicly available.[125]

The contentiousness in putting the Pact together and seeking buy-in from Member States is obvious from the themes it stresses. 'Solidarity' appears front and centre in the Pact, reflecting a means to ensure that Member States take their (general) Treaty-based obligations seriously,[126] but also to try to ensure the success of the Commission's delicate balancing act between the role of guardian of the Treaties and that of 'honest broker' via a 'realpolitik' approach.[127] 'Flexible solidarity' is a clear attempt to break the impasse of the Dublin Regulations, though the contours of what solidarity means here have been fiercely critiqued as fundamentally different from undifferentiated responsibility for all, as per the Court of Justice's characterization when refusing Hungary and Slovakia's challenge to

[119] Commission Recommendation (EU) 2020/1366 of 23 September 2020 on an EU mechanism for preparedness and management of crises related to migration [2020] OJ L 317/26.

[120] Commission Recommendation (EU) 2020/1364 of 23 September 2020 on legal pathways to protection in the EU: promoting resettlement, humanitarian admission and other complementary pathways [2020] OJ L 317/13.

[121] Commission Recommendation (EU) 2020/1365 of 23 September 2020 on cooperation among Member States concerning operations carried out by vessels owned or operated by private entities for the purpose of search and rescue activities [2020] OJ L 317/23.

[122] Commission, 'Communication from the Commission, Commission Guidance on the implementation of EU rules on definition and prevention of the facilitation of unauthorised entry, transit and residence 2020/C 323/01' [2020] OJ C 323/1.

[123] Commission, 'Common Implementation Plan to turn the Pact on Migration and Asylum into a reality' (*European Commission: Migration and Home Affairs*, 12 June 2024) https://home-affairs.ec.europa.eu/news/common-implementation-plan-turn-pact-migration-and-asylum-reality-2024-06-12_en#:~:text=2%20min%20read-,Common%20Implementation%20Plan%20to%20turn%20the%20Pact%20on%20Migration%20and,rules%20on%20migration%20into%20practice, accessed 9 June 2025; Commission, 'Communication from the Commission to the European Parliament, the Council, the European Economic and Social Committee and the Committee of the Regions: Common Implementation Plan for the Pact on Migration and Asylum' COM(2024) 251 final 1.

[124] COM(2024) 251 final.

[125] See European Union Agency for Asylum, 'Situational Update: National Implementation Plans and National Strategies under the EU Pact on Migration and Asylum' (2026) https://www.euaa.europa.eu/sites/default/files/publications/2026-03/2026_national_implementation_plans_strategies_asylum_EN.pdf, accessed 30 March 2026

[126] Article 80 TFEU: 'The policies of the Union set out in this Chapter and their implementation shall be governed by the principle of solidarity and fair sharing of responsibility, including its financial implications, between the Member States. Whenever necessary, the Union acts adopted pursuant to this Chapter shall contain appropriate measures to give effect to this principle.'

[127] Daniel Thym, 'European Realpolitik: Legislative Uncertainties and Operational Pitfalls of the "New" Pact on Migration and Asylum' (*Immigration and Asylum Law and Policy Blog*, 28 September 2020) http://eumigrationlawblog.eu/european-realpolitik-legislative-uncertainties-und-operational-pitfalls-of-the-new-pact-on-migration-and-asylum/, accessed 7 June 2025.

mandatory relocation quotas in 2015.[128] As such, the New Migration Pact emphasizes the combination of law with flexibility and the emphasis on innovation. At the same time, there is a need for mainstream parties on the left and right to portray themselves as 'efficient legislators'—that is, to demonstrate to European public(s) that action on migration is possible, as a means to prevent the domination of discourse by the far right, while simultaneously co-opting long-running themes promoted by the far right.[129] Some scholars have noted that the New Pact appears to mark a more fundamental shift away from a human-centred approach to migration, given the emphasis on inter-institutional bargaining.[130] Rijpma, for instance, sees convergence between the institutions who see 'the respect for fundamental rights [as] an obstacle to the management of the EU's external borders, rather than part and parcel thereof'.[131] This point can be made of the application of fairness in migration decision-making.[132]

The main challenge for the Commission was to overcome the opposing viewpoints between Member States advocating for mandatory relocations of asylum seekers from EU border states to other EU states and Member States who opposed any form of solidarity premised on such mandatory relocations.[133] It does so via some innovations allowing Member States to avoid receiving migrants but instead allowing them to engage in return sponsorship, by which they have 'the flexibility to decide whether and to what extent to share their effort between persons to be relocated and those to whom return sponsorship would apply'.[134]

The Pact, with legislation at its core, might appear to reverse the trend observed in this chapter and the previous chapter of legislation taking a back seat in EU migration governance, but as Goldner Lang has observed, the increasing phenomenon of Member State infringements of EU migration and asylum law reached a peak during the 'crisis' of 2015–16 but has continued according to data

128 Joint Cases C-643/15 and C-647/15, *Slovakia and Hungary v Council*, ECLI:EU:C:2017:631, paras 291–293. See Eleni Karageorgiou and Gregor Noll, 'What Is Wrong with Solidarity in EU Asylum and Migration Law?' (2022) 4 Jus Cogens 131.

129 Sarah Wolff, 'The New Pact on Migration: Embedded Illiberalism?' 62(S1) JCMS: Journal of Common Market Studies 113.

130 See, for example, Jouni Häkli, Gintarė Kudžmaitė, and Kirsi Kallio, 'Devaluing Personhood: The Framing of Migrants in the EU's New Pact on Migration and Asylum' (2024) 49(4) Transactions of the Institute of British Geographers e12676; Sofyan Essarraoui, 'The EU's New Migration Pact: A Historic Move Forward or a Replication of Past Mistakes?' (2024) 3(2) Moroccan Journal for Research in the Humanities and Social Sciences 280.

131 Jorrit J Rijpma, 'Watching the Guards: Ensuring Compliance with Fundamental Rights at the External Borders' (2024) 30(1–2) European Law Journal 74.

132 Leandro Mancano, 'Sketches of Fairness in EU and International Law: Focus on the Asylum and Migration Pact' (2025) 4(3) European Law Open 481–504.

133 Olivia Diez, Florian Trauner, and Marie De Somer, 'Return Sponsorships in the EU's New Pact on Migration and Asylum: High Stakes, Low Gains' (2021) 23(3) European Journal of Migration and Law 219; Steve Peers, 'The New EU Asylum Laws: Taking Rights Half-Seriously' (2024) Yearbook of European Law 1, 26.

134 COM(2020) 609 final 5.

on infringement proceedings launched by the Commission.[135] Taking this point to its logical conclusion, if the Member States' commitment to adhering to EU law is starting look less certain—especially if widespread in other areas—then the idea of solidarity holding the Member States together must also be considered to lack a full foundation too.

Ensuring that a 'pact' is capable of forging a common approach is thus questionable, whether on the basis of formal (legislation and agreements based on Treaty competences) or less formal (undefined instruments centring on cooperation) means. As a result, while legislation is designed to provide the bedrock of EU migration governance, it is the coordination aspects of the 'flexible solidarity' concept that may prove both difficult to enforce and (overly) reliant on Member States adhering to both the principle and practice. While solidarity is at the heart of the Treaties, there is a strong risk of fragmentation across the legislation due to the broad margins of discretion accorded to the Member States. Thus, even when in force, the outcomes of the Pact will be far from the harmonising spirit of the Treaty and objective of the Common European Asylum System (CEAS).[136]

It is worth highlighting some of the innovations contained in the Pact and its legislative package which demonstrate both where the legislative and coordination aspects are most visible, and where concerns about adherence to fundamental rights have been raised.[137] The Pact speaks of the institutional arrangements more than of migrants themselves. This is important for the framing of the Pact and its intended audience, suggesting that it is in essence more of a question of institutional competence, power, and balance rather than the individuals concerned.[138]

As part of the Pact, of particular note to highlight here is the Asylum and Migration Management Regulation (AMMR). The Regulation modifies the previous Dublin system, and sets out the principle that when a Member State is faced with actual or potential migratory pressure, defined as 'a situation brought about by arrivals by land, sea or air or applications of third-country nationals or stateless persons, that are of such a scale that they create disproportionate obligations on a Member State, taking into account the overall situation in the Union',[139] then a 'solidarity pool' can be engaged.[140] The innovation lies in the Member States being able to choose whether to contribute by relocating asylum seekers, or supporting

[135] Iris Goldner Lang, 'No Solidarity Without Loyalty: Why Do Member States Violate EU Migration and Asylum Law and What Can Be Done?' (2020) 22(1) European Journal of Migration and Law 39.

[136] Vasiliki Apatzidou, 'Derogations in Exchange of Increased Responsibility: How Can This Fix the Broken Promise for More Solidarity in the EU?' (2024) 26(3) European Journal of Migration and Law 317.

[137] As explored further in Chapter 7.

[138] See, for example, Häkli, Kudžmaitė, and Kallio, 'Devaluing Personhood: The Framing of Migrants in the EU's New Pact on Migration and Asylum' (n 130).

[139] Regulation (EU) 2024/1351 [2024] OJ L 2024/1351, Article 2(24).

[140] ibid, Article 56 et seq.

the return of migrants without permission to remain through return sponsorships, or through financial or operational assistance, or a combination of these.[141] This is a rather different model to the traditionally conceived 'command-and-control' nature of Regulations, and brings into focus how the Commission might reasonably, as guardian of the Treaties, enforce its complex terms and avoid accusations of doing so against certain Member States only. Karageorgiou and Noll claim that the proposed system is 'responsive by design', and heavily reliant on the Commission deciding which contributions will be considered proportional and appropriate in the case that voluntary pledges are not sufficient.[142] Furthermore, core to the concept of solidarity here is that derogations are explicitly regarded as solidarity measures to support states facing migratory pressures.[143] While solidarity is often expressed as a response to a particular set of difficulties experienced by one or more Member States—or the Union as a whole—the framing of solidarity vis-à-vis migration here appears as a state of permanent crisis, putting the rights of migrants on the backseat.[144]

The Regulation makes a direct link with some of the instances of 'formal informality' detailed in the following chapters. In particular, it reinforces the obligation of Member States to cooperate closely to prevent and reduce irregular migration to the territories of the Member States,[145] Article 6 refers to the 'Permanent EU Migration Support Toolbox'. The 'Toolbox' indicates a non-exhaustive list ('shall include at least') of funds,[146] derogations,[147] 'measures to facilitate return and reintegration activities, including through cooperation with third countries',[148] and 'promoting legal migration and well-managed mobility, including by strengthening bilateral, regional and international partnerships on migration, forced displacement, legal pathways and mobility partnerships'.[149]

With 'legal pathways' reduced to only one clause as a potential for Member States to use, the AMMR demonstrates once again that the centre of gravity of EU migration governance appears even more firmly anchored in combating irregular migration, to the detriment of working towards a more coherent system for facilitating migration for work. As a consequence, the Member States will continue to formulate separate, and competing, national policies unless the 'Talent Pool'

[141] Diez, Trauner, and Somer, 'Return Sponsorships in the EU's New Pact on Migration and Asylum' (n 133).

[142] See Karageorgiou and Noll, 'What Is Wrong with Solidarity in EU Asylum and Migration Law?' (n 128).

[143] Apatzidou, 'Derogations in Exchange of Increased Responsibility' (n 129).

[144] Violeta Moreno-Lax, 'Crisis as (Asylum) Governance: The Evolving Normalisation of Non-Access to Protection in the EU' (2024) Queen Mary Law Research Paper No. 423/2024.

[145] Regulation (EU) 2024/1351 [2024] OJ L 2024/1351, Article 6(2)(c).

[146] ibid, 6(3)(b).

[147] ibid, Article 6(3)(c).

[148] ibid, Article 6(3)(e).

[149] ibid, 6(3)(j).

(discussed in what follows) becomes effective.[150] At the very least, the Regulation demonstrates a variation of what Regulations look like and how they are used, which befits the advanced stage of governance the EU finds itself at.

4.9.1 Pre-entry screening and the new border procedures

A Regulation for a screening of third country nationals will be applicable to migrants crossing the EU's external borders without authorization.[151] The aim of the screening is, according to the Preamble, to 'contribute to the new comprehensive approach to migration and mixed flows by ensuring that the identity of the persons but also any health and security risks are quickly established and that all third-country nationals who are present at the external border without fulfilling entry conditions or after disembarkation following a search and rescue operation are swiftly referred towards the applicable procedure'.[152] More precisely, the screening should direct all third country nationals who cross borders other than at regular crossings (and who are thus fingerprinted as per the Eurodac Regulation) or via search and rescue operations to the appropriate procedures as early as possible. Consequently, this procedure should lower the risk of absconding after entrance in the territory to reach a different state than the one of arrival. The screening should contribute to curbing secondary movements, which is a policy target highly relevant for many northern and central European Member States.

There are significant doubts regarding how to qualify the legal situation of those undergoing the screening process. Given that the process will be obligatory and may take time, there is a lack of clarity over whether this would qualify as detention or not as well as on the practical questions of 'hot spots' and transit zones, availability facilities, and access to essential services. It is noted that in the CJEU's decision on Hungarian transit zones,[153] the Court of Justice has decided that being held in the Röszke transit zone qualified as 'detention'. Therefore, it can be argued that the logic in that case could also be applied to the case of migrants during the screening phase.[154]

Pre-screening is seen as a panacea for the problems experienced by the Member States, insofar as it should resolve some of the challenges of post-entry movement

150 Paul Minderhoud, 'Regulation of EU Labour Migration: At a Crossroads after the New Pact on Migration and Asylum?' (2021) 17(4) Utrecht Law Review 31.

151 Commission, Proposal for a Regulation of the European Parliament and of the Council introducing a screening of third country nationals at the external borders and amending Regulations (EC) No 767/2008, (EU) 2017/2226, (EU) 2018/1240 and (EU) 2019/817 COM 612 final.

152 ibid, preamble.

153 C-924/19 and C-925/19 *FMS and Others v Országos Idegenrendészeti Főigazgatóság Dél-alföldi Regionális Igazgatóság and Országos Idegenrendészeti Főigazgatóság* ECLI:EU:C:2020:367.

154 Jean-Pierre Cassarino and Luisa Marin, 'The Pact on Migration and Asylum: Turning the European Territory into a Non-Territory?' (2022) 24(1) European Journal of Migration and Law 1.

across different Member States and their jurisdictions. However, some screening is already provided in the Recast Asylum Procedures Directive,[155] where it is stated that Member States may provide for procedures on the admissibility or substance of an application. Yet, the transposition and application of current EU law by the Member States show significant challenges and shortcomings.[156] The bureaucracy and resources required to fully adhere to the terms of the Regulation would appear, however, to disadvantage those Member States on the EU's external borders and increase tensions with the third states who are increasingly being relied upon to prevent migrants arriving at the border, thus leading to their instrumentalization.[157]

4.9.2 The Common Procedure for International Protection Regulation

In addition, an amended proposal for a border procedure Regulation[158] emerged as part of the New Migration Pact and is designed to link claims for asylum with returns. It was adopted in May 2024. Under the amended Regulation,[159] the procedure is obligatory for Member States for applicants who arrive irregularly at the external border or via disembarkation. Entry to the EU is not granted during the border procedure and the individual's request for protection will be denied if in addition he/she is deemed to represent a risk to national security or public order; or has provided false information or documents or withheld relevant information; or the applicant comes from a third country for which the share of positive decisions in the total number of asylum decisions is below 20 per cent.

While this may expedite procedures and provide some certainty for the Member States, there is a strong risk that the criteria could be interpreted differently by national administrations, especially those who have taken a particularly strong line against accepting migrants, and again places the burden on some—rather than all—Member States.[160]

[155] Directive 2013/32/EU of the European Parliament and of the Council of 26 June 2013 on common procedures for granting and withdrawing international protection (recast), Article 43 (1)(a) and (b).

[156] Galina Cornelisse and Marcelle Reneman, 'Border Procedures in the Commission's New Pact on Migration and Asylum: A Case of Politics Outplaying Rationality?' (2021) 26(3–4) European Law Journal 181.

[157] Joana Uriate, 'The European Pact on Migration and Asylum: Border Containment and Frontline States' (2022) 24(4) European Journal of Migration and Law 463.

[158] Commission, Amended proposal for a Regulation of the European Parliament and of the Council establishing a common procedure for international protection in the Union and repealing Directive 2013/32/EU COM 611 final.

[159] Regulation (EU) 2024/1348 of the European Parliament and of the Council of 14 May 2024 establishing a common procedure for international protection in the Union and repealing Directive 2013/32/EU.

[160] Cassarino and Marin, 'The Pact on Migration and Asylum' (n 154).

4.9.3 The Crisis and Force Majeure Regulation

This Regulation, adopted in 2024,[161] aims to codify the approaches to a crisis in migration—in terms of the numbers of (potential) migrants arriving, as experienced in 2015–16 in the Mediterranean/Aegean, and the different circumstances of the instrumentalism of crossing from Belarus in 2021[162] and displacement of Ukrainians towards the EU since 2022. The Regulation addresses 'exceptional situations of crisis' with the use of 'temporary measures'.[163] The definition of crisis is one where the numbers of arrivals risk rendering a Member State's asylum and reception services 'non-functional', which could have 'serious consequences for the functioning of the Common European Asylum System'.[164] Force majeure occurs in cases of, 'abnormal and unforeseeable circumstances' outside the control of the Member State. It is likely, thus, that only the Member States on the external borders, such as Italy and Greece, may seek to engage the Regulation's terms. However, although defining what a crisis or force majeure situation consists of in the Regulation, there is a disconnect with the obligations under EU law triggered by a criterion which is, by its nature, dependent on capacity rather than numbers. There is significant scope here for the Regulation to be mis-applied or misused. As Ineli-Ciger has noted, 'the large-scale arrival of refugees and migrants rendering a Member State's return system non-functional should not be accepted as a criterion to determine the existence of a situation of crisis or a mass influx situation since return capacity of the host state alone has nothing to do with the existence of a mass influx and cannot justify derogating from state responsibilities under international or EU law'.[165]

If a Member State seeks to engage the Regulation, for which a proposal from the Commission must be accepted by the Council,[166] a number of derogations may be triggered. All of these rely on enhanced solidarity from other Member States, such as relocation of migrants from the Member States and exemptions from other pieces of CEAS legislation. The derogations include taking longer to process asylum applications, prolonging detention under the borders Common Procedure,[167] and expediting asylum decision-making. As might be expected,

[161] Regulation (EU) 2024/1359 of the European Parliament and of the Council of 14 May 2024 addressing situations of crisis and force majeure in the field of migration and asylum and amending Regulation (EU) 2021/1147.

[162] Jari Piriola, 'Hostile Instrumentalized Migration and the Right to Seek Asylum: Reflecting the European Legal Framework' (2025) 27(1) European Journal of Migration and Law 1.

[163] Regulation (EU) 2024/1359, Article 1.

[164] Regulation (EU) 2024/1359, Article 1(4)(a).

[165] Meltem Ineli-Ciger, 'Navigating the labyrinth of derogations: a critical look at the Crisis Regulation' (EU Immigration and Asylum Law and Policy blog, 10 June 2024) https://eumigrationlawblog.eu/navigating-the-labyrinth-of-derogations-a-critical-look-at-the-crisis-regulation/, accessed 7 June 2025.

[166] Regulation (EU) 2024/1359, Article 4 (1)–(5).

[167] See the previous section.

the derogations have attracted the most criticism, due to a potential lack of legal certainty over their scope[168] and the normalization of arbitrary immigration detention, racial profiling, and pushbacks.[169] As a result, the risk of the Regulation being triggered may undermine the ability of individuals to seek asylum and thus see greater externalization and a shift of responsibility to non-EU countries. The Regulation was subject to special criticism by Amnesty International directed at the European Parliament and its agreement to the legislative packages.[170]

4.10 The Skills and Talent Mobility Package

Officially separate to the New Pact on Migration and Asylum, but playing a supporting role, is the Skills and Talent Mobility Package. This series of measures was proposed by the Commission's Directorate General for Migration and Home Affairs in November 2023. The package recognizes the growing labour shortages across the EU, and aims to increase capacity to attract, retain, and effectively use skilled talent from third countries.

A central component of the package is the proposed Regulation establishing an EU 'Talent Pool', as an EU-wide platform to match skilled jobseekers from non-EU countries with vacancies in sectors experiencing labour shortages.[171] The Commission's hope is that this will streamline international recruitment and reduce the complexity and cost associated with cross-border hiring. However, the voluntary nature of the pool for Member States and employers within them and the lack of replacement of any national schemes limit its potential usefulness.

The package is representative of the mix of tools. Alongside the proposal for a Regulation as a formal or 'hard' law instrument—albeit one which does not harmonize and is merely open to voluntary participation—are initiatives which are beyond the EU's legal competences but which help contribute to skills gaps via approaches familiar to those explored as part of the new modes of governance debate since the 1990s.[172] These include a Council Recommendation titled 'Europe on

[168] Alberto-Horst Neidhardt, 'The Crisis and Force Majeure Regulation: Towards Future-Proof Crisis Management and Response?' (Foundation for Progressive Studies, Friedrich-Ebert-Stiftung and European Policy Centre 2024) https://library.fes.de/pdf-files/bueros/bruessel/21303.pdf, accessed 7 June 2025.

[169] Open Letter, 'Over 50 NGOs pen eleventh-hour open letter to EU on human rights risks in Migration Pact' (*PICUM*, 18 December 2023) https://picum.org/blog/open-letter-eu-human-rights-risks-migration-pact/, accessed 7 June 2025.

[170] Amnesty International, 'EU: Migration and Asylum Pact reforms will put people at heightened risk of human rights violations' (*Amnesty International*, 4 April 2024) https://www.amnesty.org/en/latest/news/2024/04/eu-migration-asylum-pact-put-people-at-risk-human-rights-violations/, accessed 7 June 2025.

[171] Proposal for a Regulation of the European Parliament and of the Council establishing an EU Talent Pool COM(2023) 716 final. This was discussed in more detail in Chapter 3.

[172] See the discussion in Chapter 2.

the Move', which promotes learning mobility as a standard part of education and training pathways. It sets targets such as increasing the share of vocational education and training students participating in mobility programmes to 15 per cent by 2030. The package also includes measures to support apprentice mobility and improve the recognition of qualifications obtained outside the EU. All of these would require Member States to engage in coordination, but matched with the political will to do at the European level, rather than merely nationally.

4.11 Conclusion

The recent history of migration governance in the EU since the Treaty of Amsterdam is one where legislation has played—and continues to play—a central role. The enthusiasm within the institutions, however, when the Treaty of Amsterdam first introduced the express legal competences on migration dissipated when the difficulties in moving from the proposal stage to the final agreement on texts became apparent. These difficulties appear to have only increased over time as migration has continued to dominate the national and European agendas.

As a result, migration law represents something of a quandary. On the one hand, there is the expectation that migration as an issue, and one which has been increasingly susceptible to the language of crisis, would be the object of increased focus of legislation. Although often presented as the contrary, EU-led harmonization does not necessarily entail a loss of state power or sovereignty, but rather an opportunity to maximize it.[173]

In reality, however, this has not been the case. Rather, this chapter has considered how a succession of strategic documents on JHA and AFSJ, external relations, and foreign and security policy have all stressed how important it is for the EU to confront the challenges of migration, but not through the central means by which other areas within the sphere of interest of the EU and its Member States have used. Rather, the slow pace of passing legislation, coupled with a sense of (general) legislative fatigue and other crises permeating the EU, plus the urgency for the institutions (particularly the Commission) to ensure the continued relevance of the EU in this important domain, have led to more innovative solutions than reliance on traditional legislation.

Since both the regulation of migration and its enforcement are a complex mix of EU and national competences, the result is a patchwork of legislation which faces constant criticism, from those concerned with the effects on migrants themselves to those who see missed opportunities for a 'better' system (whatever this may

[173] Theodora (Dora) Kostakopoulou, 'The "Protective Union": Change and Continuity in Migration Law and Policy in Post-Amsterdam Europe' (2000) 38(3) JCMS: Journal of Common Market Studies 497, 514.

mean). EU migration policy is used as a means of critiquing the EU itself by some Member States, particularly those where there has been backsliding in the rule of law. as a consequence, we can even question whether it is possible to even speak of a common policy or approach to refugees and asylum.[174] The Court of Justice has found itself in the position of gap-filling in legislation between the different levels of competences but also the variations in the application of standards in the different Member States. A series of recent decisions exemplify the different tensions: the Court has favourably interpreted procedural rights in favour of individuals caught by the Dublin system, while at the same time prioritizing mutual trust between Member States over the potential for *non-refoulement*, in contrast to the European Court of Human Rights.[175]

As a result, the narrative of EU migration law only partly reflects the traditional account of integration via law-making. Told via the lens of the Commission, as the motor of integration, legislation forms the backbone of the EU polity and, when new ways of doing things emerge that appear to downplay legislation or threaten the monopoly of the Commission on introducing legislation, there have been attempts to recapture the narrative. The White Paper on Governance 2001, unrelated to migration as a policy area, is one such example.[176] The Commission's attempt to both set the public-facing agenda and ensure that it does not lose the confidence of Member State governments can be observed in discourse such as 'Striking a balance on migration: an approach that is both fair and firm', to quote a recent communication.[177]

But the story of EU migration law is not one where competences simply emerged in the Treaty, and its late entrance to the scene and political salience mean that it should not necessarily be expected to follow the same script as in other areas. The gradual building up of interactions between the Member States and contemporaneous efforts to spearhead cooperation on removing internal frontiers (which led to Schengen) and on foreign policy matters (which led to European Political Cooperation and the Common Foreign and Security Policy) prompted institutional bargaining beyond the formal, legal competences. Informality and

[174] Magnus Henrekson, Özge Öner, and Tino Sanandaji, 'The Refugee Crisis and the Reinvigoration of the Nation-State: Does the European Union Have a Common Asylum Policy?' in Antonina Bakardjieva Engelbrekt and others (eds), *The European Union and the Return of the Nation State* (Palgrave Macmillan 2020).

[175] See Joint Cases C-228/21, C-254/21, C-297/21, C-315/21, and C-328/21 *Ministero dell'Interno, Dipartimento per le Libertà civili e l'Immigrazione—Unità Dublino and Others v CZA and Others*, ECLI:EU:C:2023:934. See, for comment, Marco Gerbaudo, 'Paving the Way to the New Pact on Migration and Asylum: Some Reflections on Ministero dell'Interno (Joined Cases C-228/21, C-254/21, C-297/21, C-315/21, C-328/21)' (2025) 31(5) Maastricht Journal of European and Comparative Law 647.

[176] See the discussion in Chapter 2.

[177] Commission, 'Communication from the Commission to the European Parliament, the European Council and the Council—Striking a balance on migration: an approach that is both fair and firm' COM(2024) 126 final.

cooperation outside the Treaty framework therefore provided the foundations for the later binding measures.

Political wrangling explains only some of the story as told through the multiple attempts to move migration law and policy forward. Migration is by no means alone in finding legislation difficult, and this is not a new phenomenon in the history of the EU, as the stagnation over free movement in the 1960s and 1970s demonstrates. Neither is the time taken to pass core legislation enough alone to mark out migration as substantially different to other fields. However, a combination of these factors along with political sensitivity and public awareness, the changing roles of the institutions, and the language of 'crisis' mark migration out as different. This helps to explain why there are so many attempts to reset migration law and policy and note each one as a 'fresh start' despite the policy stability of the goals.[178]

The nature of governance has shifted too. At the outset of the process, the emphasis was on combating irregular immigration but also ensuring minimum reception standards for arrivals across the Member States. Migration was not mentioned as a relevant factor in the ESS in 2003. Just over a decade later, in 2016, the Global Strategy placed migration front and centre as a security risk. Thus arose the synergy between migration law as a 'first pillar' set of competences similar to those where extensive legislation had been produced and the CFSP, which did not rely on the same kind of instruments. Migration thus is a foreign policy issue, with the competence and institutional problems that go with it, particularly vis-à-vis its relationship with Member State sovereignty. The European Council has continued to exert a strong influence on migration governance, which underlines the intergovernmental dimension to migration but also places the Commission in a space where it is forced to attempt to regain control, and its monopoly on the proposals for legislation is of course the main way for it to do so.

As a result, the lack of legislation opens up a space for innovation and informal means to achieve goals. These goals can be those set out in the Treaty, or those evidenced from the successive policy strategies (i.e. externalization, securitization), or even those presented to safeguard other areas of integration such as Schengen.[179]

The problem is that there is a limit to how far this can go, especially when it concerns the aims of the Dublin Regulation and the expectation that formal rules will undertake the important task of defining which Member State has responsibility, when, and how. The choice is either full harmonization and a greater role for competence of the institutions (politically unviable) or differentiated integration (which would also be self-defeating in this context).

[178] Leila Abdou and Andrea Pettrachin, 'Exploring the EU's Status Quo Tendency in the Migration Policy Field: A Network-Centred Perspective' (2023) 30(6) Journal of European Public Policy 1013.

[179] Michela Ceccorulli, 'The EU's Normative Ambivalence and the Migrant Crisis' in Michela Ceccorulli, Enrico Fassi, and Sonia Lucarelli (eds), *The EU Migration System of Governance* (Palgrave Macmillan 2021).

Nevertheless, the New Pact on Migration and Asylum appears to have swung the pendulum back in favour of legislation as sitting at the core of migration governance, with—for the first time in a long period—renewed efforts both to reform existing law and to introduce new legislative provisions too. In the past, this would have appeared to confirm a narrative of legal integration, but there are two notes of caution here. The first is the ability and capacity for enforcement of the law, in an area where Member States might be prepared—individually or in groups—to publicly challenge their obligations to do so, especially if it can be turned to (domestic) political advantage. To do so is to undermine faith in the law and its overall purpose,[180] and risks destabilizing not only migration governance but the EU as a polity as a whole.

The second is that the legislation will not enter into force for some time, and given the permanent state of 'crisis' in migration governance, the New Pact might find itself overtaken by events, especially as responses since 2013 have largely prioritized short-term solutions over long-term planning.[181] As per Bauböck, even though the EU institutions are powerful and 'in a nearly optimal position to establish an effective regime of burden-sharing involving all its Member States',[182] many aspects of the CEAS have been shown to be largely unworkable in practice. The result is that the institutions are faced with either a situation where legislation is not complied with by the Member States, which would undermine the whole legal order of the EU at a time when it is already facing pressures, or the need to seek solutions which diverge from the traditional way of doing things in EU governance. The following chapter traces how the institutions have engaged in informality as a departure from law-making.

[180] Daniel Thym, 'The "Refugee Crisis" as a Challenge of Legal Design and Institutional Legitimacy' (2016) 53(6) Common Market Law Review 1547.

[181] Giuseppe Campesi, 'Defining "Crisis" in Migration Governance: A Critical Legal Mapping of EU Crisis Response Mechanisms' (2024) 26(1) European Journal of Migration and Law 26.

[182] Rainer Bauböck, 'Refugee Protection and Burden-Sharing in the European Union' (2018) 56(1) JCMS: Journal of Common Market Studies 141.

5

The EU Institutions and Approaches in Formal and Informal Law-Making

The institutional approach adopted by this book necessitates, by its very nature, a deeper consideration of the interactions between the different formal institutions of the European Union and the Member States. Both have contributed to the migration acquis, but also to the opportunities for innovation and the emergence of new forms of governance during the EU integration process.

This chapter picks up the thread on the place of migration within both internal law and policymaking and external relations, to dissect the inter-institutional competences, where the balances of power lie, and frameworks for cooperation between Member States. This is a significant aspect of the core argument, given the shared competences over migration, the emergence of measures that do not rely on formal legislative frames, and the creation of bodies (i.e. agencies such as Frontex) that are both familiar within frames of governance and uncertain in terms of their role and responsibility. Only by doing this can we appreciate how the institutions position themselves, but also how informality arises and is supported.

Shifts in migration governance are highly dependent on the ways in which the EU institutions have themselves (re)conceptualized their own roles and their inter-institutional relationships. This is true of any number of law and policy areas across the EU, and helps explain both where there has been extensive activity and where there has been relative inertia. The specificities of migration are found both in its national and EU political salience and in the way in which the area has moved, although not entirely, from the intergovernmental to a 'Lisbonized' sphere. In a maturing legal–political system of governance, tracking the ways in which the EU institutions have individually and collectively found ways to innovate in migration is important in understanding why the contemporary state of external migration governance has taken on informal as well as formal characteristics.

Previous chapters have referred to the tools associated with the governance of migration in the EU. The institutions responsible for the use of such tools merit further examination. The institutional dimension to any EU policy has always been paramount across legal and political science scholarship: the institutions themselves, empowered with the tasks of ensuring 'an ever closer Union', have developed their own roles based on the often uncertain limits of the Treaties. In migration, this has not necessarily led to harmonization in a traditionally understood sense, but the weight of activity on migration means that something is happening.

The Governance of Migration in the European Union. Paul James Cardwell, Oxford University Press.
 DOI: 10.1093/9780191946592.003.0006

The question of what is covered in Chapters 6 and 7, and this chapter considers the question by whom.

The governance approach adopted in this book prioritizes the role of institutionalism. This does not restrict itself to the formal institutions (in the sense of the EU Treaties) but rather considers the creation of (legal) institutions via formal and informal interactions. Nevertheless, understanding the way in which the EU institutions have contributed to the emergence of newer forms of governance in migration and using the knowledge and experience drawn from other dimensions of EU integration and cooperation is pertinent.

5.1 The Commission

Most classic accounts of the role and composition of the Commission begin by attempting to place it somewhere between a national executive or government and the secretariat of an international organization.[1] The Commission shares some features of both, but with some fundamental differences, which makes this attempt to categorize the institution difficult. This is particularly the case for migration, given the context of evolution in which the Treaty powers have changed from a largely intergovernmental arrangement where the Commission's role has not been at the forefront.

For legal scholars, the Commission is most associated with enjoying the monopoly on the proposal of EU legislation, ensuring the application of the EU Treaties (Article 17 TEU), and enforcing EU law as the 'guardian of the Treaties'. In this respect, the Commission has played a lead role in proposing the set of Regulations and Directives that form the backbone of the framework of EU migration law as detailed in the previous chapter. As previously explored,[2] the extensive experience gained by the Commission in driving forward the single market plans in the late 1980s[3] enabled it to be well positioned to use the newly gained competences in the Treaty of Amsterdam to realize the Treaty objectives in migration.

When difficulties in adopting proposals have arisen—which, as we have seen, occurred relatively soon after the entry into force of the Treaty of Amsterdam—the Commission was equally responsible for redrafting them in a way that would be acceptable to the Council and Parliament. Seeing the Commission's role through a limited lens of proposer (and later enforcer) of legislation suggests that an ability to succeed in passing legislation would render its role severely curtailed. The regular back-and-forth of the earliest pieces of legislation post-Amsterdam and the limited

[1] See, inter alia, Peter Ludlow, 'The European Commission' in Robert O Keohane and Stanley Hoffman (eds), *The New European Community* (Routledge 1991).

[2] See Chapters 3 and 4.

[3] Kenneth Armstrong and Simon Bulmer, *The Governance of the Single European Market* (Manchester University Press 1998).

success in passing subsequent legislation makes a regular characterization of the Commission's role one where it is not in tune with the political realities and ambitions of the Council, whether or not the legislation is workable. The Commission has, therefore, had to adapt and become strategic in its ways of working to maintain its position at the heart of the institutional processes.

Turning Treaty-based obligations such as solidarity into proposals for binding and enforcement legislation is a difficult task, especially when redrafting requires a shift in the extent to which measures substantially advance the Treaty goals. As Scipioni notes, 'The Employment Directive was bold and far-reaching, as it embraced both employed and self-employed workers and provided a single procedure to govern admission and residence rights for TCNs for employment purposes. It took nearly four years and three different proposals to negotiate the Family Reunification Directive, and the Commission had to table a second proposal on the Asylum Procedure Directive after the Council spent over a year in internal wrangling over its first proposal.'[4] The Council's attitude towards many of these early efforts by the Commission is perhaps best summarized by former German Chancellor Gerhard Schroeder's statement: 'The Commission's fantasies have been rationalised.'[5]

The right of initiation of legislation is strongly associated with the enforcement procedures endowed on the Commission in its role as the 'guardian of the Treaties'. The use of the enforcement procedure generally by the Commission has been under pressure in an enlarged EU with more detailed, complex legislation to pick apart. Recent research has explored the nature of the Commission's powers as a political tool, and how launching infringement powers is only the last resort in a set of powers where informal compliance is encouraged.[6] Rather, the Commission has supported the use of the preliminary reference procedures by national courts, thus sharing both the burden of enforcement and, with national courts, the role of guardian of the Treaties.[7] In 'sacrificing' its central role in enforcement, Keleman and Pavone claim that over a longer-term period since 2004, the Commission has lowered the risk of a lack of engagement from Member State governments and thus safeguarded its place as the motor of enforcement.[8]

Nevertheless, the Commission has not shied away from opening infringement cases against Member States for incorrect or incomplete transposition of

[4] Marco Scipioni, 'Failing Forward in EU Migration Policy? EU Integration after the 2015 Asylum and Migration Crisis' (2018) 25(9) Journal of European Public Policy 1357.

[5] As quoted in ibid at 1362.

[6] Melanie Smith, 'The Visible, the Invisible and the Impenetrable: Innovations or Rebranding Regulatory Goals and Constitutional Values' in S Drake and M Smith (eds), *New Directions in the Effective Enforcement of EU Law and Policy* (Edward Elgar 2016).

[7] Andreas Hofmann, 'Is the Commission Levelling the Playing Field? Rights Enforcement in the European Union' (2018) 40(6) Journal of European Integration 737.

[8] Roger Kelemen and Tommaso Pavone, 'Where Have the Guardians Gone? Law Enforcement and the Politics of Supranational Forbearance in the European Union' (2023) 75(4) World Politics 779.

Common European Asylum System (CEAS) directives. In 2023, these included Member States having failed in their obligations in the transposition of the Reception Conditions Directive and Qualification Directive[9] and regular migration Directives, including cases against no less than eighteen Member States alleged to have infringed the Seasonal Workers Directive. The extent to which the Commission uses its discretion in the enforcement of components of the New Pact on Migration will be a telling indication.

If the Commission's role has been largely understood—by legal scholars at least—as one which is structured about its Treaty-based role in the production, supervision, and enforcement of legislation, then the innovations associated with the emerging instruments generally and in the AFSJ, and migration risk bringing into question the Commission's role as the motor of integration, especially if 'integration' is replaced by looser or more flexible forms of question.

The emergence of instruments in migration as identified in this book must be understand against the background of the changing patterns of EU governance. As explored earlier in this book,[10] new dynamics of legal integration observed in the 1980s and 1990s have become a permanent fixture of governance.[11] The common thread of the emergence of new instruments is that they depart from the 'integration through law' approach as exemplified by the Community Method of law-making. Ergo, any potential diminishment in the core use of the Community Method (which relies on the Commission playing a key role via both the tasks above) would seemingly threaten the Commission.

Assuming that institutions tend to try to maximize their influence and power over the long term,[12] the Commission has on occasions asserted the centrality of law in European integration and cooperation. This was evident in the Commission's White Paper on Governance,[13] which, although not referring to specific policy

[9] In 2023, the Commission initiated infringement proceedings against Belgium, Greece, Spain, and Portugal for improperly transposing the Reception Conditions Directive. It also enforced the Qualification Directive, addressing incomplete transposition by Czechia and incorrect implementation by Greece, Portugal, and Finland. The Commission also launched an infringement procedure against Hungary for violating the Facilitators Package aimed at combating migrant smuggling. To uphold legal migration standards, it also opened infringement cases against 18 Member States over the incorrect transposition or application of the Seasonal Workers Directive. Furthermore, the Commission continued monitoring compliance with the Long-Term Residents Directive, notably by pursuing a case against Malta based on two petitions to the European Parliament. Commission, 'Report from the Commission: Monitoring the application of European Union law 2023 Annual Report' COM(2024) 358 final 39.

[10] See the discussion in Chapter 2.

[11] Jo Shaw and Gillian More, *The New Legal Dynamics of European Union* (Clarendon Press 1995).

[12] See, inter alia, Miriam Hartlapp, 'How Time Empowers Agency: Combining the EU Commission's Political Powers and Its Administration's Advantage of Acting from a Long-Term Perspective' (2016) 29(3) Journal of European Integration 303; Antonis Ellinas and Ezra Suleiman, *The European Commission and Bureaucratic Autonomy: Europe's Custodians* (Cambridge University Press 2012); Gijs Brandsma and Jens Blom-Hansen, 'Controlling Delegated Powers in the Post-Lisbon European Union' (2015) 23(4) Journal of European Public Policy 531; Anu Bradford, *The Brussels Effect: How the European Union Rules the World* (Oxford University Press 2020).

[13] Commission, 'European governance—A white paper' [2001] COM 428 final.

areas, attempted to structure the emergence of new modes of governance around variations on the Community Method. As the Commission alluded to in the White Paper, any moves away from the Community Method of decision-making risk disrupting the process of European integration. By extension, this would imply the Commission, and one of its primary functions would be sidelined. This approach can be interpreted as an attempt to neutralize the 'threat' that alternative governance approaches risk reducing or sidelining the Commission's traditional role in favour of deliberative solutions with the Council. By the turn of the millennium, the emphasis on total harmonization, which gives the Community exclusive competence over a given policy area, had been eroded by the rise of more flexible, non-binding tools, instruments, and practice that do not rely solely on the Community Method. Finally, the Treaties of Maastricht and Amsterdam explicitly excluded harmonization for most new competences.

It is thus relatively easy to find instances where the Commission has expressed criticism of any measures which fall outside the Community Method and sideline it. This includes evaluations of Action Plans in migration which centre on resolutions and recommendations and have no formal monitoring arrangements.[14] Nevertheless, the Commission has long had a role in 'soft' law and tools of governance, such as post-legislative guidance. It also, as referred to above, has its own 'tool box' approach to the monitoring and enforcement of EU law. The distinction, however, is that these examples are generally those which build on—rather than replace—the core legislation.[15] The Commission has long been reconciled to the lack of will for 'total harmonization' and the gradual increase in legislation built on optional and minimum harmonization, the importance of non-binding technical standards, and mutual recognition.[16]

Replacing legislation with bargaining in the Council appears to be a natural consequence of the intergovernmental roots of both migration, as part of Justice and Home Affairs, and the CFSP. As explored in earlier chapters, the Commission was initially largely excluded from the intergovernmental pillars of CFSP and Justice and Home Affairs (JHA), due to the need for (some of) the Member States to keep

[14] Scipioni, 'Failing Forward in EU Migration Policy?' (n 4); Council, 'Action Plan of the Council and the Commission on how best to implement the provisions of the Treaty of Amsterdam on an area of freedom, security and justice' [1999] OJ C 19/1.

[15] See Paul James Cardwell and Tamara Hervey, 'The Role of Law in a New Intergovernmentalism European Union' in Christopher J Bickerton, Dermot Hodson, and Uwe Puetter (eds), *The New Intergovernmentalism: States and Supernational Actors in the Post-Maastricht Era* (Oxford University Press 2015); see also Joanne Scott, 'In Legal Limbo: Post-Legislative Guidance as a Challenge for European Administrative Law' (2011) 48(2) Common Market Law Review 329; Steven Vaughan, 'Differentiation and Disfunction: An Exploration of Post-Legislative Guidance Practices in 14 EU Agencies' (2015) 17 Cambridge Yearbook of European Legal Studies 66; Oana Stefan, 'Soft Law and the Promise of Transparency in the Member States' in Mariolina Elianronio, Emilia Korkea-aho, and Oana Stefan (eds), *EU Soft Law in the Member States* (Hart Publishing 2021).

[16] Giandomenico Majone, 'The European Commission: The Limits of Centralization and the Perils of Parliamentarization' (2002) 15(3) Governance 375.

the supranational aspect of EU integration as represented by the Commission out of the picture. Although many accounts of the Commission's post-Maastricht position point to its less central role in European integration, over the longer term a more complex picture emerges where the Commission has adapted its place in the institutional machinery.[17] The rise of intergovernmentalism spearheaded by the second and third pillars, plus the central role of the Council in the headline issues of the day (including migration, but also economic policy and the recovery from the Covid pandemic), has not prevented the Commission as a 'competence maximiser'[18] from developing its networking role, in conjunction with Member State actors. The Commission has, since the 1990s, been identified as striving to be both the EU's 'policy entrepreneur' and 'policy manager',[19] suggesting a more behind-the-scenes role than that of the (national) politicians front and centre in the Council, especially when responding to crises. The Commission has not always succeeded in doing so, hence the limited progress on some of the legislative instruments it has proposed, particularly in the earlier days of the post-Amsterdam arrangements.[20] But alongside a renewed, central role of the Council and the Member States, the proliferation of agencies, including in migration, has been one of the most obvious developments in EU governance in the past two decades.[21] Since the Commission does not possess its own agencies with the Member States who are able to implement or oversee policies, the Commission has instead built close cooperation with a variety of agencies across different policy areas, which have varied powers delegated to them.[22] The Commission has assumed the role of mediator in cases of interinstitutional conflict, signalling a willingness (rather than an opposition) to legitimize resource expansion.[23] Given the prominence of the European Border and Coast Guard Agency (Frontex) and the European Asylum

[17] John Peterson, 'The Commission and the New Intergovernmentalism: Calm with the Storm?' in Christopher J Bickerton, Dermot Hodson, and Uwe Puetter (eds), *The New Intergovernmentalism: States and Supranational Actors in the Post-Maastricht Era* (Oxford University Press 2015) 206.

[18] Mark Pollack, 'Creeping Competence: The Expanding Agenda of the European Community' (1994) 14 Journal of Public Policy 95.

[19] Brigid Laffan, 'From Policy Entrepreneur to Policy Manager: The Challenge Facing the European Commission' (1997) 4(3) Journal of European Public Policy 422.

[20] Georg Menz, 'The European Commission as a Policy Entrepreneur in European Migration Policy Making' (2013) 3(3) Regions and Cohesion 86.

[21] See, inter alia, Morten Egeberg and Jarle Trondal, 'Researching European Union Agencies: What Have We Learnt (and Where Do We Go from Here)?' (2017) 55(4) JCMS: Journal of Common Market Studies 675; Madalina Busuioc, Martijn Groenleer, and Jarle Trondal, *The Agency Phenomenon in the European Union: Emergence, Institutionalisation and Everyday Decision-Making* (Manchester University Press 2012); Berthold Rittberger and Arndt Wonka, 'Agency Governance in the European Union' (2011) 18(6) Journal of European Public Policy 780.

[22] Morton Egeberg, 'The European Commission' in Michelle Cini and Nieves Borragán, *European Union Politics*, 7th edn (Oxford University Press 2022) 152; Peterson, 'The Commission and the New Intergovernmentalism' (n 17) 206.

[23] Michalis Moutselos, 'Expansion Without Mandates: Border and Asylum Agencies in European Union Migration Governance' (2024) 38(1) *Governance* 1.

Support Office (EASO), migration governance, including with agencies working in border zones and 'hot spots', is no exception.[24]

A singular view of the Commission as an institution that seeks greater integration and harmonization above all else, and often in opposition to Member States, is not borne out by the development of migration law and governance. Rather, as Lahav and Luedtke observe, the Commission has been at pains to show itself an 'ally [to Member States] in tougher border control and immigration enforcement'.[25] This aim does not negate its role as either the guardian of the Treaties or the motor of integration, since tougher EU controls might well be indicative of cooperation or even harmonization. However, there is a tension between the Commission maintaining its independence from the Member States and seeking to maximize its function as a central force in migration.

An example of this tension can be seen in the conclusion of Readmission Agreements. The Commission has long argued that these are essential in the fight against illegal/irregular migration. The Commission receives a negotiating mandate with a third country from the Council, placing itself at the centre of the process. The Commission has also tried to maximize its role, and inter alia the coordination of EU-wide policy, by including third country nationals who have transited through the partner state.[26] The problem then becomes one of actually concluding a Readmission Agreement with a third state: accepting the return of citizens of that country (assuming that their nationality has been established by the authorities in the Member State) is part of international law and numerous multilateral texts concluded between the EU and third states,[27] but accepting nationals of other states who have transited (or assumed to have done so) places a potentially large and unspecific burden on the partner. This is one of the reasons why Readmission Agreements have not been successfully concluded to the extent that the Commission or the Member States would like, and the lack of such

[24] Chiara Loschi and Peter Slominski, 'Interagency Relations and the EU Migration Crisis: Strengthening of Law Enforcement through Agencification?' in Johannes Pollak and Peter Slominski (eds), *The Role of EU Agencies in the Eurozone and Migration Crisis: European Administrative Governance* (Palgrave Macmillan 2021); Chiara Loschi and Peter Slominski, 'The EU Hotspot Approach in Italy: Strengthening Agency Governance in the Wake of the Migration Crisis' (2022) 44(6) Journal of European Integration 769.

[25] Gallya Lahav and Adam Luedtke, 'Immigration Policy' in C Bretherton and M Mannin (eds), *The Europeanization of European Politics* (Palgrave Macmillan 2013) 111.

[26] Annabelle Roig and Thomas Huddleston, 'EC Readmission Agreements: A Re-Evaluation of the Political Impasse' (2007) 9(3) European Journal of Migration and Law 363.

[27] See, for instance, the Khartoum Process launched between the EU and states in the Horn of Africa, including the Joint Valletta Action Plan: European Council, 'Valletta Summit, 11–12 November 2015 Action Plan' (11–12 November, Valletta, 2015) https://www.consilium.europa.eu/media/21839/action_plan_en.pdf, accessed 7 June 2025; and the Cairo Declaration and Action Plan, 9 April 2025, which includes commitments to '[e]nhance international, regional and bilateral cooperation on return and readmission, based on States' obligation under international law and bilateral agreements to readmit their own nationals': Khartoum Process, 'Cairo Action Plan' (9 April, Cairo, 2025) https://www.khartoumprocess.net/resources/political-documents/cairo-action-plan/download, accessed 7 June 2025.

agreements providing a catalyst for the pursuit of alternative methods to achieve the same aim.[28]

For the Commission, therefore, being in the driving seat of this type of negotiation has a dual advantage. First, it is placed at the core of the decision-making process. Second, and relatedly, it engages the principles of loyal cooperation and largely prevents Member States from acting unilaterally. Molinari has argued that the Commission deftly uses the requirement for sincere cooperation between the Member States (as set out in the Treaty)[29] to set out at an early stage when requesting a negotiation mandate the Union's consorted action. As a result, this imposes on the Member States 'special duties of action and abstention'.[30]

As a result, by adopting the same language of exclusion and 'fortress Europe' as the Member States, the Commission is able to position itself as an ally and shield itself against any attempt to exclude it from this dynamic area of cooperation which has become central to the EU agenda. It has not, however, used its privileged position as being removed from direct electoral scrutiny to either resist the moves towards 'fortress Europe' or steer the policy towards other aspects of the GAMM.

In the emergence of new forms of governance, the Commission has sought to place itself at the centre, or as closest to, the centre of decision-making and innovation. This has partly been through the synergy with migration as foreign policy/external relations. As such, speaking about 'the Commission' as a coherent whole requires a further depth of analysis due to the different logics applying across the Directorates-General,[31] and the different levels of contact with external actors.[32] The cluster in the European Commission focusing on external action (the 'Commissioners Group on External Action') was originally chaired by the HRVP but did not include the Commissioner responsible for migration and home affairs. In late 2016 it was expanded to this effect, with foreign policy actors in the EEAS and the Commission working closely with Commission home affairs officials and JHA agencies in the development of the Migration Partnerships with African countries.[33]

Therefore, while the Commission might have been expected to be placed on the sidelines as migration policy moves away from the more traditional forms

[28] See the discussion in Chapter 7.

[29] Article 4(3) TEU.

[30] Caterina Molinari, 'Sincere Cooperation Between EU and Member States in the Field of Readmission: The More the Merrier?' (2021) 23 The Cambridge Yearbook of European Legal Studies 269, 282.

[31] Yves de Neuilly, 'Y a-t-il un pilote dans la gestion des crises? Attentes et enjeux de cohérence dans les interventions européennes extérieures' (2022) 181(1) Revue française d'administration publique 149, 158.

[32] Pierre Alayrac and others, 'Des bureaucraties poreuses? Les interactions de la commission européenne et du secrétariat du conseil avec leur environnement, et leur influence sur leurs préférences en termes de gouvernance' (2022) 181(1) Revue française d'administration publique 41.

[33] Nathalie Tocci, 'Resilience and the Role of the European Union in the World' (2020) 41(2) Contemporary Security Policy 176. Migration Partnerships are discussed in detail in Chapter 7.

of governance, it has remained a central actor. The GAMM points clearly to the Commission as the lead in the development of such tools as Migration Partnerships and the initiatives and projects carried out under them (see GAMM).[34] On the EU–Türkiye Statement, rather than decrying its lack of central role, it has done the opposite and cited the Statement as a successful model to follow. It was able to position itself as a broker of the 'deal', relying on its technical expertise, networks, and personal links between individual Commissioners and the government of Türkiye.[35] And, despite the emphasis it places on the Treaty-based obligations for sincere cooperation, the Commission—via its President—has not been reticent in lauding the benefits of bilateral 'deals' between Member States and third countries, such as Italy and Albania, in the 'fight' against irregular migration.[36]

While the text of the Treaty might have changed relatively little in terms of its role, accounts of the Commission as a technically focused executive arm with the integration of the EU through legislation as its only goal are outdated. The Commission is a large and multi-faceted actor, and much like national government, comprising ministers and ministries with varying interests and levels of influence, is not a monolithic actor. In migration, different DGs have a variety of approaches to crises, depending on whether they are cast as humanitarian or security-based[37] and how these logics play out in the public sphere.[38]

Yet, in its most visible public role as a key EU institution, the Commission is, after all, largely headed by experienced politicians drawn from national systems who appreciate and understand how to adapt the institution, or at the very least to mould it. As the 'EU in crisis' term took hold in the mid-2010s, the role of the Commission in its relations with Member States and need to engage with them as a means to confront these crises has become prominent.[39] The increasingly important—and visible—role of the Commission President and Vice-Presidents, for which it is now the norm to choose former senior national politicians from

[34] Commission, 'Communication from the Commission to the European Parliament, The Council, The European Economic and Social Committee and the Committee of the Regions: The Global Approach to Migration and Mobility' COM(2011) 743 final (GAMM).

[35] Elena Baracani and Virginia Sarotto, 'The European Commission's Role in EU–Turkey Migration: Political Leadership through Strategic Framing' (2022) 46(3) West European Politics 573; David Moloney, 'From Turkey to Belarus: Exploring the EU's Response to Migration Crises through the Lens of Functional Spillover' (2026) Journal of Ethnic and Migration Studies, early view, doi:10.1080/1369183X.2026.2631128, accessed 30 March 2026.

[36] Letter from Ursula von der Leyen to the European Council (13 December 2023) https://www.eerstekamer.nl/overig/20231222/letter_to_eu_leaders_on_migration/document3/f=/vm9piyytumzb.pdf, accessed 7 June 2025.

[37] Alexandra Berger and Christof Roos, 'The European Commission and the Migration–Development Nexus: Accessing Resources and Increasing the Mandate' (2024) 51(1) Journal of Ethnic and Migration Studies 268.

[38] David Moloney and Sebastiaan Princen, 'Assessing the Role of the European Council and the European Commission during the Migration and COVID-19 Crises' (2023) 47(7) West European Politics 1556; De Neuilly, 'Y a-t-il un pilote dans la gestion des crises?' (n 31) 158.

[39] John Peterson, 'Junker's Political European Commission and an EU in Crisis' (2017) 55(2) JCMS: Journal of Common Market Studies 349.

a Member State, positions the Commission as a rather different actor than the 'technocratic' label often suggests. As a result, neither the supranational versus intergovernmental nor the Commission versus Council labels, in their binary terms, can tell us very much about the contemporary state of EU migration governance,[40] or crisis governance more generally.[41] Rather, the Commission has accepted the role of informality or soft instruments in which it is not visibly in the driving seat, but where it has a significant role to play as an agenda-setter.[42] The advantage here for the Commission is found in the ability to be a significant player even where its attempts to introduce legislation have not succeeded. As a result, the Commission has increased its capability to use interpretative documents aimed at exploiting the gaps and ambiguities of the Directive.[43]

Migration, the rise of informality, and the general conditions of 'crisis' since the 2010s have thus contributed to a changing role for the Commission, and arguably more so than any of the other institutions. The Commission's role in migration remains central, and the emphasis it places on the traditional integration-through-law model is evident in the most recent Migration Pact. However, the Commission's involvement in informality is more obscured, including by the Council and Member States playing a more front-and-centre role. But this in turn helps us see how the Commission has managed to position itself as a key actor in such as highly politicized field as migration,[44] where it is difficult to conceive of a previous long-term issue to which so much national and European political capital has been attached.

5.2 The Council of the European Union (Council of Ministers)

The Council took centre stage in the second and third pillars after the Treaty of Maastricht. At the time, there was much speculation as to the role of the Council, and in particular what this meant for the Commission[45] and the legal dynamics of

[40] See further, Pierre Bocquillon, 'Setting the European Agenda in Hard Times: The Commission, the European Council and the EU Polycrisis' (2024) 46(4) Journal of European Integration 567.

[41] See Isabel Camisão and Paulo Maior, 'A Convincing Narrative to Control the Crisis Response? The Role of the President of the European Commission during the COVID-19 Pandemic' (2024) 63(3) JCMS: Journal of Common Market Studies 821.

[42] Neil Nugent and Mark Rhinard, 'Is the European Commission Really in Decline?' (2016) 54(5) JCMS: Journal of Common Market Studies 1199.

[43] Peter Slominski and Florian Trauner, 'Reforming Me Softly—How Soft Law Has Changed EU Return Policy since the Migration Crisis' (2020) 44(1) West European Politics 93, 100.

[44] Galina Cornelisse and Marcelle Reneman, 'Border Procedures in the Commission's New Pact on Migration and Asylum: A Case of Politics Outplaying Rationality?' (2020) 26(3–4) European Law Journal 181.

[45] See, for example, Robert Lane, 'New Community Competences under the Maastricht Treaty' (1993) 30 Common Market Law Review 939; Trevor Hartley, 'Constitutional and Institutional Aspects of the Maastricht Agreement' (1993) 42(2) International and Comparative Law Quarterly 213; Brigid Laffan, 'The Treaty of Maastricht: Political Authority and Legitimacy' in Alan W Catruny and Glenda G Rosenthal (eds), *The State of the European Community: The Maastricht Debates and Beyond* (Lynne Rienner Publishers 1993); Daniel Wincott, 'Is the Treaty of Maastricht an Adequate "Constitution" for the European Union?' (1994) 72(4) Public Administration 573.

integration.[46] The immediate consequence of the pillar structure was that 'intergovernmental' has remained a characteristic of CFSP, and to a lesser extent JHA/FSJ too. Yet 'intergovernmentalist' has been the dominant frame for migration, even after the *Communitarization* or *Lisbonization* of migration as a policy area.[47]

The new pillars were endowed with new instruments—joint actions, common strategies, decisions, resolutions and conclusions—and deliberately distinct from the familiar Regulations and Directives of the first, Community, pillar. It took time for the qualities and contours of the new instruments to 'settle in' to the system of governance.[48] Some were underused—for example, Common Strategies in the CFSP[49]—and in JHA there was widespread recognition that the third pillar instruments were inadequate. While the non-binding or enforceable nature of instruments adopted for the CFSP might be justifiable, they were unlikely to function for migration. The exclusion of the CJEU did not help to develop whatever legal qualities they might have.[50]

With the Commission's role (initially) more limited, the Council became the focal point of the development of migration law and policy. In the post-Maastricht search for the next steps in European integration, the Council gradually assumed a leadership role, in sharp contrast to its pre-1992 position.[51]

There is a paradox, however, which is mirrored in the areas formerly under both the second and the third pillar. On the one hand, the Council—as composed of Member States—permitted the granting of competences to the Commission to propose legislation in areas which feature as an almost constant on the EU's agenda. And yet, when those proposals are made, they are subject to intense discussion and 'watering down'. The post-Amsterdam experience of the first Directives on migration demonstrates that the time taken for them to be passed in some form does not demonstrate an enthusiasm to capitalize on the new competences and meet the goals of the revised Treaty. Denza argued in 2002 that difficulties relating to the need for 'cross-pillar action' might be the source of institutional conflict.

[46] Shaw and More, *The New Legal Dynamics of European Union* (n 11).

[47] Saskia Bonjour, Ariadna Servent, and Eiko Thielemann, 'Beyond Venue Shopping and Liberal Constraint: A New Research Agenda for EU Migration Policies and Politics' (2018) 25(3) Journal of European Public Policy 409, 409.

[48] Monica Den Boer, 'An Area of Freedom, Security and Justice: Bogged Down by Compromise' in David O'Keefe and Patrick M Twomey (eds), *Legal Issues of the Amsterdam Treaty* (Hart 1999) 303.

[49] Claire Spencer, 'The EU and Common Strategies: The Revealing Case of the Mediterranean' (2001) 6 European Foreign Affairs Review 31.

[50] Eileen Denza, *The Intergovernmental Pillars of the European Union* (Oxford University Press 2002) 202–03.

[51] See, inter alia, Fiona Hayes-Renshaw and Helen Wallace, 'Executive Power in the European Union: The Functions and Limits of the Council of Ministers' (1995) 2(4) Journal of European Public Policy 559; Robert Thomson and Madeleine Hosli, 'Who Has Power in the EU? The Commission, Council and Parliament in Legislative Decision-Making' (2006) 44(2) JCMS: Journal of Common Market Studies 391; Uwe Puetter, 'Europe's Deliberative Intergovernmentalism: The Role of the Council and European Council in EU Economic Governance' (2012) 19(2) Journal of European Public Policy 161.

However, the rapid development of techniques to deal with the post-Amsterdam set of competences suggests that institutions find ways of working through the complexities.[52] The lack of political will amongst the Member States to see through the legislative measures foreseen in the Treaty competences on irregular migration is even more evidence in the lack of movement towards cooperation in legal or regular migration.

At the same time, the theme of migration as a crisis and the role of the EU (or not) in confronting this and other crises since the 2010s demonstrates the 'up-loading' of national priorities from Member States to the Council. A look at the agendas and Council conclusions since 2010 demonstrates that migration features as a constant, and very often as the headline issue. As Tocci notes:

> While massive security threats, ranging from climate change to the weakening of the nuclear arms control regime, have represented subjects of expert discussion, the migration phenomenon has often appeared to be the be all and end all of many EU governments, and consequently of the Council of Ministers and European Council.[53]

The default position of the Council is therefore assumed to be restrictive towards all types of migration, and reticent towards enhancing any common standards which might be politically difficult to justify domestically or might risk 'attracting' irregular migration. Fink has shown that party politics and public opinion matter for EU Member States' positioning on migration policy, and the more right-wing parties there are in national governments, the more likely it is that a restrictive position is taken.[54] The EU level is not insulated from domestic politics and the confidentiality of the Council cannot be used to 'hide' from national-level scrutiny. Rather, Member States governments use positioning on EU migration as a response to—but also to cater to—domestic public opinion. This is particularly the case for external migration rather than intra-EU migration, and potentially translates to anti-EU integration too.[55] It is no accident that migration law and policy is the clearest example of differentiated integration, a logic which permeates the intergovernmental foundations of JHA and the AFSJ.[56]

[52] Denza, *The Intergovernmental Pillars of the European Union* (n 50) 309.

[53] Tocci, 'Resilience and the Role of the European Union in the World' (n 33).

[54] Simon Fink, 'Party Politics and the Shaping of Migration Policy in the Council of Ministers' (2023) 10(1) European Policy Analysis 128.

[55] Cigdem Kentmen-Cin and Cengiz Erisen, 'Anti-Immigration Attitudes and the Opposition to European Integration: A Critical Assessment' (2017) 18(1) European Union Politics 3.

[56] Ariane d'Appollonia, 'EU Migration Policy and Border Controls: From Chaotic to Cohesive Differentiation' (2019) 17(5) Comparative European Politics 192; Nadia El-Enany, 'The Perils of Differentiated Integration in the Field of Asylum' in Bruno De Witte, Andrea Ott, and Ellen Vos (eds), *Between Flexibility and Disintegration: The Trajectory of Differentiation in EU Law* (Edward Elgar 2017) 362.

In this scenario, and given the national importance of migration on agendas across all the Member States, there is a debate about whether the EU institutions act as a 'liberal constraint' on the Council as representing the restrictive end of migration policymaking. This argument has been advanced in relation to the Commission, Court, and Parliament,[57] in relation to rights and particularly family migration rights.[58] The Court has generally been regarded as upholding adherence to the rule of law and acting as a brake on excessively harsh rules,[59] though is often criticized for vagueness, lack of consistency, and leaving too much interpretation to the Member States.[60]

The danger here is to assume that the Council is always capable of acting as a single actor with a singular approach to legislation. Looking below the surface, there is in fact a wide variety of approaches amongst the Member States, and migration is perhaps the best example of where these differences are most sharply felt. The Dublin Regulations have been contested intently since their existence by Member States in the south of the EU, who feel—or at the least claim—that the Regulations impose an undue or unfair burden on them. Refugee 'quotas', passed by Qualified Majority Voting, were challenged by Hungary and Slovakia. This is not the first time that a Member State has challenged the law-making process in the Court of Justice, but the political salience of migration and characterization of 'Brussels' as an enemy attempting to change the nature of a Member State has (electoral) resonance. When, at the same time, there is an expectation that the institutions will respond to the 'challenge' or 'crisis' posed by migration, the potential for deadlock in the Council and failure to respond also carries risks for both the Council as an institution and the Member States.[61]

The use of informal and newer modes of governance in migration has been encouraged by the Council. In this respect, the strategy documents ranging from the Hague and Stockholm Programmes to the GAM/GAMM and the more recent 'pacts' underline the importance of the use of innovative means, particularly to combat irregular migration and operating out of public view and scrutiny. One key way of pursuing informality is seeking the cooperation of third states, which may involve the signing of agreements.[62] The post-Lisbon arrangements for the

[57] Christian Kaunert and Sarah Léonard, 'The Development of the EU Asylum Policy: Venue-Shopping in Perspective' (2012) 19(9) Journal of European Public Policy 1396.

[58] Laura Block and Saskia Bonjour, 'Fortress Europe or Europe of Rights? The Europeanisation of Family Migration Policies in France, Germany and the Netherlands' (2013) 15(2) European Journal of Migration and Law 203.

[59] Diego Acosta and Andrew Geddes, 'The Development, Application and Implications of an EU Rule of Law in the Area of Migration Policy' (2013) 51(2) Journal of Common Market Studies 179.

[60] Marie-Laure Basilien-Gainche, 'Immigration Detention under the Return Directive: The CJEU Shadowed Lights' (2015) 17(1) European Journal of Migration and Law 104–26; Janine Silga, 'Differentiation in the EU Migration Policy: The "Fractured" Values of the EU' (2022) 7(2) *European Papers: A Journal on Law and Integration* 909.

[61] Christof Roos, 'How to Overcome Deadlock in EU Immigration Politics' (2013) 51(6) International Migration 67.

[62] See Chapter 6 for detailed discussion.

negotiation and signing of agreements have lacked clarity in terms of the respective powers of the Council and the Commission, and have resulted in a series of cases before the CJEU. On this point, the Court of Justice has clarified the terms of the Treaty, particularly Article 218 TFEU,[63] where the Commission successfully challenged the Council's decision allowing a protocol on fisheries with Gabon to be signed by Portugal on behalf of the Council.[64] The rationale for doing so was on the basis of the Commission's role in the representation of the Union as per Article 17(1) TEU. Yet, it broke with a long-standing tradition of both the Council and Commission signing agreements, and leaves open the question of how both institutions will act in the future.[65]

Non-binding instruments—for which the EU is not alone responsible for their increased use[66]—have represented a 'normative transformation' in EU external relations[67] and its legal architecture.[68] These are covered in more detail later,[69] but their increase in use sheds light on the Council–Commission relationship and their willingness to make 'soft' agreements with third countries that do not fall within the scope of Article 218 TFEU and thus also evade scrutiny by the Court.[70] The Council has been willing to let the Commission engage in this kind of agreement-making, even against the background of the inter-institutional battles played out in the Court.[71] As a result of a CJEU judgment[72] which annulled

[63] Case C-551/21 *Commission v Council (Signature d'accords internationaux)* ECLI:EU:C:2024:281.

[64] For comment, see Gesa Kübek, 'Reflections on the Signature of EU International Agreements and the Court of Justice's Judgment in Case C-551/21, Commission v Council' (*EU Law Live*, 23 April 2024) https://eulawlive.com/op-ed-reflections-on-the-signature-of-eu-international-agreements-and-the-court-of-justices-judgment-in-case-c%E2%80%91551-21-commission-v-council-by-gesa-kubek, accessed 7 June 2025; Felipe de Souza, 'Who You Gonna Call? Insights from the ECJ's Case C-551/21 on the Signature of International Agreements' (2024) 9(1) European Papers 121.

[65] Davide Genini, 'Breaking a Tradition: How Signing of Agreements Is No Longer a Matter for the Council' (2024) 9(1) European Papers 145.

[66] See, inter alia, Curtis Bradley, Jack Goldsmith, and Oona Hathaway, 'The Rise of Nonbinding International Agreements: An Empirical, Comparative, and Normative Analysis' (2023) 90(5) University of Chicago Law Review 128; Joost Pauwelyn, Ramses Wessel, and Jan Wouters, 'When Structures Become Shackles: Stagnation and Dynamics in International Lawmaking' (2014) 25(3) European Journal of International Law 733.

[67] Ramses Wessel, 'Normative Transformations in EU External Relations: The Phenomenon of "Soft" International Agreements' (2021) 44(1) West European Politics 72; Sabine Saurugger and Fabien Terpan, 'Normative Transformations in the European Union: On Hardening and Softening Law' (2020) 44(1) West European Politics 1.

[68] Graham Butler, 'EU Foreign Policy and Other EU External Relations in Times of Crisis: Forcing the Law to Overlap?' in Elżbieta Kużelewska, Amy Weatherburn, and Dariusz Kloza (eds), *Irregular Migration as a Challenge for Democracy* (Cambridge University Press 2018); Paula Andrade, 'EU External Competences in the Field of Migration: How to Act Externally When Thinking Internally' (2018) 55(1) Common Market Law Review 157.

[69] See Chapters 6 and 7.

[70] Paula Andrade, 'The Distribution of Powers Between EU Institutions for Conducting External Affairs through Non-Binding Instruments' (2016) 1(1) European Papers 115.

[71] Andrea Ott, 'Informalization of EU Bilateral Instruments: Categorization, Contestation, and Challenges' (2020) 39 Yearbook of European Law 569.

[72] Case C-660/13 *Council of the EU v Commission* (MoU with Switzerland) ECLI:EU:C:2016:616; see further, Thomas Velleren, 'On Conferral, Institutional Balance and Non-binding International

the Commission's decision to sign a non-binding addendum to an agreement with Switzerland on the basis that the Commission infringed the principle of distribution of powers (Article 13(2) TEU) and the principle of institutional balance, the Council and Commission made procedural arrangements for the conclusion of non-binding instruments.[73]

Finally, the High Representative for Foreign Affairs and Security Policy has, since the Treaty of Lisbon, straddled both the Council and the Commission, where in the latter the post-holder is a Vice President. The High Representative for Foreign and Security Policy was initially VP of the Council, later becoming also a VP of the Commission in a 'double-hatted' role. The aim was to provide a voice and face to EU foreign policy and external relations and provide an institutional boost to the coherence of the EU's policies.

The mandate of the High Representative is focused on foreign policy, but given that migration is an inherent part of the EU's external relations and that relationships with third countries both near and far from the EU's borders are constantly featured high on the EU's agenda, the institutional position of the HR/VP needs further exploration.

The aim, as per the Treaty, is to 'ensure the consistency of the Union's external action'. This institutional innovation, which was originally intended in the Constitutional Treaty to have the title of Foreign Minister, has largely had a workload responding to sets of global challenges while at the same time working out the intricate mechanisms in the EU's complex system of governance and competences. Migration is one such challenge, and 'a key element in our overall foreign policy' as per Josep Borrell, High Representative from 2019 to 2024.[74]

With the fourth High Representative in the post-Lisbon period having taken office,[75] detailed comparison of the personalities, priorities, and politics of the post-holders has been possible.[76] The main task of the High Representative in promoting and ensuring coherence is a difficult one, especially in situations where

Agreements: The Swiss MoU Case' (2016) 1(3) European Papers 1225; Ivan Smyth. 'The Use of Soft Law Instruments in the European Union's External Relations: A Delicate Balance between Pragmatism, Transparency and Democratic Oversight' in Stephan Marquardt and Steven Blockmans (eds), *The European Union's Contribution to International Peace and Security* (Brill Nijhoff 2023).

[73] Council Decision (EU) 2017/684 of the European Parliament and of the Council of 5 April 2017 on establishing an information exchange mechanism with regard to intergovernmental agreements and non-binding instruments between Member States and third countries in the field of energy, and repealing Decision No 994/2012/EU.

[74] Joseph Borrel, 'Migration is a key element of our foreign policy' (*European Union External Action*, 7 February 2023) https://www.eeas.europa.eu/eeas/migration-key-element-our-foreign-policy_en, accessed 7 June 2025.

[75] Kaja Kallas was appointed in December 2024, following Catherine Ashton (2009–14), Federica Mogherini (2014–19), and Josep Borrell (2019–24). The High Representative is appointed by the European Council (Article 18(1) TEU).

[76] See, in particular, Niklas Helwig, *The EU High Representative: Foreign Policy Leadership in a Changing World* (Palgrave Macmillan 2024).

Member States have adopted positions which are contrary to agreed positions, for example on the Global Compact for Migration in 2018.[77]

5.3 The European Council

The European Council, which brings together the heads of state or government of the Member States with its own President, the President of the Commission, and the High Representative for Foreign and Security Policy,[78] began life as an informal grouping in 1974.[79] It gained the status of an institution of the EU in the TEU.[80] Its role, as per the TEU, is to give 'the necessary impetus' for the EU's development and it 'shall define the general political directions and priorities thereof'.[81]

Unlike the Council of the EU (Council of Ministers), it does not have legislative power but plays a crucial role in shaping high-level policies, including on migration. While it does not directly legislate or have a formal role in the legislative process, the European Council sets strategic guidelines that influence legislative and operational responses to migration challenges. Many of the documents explored in the previous chapters are under the auspices of the European Council.[82] The European Council's role as a decision-maker has come to prominence in the Brexit process, as the key institution responsible for setting out the parameters for future relations with an ex-Member State.[83] Subsequently, the Covid-19 pandemic and the recovery plan for Europe placed the European Council as a central institution for both decision-making and crisis-managing,[84] and an opportunity for policy learning.[85] Some doubt, however, whether this public image as a 'locus' is matched with an ability to produce meaningful and legally sound solutions which can become operational within the EU framework.[86] Simultaneously, the rule of

[77] Pauline Melin, 'The Global Compact for Migration: Lessons for the Unity of EU Representation' (2019) 21(2) European Journal of Migration and Law 194, 202.

[78] Article 15(2) TEU.

[79] Wolfgang Wessels, 'The Maastricht Treaty and the European Council: The History of an Institutional Evolution' (2012) 34(7) Journal of European Integration 753.

[80] Now Article 13(1) TEU.

[81] Article 15(1) TEU.

[82] See also Uwe Puetter, 'The European Council' in Christopher J Bickerton, Dermot Hodson, and Uwe Puetter (eds), *The New Intergovernmentalism: States and Supranational Actors in the Post-Maastricht Era* (Oxford University Press 2015) 170.

[83] Birgit Bujard and Wolfgang Wessels, 'The European Council and Brexit: From Accommodating an Awkward Partner towards Managing a Conflictual Relationship?' in John Fossum and Christopher Lord (eds), *Handbook on the European Union and Brexit* (Edward Elgar Publishing 2023).

[84] See Lucas Schramm, Ulrich Krotz, and Bruno De Witte, 'Building "Next Generation" after the Pandemic: The Implementation and Implications of the EU Covid Recovery Plan' (2022) 60 JCMS: Journal of Common Market Studies 114; Lucas Schramm and Wolfgang Wessels, 'The European Council as a Crisis Manager and Fusion Driver: Assessing the EU's Fiscal Response to the COVID-19 Pandemic' (2023) 45(2) Journal of European Integration 257.

[85] Stella Ladi and Dimitris Tsarouhas, 'EU Economic Governance and Covid-19: Policy Learning and Windows of Opportunity' (2020) 42(8) Journal of European Integration 1041.

[86] Sandrino Smeets and Derek Beach, 'New Institutional Leadership Goes Viral: EU Crisis Reforms and the Coming About of the Covid Recovery Fund' (2023) 62(2) European Journal of Political

law conditionality relating to 'backsliding' in several Member States, which became intertwined with both migration policy and the post-Covid recovery, has placed the European Council in the unenviable position of seeking to bring together (very) divergent and publicly expressed views of Member States on high politics issues.[87]

Since the 2015 migration 'crisis', the Council has been at the forefront of efforts to manage migration flows, enhance border security, and coordinate asylum policies among Member States. Its decisions have led to significant policy shifts, such as strengthening the role of Frontex[88] and deepening cooperation with third countries to curb irregular migration.[89] Such is its increased prominence in the institutional governance of the EU that it can be indicative of a reversal in the supranational development of EU.[90]

The European Council has been the key architect of externalization in migration governance and promoting cooperation and conditionality with third countries. Leveraging the bilateral relations between heads of state and government in the Council and the governments of third countries has allowed the European Council to broker such instruments as the EU–Türkiye Statement (although when challenged, the General Court made a distinction between the European Council as an institution and the Member States within it acting collectively).[91] Similarly, the European Council has supported Migration Partnerships with North African countries, such as Libya and Tunisia, to prevent departures and facilitate migrant returns. As a result, the European Council has found itself the focus of criticism for the process of outsourcing migration control to countries with poor human rights records, raising concerns about the treatment of migrants and the EU's adherence to international legal obligations.

Despite these possibilities and leverage, the European Council continues to face internal divisions among Member States on migration policy. Disagreements persist over issues such as burden-sharing, asylum reform, and solidarity mechanisms for frontline states such as Italy and Greece. While some countries advocate for a fair distribution of asylum-seekers across the EU, others, particularly in Central

Research 377; Sandrino Smeets and Derek Beach, 'Intergovernmentalism and Its Implications: New Institutional Leadership in Major EU Reforms' (2020) 27(8) Journal of European Public Policy 1137.

[87] Louise Fromont and Arnaud Van Waeyenberge, 'Trading Rule of Law for Recovery? The New EU Strategy in the Post-Covid Era' (2021) 27(1–3) European Law Journal 132.

[88] See below.

[89] European Council, 'Conclusions by the President of the European Council on the external dimension of migration' (*European Council of the European Union*, 30 June 2023) https://www.consilium.europa.eu/en/press/press-releases/2023/06/30/conclusions-by-the-president-of-the-european-council-on-the-external-dimension-of-migration/, accessed 7 June 2025.

[90] Anders Wivel, 'The EU's Soft Balancing Governance Model: Origins, Characteristics and Prospects for the Future' (2025) 101(1) International Affairs 17; see also Wolfgang Wessels, *The European Council* (Palgrave 2016).

[91] See the discussion of Case T-192/16 *NF v European Council* ECLI:EU:T:2017:128 below.

and Eastern Europe, oppose mandatory quotas. These tensions have hindered progress on a comprehensive and unified migration policy, forcing the Council to rely on ad hoc agreements and crisis-driven solutions rather than long-term structural reforms. As migration remains a key political challenge for the EU, the European Council's ability to forge consensus and implement effective policies will be critical in shaping the future of European migration governance.

5.4 The European Parliament

The European Parliament's previous lack of formal role in migration governance did not square with its long-standing interest in issues of migration. In the 1970s and 1980s, the European Parliament passed resolutions which demonstrated the interest of its members in the relationship between European integration and migration both from outside and within the EU.[92] The European Parliament was long regarded as a 'friend' of third country nationals, from the Vetter report in the 1970s which called for rights of political participation for migrants to its support of the European Migrants' Forum and numerous declarations on anti-racism.[93] Geddes noted in 2000 that pro-migration lobbies tended to see the European Parliament as a sympathetic institution, and thus the focus of alliance-building to counter the 'lowest common denominator' of Council-based decision-making.[94]

As an externally facing law and policy domain, the Parliament's formal role in migration has been limited. Successive Treaty reforms have increased the powers of the European Parliament, making it the EU institution that has witnessed the most profound changes in structure, identity, and role over the course of the European integration process.[95] In migration, however, its role was limited in the first moves towards progress in integration (or rather cooperation). The architects of the Treaty changes—that is, the Member States—feared the impact of involving the European Parliament in areas where sovereignty concerns remained high. The Treaty on European Union 1992 required consultation of the European Parliament for third pillar measures, but reports from MEPs in the 1990s revealed the frustrations of the institution, which found itself largely excluded.[96]

[92] See Maria Belloni, 'A Common Policy on Migration: A Step towards Citizens' Europe' (1987) 52(3) Il Politico 437, 441–42.

[93] Virginie Guirandon, 'European Integration and Migration Policy: Vertical Policy-Making as Venue Shopping' (2000) 38(2) JCMS: Journal of Common Market Studies 251, 264.

[94] Andrew Geddes, 'Lobbying for Migrant Inclusion in the European Union: New Opportunities for Transnational Advocacy?' (2000) 7(4) Journal of European Public Policy 632.

[95] See, inter alia, Ariadna Ripoll Servent, *The European Parliament* (Bloomsbury 2017); Ariadna Servent and Olivier Costa, 'The European Parliament: Powerful but Fragmented' in Dermot Hodson and others (eds), *The Institutions of the European Union* (Oxford University Press 2021); Richard Corbett and others, *The European Parliament*, 10th edn (John Harper Publishing 2024); Stelios Stavridis and Daniela Irrera, *The European Parliament and Its International Relations* (Routledge 2015).

[96] See Guirandon, 'European Integration and Migration Policy' (n 93) 264; Jean-Louis Bourlanges and David Martin, 'Report on the functioning of the Treaty on European Union with a view to the

The institutional position of the Parliament after the Treaty of Amsterdam did not improve, and, as Guirandon wrote soon after the entry into force of the Treaty, 'MEPs have mostly expressed their anger by rejecting Commission proposals in related areas, for instance on visa policy. Amsterdam sets a very high hurdle for the EP to have a policy role. During the five-year transitional period, the EP will have only a consultative role. Afterwards, co-decision may be extended to cover all or part of the areas covered by Title IV only after a unanimous vote by Council members.'[97]

Despite this deliberate limitation of its role, in migration and a number of other externally focused areas the Parliament has eked out a role and stamped its authority. Even where it lacks a legislative role, it has used its budgetary powers and other levers (such as the approval of the new Commission) to gain influence.[98] This has been the case, for example, in development policy, which is generally characterized as 'low' rather than the 'high' politics associated with the CFSP, or major trade agreements such as the EU–Canada Comprehensive Economic and Trade Agreement (CETA), the EU–US Transatlantic Trade and Investment Partnership (TTIP), or Brexit.[99] The European Parliament has been particularly effective in using times of crisis to expand its role beyond that which has been formally granted the institution, both formally and informally.[100] However, there is also evidence that this influence might be limited in areas close to state sovereignty, which would include migration alongside economic governance.[101] Alongside the growing

1996 Intergovernmental Conference' (European Parliament Committee on Institutional Affairs, A4–0102/95, 4 May 1995); Jean-Louis Bourlanges and David Martin, 'Note on the European Parliament's Priorities for the ICG and the New Amsterdam Treaty: Report and Initial Evolution of Results' (European Parliament, 15 July 1997).

[97] Guirandon, 'European Integration and Migration Policy' (n 93) 264.

[98] Johannes Pollak and Peter Slominski, 'The European Parliament: Adversary or Accomplice of the New Intergovernmentalism' in Christopher J Bickerton, Dermot Hodson, and Uwe Puetter (eds), *The New Intergovernmentalism: States and Supranational Actors in the Post-Maastricht Era* (Oxford University Press 2015) 248; Magnus G Schoeller and Peter Slominski, 'Scrutinising Frontex: The European Parliament and Accountability through Discharge' (2026) JCMS: Journal of Common Market Studies, early view, https://doi.org/10.1111/jcms.70097, accessed 30 March 2026.

[99] Paul James Cardwell and Davor Jančić, 'The European Parliament and Development Cooperation: Democratic Participation in the "Low Politics" of EU External Relations' (2019) 41(3) Journal of European Integration 365; Guri Rosén and Kolja Raube, 'Influence beyond Formal Powers: The Parliamentarisation of European Union Security Policy' (2018) 20(1) The British Journal of Politics and International Relations 69; Davor Jančić, 'TTIP and Legislative–Executive Relations in EU Trade Policy' (2017) 40(1) West European Politics 202; Katharina Meissner, 'Democratizing EU External Relations: The European Parliament's Informal Role in SWIFT, ACTA, and TTIP' (2016) 21(2) European Foreign Affairs Review 269.

[100] Carlos Closa, Felipe de León, and Gisela González, 'Pragmatism and the Limits to the European Parliament's Strategies for Self-Empowerment' (2021) 9 Politics and Governance 163; See also contributions to Adrienne Héritier and others (eds), *European Parliament Ascendant* (Palgrave Macmillan 2019).

[101] Edoardo Bressanelli and Nicola Chelotti, 'The European Parliament and Economic Governance: Explaining a Case of Limited Influence' (2018) 24(1) The Journal of Legislative Studies 72; Ariadna Servent and Florian Trauner, 'Do Supranational EU Institutions Make a Difference? EU Asylum Law before and after "Communitarization"' (2014) 21(8) Journal European Public Policy 1142.

significance of agencies in EU governance—not least Frontex[102]—the Parliament has also managed to shape its institutional design, which has had a positive effect on its accountability, even in the 'maximal sovereignty' domain of borders.[103]

There is a principal narrative of the European Parliament and migration, which helps to explain both the reason for its exclusion from law and policymaking on migration and its attempts to be further involved. Such narrative is that the European Parliament has established a reputation for openness towards different forms of migration, the elevation of reception standards for those seeking protection, and the linkage of migration with European values. As noted above, such reputation was established in the years before the Parliament was directly elected at the end of the 1970s.

However, the point at which the European Parliament gained institutional competence in law-making coincided with the emergence of a new narrative that its traditional openness and liberalism towards migration was shifting. In the specific example of the Returns Directive, Acosta makes the case that the Parliament could still be regarded as more sympathetic to migrants and their rights than the Council, but did not use its powers of influence to such an effect in the passing of this Directive.[104] Similarly, Vinciguerra's analysis of the legislative passage of two Directives in 2015 supports the view that the European Parliament's orientation is, at the very least, more nuanced than was previously assumed to be the case.[105] In a plenary vote in March 2026, the European Parliament agreed to proceed to the next stage of the legislative process for an updated EU common system for the return of third country nationals staying illegally in the EU via 'return hubs'. This attracted much comment on the punitive nature on the proposal itself, but also the way in which it was passed by the centre-right with support from the far-right groups in the Parliament.[106]

[102] See further in this chapter. Subsequent to the OLAF investigation into Frontex in 2022, the Parliament decided to postpone the discharge of Frontex's budget on the ground of lacking information with regard to the subject of the OLAF report. See Michele Gigli, 'The Potential of Budgetary Discharge for Political Accountability: Which Lessons from the Case of Frontex?' (2024) 30(1–2) European Law Journal 238.

[103] Pollack and Slominski, 'The European Parliament: Adversary or Accomplice of the New Intergovernmentalism' (n 98) 258; Katrin Huber, 'The European Parliament as an Actor in EU Border Policies: Its Role, Relations with Other EU Institutions, and Impact' (2015) 24(3) European Security 420.

[104] Diego Acosta, 'The Good, the Bad and the Ugly in EU Migration Law: Is the European Parliament Becoming Bad and Ugly? (The Adoption of Directive 2008/15: The Returns Directive)' (2009) 11(1) European Journal of Migration and Law 19.

[105] Maria Vinciguerra, 'Punching Below Its Weight: The Role of the European Parliament in Politicised Consultation Procedures' (2021) 9(3) Politics and Governance 29.

[106] David Colombi, 'The Return Regulation Will "ICE-ify" the EU's Migration Policy' (CEPS briefing, 26 March 2026) https://www.ceps.eu/the-return-regulation-will-ice-ify-the-eus-migration-policy/ accessed 30 March 2026; María Teresa Gil Bazo, 'EU "return hubs": what are they, and how will they change the rights of migrants and asylum seekers?' (*The Conversation*, 1 April 2026), https://theconversation.com/eu-return-hubs-what-are-they-and-how-will-they-change-the-rights-of-migrants-and-asylum-seekers-279692, accessed 1 April 2026.

How can this shift in institutional role in the EU's system of migration be explained? First, as a unitary actor, the political shifts within the institution are even more identifiable than in the Council. The rise to prominence of the main centre-right grouping, the EPP, from the 1990s/2000s placed the Parliament in parallel to the main tendencies of many of the Member State governments and signalled its openness towards more restrictive policies, particularly those on irregular migration—since this is where the bulk of the legislation on migration could be found[107]—rather than human rights. Enthusiasm for greater communitarization of EU migration law and policy was, even by the mid-2000s, muted among Members of the European Parliament, who appeared to prefer national regulation.[108] Some groups, particularly the Socialist (PES) and Liberal ALDE groups, underwent their own shifts, with a greater diversity of views within them.[109] Where the European Parliament did adopt a position supporting reform of the CEAS and strengthening the European dimension, it did not have the required effect on the Council.[110]

As a result, the Parliament has been regarded as adopting a much less liberal position on migration since its acquisition of full legislative power, and a position that has generally shifted closer to that of the Council. Various scholars have argued that the Parliament has tended to adopt much less liberal and more consensual positions since it has been granted full legislative power.[111] At the same time, the European Parliament's approach could equally be seen as one which is maximizing its position of influence, including appreciation of the direction of travel in the Council towards greater restrictiveness in policymaking.[112] With the advent of the multiple crises in the EU and the sheer volume of legislative and policymaking

[107] Ariadna Ripoll Servent, 'When Words Do Not Follow Deeds: An Analysis of Party Competition Between Centre-Right and Eurosceptic Radical-Right Parties in the European Parliament' in Petra Ahrens, Anna Elomäki, and Johanna Kantola (eds), *European Parliament's Political Groups in Turbulent Times* (Springer 2022).

[108] Gallya Lahav and Anthony Messina, 'The Limits of a European Immigration Policy: Elite Opinion and Agendas within the European Parliament' (2005) 43(4) JCMS: Journal of Common Market Studies 851.

[109] Esther Lopatin, 'The Changing Position of the European Parliament on Irregular Migration and Asylum under Co-Decision' (2013) 51(4) JCMS: Journal of Common Market Studies 740, 751.

[110] Jan Krotký and Petr Kaniok, 'Who Says What: Members of the European Parliament and Irregular Migration in the Parliamentary Debates' (2021) 30(2) European Security 178; Ariadna Ripoll Servent, 'Failing under the "Shadow of Hierarchy": Explaining the Role of the European Parliament in the EU's Asylum Crisis' (2019) 41(3) Journal of European Integration 293.

[111] Florian Trauner and Ariadna Servent, 'The *Communitarization* of the Area of Freedom, Security and Justice: Why Institutional Change Does Not Translate into Policy Change' (2016) 54(6) JCMS: Journal of Common Market Studies 1417; Ariadna Ripoll Servent, *Institutional and Policy Change in the European Parliament: Deciding on Freedom, Security and Justice* (Palgrave Macmillan 2015); Lopatin, 'The Changing Position of the European Parliament on Irregular Migration and Asylum under Co-Decision' (n 109); Bonjour, Servent, and Thielemann, 'Beyond Venue Shopping and Liberal Constraint' (n 47).

[112] Ariadna Servent, 'Point of No Return? The European Parliament after Lisbon and Stockholm' (2010) 19(2) European Security 191; Ariadna Servent, 'Playing the Co-Decision Game? Rules' Changes and Institutional Adaptation at the LIBE Committee' (2011) 34(1) Journal of European Integration 55.

activities, the Parliament has had to selectively pick its battles with the other institutions.[113]

The use of informal and newer tools of governance is largely the product of the Commission and Council working in a cooperative relationship outside of the formal Treaty processes. As one might expect, the Parliament has neither the access nor the ability to be involved. Here, therefore, and despite the synergy in recent years between the Parliament and Council's positions as detailed above, the Parliament has adopted the stance of a critical observer. The Parliament does have the opportunity to challenge courses of action which do not follow established procedures before the Court of Justice, but only insofar as it is, first, aware of them and, second, able to form an admissible argument. The Parliament's objections to informality have therefore been the result of not their involvement but rather the lack of it in the negotiation of informal agreements and in their implementation. A Readmission Agreement, as a 'formal' agreement concluded until Article 79(3) TFEU and Article 218(6) TFEU, requires the consent of the Parliament, but this is not the case for informal agreements, which operate outside the Treaty framework.[114]

Given the centrality of the European Parliament's *raison d'etre* as representative of the citizens of the EU in the EU's system of governance and institutional machinery, its exclusion from the types of modes of governance that are highlighted as a success is concerning.[115] Indeed, the European Parliament's 2021 Resolution on Human Rights and EU External Migration Policy[116] makes specific reference to the fact that 'the EU has concluded at least 11 informal agreements but only one new readmission agreement; whereas informal agreements between the EU and third countries do not provide a predictable policy or any stable and coherent statutory framework provisions on irregular migration' and to 'the absence of operational, reporting, monitoring, evaluation and accountability mechanisms for individual cases which track and respond to potential violations, as well as the lack of effective

[113] Marine Bardou and Tom Delreux, 'How the European Parliament Chooses Its Battles: Parliamentary Resolutions on the Negotiation of International Agreements' (2025) JCMS: Journal of Common Market Studies, early view, https://onlinelibrary.wiley.com/doi/full/10.1111/jcms.13720, accessed 7 June 2025.

[114] Sara Poli, 'The Integration of Migration Concerns into EU External Policies: Instruments, Techniques and Legal Problems' (2020) 5(1) European Papers 71.

[115] Martino Reviglio, 'The Shift to Soft Law at Europe's Borders: Between Legal Efficiency and Legal Validity' (2023) 23(1) Global Jurist 23; Christina Eckes, 'How the European Parliament's Participation in International Relations Affects the Deep Tissue of the EU's Power Structures' (2014) 12(4) International Journal of Constitutional Law 904; Ariadna Servent, 'The Role of the European Parliament in International Negotiations after Lisbon' (2014) 21(4) Journal of European Public Policy 568; Juan Vara, 'The European Parliament in the Conclusion of International Agreements Post-Lisbon: Entrenched Between Values and Prerogatives' in Juan Santos Vara and Soledad Rodríguez Sánchez-Tabernero (eds), *The Democratisation of EU International Relations through EU Law* (Routledge 2018).

[116] European Parliament, 'Human rights protection and the EU external migration policy European Parliament resolution of 19 May 2021 on human rights protection and the EU external migration policy' (2020/2116(INI)).

judicial remedies for persons whose rights are allegedly violated as a consequence of informal EU agreements and financial cooperation', and 'notes with concern that this blending of executive responsibilities has created a lack of sufficient and coherent oversight of the Commission's activities that would enable Parliament to exert democratic scrutiny over the EU's external migration policy'.[117]

Sebastião has suggested that there are 'signs of the creation of a pro-security grand coalition comprising centre-left, centre-right and right in asylum issues'.[118] Thus, while the political orientation of the Parliament in recent years might have made it—as an institution—more inclined to find common ground on the restrictive stances adopted by the Council, its exclusion from the search for newer, informal modes of governance has pointed the Parliament back towards its familiar terrain of highlighting the importance of (human) rights and ensuring that its powers and competences are not usurped. The more complex, polarized, and changing nature of the European Parliament's traditionally held positions, such as advocating for Social Europe, has been noted by other observers too.[119]

5.5 The Court of Justice of the European Union

The Court of Justice sits apart from the other institutions in the EU's system of migration governance insofar as it plays a reactive role. The Court's role, as defined in the Treaties, is to 'ensure that in the interpretation and application of the Treaties the law is observed'.[120] The Court has long been called upon to rule on migration rights regarding third country nationals, particularly those from Türkiye.[121] As such, the Court enjoyed a familiarity with the kind of cases that began to reach it after the Treaty of Amsterdam. The Treaty gave the Court jurisdiction over all JHA measures, split between the issues of immigration, asylum, and civil law, as well as policing and criminal law. However, jurisdiction over each of these matters was

[117] ibid para L.

[118] Dina Sebastião, 'Politicisation of Asylum and Refugee and the Signs of Political Contagion Effect in European Parliament' (2025) 31(2) The Journal of Legislative Studies 399.

[119] See, for instance, Paul Copeland, Anna Elomäki, and Barbara Gaweda, 'Filtering Politicisation towards a More Social Europe? The European Parliament and EU Social Legislation' (2024) 32(6) Journal of European Public Policy 1467.

[120] Article 19 TEU.

[121] Notably, Case C-12/86 *Meryem Demirel v Stadt Schwäbisch Gmünd* ECLI:EU:C:1987:400 and Case C-434/93 *Ahmet Bozkurt v Staatssecretaris van Justitie* ECLI:EU:C:1995:168. See further, Kees Groenendijk, 'The Court of Justice and the Development of EEC–Turkey Association Law' in Daniel Thym and Margarite Zoeteweij-Turhan (eds), *Rights of Third-Country Nationals under EU Association Agreements* (Brill Nijhoff 2015); AP Van der Mei, 'The Bozkurt-Interpretation Rule and the Legal Status of Family Members of Turkish Workers under Decision 1/80 of the EEC–Turkey Association Council' (2009) 11(4) European Journal of Migration and Law 367; Narin Tezcan/Idriz, 'Free Movement of Persons Between Turkey and the EU: To Move or Not to Move? The Response of the Judiciary' (2009) 46(5) Common Market Law Review 1621.

subject to special rules.[122] Of particular note was that only final courts in Member States could refer to the CJEU.[123] The rationale was the risk of overload for the Court, as a single court potentially facing a huge number of contested decisions, especially on asylum, from Member States who often have immigration as a separate jurisdiction with multiple, specific courts. This risk was, at the time, the focus of critique as having the potential to undermine legal certainty and the consistent interpretation of EU law without the input of the CJEU that has been so vital in other areas of law.[124] The removal of the restriction led to an increase in cases referred to the Court from national courts, and extensive opportunities for the Court to be involved in shaping the law.[125] The role of the Court has, in migration as in foreign policy, engaged a certain amount of boundary-testing in terms of what the Treaty intended. This has also allowed the Court to establish general principles of law to be applied.[126]

As explored in Chapter 3, the Court has had a strong role to play in the constitutionalization of migration as part of JHA and the AFSJ and the EU's legal order.[127] As such, the Court's role rests on a balancing act: its constitutional role to uphold the Treaties, including provisions on loyal cooperation among the Member States, recognizing and enforcing the protection of rights, including the scope, contents, and effects of migrants' rights, and at the same time the need to be mindful of the shared competence in migration between the EU institutions and the Member States.[128] Unlike in CFSP, where foreign policy was 'ring-fenced' from the rest of the Treaty provisions and in particular the purview of the Court,[129] the Court is acutely aware of its need to balance both the protection of rights and the need to recognize the political will of the institutions (including the Parliament) in enforcing returns under the terms of the Directive.

Beyond the initial phase of migration legislation, the post-Lisbon period appears to be best characterized as an era of recasting of existing Directives rather than new legislative measures. It is the Court which has been vigorous in its interpretation of

[122] Steve Peers, 'The Future of the EU Judicial System and EC Immigration and Asylum Law' (2005) 7 European Journal of Migration and Law 263, 265.

[123] Article 68(1) Treaty of Amsterdam.

[124] Theodora Kostakopoulou, 'The "Protective Union": Change and Continuity in Migration Law and Policy in Post-Amsterdam Europe' (2000) 38(3) JCMS: Journal of Common Market Studies 497.

[125] Diego Acosta Arcarazo and Andrew Geddes, 'The Development, Application and Implications of an EU Rule of Law in the Area of Migration Policy' (2013) 51 JCMS: Journal of Common Market Studies 179; Scipioni, 'Failing Forward in EU Migration Policy?' (n 4).

[126] See, for example, Roberto Angrisani, *La CJUE et la protection des droits fondamentaux face à la répression des migrations irrégulières* (Bruylant 2024).

[127] Jean-Pierre Cassarino and Luisa Marin, 'The Pact on Migration and Asylum: Turning the European Territory into a Non-Territory?' (2022) 24(1) European Journal of Migration and Law 1.

[128] Madalina Moraru, 'The European Court of Justice Shaping the Right to Be Heard for Asylum Seekers, Returnees, and Visa Applicants: An Exercise in Judicial Diplomacy' (2022) 14 European Journal of Legal Studies 21.

[129] Paul James Cardwell, 'On "Ring-Fencing" the Common Foreign and Security Policy in the Legal Order of the European Union' (2013) 64(4) Northern Ireland Legal Quarterly 443.

the legislation—and in particular the Returns Directive—to allow us to understand where migration law stands today. Despite the increase in workload of the Court in migration-related cases, is not straightforward to characterize an overall approach by the Court to the tensions between the protection of rights and narratives of security or exclusion. On the one hand, the Court has been instrumental in ensuring the legal effectiveness of the Charter of Fundamental Rights and the respect for the European Convention on Human Rights.[130] It has found that common standards and procedures set out in the relevant Directive[131] preclude Member States from, for example, imprisoning irregularly staying third country nationals on the sole ground that they remain on the territory of the Member State, contrary to an order to leave the territory.[132]

The Court has not been impressed by arguments by the Member States that they are unable to comply with EU migration law. In Case C-715/17 *Commission v Poland, Hungary and Czechia*,[133] the Court found that these Member States violated EU law by failing to comply with binding Council Decisions to relocate asylum-seekers from Italy and Greece under the 2015 emergency relocation mechanism. The Court rejected their arguments based on national security and administrative burden, reaffirming the binding nature of EU solidarity mechanisms under Article 80 TFEU.[134] Soon after, two cases involving Hungary's detention of migrants in border 'transit zones' were referred to the Court.[135] The CJEU held that detention, when not subject to judicial oversight and without adequate procedural safeguards, violated the Reception Conditions Directive[136] and the Charter of Fundamental Rights of EU Articles 6 (liberty) and 47 (right to an effective remedy). The decisions led to the closure of the transit zones. The Court also found Hungary in breach of EU law for its criminalization of assistance to asylum-seekers.[137]

The Court has similarly been reticent to allow Member States to revoke international protection when they claim that the situation in the county of origin has improved. It has underlined that the instances where Member States consider an application for international protection as inadmissible, as listed in Article 33 of the

[130] Dorota Leczykiewicz, 'Human Rights and the Area of Freedom, Security and Justice' in Maria Fletcher, Ester Herlin-Karnell, and Claudio Matera (eds), *The European Union as an Area of Freedom, Security and Justice* (Routledge 2017) 107.

[131] Directive 2008/115/EC of the European Parliament and of the Council of 16 December 2008 on common standards and procedures in Member States for returning illegally staying third-country nationals [2008] OJ L 384/98.

[132] Case C-61/11 *Hassen El Dridi, alias Soufi Karim* ECLI:EU:C:2011:268.

[133] Case C-715/17 *Commission v Republic of Poland and Others* ECLI:EU:C:2020:257.

[134] ibid para 80.

[135] Joined Cases C-924/19 and C-925/19 *FMS and Others v Országos Idegenrendészeti Főigazgatóság Dél-alföldi Regionális Igazgatóság and Országos Idegenrendészeti Főigazgatóság* ECLI:EU:C:2020:367.

[136] Directive 2013/33/EU of the European Parliament and of the Council of 26 June 2013 laying down standards for the reception of applicants for international protection (recast) [2013] OJ L 180/96.

[137] Case C-821/19 *Commission v Hungary* ECLI:EU:C:2021:930.

Asylum Procedures Directive,[138] are exhaustive.[139] In a series of cases[140] relating to the concept of a 'safe third country' and the ability of Member States to add their own qualifications to admissibility for international protection, the Court took a highly restrictive view, also finding that Hungary breached EU law by rejecting applications for protection from individuals who arrived via a state where they were not at risk of persecution.[141] The Court returned to this question more recently when it allowed Greece to designate Türkiye as a 'safe third country' (pursuant to the EU–Türkiye Statement) despite the latter's refusal to readmit asylum-seekers from Greece.[142] The Court nevertheless underlined 'that Member State must ensure that each of the applicants concerned has the right to access a procedure for the examination of his or her application for international protection'.[143]

And yet, the Court has also ruled in *Zaizoune*[144] that failure to enforce removal of those with no legal status is a breach of EU law, thus limiting the Member States' scope and ability to treat irregular migrants more favourably.[145] In certain cases, the Court has appeared to place excessive weight on Member State interests or restrictive interpretations of EU law, potentially at the expense of human rights standards.

[138] Directive 2013/32/EU of the European Parliament and of the Council of 26 June 2013 on common procedures for granting and withdrawing international protection (recast) [2013] OJ L 180/60, Article 33: Member States may consider an application for international protection as inadmissible only if: (a) another Member State has granted international protection; (b) a country which is not a Member State is considered as a first country of asylum for the applicant, pursuant to Article 35; (c) a country which is not a Member State is considered as a safe third country for the applicant, pursuant to Article 38; (d) the application is a subsequent application, where no new elements or findings have arisen (e) a dependant of the applicant lodges an application, and there are no facts relating to the dependant's situation which justify a separate application.

[139] Joined Cases C-297/17, C-318/17, C-319/17, and C-438/17 *Bashar Ibrahim and Others v Bundesrepublik Deutschland and Bundesrepublik Deutschland v Taus Magamadov* ECLI:EU:C:2019:219; Case C-720/20 *RO v Germany* ECLI:EU:C:2022:603; reaffirmed in Case C-216/22 *AA v Germany* ECLI:EU:C:2024:122.

[140] Case C-564/18 *Bevándorlási és Menekültügyi Hivatal (Tompa)* ECLI:EU:C:2020:218 and C-924/19 (n 135).

[141] Case C-821/19 *Commission v Hungary* (n 137).

[142] Case C-134/23 *Elliniko Symvoulio gia tous Prosfyges and Ypostirixi Prosfygon sto Aigaio* ECLI:EU:C:2024:838. See comment by Steve Peers, 'Pyrrhic victory for the Greek government: the CJEU rules on Turkey as a "safe third country"' (*EU Law Analysis*, 11 October 2024) https://eulawanalysis.blogspot.com/2024/10/pyrrhic-victory-for-greek-government.html, accessed 9 June 2025, and Agostina Pirrello, 'Turkey as a "Safe Third Country"? The Court of Justice's Judgment in C-134/23 Elliniko Symvoulio' (*European Law Blog*, 4 December 2024) https://doi.org/10.21428/9885764c.0371eca2, accessed 9 June 2025.

[143] Case C-134/23 (n 142), para 48.

[144] Case C-38/14 *Subdelegación del Gobierno en Guipuzkoa—Extranjeria v Samir Zaizoune* ECLI:EU:C:2015:260.

[145] Steve Peers, 'The Rise and Fall of EU Justice and Home Affairs Law' in Maria Fletcher, Ester Herlin-Karnell, and Claudio Matera (eds), *The European Union as an Area of Freedom, Security and Justice* (Routledge 2017) 25.

Such an example is the Court's decision in *Jafari*,[146] where the CJEU interpreted the Dublin III Regulation.[147] The case concerned asylum-seekers who had entered the EU during the 2015 crisis and travelled onward from their first country of entry without being registered. The Court held that even where a Member State allowed entry on humanitarian grounds, it remained responsible for processing the asylum application under Dublin rules, and the 'fact that admission to the territory of the Member State concerned occurs in a situation characterised by the arrival of an unusually large number of third-country nationals seeking international protection does not alter that conclusion'.[148] Critics argued that this interpretation prioritized procedural order over the practical realities of mass displacement and ignored the deficiencies in reception conditions in frontline Member States, such as in Greece.[149]

Similarly, in *Commission v Hungary*,[150] although the Court ultimately found Hungary in breach of EU law for imposing unlawful restrictions on asylum procedures and return measures, the ruling was criticized for arriving too late to effectively address the human rights violations that had occurred. By the time of the judgment in 2020, Hungary had already made structural changes that further restricted asylum access, thus prolonging rights violations in breach of the Charter of Fundamental Rights, particularly Article 18 (right to asylum) and Article 47 (right to an effective remedy).

Finally, although the CJEU has often upheld key procedural rights for migrants, it has sometimes allowed national practices that arguably fall short of international human rights standards. In the cases *C.K. and others v Slovenia* and *Jawo v Germany*,[151] the Court recognized the need to suspend transfers under Dublin III where they would result in inhuman or degrading treatment due to medical conditions. However, critics noted the narrow factual framing of the case, which limited its broader applicability and left other vulnerable groups without similar protections.[152] More recently, in *Ministero dell'Interno*,[153] the Court adopted a conversative approach, prioritizing the requirements for mutual trust between the

[146] Case C-646/16 *Proceedings brought by Khadija Jafari and Zainab Jafari* ECLI:EU:C:2017:586.

[147] Regulation (EU) No 604/2013 of the European Parliament and of the Council of 26 June 2013 establishing the criteria and mechanisms for determining the Member State responsible for examining an application for international protection lodged in one of the Member States by a third-country national or a stateless person (recast) [2013] OJ L 180/31.

[148] Case C-646/16 (n 146), para 54.

[149] Evangelia (Lilian) Tsourdi and Cathryn Costello, '"Systemic Violations" in EU Asylum Law: Cover or Catalyst?' (2023) 24(6) German Law Journal 982.

[150] C-808/18 *Commission v Hungary* ECLI:EU:C:2020:1029.

[151] Case C-578/16 *PPU C K and Others v Slovenia* ECLI:EU:C:2017:127 and Case C-163/17 *Abubacarr Jawo v Bundesrepublik Deutschland* EU:C:2019:218.

[152] See also Moraru, 'The European Court of Justice Shaping the Right To Be Heard for Asylum Seekers, Returnees, and Visa Applicants' (n 128).

[153] Joined Cases C-228/21, C-254/21, C-297/21, C-315/21, and C-328/21, *Ministero dell'Interno, Dipartimento per le Libertà civili e l'Immigrazione—Unità Dublino and Others v CZA and Others*, ECLI:EU:C:2023:934.

Member States, limiting the risks of indirect refoulement under Dublin transfer to where there are 'systemic flaws',[154] and declining to use the exceptions provided for in *C.K.* and *Jawo* or a wide, rights-based approach.[155]

The discussion above largely pertains to the CEAS, and the interpretation of the Regulations and Directives which structure it. The limitations placed on the Member States via their own commitments in the Treaty is a hallmark, including with reference to the Charter of Fundamental Rights, comes through as a set of legal principles. What is less certain, however, is how that might evolve with the future changes brought about the New Migration Pact.[156] A similar question—and the core theme of this book—is how the Court approaches the less formal mechanisms in migration governance.

Certainly, there are calls for the Court to have a stronger role in setting the limits of what is permitted, given the perceived politicization of the Commission.[157] But this is difficult to do if the Court is not given the opportunity to rule on matters which do not involve instruments of EU law as recognized by the Treaty—or indeed if the Court declines to so do.

The Court has long had opportunities to consider how non-binding instruments in EU governance should be given weight. In a line of case-law stretching back to the 1980s,[158] the Court has found that measures such as Recommendations and Opinions have an interpretative value that must be used by national courts when interpreting national law.[159] However, Recommendations and Opinions are, after all, provided for in the Treaty and thus can be seen as a special case. More difficult is when legal effects are (seemingly) produced and non-binding measures can be understood as creating some kind of legal effect or legitimate expectation, both of which the Court has recognized.[160] The role of the Court in attempting to set out whether, in the absence of direct effect of the measures in question, such measures

[154] Regulation (EU) No 604/2013 of the European Parliament and of the Council of 26 June 2013 establishing the criteria and mechanisms for determining the Member State responsible for examining an application for international protection lodged in one of the Member States by a third-country national or a stateless person (recast) [2013] OJ L 180/31 (Dublin III); Article 3(2).

[155] For comment, see Marco Gerbaudo, 'Paving the Way to the New Pact on Migration and Asylum: Some Reflections on Ministero dell'Interno (Joined Cases C-228/21, C-254/21, C-297/21, C-315/21, C-328/21)' (2025) 31(5) Maastricht Journal of European and Comparative Law 647.

[156] Cassarino and Marin, 'The Pact on Migration and Asylum' (n 127).

[157] Cornelisse and Reneman, 'Border Procedures in the Commission's New Pact on Migration and Asylum' (n 44).

[158] See further, Francis Snyder, 'Soft Law and Institutional Practice in the European Community' in Stephen Martin (ed), *The Construction of Europe* (Kluwer Academic Publishers 1994) 198; Linda Senden, *Soft Law in European Community Law* (Hart Publishing 2004).

[159] Case C-322/88 *Salvatore Grimaldi v Fonds des maladies professionnelles* ECLI:EU:C:1989:646. The Court stated, at para 18, 'it must be stressed that the measures in question cannot therefore be regarded as having no legal effect. The national courts are bound to take recommendations into consideration in order to decide disputes submitted to them, in particular where they cast light on the interpretation of national measures adopted in order to implement them or where they are designed to supplement binding Community provisions.'

[160] Case C-706/18 *X v Belgium* ECLI:EU:C:2019:993; Case C-515/08 *Criminal proceedings against Vítor Manuel dos Santos Palhota and Others* ECLI:EU:C:2010:589.

can be characterized as law has been contested over a long period.[161] This is partly a result of the EU's maturing system of governance and reliance on innovation, but also due to the differences in the national legal traditions among the Member States[162] and a similarly vigorous debate in international law.[163] While in the interests of transparency, placing the weight on the 'real' effects of non-binding instruments is a legitimate argument, there is also a danger of bypassing the established frames of law-making (as set out, in the case of the EU, in the Treaties), which goes to the heart of the argument in this book about the risks of 'formal informality'. The Court is only one player in improving the potential transparency of non-binding instruments; this would rely on other actors, including the Commission, to strengthen the visibility and dissemination of such instruments.[164]

The role of the courts has come to the fore in migration in ways which distinguish it from other policy areas. This is largely because of a focus on relationships with non-EU Member States and 'agreements' (although not termed as such) which are capable of having legal effects on individuals. This is examined in more detail in subsequent chapters, but on the main opportunity the Court has had to rule on the best known example of such an instrument, the EU–Türkiye Statement of 2016, it declined to do so. The General Court in *NF v European Council* stated that 'the EU–Turkey statement . . . cannot be regarded as a measure adopted by the European Council, or, moreover, by any other institution, body, office or agency of the European Union, or as revealing the existence of such a measure that corresponds to the contested measure'.[165] As such, the action was dismissed on the ground of the Court's lack of jurisdiction to hear and determine it. This reasoning—found to be 'frankly bizarre', in the words of Peers[166]—did not help on the question of whether the Statement is binding. The General Court focused only on the Statement's authorship, presenting the Statement as authored by the Heads of Government of the Member States, rather than by the EU institution they were meeting to agree the terms with Türkiye.[167] As such, it raised more questions than answers, although the academic commentary on the decision—which was dismissed on appeal to the CJEU—has been almost universally critical.[168]

[161] Allan Rosas, *Soft Law and the European Court of Justice* (Nomos Verlagsgesellschaft mbH & Co. KG 2012).

[162] See the contributions to Mariolina Eliantonio, Oana Stefan, and Emilia Korkea-aho (eds), *EU Soft Law in the Member States* (Hart Publishing 2021).

[163] See Christine Chinkin, 'The Challenge of Soft Law: Development and Change in International Law' (1989) 38(4) International & Comparative Law Quarterly 850 and for a more recent analysis, Emily Crawford, *Non-Binding Norms in International Humanitarian Law: Efficacy, Legitimacy, and Legality* (Oxford University Press 2022).

[164] Stefan, 'Soft Law and the Promise of Transparency in the Member States' (n 16).

[165] Case T-192/16 *NF v European Council* ECLI:EU:T:2017:128.

[166] Peers, 'Pyrrhic victory for the Greek government: the CJEU rules on Turkey as a "safe third country"' (n 142).

[167] The European Court of Human Rights, however, also came to the same conclusion: *JR and Others v Greece* App No 22696/16 (Judgment, 25 January 2018).

[168] Eva Kassoti and Alina Carrozzini, 'One Instrument in Search of an Author: Revisiting the Authorship and Legal Nature of the EU–Turkey Statement' in E Kassoti and N Idriz (eds), *The*

If accepting that the presence of a variety of instruments producing effects is here to stay, calls to recognize—or even embrace[169]—the hybridity and for the Court to set out procedural requirements could be a way in which to bring the legal effects of informal mechanisms within the scope of EU law. The opaque institutional format for making such important 'statements', the lack of use of established procedures, and the procedural hurdles such as the rules on standing and lack of preliminary reference opportunities for individuals and courts have been the focus of much of the criticism.[170] The Court is not precluded from adopting a more stringent line on soft law or instances of formal informality in the future, but can be expected to be cautious in doing so in politically contentious cases, of which migration sits at the top of the list.

5.6 The role of agencies in migration governance: Frontex and the EASO/EUAA

Agencies have been a long-standing feature in the EU's system of governance, with the first created in the 1970s. More than thirty EU decentralised agencies now exist, having been created on an ad hoc basis to meet certain needs in specific policy areas. The 'agencification' of EU administration took off in the 1990s,[171] with a marked increase in scholarly attention to the phenomenon only occurring some years later.[172] Beyond case studies of individual agencies which attempt to construct a typology of what agencies do and how, most agencies have not themselves been the focus of attention.

Informalisation of the EU's External Action in the Field of Migration and Asylum (Asser Press/Springer 2021); Gloria Arribas, 'The EU–Turkey Statement, the Treaty-Making Process and Competent Organs. Is the Statement an International Agreement?' (2017) 2(1) European Papers 309; Mauro Gatti and Andrea Ott, 'The EU–Turkey Statement: Legal Nature and Compatibility with EU Institutional Law' in Sergio Carrera, Juan Santos Vara, and Tineke Strik (eds), *Constitutionalising the External Dimensions of EU Migration Policies in Times of Crisis* (Edward Elgar Publishing 2019).

[169] Mariolina Eliantonio and Oana Stefan, 'Soft Law before the European Courts: Discovering a "Common Pattern"?' (2018) 37 Yearbook of European Law 457.

[170] Virginia Passalacqua, 'Who Mobilizes the Court? Migrant Rights Defenders before the Court of Justice of the EU' (2022) 15(2) Law and Development Review 381; Annick Pijnenburg, 'The Informalisation of Migration Deals and Human Rights of People on the Move: Does It Matter?' in E Kassoti and N Idriz (eds), *The Informalisation of the EU's External Action in the Field of Migration and Asylum* (Asser Press/Springer 2021).

[171] Michelle Everson, 'Independent Agencies: Hierarchy Beaters?' (1995) 1(2) European Law Journal 180.

[172] See, for example, Madalina Busuioc, Martijn Groenleer, and Jarle Trondal (eds), *The Agency Phenomenon in the European Union* (Manchester University Press 2012); Michelle Everson, Cosimo Monda, and Ellen Vos (eds), *European Agencies In Between Institutions and Member States* (Wolters Kluwer 2014); David Levi-Faur, 'Regulatory Networks and Regulatory Agencification: Towards a Single European Regulatory Space' (2011) 18(6) Journal of European Public Policy 810.

In more recent years, agencies have risen to prominence and are often seen as a necessary—or at least desirable—institutional contribution to particular policy areas, either due to functional/technical needs or to avoid the appearance of over-delegation to the (supranational) Commission.[173] Furthermore, the politicization of agencies has often been centred on their location rather than their role. Member States are keen to have the benefits—in both economic and reputational terms—of an agency located on their territory. The intense competition to rehome the two EU agencies leaving post-Brexit London serves as evidence of their importance in material and symbolic terms.[174] The possibility for future UK involvement in agencies even though this would not be possible in the full-fledged EU institutions is one potential route to future EU–UK cooperation.[175] Indeed, agencies are often capable of involving third states in activities in a way which is not possible in the 'regular' institutions, including in situations where full enlargement processes have stalled.[176] The role and function of agencies—either singularly or collectively—has rarely attracted widespread public attention.

Agencies have also risen to prominence in discussions on the types of EU governance at play due to their proliferation and lack of easy categorization as supranational, intergovernmental, or hybrid bodies.[177] Such has been their increase and diversity of roles, size, and competences that a joint statement by the Parliament, Council, and Commission in 2012 attempted to set some ground rules for what agencies should be called, what they should do, and how.[178] The risk associated with a proliferation of agencies is at best, uncertainty as to their role and purpose, and at worst, a lack of transparency and accountability, which can have a negative impact on the EU system as a whole, public confidence within it, and the protection and promotion of fundamental rights. When set alongside the 'regular'

[173] Egeberg and Trondal, 'Researching European Union Agencies' (n 21).

[174] The European Medicines Agency and the European Banking Authority. See Martin Banks, 'Fierce competition to host European Medicines Agency' (*The Parliament*, 20 Nov 2017) https://www.theparliamentmagazine.eu/news/article/fierce-competition-to-host-european-medicines-agency, accessed 7 June 2025; Fiona Maxwell, 'Paris wins battle to host European Banking Authoirty' (*Politico*, 20 November 2017) https://www.politico.eu/article/paris-wins-european-banking-authority/#:~:text=A%20vote%20among%20the%20remaining,to%20ensure%20a%20smooth%20transition, accessed 7 June 2025.

[175] See, for example, Michael Kaeding, 'EU Agencies and Brexit: Assessing the Implications of Brexit for EU Agencies' in John Fossum and Christopher Lord (eds), *Handbook on the European Union and Brexit* (Edward Elgar Publishing 2023); Andrea Ott, 'Brexit and EU Agencies: Opting-In from the Outside?' in Juan Santos Vara and Ramses A Wessel (eds), *The Routledge Handbook on the International Dimension of Brexit* (Routledge 2020).

[176] Matis Poussardin, 'The Agencies of the European Union: A Glimmer of Hope for Enlargement?' (2026) JCMS: Journal of Common Market Studies, early view, https://doi.org/10.1111/jcms.70095, accessed 30 March 2026.

[177] Egeberg and Trondal, 'Researching European Union Agencies' (n 21) 676–77.

[178] European Union, 'Joint statement of the European Parliament, the Council of the EU and the European Commission on decentralised agencies' (19 July 2012), https://european-union.europa.eu/document/download/d4199ff4-1e3d-45e6-af7e-90cf1a7b10bc_en?filename=joint_statement_on_decentralised_agencies_en.pdf, accessed 7 June 2025.

institutions discussed in this chapter, agencies can also be seen to have a number of different features which have an impact upon the type of system of governance to which they contribute. The involvement of third states in agencies and their ability to participate in and influence the work of the agency is a prominent example.[179] Needless to say, in migration the protection of human rights, transparency, and accountability for actions is paramount, and it is no surprise that much of the general attention focused on EU agencies has been motivated by the two agencies under scrutiny here, Frontex and the European Asylum Support Office/EU Agency for Asylum.[180] Both have direct roles in the governance of migration and are considered in some detail in what follows.[181]

5.6.1 European Border and Coast Guard Agency—Frontex

The European Border and Coast Guard Agency, known as Frontex, was established via Council Regulation 2007/2004 in 2004, with a seat in Warsaw.[182] Officially, and front and centre on its website, its role is to 'support' Member States and Schengen-associated countries 'in the management of the EU's external borders and the fight against cross-border crime'.[183]

With migration and borders occupying such a central place on the EU and national agendas, but with a lack of physical harmonization or general competence on the part of the EU to deal with this area, a coordination body at arm's length from the other institutions would be required. Frontex began life as such a body, which is in itself a hallmark of new governance[184] and reflective of national modes

[179] See, inter alia, Marja-Liisa Öberg, 'Third Countries in EU Agencies: Participation and Influence' in Herwig CH Hofmann, Ellen Vos, and Merijn Chamon (eds), *The External Dimension of EU Agencies and Bodies* (Edward Elgar Publishing 2019); Tarjei Bekkedal, 'Third State Participation in EU Agencies: Exploring the EEA Precedent' (2019) 56(2) Common Market Law Review 56; Sandra Lavenex and Philipp Lutz, 'Third Country Access to EU Agencies: Exploring Spaces for Influence' (2023) 61(6) JCMS: Journal of Common Market Studies 1563.

[180] See, for example, Editorial, 'Migration: Frontex cannot be free of European values' (*Le Monde*, Paris, 2 May 2022) https://www.lemonde.fr/en/opinion/article/2022/05/02/migration-frontex-cannot-be-free-of-european-values_5982218_23.html, accessed 7 June 2025.

[181] It should also be noted that two other JHA-focused agencies, Europol and Eurojust, are also involved in some migration-related aspects of EU governance, for example the operation of 'hotspots'. See further, Aida Halilovic, 'Executive Migration Governance and Law-Making in the European Union: Towards a State of Exception' (2024) 9(2) European Papers—A Journal on Law and Integration 513.

[182] Council Regulation (EC) No 2007/2004 of 26 October 2004 establishing a European Agency for the Management of Operational Cooperation at the External Borders of the Member States of the European Union [2004] OJ L 349/1.

[183] Frontex, 'Who we are' (Frontex: European Border and Coast Guard Agency) https://www.frontex.europa.eu/about-frontex/who-we-are/tasks-mission/, accessed 7 June 2025; Council Regulation (EC) No 2007/2004 [2004] OJ L 349/1 (n 182), Article 2.

[184] See discussion in Chapter 2 and, inter alia, Giandomenico Majone, 'The New European Agencies: Regulation by Information' (1997) 4(2) Journal of European Public Policy 262.

towards the creation of specialized agencies in both the EU Member States and beyond.[185]

Frontex operates at the very heart of state sovereignty, engaging with one of its most fundamental aspects: control over who can and cannot enter a state's territory. This authority lies at the core of national self-determination and is traditionally regarded as an essential function of the state. Within the EU, however, this area has undergone a degree of harmonization, particularly through the development of the Schengen area. While internal borders have been largely eliminated, this has not erased tensions—especially when it comes to differing national perspectives on border management and the uneven implementation of Schengen rules.

The original 2004 Frontex Regulation saw the agency as primarily supporting and coordinating operational cooperation in external border management. Its task list consisted, as per the Regulation, in coordinating Member State cooperation and assisting with technical or operation assistance, carrying out risk analyses, 'follow up' on relevant research on borders, and providing support for joint return operations.[186] The only mention of fundamental rights was contained in the preamble.[187] The mandate thus appears rather limited, and it is telling how the opportunity to coordinate joint operations and 'pilot projects at external borders' has been used to incrementally position Frontex as a major institutional player.[188] In this respect too, Frontex is at the forefront of the types of governance exhibited via 'formal informality'.

Frontex's legal basis has been frequently changed, via Regulations in 2016[189] and 2019.[190] Frontex Regulation 2016 marked a major development in the EU's substantive approach to border security. Adopted on 14 September 2016, this Regulation transformed Frontex from 'the European Agency for the Management of Operational Cooperation at the External Borders' into the 'European Border and Coast Guard Agency'. It aimed to respond to the migration crisis and growing security concerns by strengthening the EU's ability to manage its external borders more effectively and coherently.

[185] Michelle Everson and others, *The Role of Specialised Agencies in Decentralising EU Governance* (EIPA 1999); Martin Shapiro, 'The Problems of Independent Agencies in the United States and the European Union' (1997) 4(2) Journal of European Public Policy 276.

[186] Council Regulation (EC) No 2007/2004 [2004] OJ L 349/1 (n 182), Article 2(1).

[187] ibid Preamble, para 22: 'This Regulation respects the fundamental rights and observes the principles recognised by Article 6(2) of the Treaty on European Union and reflected in the Charter of Fundamental Rights of the European Union.'

[188] ibid Article 3.

[189] Regulation (EU) 2016/1624 of the European Parliament and of the Council of 14 September 2016 on the European Border and Coast Guard and amending Regulation (EU) 2016/399 of the European Parliament and of the Council and repealing Regulation (EC) No 863/2007 of the European Parliament and of the Council, Council Regulation (EC) No 2007/2004 and Council Decision 2005/267/EC [2016] OJ L 251/1.

[190] Regulation (EU) 2019/1896 of the European Parliament and of the Council of 13 November 2019 on the European Border and Coast Guard and repealing Regulations (EU) No 1052/2013 and (EU) 2016/1624 [2019] OJ L 295/1.

The Regulation enhanced Frontex's mandate significantly, granting it broader operational powers and responsibilities. It established a reserve pool of 1,500 border guards that could be rapidly deployed in emergencies alongside national coast guards responsible for border control as a 'shared responsibility'.[191] Member States were required to contribute personnel and equipment to ensure readiness. The agency was also given a stronger role in coordinating return operations for irregular migrants and supporting border surveillance and risk analysis.

Importantly, Regulation 2016/1624 gave Frontex a more proactive role in monitoring Member States' border control capacities. If a Member State failed to take adequate measures in a crisis, 'to such an extent that it risks jeopardising the functioning of the Schengen area',[192] the Commission could propose to the Council direct intervention by Frontex.[193] This was a shift towards shared responsibility at the EU level, aiming to close security gaps and ensure a uniform standard of border control.

The Regulation also strengthened cooperation with non-EU countries, particularly those neighbouring the EU, in order to improve border management and migration control. References to cooperation with third countries are found throughout the Regulation, including technical assistance and joint operations with neighbouring countries.[194]

Overall, the 2016 Frontex Regulation signified the EU's move towards a more integrated, centralized approach to border management as an area of 'shared responsibility' with the Member States. The Regulation marked a shift from a supporting or coordinating body to one directly involved in border management via an expanding task list, heavily focused on practical engagements. While the legal regime aimed to enhance security and solidarity, it also raised concerns regarding accountability, human rights protections (particularly via the 'complaint mechanism'[195] and in rescue tasks),[196] and the balance between national sovereignty

[191] Regulation 2016/1624 [2016] OJ L 21/1 (n 189), Article 3(1) and 5(1).

[192] ibid Article 19(1); see further, Juan Santos Vara, *La gestión de las fronteras exteriores de la UE: los nuevos poderes de la Agencia Frontex* (Tirant lo Blanch 2021).

[193] Regulation 2016/1624 [2016] OJ L 21/1 (n 189), Article 19(1). Procedurally, the Council could 'adopt without delay a decision by means of an implementing act, identifying measures to mitigate those risks to be implemented by the Agency and requiring the Member State concerned to cooperate with the Agency in the implementation of those measures'.

[194] For example, Regulation 2016/1624 [2016] OJ L 21/1 (n 189), Article 8(1)(f); Article 14(2), Article 19(2)(c).

[195] David Rojo, 'Reglamento 2016/1624: de FRONTEX a la Guardia Europea de Fronteras y Costas' (2017) 41 Revista General de Derecho Europeo 203.

[196] See, inter alia, Francina Esteve, 'The Search and Rescue Tasks Coordinated by the European Border and Coast Guard Agency (Frontex) Regarding the Surveillance of External Maritime Borders' [2017] (5) *Paix et Securité Internationales* 93; Giuseppe Campesi, 'European Border and Coast Guard (Frontex): Security, Democracy, and Rights at the EU Border' in *Oxford Research Encyclopedia of Criminology and Criminal Justice* (Oxford University Press 2018).

and EU authority, given the unprecedented executive power now exercised by Frontex as a 'superagency'.[197]

Only three years later, a further Frontex Regulation, adopted on 13 November 2019, marked a significant upgrade of the European Border and Coast Guard Agency (Frontex), building on its 2016 reform.[198] This Regulation was a response to the persistent challenges of irregular migration, cross-border crime, and the need for stronger EU external border management. It expanded Frontex's mandate, resources, and operational capacity, solidifying its role as a central player in the EU's border and migration policy. It repealed the 2016 Frontex Regulation.

A major feature of the 2019 Regulation foresaw the creation of a standing corps of up to 10,000 operational staff by 2027. This corps includes Frontex-employed border guards and personnel seconded from Member States, enabling the agency to respond more swiftly and independently to crises at EU borders. The standing corps significantly increased the EU's direct control over border management and reduced its reliance on the voluntary contributions of Member States.

The emphasis in the 2019 Regulation on operational powers enhanced Frontex's capacity to conduct joint operations, return third country nationals, and cooperate with non-EU countries, including deploying liaison officers and concluding operational agreements. It also expanded the agency's role in supporting the development of border control technologies, training, and the coordination of return operations.[199] Nevertheless, this operational focus was not accompanied by a shift towards more centralized border management. Rather, the monitoring of effective practices came to the fore.[200]

Another key element was the strengthening of Frontex's fundamental rights safeguards. The Regulation required the appointment of a Fundamental Rights Officer and a pool of fundamental rights monitors, aiming to ensure that border operations respect EU and international law, including asylum and human rights obligations. While Regulation 2019/1896 empowered Frontex to become a more robust and autonomous agency, it also intensified scrutiny regarding transparency, accountability, and the agency's involvement in controversial border practices against a background of a 'crisis' or 'emergency' narrative.[201]

[197] Trym Fjørtoft, 'More Power, More Control: The Legitimizing Role of Expertise in Frontex after the Refugee Crisis' (2022) 16(2) Regulation & Governance 557. The term 'superagency' comes from Vittoria Meissner, 'The European Border and Coast Guard Agency Frontex after the Migration Crisis: Towards a "Superagency"?' in Johannes Pollack and Peter Slominski (eds), *The Role of EU Agencies in the Eurozone and Migration Crisis: Impact and Future Challenges* (Palgrave Macmillan 2021).

[198] Regulation (EU) 2019/1896 [2019] OJ L 295/1 (n 190).

[199] Romain Tinière, 'Règlement 2019/1896 et le renforcement des compétences de Frontex' (2021) No 275 Journal de Droit Européen 10.

[200] David Fernandez-Rojo, 'The European Border and Coast Guard's Executive Powers: From Regulation 2016/1624 to Regulation 2019/1896' (2020) 60 Revista Catalana de Dret Públic 181.

[201] Mariana Gkliati and Jane Kilpatrick, 'Crying Wolf Too Many Times: The Impact of the Emergency Narrative on Transparency in FRONTEX Joint Operations' (2022) 17(4) Utrecht Law Review 57.

Over time, Frontex's mandate has significantly expanded, in parallel to its growth in operational capacity. This rapid evolution has not been without controversy or conflict. Further, the process has been far from smooth, marked by resistance from some Member States and criticism from human rights organizations. In many ways, Frontex has become a 'victim of its own success',[202] growing in both size and influence, but also attracting greater scrutiny and facing higher expectations from multiple sides.

As noted above, one of the more striking developments in recent legislation is the provision that, under certain circumstances, Frontex can take action even against the wishes of a Member State. This introduced a significant shift in the balance between national sovereignty and supranational authority. The agency has been granted new powers that include deploying border guards and equipment without prior national consent if there is a serious threat to the Schengen area.[203] Such provisions point to an emerging model of shared sovereignty in border control, but one that is still contested and politically sensitive. The extent to which Frontex is truly autonomous is only partly discernible from the text of the Regulations but requires a more careful examination of its work in practice.[204]

Although Frontex is formally a JHA agency, its activities are heavily focused on the external dimension of EU policy, particularly through cooperation with third countries, extending well beyond those involved in the enlargement process.[205] This external orientation has made Frontex distinct among EU agencies, as it plays a critical role in managing the EU's borders and in shaping migration and security relationships with countries outside the Union.[206]

As a result, Frontex has attracted significantly more public and political attention than many other EU agencies, despite its relatively short existence. Its operations and partnerships—often with countries with which the EU has complex or politically sensitive relationships—have become the subject of detailed scrutiny. Numerous case studies have examined how Frontex engages bilaterally with third countries, as well as how it operates at the EU's external borders, where practices have sometimes clashed with human rights norms and EU values.

[202] Luisa Marin, 'Frontex at the Epicentre of a Rule of Law Crisis at the External Borders of the EU' (2024) 30(1–2) European Law Journal 11.

[203] Council Regulation (EC) No 2007/2004 [2004] OJ L 349/1 (n 182), Article 19; Juan Santos Vara, *La gestión de las fronteras exteriores de la UE: los nuevos poderes de la Agencia Frontex* (Tirant lo Blanch 2021).

[204] Åsa Gustafsson, 'The Baltic Sea Region Border Control Cooperation (BSRBCC) and Border Management in the Baltic Sea Region: A Case Study' (2018) 98 Marine Policy 309.

[205] Eleonora Frasca, 'Informal Agreements and Quasi-Legal Mechanisms in EU–Africa Cooperation on Migration: How the EU Takes Advantage of the GCM Commitments' (2023) 5 Frontiers of Human Dynamics 1; Yichen Zhong and Helena Carrapico, 'Frontex Goes Global: A Two-Level Experimentalist Governance Analysis of Frontex's International Action and Its Role within the Externalisation of EU Borders' (2024) 2(1) Contemporary European Politics e7.

[206] For a comprehensive literature review on Frontex, see Jori Kalkman, 'Frontex: A Literature Review' (2021) 59(1) International Migration 165.

Public interest in Frontex intensified further in 2022 with the high-profile resignation of its executive director, Fabrice Leggeri. His departure followed sustained media coverage of alleged unlawful violence and misconduct at the EU's external borders, particularly involving so-called pushbacks of migrants and asylum-seekers.[207] These reports prompted an investigation by the European Anti-Fraud Office (OLAF),[208] which raised serious questions about the agency's accountability and adherence to EU law and the protection of fundamental rights. Leggeri himself was elected as an MEP for the French far-right party Rassemblement national (National Rally) in 2024. He was later placed under investigation by the French judiciary for possible complicity in crimes against humanity and acts of torture during his tenure at Frontex.[209]

The Court of Justice has been facing a number of claims into 'pushback' practices, reflecting broader concerns over how the EU balances effective border control with the protection of fundamental rights in its external action.[210] In December 2025, the Grand Chamber delivered two judgments on appeal from the General Court brought by individuals against Frontex and seeking compensation under the right to an effective remedy under the Charter of Fundamental Rights.[211] The General Court required an unrealistically high evidentiary standard of burden of proof and formulated its decision in terms of Frontex merely supporting Member States, who retain responsibility. The Court, however, found that Frontex could not evade legal responsibility under the Charter, EU law, and international law in return operations. A failure to check national decisions for the return of an individual in each case could lead to a fundamental rights violation. The highly anticipated decisions were welcomed in terms of ensuring the effective protection of rights of vulnerable individuals and the ability to enforce EU law. This did, however, shine a light on the extent of 'lawless borders',[212] the legal and practical problems inherent in the CEAS, and the emphasis on uncertainty in questions of legal responsibility.[213]

[207] The Guardian, 'Head of EU border agency Frontex resigns amid criticisms' (The Guardian, 29 April 2022), https://www.theguardian.com/world/2022/apr/29/head-of-eu-border-agency-frontex-resigns-amid-criticisms-fabrice-leggeri, accessed 30 March 2026.

[208] Elspeth Guild, 'Frontex and Access to Justice: The Need for Effective Monitoring Mechanisms' (2024) 30(1–2) European Law Journal 136; Salvatore Nicolosi, 'The European Border and Coast Guard Agency (Frontex) and the Limits to Effective Judicial Protection in European Union Law' (2024) 30(1–2) European Law Journal 149.

[209] *Le Monde*, 'Fabrice Leggeri, ex-directeur de Frontex et eurodéputé RN, visé par une enquête pour complicité de crimes contre l'humanité' (*Le Monde*, 24 March 2026), https://www.lemonde.fr/societe/article/2026/03/24/fabrice-leggeri-ex-directeur-de-frontex-et-eurodepute-rn-vise-par-une-enquete-pour-complicite-de-crimes-contre-l-humanite_6674028_3224.htm, accessed 30 March 2026.

[210] Case T-136/22 *Hamoudi v Frontex* ECLI:EU:T:2023:821, on appeal as Case C-136/24 P *Hamoudi v Frontex* ECLI:EU:C:2025:977, and Case T-600/21 *WS and Others v Frontex* EU:T:2023:492, on appeal as C-679/23 P *WS and Others v Frontex* ECLI:EU:C:2025:976.

[211] Articles 2 and 47.

[212] Elspeth Guild, Valsamis Mitsilegas, and Niovi Vavoula, *Lawless Borders* (Bristol University Press 2025).

[213] For comment, see Mohammad Rakraki, 'La responsabilité extracontractuelle de Frontex à la lumière des conclusions des avocats généraux dans les affaires Hamoudi et WS e.a.' (2026) 25 Journal

It is not only the substantial role of Frontex that distinguished it from other EU agencies. The other characteristic which marks it out is its size and projected growth. Over time, it has witnessed an increase in resourcing, size, and role which is unusual for an EU agency. Originally launched with a modest budget of around €6 million, Frontex's financial resources have expanded rapidly, particularly in response to the 2015 migration crisis and subsequent, sustained political pressure to strengthen external border control.[214]

By 2021, Frontex's budget had surpassed €500 million, making it the EU's highest-funded agency. The multiannual financial framework for 2021–27 allocated around €5.6 billion to Frontex, underlining its central role in the EU's migration and security strategy. Frontex's revenue has increased from €688 million in 2022 to €922 million in 2024,[215] and a projected €1124 million in 2025.[216] This funding supports a wide range of activities, including joint operations at land and sea borders, the deployment of the European Border and Coast Guard standing corps, return operations for irregular migrants, and cooperation with third countries. A reported proposal in early 2025 was for Frontex staffing to reach 30,000 employees, which would be more even than the Commission.[217] The rationale is the continued emphasis on borders as a critical mission for the EU, but also to tackle a series of other interconnected threats. This would take Frontex quite far from its original intention for border coordination with Member States, and would seem to make an argument for it to be treated as a full-fledged institution.[218]

d'Actualité du Droit International et Européen, https://revue-jadie.eu/article/view/9742, accessed 30 March 2026; Catharina Ziebritzki, 'With great power comes great responsbility: Why WS el al and Hamoudi vs Frontex Mark a Turning Point' (*Verfassungsblog*, 4 January 2026) https://verfassungsblog.de/w-s-et-al-and-hamoudi-vs-frontex/, accessed 30 March 2026; Lea Schubert, 'Asylum seekers as vulnerable applicants—the CJEU's approach to causation and evidence in the Frontex appeal judgments' (*European Law Blog*, 8 January 2026), https://www.europeanlawblog.eu/pub/16zd10nh/release/1, accessed 30 March 2026; Tamás Molnár, 'Frontex' Responsibility for Human Rights Violations: The CJEU and Certain Aspects of the International Responsibility of International Organisations' (*EJIL: Talk!*, 29 January 2026) https://www.ejiltalk.org/frontex-responsibility-for-human-rights-violations-the-cjeu-and-certain-aspects-of-the-international-responsibility-of-international-organisations/, accessed 30 March 2026.

[214] European Court of Auditors, 'Audit Preview: Frontex' (January 2020) https://www.eca.europa.eu/lists/ecadocuments/ap20_02/ap_frontex_en.pdf, accessed 7 June 2025.

[215] See 'Statement of revenue and expenditure for the 2024 financial year—European Border and Coast Guard Agency (Frontex)' [2024] OJ C 2024/1731.

[216] See Frontex, 'Budget 2025: Voted Budget (VOBU)' (20 December 2024) https://prd.frontex.europa.eu/wp-content/themes/template/templates/cards/1/dialog.php?card-post-id=2722&document-post-id=17396, accessed 7 June 2025.

[217] Sam Clark, 'EU wants to beef up border agency to 30,000 staffers' (*Politico*, 1 April 2025) https://www.politico.eu/article/eu-wants-new-police-border-powers-to-counter-very-alarming-security-threats/, accessed 7 June 2025. The current staffing list, according to Frontex's website, is 2500 employees from 29 countries, an increase from 749 in 2019: Frontex, 'Why us' (*Frontex: Careers*) https://www.frontex.europa.eu/careers/who-we-are/why-us/, accessed 7 June 2025.

[218] This would, however, require a change in the Treaty which limits 'institutions' to those listed in Article 13 TEU (the European Parliament, the European Council, the Council, the European Commission, the Court of Justice of the EU, the European Central Bank, and the Court of Auditors). It should be noted that elsewhere in the Treaty there are references to 'institutions, bodies, offices and

This evolution carries significant implications. The agency's increasing presence at Europe's borders has raised alarms about Frontex (and thus also the EU more generally) contributing to rule of law violations in the border zones.[219] The perceived growing threat of instrumentalization of migrants in geopolitical standoffs also places the role of Frontex and its inter-institutional and Member State relations under scrutiny.[220] Moreover, the symbolic power of Frontex's name underscores the shift—although perhaps, given the connotation of 'front' in its name, the link with (hybrid) forms of warfare is not as distant as might be expected, also bearing in mind the discourse on 'protection' of Europe and European populations and society from 'others'. As Maurits notes, 'front' evokes imagery of warfare, while 'ex' hints at expulsion,[221] even when engaged in missions which are classed as humanitarian.[222] Frontex, then, can be read as an entity engaged in a battle to repel and remove; framing migration as a threat, and protection as exclusion.

The growing militarization of Europe's border apparatus, and the accompanying discourse of defending European society from external 'others', pushes the future potential role for Frontex far beyond its original scope. The agency now stands at the intersection of law enforcement, military logic, and identity politics, a reflection of Europe's struggle to reconcile openness with security in an era of uncertainty. Carrera, den Hertog, and Parkin observe that there is a widening of the powers of the agencies which has not only taken place through the legislative process but also developed through agencies' de facto expansions and 'learning by doing'-like interventions. Therefore, they discuss both de jure and de facto competences that the agencies have in order to suggest that human rights violations are not uncommon and pose a major issue.[223]

Frontex has undertaken a number of initiatives with a view to integrating fundamental human rights in its activities, such as the Frontex Fundamental Rights

agencies' to which, for example, the principle of equality of citizens applies (Article 9 TEU), to openness and right of access to documents (Article 15(3) TFEU), and to who may intervene in cases before the CJEU (Article 40 TEU).

[219] Marin, 'Frontex at the Epicentre of a Rule of Law Crisis at the External Borders of the EU' (n 202).

[220] Sofia Galani, 'The Instrumentalization of Migration as a Hybrid Threat against the EU: Can Human Rights Become "Hybrid" Too?' in Alexander Lott (ed), *Maritime Security Law in Hybrid Warfare* (Brill | Nijhoff 2024); Jari Pirjola, 'Hostile Instrumentalized Migration and the Right to Seek Asylum: Reflecting the European Legal Framework' (2025) 27(1) European Journal of Migration and Law 1; Stefania Panebianco, 'The EU and Migration in the Mediterranean: EU Borders' Control by Proxy' (2020) 48(6) Journal of Ethnic and Migration Studies 1398; Martin Faix, 'Development of Frontex vis-a-vis Instrumentalization of Migration as a Tool of Hybrid Warfare-More Institutionalisation the Answer?' (2024) 13 Polish Review of International and European Law 119.

[221] Peter Maurits, 'Vanishing Migrants and the Impossibility of a European Union' (2015) 17(4) Interventions 503.

[222] On 'Operation Triton', see Martina Tazzioli, 'Border Displacements: Challenging the Politics of Rescue between Mare Nostrum and Triton' (2016) 4(1) Migration Studies 1.

[223] Sergio Carrera, Leonhard den Hertog, and Joanna Parkin, 'The Peculiar Nature of EU Home Affairs Agencies in Migration Control: Beyond Accountability versus Autonomy?' (2013) 15(4) European Journal of Migration and Law 337.

Strategy, the Frontex Consultative Forum on human rights, and the appointment of a Fundamental Rights Officer. The latest Regulation shows that Frontex surveillance sea operations are subject to international obligations stemming from the main human rights instruments, and, in particular, to the principle of non-refoulement. Additionally, despite the Regulation not applying to the territorial waters of third countries, Member States remain subject to their international human rights obligations when they are involved in border surveillance activities extraterritorially.[224] However, the question of discretion remains as to how strictly these, and the principle of non-refoulement, are adhered to. In the earlier days of the agency's operation, the regular practice of diverting intercepted migrants back to their port of departure was sharply criticized.[225] More recently, legal scholars have emphasized that Frontex should comply with the principle of *non-refoulement* regardless of where operations take place, since diverting people to places where they may be mistreated can never be allowed.[226]

Returning to the status of Frontex and how this relates to its institutional position within the EU's governance migration, and its accountability, is vital. The characterization of agencies as 'hybrid' bodies operating in the space between EU institutions and national institutions is apt here.[227] There is little doubt that Frontex has facilitated migration cooperation among Member States and agencies.[228] But the nature of the relationship remains uncertain. Initial accounts of the role of Frontex focused on its supporting role for Member States in a core domain of state sovereignty in a functional sense,[229] without the overall ambition for integration or even common approaches or solutions for border management.[230] The changes over time to the role and function of Frontex suggest that a more nuanced approach is needed which fits neatly into neither an intergovernmental, supportive box nor a fully supranational one. For instance, given the domestic political pressures and

[224] Juan Vara and Soledad Sánchez-Tabernero, 'In Deep Water: Towards a Greater Commitment for Human Rights in Sea Operations Coordinated by Frontex?' (2016) 18(1) European Journal of Migration and Law 65.

[225] Luisa Marin, 'Policing the EU's External Borders: A Challenge for the Rule of Law and Fundamental Rights in the Area of Freedom, Security and Justice? An Analysis of Frontex Joint Operations at the Southern Maritime Border' (2011) 7(4) Journal of Contemporary European Research 468.

[226] Efthymios Papastavridis, '"Fortress Europe" and Frontex: Within or Without International Law?' (2010) 79(1) *Nordic Journal of International Law* 75; Violeta Moreno-Lax, 'Seeking Asylum in the Mediterranean: Against a Fragmentary Reading of EU Member States' Obligations Accruing at Sea' (2011) 23(2) International Journal of Refugee Law 174; Juan Vara and Soledad Sánchez-Tabernero, 'In Deep Water: Towards a Greater Commitment for Human Rights in Sea Operations Coordinated by Frontex?' (2016) 18(1) European Journal of Migration and Law 65.

[227] Michelle Everson, Cosimo Monda, and Ellen Vos (eds), *European Agencies In Between Institutions and Member States* (Kluwer Law International 2014) 5.

[228] Roberta Mungianu, 'Frontex: Towards a Common Policy on External Border Control' (2013) 15(4) European Journal of Migration and Law 359.

[229] Sarah Leonard, 'The Creation of FRONTEX and the Politics of Institutionalisation in the EU External Borders Policy' (2009) 5(3) Journal of Contemporary European Research 371.

[230] Sarah Wolff, 'Border Management in the Mediterranean: Internal, External and Ethical Challenges' (2008) 21(2) Cambridge Review of International Affairs 253.

salience of migration, Ripoll Servent has suggested that Frontex has become a means by which some larger Member States have sent border guards under the guise of Frontex to support or replace border management in weaker, frontier Member States.[231] The institutionalization of Frontex as a border management entity and the introduction of a European Corps of Border Guards, as well as the fact that guest officers fall under EU law, implies some degree of supranationalization over the past decade at least.[232]

Nevertheless, EU Member States' 'sovereignty clauses' for the surveillance and control of their external borders prevent the EU from fully exercising its power.[233] Focusing on joint operations, Cortinovis has argued that the introduction of elements grounded in the Regulation, such as the creation of a semi-permanent pool to which contributions were compulsory after being pledged, has resulted in a hybrid governance system in which Member States can retain their sovereignty while facilitating more effective Frontex operations.[234] Although possible, the likelihood of Frontex regularly intervening in a Member State without the latter's permission is low, and thus Frontex cannot yet be seen as fully autonomous.[235] For Mungianu, operational cooperation at the EU's external borders is the outcome of a compromise between more supranationalization in the policy area of border control and the maintenance of Member States' sovereign interests.[236]

There is an advantage for Frontex in the haziness of responsibility with the Member States, which would speak against the assumption that institutions (and especially EU bodies) seek to maximize their formal competences. Although Frontex plays a significant role operationally, its official mandate is limited to cooperating with or assisting Member States.[237] As a result, Member States are formally considered the primary actors in interactions with individuals. This distinction allows agencies such as Frontex to evade direct accountability when fundamental rights are breached, effectively using the legal responsibility of Member States as a shield.

This arrangement presents obstacles for individuals seeking judicial redress, especially when attempting to bring cases before the Court of Justice. While agencies fall under the CJEU's jurisdiction following the Lisbon Treaty, the blurred lines of responsibility complicate legal challenges and may hinder effective remedies.

[231] Ariadna Ripoll Servent, 'A New Form of Delegation in EU Asylum: Agencies as Proxies of Strong Regulators' (2017) 56(1) Journal of Common Market Studies 83.
[232] Mungianu, 'Frontex: Towards a Common Policy on External Border Control' (n 228).
[233] Lisa Heschel, *Protecting the Rights of Refugees beyond European Borders: Establishing Extraterritorial Legal Responsibilities* (Intersentia 2019).
[234] Roberto Cortinovis, 'The Evolution of Frontex Governance: Shifting from Soft to Hard Law?' (2015) 11(3) Journal of Contemporary European Research 252.
[235] Gustafsson, 'The Baltic Sea Region Border Control Cooperation (BSRBCC) and Border Management in the Baltic Sea Region' (n 204).
[236] Mungianu, 'Frontex: Towards a Common Policy on External Border Control' (n 228).
[237] Regulation (EU) 2019/1896 [2019] OJ L 295/1 (n 190), Article 10(1).

The emergence of EU agencies operating with vague competences, experimental governance approaches, and a focus on home affairs exposes a significant gap in the EU's system of fundamental rights protection. These characteristics create conditions under which agencies can sidestep their obligations under EU and international law. Consequently, the framing of autonomy versus accountability is insufficient when applied to JHA/AFSJ agencies such as Frontex.

In addition to the dynamics of Member States relations with Frontex, its mandate and oversight have been the subject of inter-institutional battles. The Parliament successfully challenged the Council's executive decision on the Schengen Borders Code and new rules for Frontex's sea operations on the basis of the Council overstepping its mandate.[238] The European Parliament sought to annul the decision. The Court found that 'the adoption of such rules constitutes a major development in the SBC system' to the extent that 'provisions on conferring powers of public authority on border guards—such as the powers conferred in the contested decision, which include stopping persons apprehended, seizing vessels and conducting persons apprehended to a specific location—mean that the fundamental rights of the persons concerned may be interfered with to such an extent that the involvement of the legislature is required'.[239] As discussed earlier in this chapter, the role of the Court of Justice in resolving inter-institutional disputes is neither new nor novel, especially in external relations.[240]

However, this case speaks to a deeper issue with the rapid development of Frontex. Its legitimacy is considered problematic for various reasons. Primarily, the overall legal basis of the agency and its involvement in operations is underregulated, despite the incremental changes brought about by the successive Regulations. Its place in European governance is significant because of its direct link with operational effects and the accountability which is materially different from the types of accountability associated with other EU institutions or agencies. Given that the emphasis has been squarely on operations at land and sea borders, the liability of deployed personnel is not clearly arranged, so that Frontex can avoid charges of violations of international or EU law by shifting legal responsibility to Member States. This means that it is very difficult for a person that was harmed by a Frontex operation to hold Frontex liable—and this goes to the heart of the Treaty-based values which the EU is supposed to be about.[241]

[238] Case C-355/10 *European Parliament v Council* ECLI:EU:C:2012:516. For comment, see Maarten den Heijer and Eljalill Tauschinsky, 'Where Human Rights Meet Administrative Law: Essential Elements and Limits to Delegation: European Court of Justice, Grand Chamber C-355/10: European Parliament v. Council of the European Union' (2013) 9(3) European Constitutional Law Review 513; Merijn Chamon, 'How the Concept of Essential Elements of a Legislative Act Continues to Elude the Court' (2013) 50(3) Common Market Law Review 849.

[239] Case C-355/10 (n 238), paras 76–77.

[240] See, inter alia, the contributions to Marise Cremona and Anne Thies (eds), *The European Court of Justice and External Relations Law: Constitutional Challenges* (Bloomsbury Publishing 2014).

[241] Carrera, Den Hertog, and Parkin, 'The Peculiar Nature of EU Home Affairs Agencies in Migration Control' (n 223).

Just as the discussion above noted that large, multifaceted institutions such as the Commission are not necessarily unitary actors and have to be understood as such, a similar point can be raised with regard to Frontex. Much of the analysis of Frontex also assumes that it itself knows what kind of an actor it is. An organizational sociology approach suggests that its attempts to build or preserve legitimacy faced with competing demands has led to an agency which is fragmented and should not be considered a unitary actor. This is particularly acute given the physical distance and understanding of different missions between staff in the headquarters in Warsaw and those deployed at the EU's borders.[242] As Frontex lacks the status of an institution, some of its working practices and (legal) accountability practices and norms are hidden from public view.[243]

This is an important point, since in relation to governance agencies are usually understood as having a limited, if influential, mandate and role. Agencies, after all, are a strong feature of contemporary governance. The fuzziness over what type of actor Frontex is can be directly linked to the type of activities it is involved in, where responsibilities lie, and whether it is a direct institutional beneficiary of a shift to informality. It would certainly seem that it is: even without the additional tasks and oversight mechanisms contained in later Frontex Regulations, its hallmark of a Europeanized form of policymaking while acting largely as an EU soft governance tool has remained present.[244]

The extensive use of informal or 'soft' mechanisms within Frontex's work is a strong indication of a shift to 'formal informality'. Frontex's 'Working Arrangements' with third countries[245] and references to 'technical' or 'operational' work give the appearance of a comprehensive system of accountability mechanisms.[246] Yet, these 'quasi-legal' instruments may have repercussions for fundamental rights of individuals, especially in those aspects related to the sharing of information, operational cooperation, and financial assistance and capacity

[242] Nina Perkowski, '"There are voices in every direction": Organizational Decoupling in Frontex (2019) 57(5) JCMS: Journal of Common Market Studies 1182.

[243] Lena Karamanidou and Bernd Kasparek, 'Fundamental Rights, Accountability and Transparency in European Governance of Migration: The Case of the European Border and Coast Guard Agency Frontex' (2020) Respond Working Paper Series: Global Migration: Consequences and Responses, https://researchonline.gcu.ac.uk/ws/files/41192917/Karamanidou_L._Kasparek_B._2020_Fundamental_Rights_Accountability_and_Transparency_in_European_Governance_article.pdf, accessed 7 June 2025.

[244] Carolyn Dudek and Carmen Pestano, 'Canaries in a Coal Mine: The Cayuco Migrant Crisis and the Europeanization of Migration Policy' (2019) 49 Revista española de ciencia política 85.

[245] Eleonora Frasca, 'More or Less (Soft) Law? The Case of Third Country Migration Cooperation and the Long-Term Effects of EU Preference for Soft Law Instruments' (2021) Queen Mary Law Journal 1; Melanie Fink, 'Frontex Working Arrangements: Legitimacy and Human Rights Concerns Regarding Technical Relationships' (2012) 28 Merkourios-Utrecht Journal of International and European Law 20.

[246] Luisa Marin, 'The Cooperation Between Frontex and Third Countries in Information Sharing: Practices, Law and Challenges in Externalizing Border Control Functions' (2020) 26 European Public Law 157; Agostina Pirrello and Mariolina Eliantonio, 'A Board of Appeals for Frontex: Panacea for Violations or Another Patch in the Incomplete System of Accountability?' (2024) 49(1) European Law Review 51.

management in border controls.[247] Although working arrangements are concluded with the cooperation of third countries, they do not fall within the Treaty definition of 'agreements'. As such, they are not covered by democratic scrutiny by the European Parliament pursuant to Article 218 TFEU. Given the vulnerability of the individuals finding themselves in land or sea border zones, especially women and children,[248] higher standards of accountability should apply with closer ongoing control over their activities, given the right to an effective remedy, judicial protection,[249] and fundamental rights at stake.[250]

The need for external cooperation with third states has, over time, been increasingly present in the EU's strategic documents on migration.[251] Here, the informality takes on a different dimension which is similarly masked by the 'technical cooperation' and 'risk analysis' foreseen in the Regulation. Frontex has, in effect, developed its own set of external relations with border authorities in a wide variety of countries. Some of these frameworks, particularly in non-EU countries such as Moldova, are embedded in broader cooperation and integration.[252] Since 2017, in African countries including Côte d'Ivoire, The Gambia, Ghana, Mauritania, Niger, Nigeria, Senegal, and Togo, Frontex has been the main driver of border control capacities and technological developments, but not without questions over the scrutiny of the practices and how rights are protected (including the right to privacy).[253]

5.6.2 European Asylum Support Office (EASO)/EU Agency for Asylum (EUAA)

The CEAS has, as seen throughout this book, been at the heart of the legalization of EU migration governance. A 2010 Regulation created the EASO with the stated aim 'to help to improve the implementation of the CEAS, to strengthen practical

[247] Carrera, Den Hertog, and Parkin, 'The Peculiar Nature of EU Home Affairs Agencies in Migration Control' (n 223); see also Ioannis Kalpouzos and Itamar Mann, 'Banal Crimes against Humanity: The Case of Asylum Seekers in Greece' (2015) 16(1) Melbourne Journal of International Law 1.

[248] Hans-Joachim Bürkner, 'Imaginaries Ready for Use: Framings of the Bordered Intersectionalised Everyday Provided by the EU's Sectoral Policies' (2018) 66 Political Geography 189.

[249] Nicolosi, 'The European Border and Coast Guard Agency (Frontex) and the Limits to Effective Judicial Protection in European Union Law' (n 208).

[250] Simone Marinai, 'The Interception and Rescue at Sea of Asylum Seekers in the Light of the New EU Legal Framework' (2016) 55 Revista de Derecho Comunitario Europeo 901.

[251] For example COM(2011) 743 final (n 34) 16: 'The capability of FRONTEX to work in partnership with non-EU authorities should be fully utilised.' See the discussion in Chapters 6 and 7.

[252] David Gazsi, 'EU Sectoral Integration in the Eastern Neighbourhood: The Case of Frontex–Moldova Relations in Border Management' (2023) 31(11) Journal of European Public Policy 3617.

[253] Frasca, 'Informal Agreements and Quasi-Legal Mechanisms in EU–Africa Cooperation on Migration' (n 205); Ngozi Uzomah, 'European Union Border Technology in Africa: Experiences En Route' (2024) 30 Population, Space and Place e2824; Marin, 'The Cooperation Between Frontex and Third Countries in Information Sharing' (n 246).

cooperation among Member States on asylum and to provide and/or coordinate the provision of operational support to Member States subject to particular pressure on their asylum and reception systems'.[254] In some ways, the development of the EASO mirrors that of Frontex, since both have fundamental roles in resolving the 'migration crisis' gripping the EU since 2015. However, since much of the public and scholarly focus has been on Frontex, which enjoys a much larger budget and list of tasks in its foundational Regulations, the EASO's dynamics and working practicalities have been somewhat neglected.[255]

In theory, the scope for the EASO to incrementally widen its mandate is limited. Asylum applications are the responsibility of the Member States, and the 'common' in CEAS refers to the legal rules rather than the implementation.[256] As such, the idea of the 'system' is one where extensive cooperation or coordination via administrative authorities was not wholly foreseen.[257] Nevertheless, despite the exclusion in the Regulation of decision-making, operational and practical cooperation began to emerge via the establishment of links with national authorities and those working within them.[258] To this extent, the EASO managed to spearhead the growth of an increasingly integrated European administrative system on asylum, despite lacking the explicit competence to do so.[259]

The EASO was eventually 'upgraded' to the EU Agency for Asylum (EUAA).[260] It has witnessed an expansion in its role and powers, but—like Frontex—not without questions over its accountability and relationship with the protection of fundamental rights.[261] Although its mission and role is distinct from Frontex, questions around privacy and data protection are highly pertinent, given the operation of the Eurodac information system at EASO/EUAA's disposal and the emergence of automated technologies.[262] Here again, a system of governance which

[254] Regulation (EU) No 439/2010 of the European Parliament and of the Council of 19 May 2010 establishing a European Asylum Support Office [2010] OJ L 132, Article 1.

[255] Salvatore Nicolosi and David Fernandez-Rojo, 'Out of Control? The Case of the European Asylum Support Office' in Miroslava Scholten and Alex Brenninkmeijer (eds), *Controlling EU Agencies* (Edward Elgar Publishing 2020).

[256] Vincent Chetail, 'The Common European Asylum System: Bric-à-brac or System?' in Vincent Chetail, Philippe De Bruycker, and Francesco Maiani (eds), *Reforming the Common European Asylum System: The New European Refugee Law* (Brill 2016).

[257] Evangelia (Lilian) Tsourdi, 'Holding the European Asylum Support Office Accountable for Its Role in Asylum Decision-Making: Mission Impossible?' (2020) 21(3) German Law Journal 506.

[258] Johan Ekstedt, 'Effects of Decoupling in Asylum Case Processing: The Case of the European Asylum Support Office in Greece' (2022) 7(1) International Journal of Migration and Border Studies 71.

[259] Tsourdi, 'Holding the European Asylum Support Office Accountable For Its Role In Asylum Decision-Making' (n 257).

[260] Regulation (EU) 2021/2303 of the European Parliament and of the Council of 15 December 2021 on the European Union Agency for Asylum and repealing Regulation (EU) No 439/2010 [2021] OJ L 468/1.

[261] See, inter alia, Françoise Comte, 'A New Agency is Born in the European Union: The European Asylum Support Office' (2010) 12(4) European Journal of Migration and Law 373; Stephanie Schneider and Carolin Nieswandt, 'EASO—Support Office or Asylum Authority? Boundary Disputes in the European Field of Asylum Administration' (2018) 43 (S1) Österreichische Zeitschrift für Soziologie 13.

[262] Derya Ozkul, 'Automating Immigration and Asylum: The Uses of New Technologies in Migration and Asylum Governance in Europe' (University of Oxford: Refugee Studies Centre, 2023) https://www.

relies on a proliferation of different actors, with a lack of clarity on responsibility and information-sharing between them, increases the risk that such a system fails to uphold fundamental rights.

5.7 Conclusion

Institutions are at the core of EU governance, providing the formal structures through which authority is exercised, decisions are made, and policies are implemented. Migration, as one of the most persistent and politically sensitive issues facing the EU, has sharply illuminated the tensions and dynamics between these institutions. While questions of institutional balance, competences, identity, and the quest for coherence are not unique to migration, this policy area has brought these issues into sharp focus.

The migration 'crisis' has acted as a stress test for the EU's institutional architecture, but also as an opportunity for some of the institutions and agencies to maximize their potential role(s). It has revealed both the friction between institutions and the necessity of cooperation across them as actors, even when individual institutions cannot be assumed to have a single identity. The role of law is central to this process, framing both the competences of institutions and the limits of their action. However, in migration governance, legal norms often collide with the political urgency to deliver fast, visible responses—generating a fertile ground for institutional experimentation and contestation. While this might be (cautiously) welcomed as a general development to counter accusations that the EU and its institutions are too slow and cumbersome to act—more generally and particularly in responding to crises—the risk of sidelining the political and legal processes designed to ensure rights becomes higher.

The proliferation of EU agencies, including in JHA and the AFSJ, is not a new phenomenon, nor one which is limited to EU governance. Yet among them, Frontex stands out as fundamentally different. It has attracted a great deal of attention and critique, both for its operational role at the EU's external borders and for the legal and ethical questions it raises. Frontex embodies the broader trend of agency expansion in EU governance, but its prominence and power mark a shift in how authority is distributed within the EU framework (including the Member States) and how responsibility for its actions can be tracked.

This proliferation of actors and agencies reflects a broader balancing act: between national sovereignty and supranational authority, and between the need for coherence and the reality of institutional fragmentation. It has led to some institutional confusion, with overlapping mandates and unclear lines of accountability,

hertie-school.org/fileadmin/2_Research/1_About_our_research/2_Research_centres/Centre_for_Fundamental_Rights/AFAR/Automating-immigration-and-asylum_Ozkul.pdf, accessed 9 June 2025.

which leads to an overall lack of transparency. In turn, the emergence of new forms of governance has raised complex questions about international legal responsibility, especially where non-EU states are involved in 'pilots', 'projects', and 'hotspots' where there is no defined (international) legal regime.

As explored in the previous chapters, the main shift in institutional dynamics over time has been striking but can only partially be explained by the changes to the Treaty text and the Regulations and Directives that have emerged. Initially, migration policy was strongly intergovernmental, with Member States firmly in control. The dominant narrative assumed that national preferences—typically more restrictive—were simply 'uploaded' to the EU level through the Council. However, this logic changed with the bringing of migration policy into the core of the legislative process, particularly following the Treaty of Lisbon, which gave the European Commission and European Parliament greater powers in this domain.

Yet this apparent deepening of EU-level control has been accompanied by a paradoxical shift back towards intergovernmentalism. In practice, Member States and EU institutions have sought new ways to bypass scrutiny by the European Parliament, legal oversight by the Court of Justice, and even the Commission's regulatory role. A case in point is the EU–Türkiye Statement of 2016, which was politically brokered and operationalized outside of standard EU legal procedures, although with the support of the Commission. This 'reverse Lisbonisation'[263] reflects a trend toward ad hoc, informal governance mechanisms that prioritize political expediency over institutional norms.

The result is a dual movement: greater formal communautarization, but also greater intergovernmental control through informal or exceptional measures. This paradox helps explain the innovation and institutional diversity observed in EU migration governance. It also reframes the role of institutions like the Commission, which has increasingly acted as an enabler, facilitating deals and solutions even when they stretch or circumvent established legal frameworks. The rationale for doing so goes to the heart of the EU's *raison d'etre*, with institutions such as the Commission keen to demonstrate that the EU is capable of acting on and responding to crises and seeking to work with the Member States on innovative solutions and, ergo, respond to political pressures which assume that action is needed to reduce migration. The ability of the EU to respond to uncertainty and recurring migration-related crises depends critically on how its institutions interact and demonstrate their resilience. The challenge, however, in this shifting space of migration governance is ensuring that transparency and the Treaty-based commitments to the protection of rights and upholding of the rule of law are not lost.[264]

[263] Sergio Carrera, Leonhard den Hertog, and Marco Stefan, 'The EU–Turkey Deal: Reversing Lisbonisation in EU Migration and Asylum Policies' in Sergio Carrera, Juan Santos Vara, and Tineke Strik (eds), *Constitutionalising the External Dimensions of EU Migration Policies in Times of Crisis* (Edward Elgar Publishing 2019).

[264] Regine Paul and Christof Roos, 'Towards a New Ontology of Crisis? Resilience in EU Migration Governance' (2019) 28(4) European Security 393, 405.

Finally, while legislation remains key to ensuring transparency and legitimacy, many of the foundational practices in JHA and migration policy originated in a shift to informal forms of governance. These early 'laboratories' for legal and policy innovation have set a precedent for a lack of transparency, embedding a tendency to privilege informal arrangements over formal legal accountability.[265] Rectifying this legacy is essential for building a migration governance system that is both resilient and democratically legitimate.

[265] Jörg Monar, 'The Dynamics of Justice and Home Affairs: Laboratories, Driving Factors and Costs' (2001) 39(4) JCMS: Journal of Common Market Studies 747.

6
Migration and EU External Relations
The 'Formal'

The horizon of formal legal instruments relating to migration spans the wide spectrum of the EU's external relations. As the previous chapters have explored, the institutional dimensions of these instruments do not follow a single governance template. Neither are they to be found in a neatly encapsulated policy area of 'migration' accompanied by a defined set of legal instruments. Rather, although some migration-specific instruments appear pursuant to provisions of the Treaty, others are found elsewhere but have no less significance for individuals.

In Chapter 4, the main pieces of legislation to emerge from the Treaty-based competences in the post-Amsterdam period were set out. The purpose of this chapter is to present the wide-ranging, but both complex and diverse, means by which the goals of the Treaty have been operationalized by formal means beyond legislation as part of the EU's external relations; that is to say, where Treaty-based procedures have been used to conclude bilateral agreements with third countries, under specific competences permitted in the Treaty.

As elsewhere in the book, this chapter considers measures and instruments relating to both regular and irregular migration. Yet it is in the latter that there has been the greatest amount of activity. This chapter considers how migration features in the agreements concluded with third states via Treaty-based processes. Bilateral agreements with third states on migration, or incorporating a migration dimension and which are not underpinned by other pieces of EU legislation, are also possible under the competences of the Treaty. Such examples include Visa Facilitation Agreements and Readmission Agreements. These are considered here as the 'formal' part but, as this book argues, cannot be considered in isolation from the informal.

The purpose is not to give an account of every piece of legislation and agreement with third states that has come into effect since the Treaty of Amsterdam (or even before). Rather, the analysis here demonstrates two things. First, just as legislation on migration writ large does not occupy the field and the mere existence of competences does not necessarily lead to legislation forthcoming, the same is also true for international agreements relating to migration. Second, the gaps left by the lack of legislation point to a system of governance where elaboration by 'softer' or 'informal' means is not only likely but—for policy-makers—essential. This chapter draws out when, where, and why this occurs, setting the case for a discussion in the

The Governance of Migration in the European Union. Paul James Cardwell, Oxford University Press.
 DOI: 10.1093/9780191946592.003.0007

following chapter of whether informality has begun to play a more prominent role in tasks which were originally destined for formal legislation and agreements.

6.1 Migration in the internal and the external spheres of governance

The place of migration, situated across the internal sphere of governance which is concerned with movement across internal borders of the EU and signified by the migration being part of an Area of Freedom, Security and Justice (AFSJ)—and yet at the same time driven by looking outwards—was considered in Chapter 1. Consequently, migration is positioned between two opposing governance frameworks: one internal, where legislation has played a key role in driving integration, and the other external, where intergovernmentalism has traditionally played a more dominant role, and integration efforts are largely secured via cooperation. Migration can 'fit' fully neither within a logic of security nor within one of economic considerations, given that it might concern regular or irregular migration across a wide spectrum of categories. If this were the case, it might help to understand which certain logics apply: we might expect regular migration (for example, for the purposes of work) to have moved further along the integration path than measures to combat irregular migration, whereas in fact the reverse is true. In addition, the scope of discretion afforded to the Member States within legislation and the reliance on dialogue both between the institutions and the Member States and between the Member States themselves are considerable. These dialogues, stemming from the assumed solidarity between Member States, have been severely tested in recent years.[1]

The further complexity is that external governance is not merely unilateral. Examples of EU migration law, such as the Blue Card Directive[2] and Family Reunification Directive,[3] are externally focused insofar as such law applies to certain categories of third country nationals who wish to migrate to the EU. This type of law does not, of course, need the agreement or acquiescence of third countries to be operationalized. By contrast, other aspects of EU law, including both regular and irregular migration, can only be effective in securing both the agreement and cooperation of third states. For regular migration, bilateral agreements allowing certain categories of individuals to migrate for the purposes of work can be agreed

[1] See, for example, Sandra Lavenex, 'Common Market, Normative Power or Super-State? Conflicting Political Identities in EU Asylum and Immigration Policy' in Sabine Saurugger and Mark Thatcher (eds), *Constructing the EU's Political Identity* (Palgrave Macmillan 2022).

[2] Directive (EU) 2021/1883 of the European Parliament and of the Council of 20 October 2021 on the conditions of entry and residence of third-country nationals for the purpose of highly qualified employment, and repealing Council Directive 2009/50/EC [2021] OJ L 382/1.

[3] Council Directive 2003/86/EC of 22 September 2003 on the right to family reunification [2003] OJ L 251/12.

at the EU or national levels.[4] For irregular migration, and especially returns, Readmission Agreements are the main way foreseen in the Treaty by which to achieve the goal of returning individuals, as a consequence providing an oft-cited 'solution' to the 'crisis' of irregular migration. Since regular and irregular migration are often considered as part of a whole within negotiations with third countries, the legal competences used can fall across a number of Treaty articles.

In this regard, there is not a single, linear line of migration as part of external relations which can be traced. In particular, Association Agreements date back to the earliest days of the Community. While many associated states have become full members, the standout example of one who has not is Türkiye. The Association Agreement between the Community and Türkiye has generated more than seventy CJEU decisions relating to protection for Turkish workers and their families, in a series of decisions stretching back much further than the Treaty of Amsterdam.[5]

The drive to include migration-related aspects in EU external relations and the relationships with third countries has become a dominant theme. The institutional documentation on both migration as part of JHA/AFSJ and external relations helps guide our understanding of the place of formal (and informal) instruments and their significance in migration. The greater synergy between these two spheres became evident as the EU emerged from the 'awkward' constitutional structure of the former third pillar[6] with the new competences found in the Treaty of Amsterdam. The conclusions of the Seville European Council 2002 made one of the clearest statements about the relationship of migration with the Union's general external relations: 'any future cooperation, association or equivalent agreement which the European Union or the European Community concludes with any country should include a clause on joint management of migration flows and on compulsory readmission in the event of illegal immigration.'[7]

[4] See, in the case of Germany, the agreements with Kenya, Uzbekistan, and Georgia https://www.bmi.bund.de/SharedDocs/pressemitteilungen/EN/2024/09/kenia_migrationsabkommen.html. Announcement of the German–Kenyan Agreement on a Comprehensive Migration and Mobility Partnership BGBL II Nr 469/2024, available at: https://www.recht.bund.de/bgbl/2/2024/469/regelungstext.pdf?__blob=publicationFile&v=3, accessed 7 June 2025; Announcement of the German–Georgian Agreement on a Migration and Mobility BGBL II Nr 14/2024, available at: https://www.recht.bund.de/bgbl/2/2024/14/VO.html, accessed 7 June 2025. The agreement with Uzbekistan does not appear to be publicly available.

[5] Daniel Thym, *European Migration Law* (Oxford University Press 2023) 82; see also Alezini Loxa, *Sustainability and EU Migration Law: Tracing the History of a Contemporary Concept* (Cambridge University Press 2025) 129–56.

[6] Grainne de Búrca, 'Institutional Development of the EU' in Paul Craig and Grainne de Búrca (eds), *The Evolution of EU Law* (1st edn, Oxford University Press 1999) 55.

[7] Council, 'Presidency Conclusions' (Seville, 21 and 22 June 2002), available at: https://www.consilium.europa.eu/media/20928/72638.pdf, accessed 7 June 2025. See also Sandra Lavenex, 'From something to "offer in return" to something to "withdraw": Retracing trade conditionality in EU readmission policy (*EU Immigration and Asylum Law and Policy Blog*, 5 September 2023) https://eumigrationlawblog.eu/from-something-to-offer-in-return-to-something-to-withdraw-retracing-trade-conditionality-in-eu-readmission-policy/, accessed 7 June 2025.

6.2 The post-Amsterdam legislative trajectory

As explored in earlier chapters, over successive multi-annual programmes, both the lenses by which migration is viewed and the role of legislation in meeting goals over time have changed. Following the 11 September attacks in the US, the association of migration with securitization—an association that had already begun in the 1990s[8]—became both more widespread and accepted as a rationale by Member States and EU institutions alike.[9] Such a logic promoted the prioritization of return (or readmission) of individuals to their home states.[10] The weight on Freedom, Security and Justice shifts over time, and depends on who is envisaged. It is no exaggeration to say that much of the emphasis on this legislation falls squarely on 'combating' or 'fighting'[11] irregular migration as the logic has shifted from 'inclusion' to 'exclusion'[12] and from 'rights' to 'security'.[13] Yet, the use of legislation as the cornerstone to do so has diminished. This helps us explain both the pace of the introduction of proposals and the ability of legislation to make its way through the institutional framework. Current discourse on migration emerging from the EU institutions continues with the theme of securitization insofar as migration is presented as a threat, or at best a challenge, to Europe.

In contrast to the Tampere Conclusions, which placed legislation at the core of the developing EU migration law acquis, the subsequent Hague and Stockholm programmes and GAM/GAMM appeared to downplay the central role of legislation, or at the very least prioritized the improvement and consolidation of existing legislation (via the recasting process) rather than suggesting new legislation. This theme has continued up to and including the most recent guiding policy, the New Pact on Migration and Asylum in 2020.[14]

[8] See, for example, Valsamis Mitsilegas, 'The Implementation of the EU Acquis on Illegal Immigration by the Candidate Countries of Central and Eastern Europe: Challenges and Contradictions' (2002) 28 Journal of Ethnic and Migration Studies 665; Ryszard Cholewinski, 'The EU Aquis on Irregular Migration: Reinforcing Security at the Expense of Rights' (2000) 2 European Journal of Migration and Law 361.

[9] Jeff Huysmans, 'The European Union and the Securitization of Migration' (2000) 38(5) JCMS: Journal of Common Market Studies 751; Thomas Faist, '"Extension du domaine de la lutte": International Migration and Security before and after September 11, 2001' (2002) 36(1) International Migration Review 7; Daniel Wunderlich, 'Implementing EU External Migration Policy: Security-Driven by Default?' (2013) 11 Comparative European Politics 406; Gabriella Lazaridis, *Security, Insecurity and Migration in Europe* (1st edn, Routledge 2011).

[10] Mariagiulia Giuffré, 'Obligation to Readmit? The Relationship between Interstate and EU Readmission Agreements' in Francesca Ippolito and Seline Trevisanut (eds), *Migration in Mare Nostrum: Mechanism of International Cooperation* (Cambridge University Press 2015).

[11] Frontex, for example, defines its operational mission as 'the fight against cross-border crime', Frontex, 'Operations' (*Frontex: European Border and Coast Guard Agency*) https://www.frontex.europa.eu/what-we-do/operations/operations/, accessed 7 June 2025.

[12] As noted by Monar: Jörg Monar, 'The Dynamics of Justice and Home Affairs: Laboratories, Driving Factors and Costs' (2001) 39(4) JCMS: Journal of Common Market Studies 747.

[13] Cholewinski, 'The EU Aquis on Irregular Migration' (n 8).

[14] Commission, 'Communication from the Commission to the European Parliament, the Council, the European Economic and Social Committee and the Committee of the Regions on a New Pact on Migration and Asylum' COM(2020) 609 final. See annual reports at: Commission, 'Pact on Migration

The purpose here is to understand if a similar trend can be detected in the EU's external relations, where the counterparts to Regulations and Directives are agreements with third states pursuant to Treaty-based competences.

Article 216(1) TFEU lays the foundation for the EU's external Treaty-making power.[15] It provides that the Union may conclude agreements where: (a) the Treaties provide for such competence; (b) it is necessary to achieve objectives of the Union; or (c) the conclusion of the agreement is likely to affect or alter existing common rules. This reflects the doctrine of implied powers, developed by the Court of Justice in cases such as *AETR/ERTA*.[16] Furthermore, the EU's legal personality, enshrined in Article 47 TEU, underpins its ability to act as a subject of international law, distinct from its Member States.

The forms of international agreements vary according to their legal and policy scope. Association agreements are based on Article 217 TFEU and aim to establish close political and economic ties with many of the countries in proximity to the EU. They go by a variety of names. Partnership and cooperation agreements often involve frameworks for political dialogue and regulatory cooperation. Trade agreements, negotiated under the Common Commercial Policy (Article 207 TFEU), fall within the EU's exclusive competence. This competence allows the Union to conclude trade deals such as the Comprehensive Economic and Trade Agreement (CETA) with Canada and the Economic Partnership Agreement (EPA) with Japan. The CJEU confirmed the broad scope of this exclusive competence in its landmark Opinion 2/15 on the EU–Singapore Free Trade Agreement, clarifying that most trade-related provisions fall under EU competence, with only limited exceptions (for example, investor-state dispute settlement and portfolio investment).[17]

Article 218 TFEU governs the procedure for negotiating and concluding international agreements. It requires the Council to authorize the opening of negotiations, adopt directives for the negotiations, and subsequently sign and conclude the agreement. The Commission acts as the lead negotiator in most cases, while the High Representative for Foreign Affairs and Security Policy or the Council may take this role in the area of the Common Foreign and Security Policy (CFSP),

and Asylum' (*European Commission*) https://commission.europa.eu/strategy-and-policy/priorities-2019-2024/promoting-our-european-way-life_en, accessed 7 June 2025.

[15] 'The Union may conclude an agreement with one or more third countries or international organisations where the Treaties so provide or where the conclusion of an agreement is necessary in order to achieve, within the framework of the Union's policies, one of the objectives referred to in the Treaties, or is provided for in a legally binding Union act or is likely to affect common rules or alter their scope.'

[16] Case C-22/70 *Commission of the European Communities v Council of the European Communities Accord européen sur les transports routiers/European Agreement on Road Transport* ECLI:EU:C:1971:32, later confirmed by Opinion 1/03 *Competence of the Community to conclude the new Lugano Convention on jurisdiction and the recognition and enforcement of judgments in civil and commercial matters* ECLI:EU:C:2006:81.

[17] Opinion 2/15 *Request for an opinion submitted by the European Commission pursuant to Article 218(11) TFEU* ECLI:EU:C:2017:376.

which is governed by procedures (Title V TEU). The European Parliament must give its consent to certain types of agreements, such as association agreements or those with significant budgetary implications, while in others it is only consulted.[18]

Where agreements address both exclusive and shared competences, they are classified as mixed agreements,[19] necessitating ratification not only by the EU institutions but also by the individual Member States in accordance with their constitutional procedures.[20] This can create procedural complexity and political sensitivity, as seen in the delayed ratification of CETA due to opposition from the Wallonia regional parliament in Belgium.[21]

Migration, particularly when linked to the Area of Freedom, Security and Justice (AFSJ), intersects with broader external competences in development (Articles 208–211 TFEU), humanitarian aid (Article 214 TFEU), and neighbourhood policy (Article 8 TEU). As such, migration can—and often does—find its way into many of the agreements the EU has concluded (or sought to conclude) with third states.

6.3 General agreements with third states

Beginning in 1995, the European Commission sought to incorporate standard readmission clauses into all association and cooperation agreements with third countries.[22] These clauses were intended to establish a general commitment by partner countries to readmit their nationals found to be irregularly present in an EU Member State. However, these provisions fall short of constituting formal

[18] Article 218(6) TFEU.

[19] See, inter alia, Joni Heliskoski, *Mixed Agreements as a Technique for Organizing the International Relations of the European Community and Its Member States* (vol 2, Martinus Nijhoff Publishers 2001); Ramses Wessel and Guillaume Van der Loo, 'The Non-Ratification of Mixed Agreements: Legal Consequences and Solutions' (2017) 54(3) Common Market Law Review 735.

[20] See further, Geert De Baere, 'The Framework of EU External Competences for Developing the External Dimensions of EU Asylum and Migration Policy' (2010) Leuven Centre for Global Governance Studies, Working Paper No 50—May 2010, available at: https://ghum.kuleuven.be/ggs/publications/working_papers/2010/50DeBaere, accessed 7 June 2025; Paula Andrade, 'EU External Competences on Migration: Which Role for Mixed Agreements?' in Sergio Carrera, Juan Santos Vara, and Tineke Strik, *Constitutionalising the External Dimensions of EU Migration Policies in Times of Crisis: Legality, Rule of Law and Fundamental Rights Reconsidered* (Edward Elgar Publishing 2019).

[21] See Dirk De Bièvre, 'The Paradox of Weakness in European Trade Policy: Contestation and Resilience in CETA and TTIP Negotiations' (2018) 53(3) The International Spectator 70; Achim Hurrelmann and Frank Wendler, 'How Does Politicisation Affect the Ratification of Mixed EU Trade Agreements? The Case of CETA' (2023) 31(1) Journal of European Public Policy 157.

[22] See, for community agreements: Council, 'Readmission—Community Agreements' (Doc 12509/95, 8 December 1995), available at https://data.consilium.europa.eu/doc/document/ST-12509-1995-INIT/en/pdf, accessed 7 June 2025; and for mixed agreements: Council, 'Council Conclusions on clauses to be inserted in future mixed agreements' (Doc 4272/96, 22 January 1996), available at https://data.consilium.europa.eu/doc/document/ST-4272-1996-INIT/en/pdf, accessed 7 June 2025, cited in Carole Billet, 'EC Readmission Agreements: A Prime Instrument of the External Dimension of the EU's Fight against Irregular Immigration. An Assessment after Ten Years of Practice' (2010) 12(1) European Journal of Migration and Law 45, 49.

Readmission Agreements. As the Commission itself has clarified, such clauses are best understood as enabling clauses; that is, they articulate a broad obligation to readmit but do not specify the procedural modalities, operational mechanisms, or enforcement frameworks necessary for effective implementation.[23]

A prominent example of this approach is Article 13 of the Cotonou Agreement, signed in 2000 between the EU and the African, Caribbean, and Pacific (ACP) group of states.[24] This article states that 'each of the ACP States shall accept the return and readmission of any of its nationals who are illegally present on the territory of a Member State of the European Union, at that Member State's request and without further formalities'. While this provision appears to establish a clear obligation, it similarly lacks detailed procedural guidance, thereby limiting its practical enforceability. It did not, however, refer to stateless persons or third country nationals. The regular migration counterpart in the Agreement was the reaffirming of the right to fair treatment of ACP workers in Member States, supporting training of ACP citizens and the provision of access to education. These are, however, only commitments, which are not accompanied by enforceable targets.[25]

The Seville European Council of June 2002 mandated that 'a clause on joint management of migration flows and on compulsory readmission in the event of illegal immigration'[26] should be included in all future external agreements. Migration was thus included as a compulsory element of external agreements, alongside human rights, good governance and anti-corruption clauses.

As a result, comparable clauses have been included in other EU agreements with third countries. However, the presence and scope of such provisions vary significantly. For instance, while many Euro-Mediterranean Association Agreements contain migration-related clauses, Morocco's agreement notably does not include a readmission clause, but merely a declaration.[27] This omission underscores the

[23] Commission, 'Communication from the Commission to the Council and the European Parliament on Immigration and Asylum Policies' COM(1994) 23 final.

[24] Partnership Agreement between the Members of the African, Caribbean and Pacific Group of States of the one part, and the European Community and its Member States, of the other part (Cotonou Agreement) [2000] OJ L317/3, Article 13.

[25] Stephen Dearden and Clara Salama, 'The New EU ACP Partnership Agreement' (2002) 14(6) Journal of International Development 899, 902.

[26] Council, 'Presidency Conclusions' (n 7); see also Karin Arts, 'ACP–EU Relations in a New Era: The Cotonou Agreement' (2003) 40(1) Common Market Law Review 95.

[27] Euro Mediterranean Agreement establishing an association between the European Communities and their Member States, of the one part, and the Kingdom of Morocco, of the other part [2000] OJ L 70/2. The Joint Declaration reads: 'The Parties hereby agree to adopt bilaterally the appropriate provisions and measures to cover readmission of their nationals in cases in which the latter have left their countries. For those purposes, in the case of the Member States of the European Union, "nationals" shall be taken to mean Member State nationals as defined for Community purposes.' See further, Sarah Wolff, *The Mediterranean Dimension of the European Union's Internal Security* (Palgrave Macmillan 2012) 145; Sarah Wolff, 'The Politics of Negotiating EU Readmission Agreements: Insights from Morocco and Turkey' (2014) 16(1) European Journal of Migration and Law 69.

political sensitivity and variability of readmission commitments across different regional contexts.[28]

Furthermore, Stabilisation and Association Agreements (SAAs) with Western Balkan countries, as well as migration clauses in broader Euro-Mediterranean frameworks, reflect the EU's evolving strategy to embed migration governance within its external relations. Nevertheless, the effectiveness of these clauses remains contingent on the willingness of partner countries to cooperate and on the EU's capacity to offer credible incentives beyond the narrow focus on return and control.

In more recent years, economic partnership agreements have included some mobility provisions, but only alongside strengthened provisions on returns. Highly skilled migration provisions were included in, for example, the partnership agreement with Caribbean states in 2008 including doctors and nurses.[29] For the renegotiated ACP agreement in 2018, this proved problematic against the background of an increasingly fragmented approach to migration on the EU side. As Carbone has noted, the Hungarian government's opposition to references to regular migration caused great difficulty in agreeing an approach. Consequently, the final text strengthened the language on irregular migration, deleted references relating to the benefits of migration, and included a clear separation between competences at national and supranational levels.[30] While the Hungarian government may have taken a particularly strong line on migration, the political shifts in Europe over the past two decades towards emphasizing the need to limit irregular migration are at odds with approaches taken towards negotiations as a partnership with other states and regions, including in Africa.[31]

6.4 Readmission Agreements

Readmission Agreements are at the heart of the aim of returning irregular migrants to their countries of origin, or countries through which they have passed en route to the territory of an EU Member State. As such, their primary purpose is to establish the procedures and obligations for the identification, documentation,

[28] Eleonora Frasca, 'Informal Agreements and Quasi-Legal Mechanisms in EU–Africa Cooperation on Migration: How the EU Takes Advantage of the GCM Commitments' (2023) 5 Frontiers in Human Dynamics 1, available at https://www.frontiersin.org/journals/human-dynamics/articles/10.3389/fhumd.2023.120762, accessed 7 June 2025.

[29] Mark Langan and Sophia Price, 'Migration, Development and EU Free Trade Deals: The Paradox of Economic Partnership Agreements as a Push Factor for Migration' (2021) 7(4) Global Affairs 505.

[30] Maurizio Carbone, 'The Calm after the Storm: Plurilateral Challenges to the Post-2020 EU–ACP Partnership' (2019) 57 JCMS: Journal of Common Market Studies 141.

[31] Franzisca Zanker, 'Managing or Restricting Movement? Diverging Approaches of African and European Migration Governance' (2019) 17(7) Comparative Migration Studies 1.

and return of third country nationals or stateless persons who do not, or who no longer, fulfil conditions for entry, presence, or residence in an EU Member State.

Reflecting the importance that the EU institutions have placed on them, these agreements have been variously described as 'the centrepiece of the external dimension of the EU's return policy'[32] and a 'standard tool to tackle irregular migration'.[33] They are premised on the generally understood obligation of states to readmit their own citizens, via the 'right to return' of individuals as found in Article 13 of the Universal Declaration on Human Rights of 12 December 1948 and Article 12.4 of the UN Convention on Civil and Political Rights of 16 December 1966 'right to return', although an explicit obligation to retake citizens is absent.

Although Readmission Agreements benefit from a specific Treaty competence and are a clear example of a migration-focused, formal legal agreement that has been concluded via an established institutional process, their origin lies in the internal sphere of governance and practices of the Member States. Prior to the consolidation of the free movement of workers, bilateral agreements between Member States of the (then) Community were used to return irregular migrants.

Multilateral Readmission Agreements have a long history in EU integration. They date back to the agreement between the Schengen states and Poland in 1991, the legal basis of which was the Convention implementing the Schengen Agreement.[34] Pre-Amsterdam, Member States also pursued bilateral agreements—in particular with states in Central and Eastern Europe.[35] As a result, the Council adopted a Resolution in 1994 to try to agree a minimum standard form for agreements between the Member States and promote third pillar cooperation.[36] This provided a template for an EU generation of Readmission Agreements foreseen in the Tampere Conclusions and starting with the EU–Hong Kong agreement in 2004.[37] The learning process that this provided within the institutional setting

[32] Peter Slominski and Florian Trauner, 'Reforming Me Softly—How Soft Law Has Changed EU Return Policy since the Migration Crisis' (2021) 44(1) West European Politics 93.

[33] Katharina Eisele, 'The EU's Readmission Policy: Of Agreements and Arrangements' in Sergio Carrera, Juan Santos Vara, and Tineke Strik (eds), *Constitutionalising the External Dimensions of EU Migration Policies in Times of Crisis* (Edward Elgar Publishing 2019).

[34] Convention implementing the Schengen Agreement of 14 June 1985 [2000] OJ L 239/19, Article 23(4): 'aliens may be expelled from the territory of that Party to their country of origin or any other State to which they may be admitted, in particular under the relevant provisions of the Readmission Agreements concluded by the Contracting Parties.'

[35] Germany, for example, concluded its own agreement with Poland almost simultaneously with that of the Community: Andrea Subhan, 'Migration and Asylum in Central Eastern Europe' (1998) European Parliament Working Paper, LIBE 104 EN, available at https://www.europarl.europa.eu/workingpapers/libe/pdf/104_en.pdf, accessed 7 June 2025, 45–51.

[36] Council, 'Council Recommendation of 30 November 1994 concerning a specimen bilateral Readmission Agreement between a Member State and a third country' [1994] OJ C 274/20; Council, 'Council Recommendation of 24 July 1995 on the guiding principles to be followed in drawing up protocols on the implementation of Readmission Agreements' [1996] OJ C 274/25.

[37] Daphné Bouteillet-Paquet, 'Passing the Buck: A Critical Analysis of the Readmission Policy Implemented by the European Union and Its Member States' (2003) 5(3) European Journal of Migration and Law 359.

has since led to a gradual but definite evolution of the scope of Readmission Agreements.

Post-Amsterdam, the legal basis was found in Article 63(3)(b) EC, which allowed the Community to take 'measures' including 'repatriation of illegal residents'. Both voluntary and forced returns are foreseen in the Returns Directive.[38] There was no express provision for Readmission Agreements; the competence relied on the general aim of meeting objectives and the implied competence underlined by the ERTA doctrine.[39] At Lisbon, a more specific objective is now found in Article 79(3) TFEU: 'The Union may conclude agreements with third countries for the readmission to their countries of origin or provenance of third-country nationals who do not or who no longer fulfil the conditions for entry, presence or residence in the territory of one of the Member States.' Readmission is hence a shared competence: Member States have concluded individual agreements and operate them whether or not there is an EU agreement.[40] This is an instance of what Cassarino has termed agreement 'dualism'.[41] Although the view of the Commission is that Readmission Agreements are 'legislative acts', 'even the broadest interpretation of the principle of parallelism is not broad enough to trigger exclusivity of the Union over readmission policy, because the treaty objective of Article 79(1) TFEU is "common migration policy" and not readmission policy'.[42] The Returns Directive states that its provisions shall be without prejudice to more favourable provisions of 'bilateral or multilateral agreements between one of more Member States and one or more third countries'.[43] As a result, there is an overlapping patchwork of agreements between the EU, Member States, and third states, though it may be surmised that an EU agreement would take precedence over a bilateral Member State agreement with the same state.[44] Since there are more bilateral agreements concluded by Member States than by the EU, the 'race to the bottom' argument is

[38] Directive 2008/115/EC of the European Parliament and of the Council of 16 December 2008 on common standards and procedures in Member States for returning illegally staying third-country nationals [2008] OJ L 348/12, Articles 3(3), 7, and 8.

[39] Case C-22/70 (n 16).

[40] France, for example, has Readmission Agreements with North African countries including Morocco, Algeria, and Tunisia, whereas the EU has not succeeded in concluding such agreements. See Tasnim Abderrahim, 'The thorny question of readmission in France-Maghreb migration talks' (*MIE: Middle East Institute*, 2 November 2021) https://www.mei.edu/publications/thorny-question-readmission-france-maghreb-migration-talks, accessed 7 June 2025.

[41] Jean-Pierre Cassarino, 'Readmission Policy in the European Union' (2010) European Parliament Committee on Civil Liberties, Justice and Home Affairs (Study), available at https://www.europarl.europa.eu/RegData/etudes/etudes/join/2010/425632/IPOL-LIBE_ET(2010)425632_EN.pdf, accessed 7 June 2025.

[42] Marion Panizzon, 'Readmission Agreements of EU Member States: A Case for EU Subsidiarity or Dualism?' (2012) 31(4) Refugee Survey Quarterly 101.

[43] Directive 2008/115/EC [2008] OJ L 348/98 (n 38), Article 4(1)(b).

[44] Finland, for example, has six bilateral agreements, although four are now EU Member States, with only Switzerland and Kosovo as the exceptions: Finnish Ministry of the Interior, 'Readmission Agreements' (*Ministry of the Interior Finland*) https://intermin.fi/en/areas-of-expertise/migration/voluntary-and-forced-return/readmission-agreements, accessed 7 June 2025.

pertinent, as is the capacity of the EU to conclude agreements or use them as bargaining tools.[45]

The stated purpose of a Readmission Agreement is to facilitate the return of individuals who do not (or who no longer) have a regular status. As a bilateral agreement, this applies to the third country and to the EU Member States[46] in the context of 'preventing and combating illegal migration'.[47] The third state commits to readmission of its own nationals 'upon application by a Member State and without further formalities' and vice versa.[48]

The aim therefore is to streamline the administrative processes, but also to act as a demotivating factor for individuals tempted to enter the EU in an irregular manner, or to overstay their legal right to stay. At their core, thus, Readmission Agreements define the criteria and mechanisms for readmitting own nationals. They may, more controversially, also cover third country nationals and stateless persons who transited through or resided in the third state. The inclusion of asylum seekers is also contentious via the method of labelling the third country as 'safe', thus removing the need for Member States to treat applications for asylum fully.[49]

The content of Readmission Agreements is largely similar. Common to all are commitments to respect international human rights agreements, and procedural safeguards in the text.[50] These have been criticized for being vague or lacking sufficiently precise safeguards, including in the related area of data protection.

[45] See the discussion that follows.

[46] As stipulated in Protocol 21 to the TFEU, Ireland (and formerly the UK also) may choose to opt in or out of readmissions agreements on a case-by-case basis, and Ireland has done so in many of the cases. Under Protocol 22 to the TFEU, Denmark has opted out of participating in justice and home affairs cooperation (of which these Readmission Agreements are part), with the exception of measures that relate to the Schengen acquis. Denmark would therefore need a separate agreement, which is also the case for the non-EU Schengen states, Iceland, Liechtenstein, Norway, and Switzerland. See further, Panizzon, 'Readmission Agreements of EU Member States' (n 2).

[47] As per, for example, Agreement between the European Union and the Republic of Belarus on the readmission of persons residing without authorisation [2020] OJ L 181/3, Article 2.

[48] As per, for example, Agreement between the European Community and the former Yugoslav Republic of Macedonia on the readmission of persons residing without authorisation [2007] OJ L 334/7, Articles 2(1) and 4(1).

[49] Hakkı Arıner and Yiğit Kader, 'On the Removal of Asylum Seekers to Third Countries and the Scope of the EU–Turkey Readmission Agreement' (2022) 34(3–4) International Journal of Refugee Law 416.

[50] For example, in the Agreement between the European Union and the Republic of Azerbaijan on the readmission of persons residing without authorisation [2014] OJ L 128/17, Article 2 requires both parties to 'ensure respect for human rights and for the obligations and responsibilities following from relevant international instruments applicable to the parties', in particular the 1948 Universal Declaration of Human Rights, the 1950 European Convention on Human Rights and Fundamental Freedoms and its protocols, the 1966 International Covenant on Civil and Political Rights, the 1984 UN Convention Against Torture, and the 1951 Geneva Convention relating to the Status of Refugees and its Protocol of 1967. It is underlined by the obligation under Article 18 that the agreement 'shall be without prejudice to the rights, obligations and responsibilities of the Union, its Member States and Azerbaijan arising from international law including from international conventions to which they are party, in particular from the international instruments listed in Article 2'. The reference to the ECHR also appears in agreements to which the third state is not a party, such as Cabo Verde.

Nevertheless, the presence of international law as a term in the agreement at the very least suggests that only states that are signatories to the relevant instruments of international law can be the subject of a 'formal' EU Readmission Agreement.

A standard agreement includes several key provisions. As noted above, the obligation on both the EU and the third state to readmit their own citizens obliges the third country to readmit any person proven to be a national of that country or EU Member State. This may be extended to the readmission of others, including stateless persons, and applies when the individual in question transited through the third country or had a visa or residence permit issued by that country. The third country must then readmit the person if the EU Member State can demonstrate these links.[51]

In procedural terms, the agreements set deadlines for responding to readmission requests (typically 14 days), issuing travel documents, and transferring the individual.[52] Failure to comply within the timeframes may result in the EU taking further diplomatic or legal steps. Some Readmission Agreements contain provisions for the transit of persons through the territory of the partner state en route to their country of origin, subject to certain safeguards.[53] Each agreement also established a Joint Readmission Committee to 'provide each other with mutual assistance in the application and interpretation' of the Readmission Agreement and to monitor implementation, resolve disputes, and propose improvements.[54] These are chaired by the Commission and the government of the third country, and may make decisions relating to implementing arrangements,[55] to be followed up by a Council decision.

There are currently eighteen Readmission Agreements concluded with third states, but not all are operational at present.[56] The first agreement was concluded with Hong Kong (by the European Community) in 2004[57] and the most recent

[51] For example, Agreement between the European Community and the Russian Federation on readmission [2007] OJ L 129/40, Article 10.

[52] For example, Agreement between the European Community and the Republic of Moldova on the readmission of persons residing without authorisation [2007] OJ L 334/149, Articles 4(4) and 6(4).

[53] For example, Agreement between the European Community and Bosnia and Herzegovina on the readmission of persons residing without authorisation—Joint Declarations [2007] OJ L 334/66, Articles 13 and 14.

[54] For example, Agreement between the European Union and the Republic of Cape Verde on the readmission of persons residing without authorisation [2013] OJ L 282/15, Article 18.

[55] For example, Council Decision (EU) 2016/551 of 23 March 2016 establishing the position to be taken on behalf of the European Union within the Joint Readmission Committee on a Decision of the Joint Readmission Committee on implementing arrangements for the application of Articles 4 and 6 of the Agreement between the European Union and the Republic of Turkey on the readmission of persons residing without authorisation from 1 June 2016 [2016] OJ L 95/9.

[56] Albania (2006), Armenia (2014), Azerbaijan (2014), Belarus (2020), Bosnia and Herzegovina (2008), Cape Verde (Cabo Verde) (2014), Georgia (2011), Hong Kong (2004), Macao (2004), Moldova (2008), Montenegro (2008), North Macedonia (2008), Pakistan (2010), Russia (2007), Serbia (2008), Sri Lanka (2005), Türkiye (2014), and Ukraine (2008).

[57] Agreement between the European Community and the Government of the Hong Kong Special Administrative Region of the People's Republic of China on the readmission of persons residing without authorisation [2004] OJ L 17/25.

with Belarus in 2020.[58] The Commission has been authorized by the Council to negotiate Readmission Agreements with six further states, though these have not been concluded despite the length of time passed: Algeria (authorized to begin negotiations in 2002); China (2002); Jordan (2015); Morocco (2000); Nigeria (2016); and Tunisia (2014).

Of the eighteen agreements in force, more than half are with European countries, some of which are also engaged in the enlargement or pre-enlargement process and others in the Eastern Partnership. All the Western Balkans states have concluded agreements, along with Russia, Moldova, Ukraine, and Belarus. In terms of enlargement, conclusion of a Readmission Agreement has been understood as a necessary precursor to an Association Agreement, with the earliest example (between Schengen states and Poland) setting the template.[59] Needless to say, the existence of a Readmission Agreement does not necessarily entail either that returns will occur or that the form of institutional cooperation foreseen via the Joint Readmission Committees will take place. Belarus unilaterally suspended the Readmission Agreement in December 2021, and there has been no Committee meeting with Russia since 2019.[60]

Since responsibility for the physical transfer of irregular migrants to the third country falls to the Member States, there are also bilateral implementing protocols concluded by some Member States with the third country—these are separate to the bilateral agreements a Member State may have separately with a third state. These protocols operationalize the Readmission Agreement and are not required of Member States. Bilateral implementation protocols are subsidiary instruments to Readmission Agreements. They provide some of the operational details necessary to translate the general obligations of a Readmission Agreement into actionable procedures. These protocols should specify concrete mechanisms such as the format for submitting readmission requests, the authorities responsible for communication, timelines for responses, means of transportation, documentation requirements (including laissez-passer documents), and the handling of disputed cases. The extent to which Member States have put in place bilateral protocols is highly varied and mostly focused on countries in proximity to the EU, particularly Armenia, Russia, and Ukraine.[61] Since they are not a requirement, bilateral

[58] Agreement between the European Union and the Republic of Belarus on the readmission of persons residing without authorisation [2020] OJ L 181/3.

[59] Claudia Charles, 'Readmission Agreements and Respect for Human Rights in Third Countries: Review and Prospects for the European Parliament' (2007) European Parliament Subcommittee on Human Rights (Briefing Paper), available at https://www.europarl.europa.eu/RegData/etudes/note/join/2007/385528/EXPO-DROI_NT(2007)385528_EN.pdf, accessed 7 June 2025, 4.

[60] Letter from Monique Pariat (Directorate-General for Migration and Home Affairs to the European Commission) to Loper Aguilar (MEP) (28 January 2022), available at https://www.statewatch.org/media/3155/eu-com-readmission-cooperation-overview-letter-to-libe-28-1-22.pdf, accessed 7 June 2025; this also covers pandemic operation.

[61] See 'Bilateral Readmission Agreements' (*EMN: European Migration Network*, September 2022) https://home-affairs.ec.europa.eu/system/files/2022-10/EMN_INFORM_bilateral_readmission.pdf, accessed 7 June 2025, 2; see, for example, Protocol between the Austrian Federal Government

protocols also present several challenges. First, they may vary significantly in scope and content, leading to inconsistencies in the application of the same Readmission Agreement across different states. Second, the negotiation and conclusion of protocols can be slow, particularly if the political relationship between the countries is strained or if there is an asymmetry in bargaining power. This is particularly in evidence if the protocol extends to respective citizens of the third state and the EU Member State, or to citizens of other states who may have transited through. While the former is always present, the latter is much rarer in a protocol. Finally, it is not always clear if bilateral protocols have been concluded, because they may not be made publicly available.[62]

6.5 Visa Facilitation Agreements

Visa Facilitation Agreements (VFAs) are separate to Readmission Agreements but share a strong bond in terms of the third states with which they have been included and their place on the agenda for cooperation in returns and readmission.

VFAs are distinct from visa liberalization, which occurs when EU Member States reduce the categories of persons needing a visa to enter the territory. VFAs apply to states whose nationals are required to possess a visa to cross an external border of the EU;[63] the existence of a VFA typically reduces the cost of visa applications, shortens processing times, and streamlines documentation requirements. VFAs apply to short-stay visas (i.e. no more than 90 days per period of 180 days). They may also include provisions for issuing multiple-entry visas for specific categories of travellers, such as students, researchers, businesspeople, and journalists.[64] The benefits of these agreements are limited to certain groups rather than extended broadly across the population, reflecting the EU's focus on mobility for selected

and the Government of Georgia on the implementation of the Agreement between the European Union and Georgia on the readmission of persons residing without authorisation BGBL III Nr 318/2013, available at https://www.ris.bka.gv.at/GeltendeFassung.wxe?Abfrage=Bundesnormen&Gesetzesnummer=20008757, accessed 7 June 2025; Implementing Protocol between the Government of the Republic of Estonia and the Cabinet of Ministers of Ukraine on the implementation of the Agreement between the European Community and Ukraine on readmission of persons, RT II 02.12.2016, available at https://www.riigiteataja.ee/akt/202122016001, accessed 7 June 2025.

62 For example, a Bulgaria–Türkiye protocol exists but is not publicly available: Orçun Ulusoy, Özgenur Yigit-Aksu, Meltem Ineli-Ciger, and Gamze Ovacik, 'Cooperation for Containment: An Analysis of the EU–Türkiye Arrangements in the Field of Migration' in Sergio Carrera Nunez, Elini Karageorgiou, Gamze Ovacik, and Nikolas-Feith Tan (eds), *Global Asylum Governance and the European Union's Role: International Perspectives on Migration* (vol 18, Springer 2025).

63 As codified by Regulation (EU) 2018/1806 of the European Parliament and of the Council of 14 November 2018 listing the third countries whose nationals must be in possession of visas when crossing the external borders and those whose nationals are exempt from that requirement (codification) [2018] OJ L 303/39.

64 See, for example, Agreement between the European Union and the Republic of Azerbaijan on the facilitation of the issuance of visas [2014] OJ L 128/49, Article 4(1)(a)–(n).

'desirable' categories—often for short-term visitors who are not considered either a security risk or at risk of becoming irregular migrants and failing to leave the territory of the EU and its Member States.

Since VFAs apply across the Schengen area in a harmonized fashion, they are generally seen as a desirable prize for the governments of third countries. Here again, many of the VFAs apply to states in the neighbourhood region, particularly the Eastern Partnership. For states including Ukraine, Moldova, and Georgia, visa facilitation (and in some cases, subsequent visa liberalization) has been tied closely to broader political and economic cooperation under the European Neighbourhood Policy (ENP).

While separate as agreements, the linkage between VFAs and Readmission Agreements has become a consistent feature of EU policy.[65] The link with readmission is now made explicit by the institutions.[66] Typically, the EU insists that visa facilitation is contingent on a functioning Readmission Agreement. This conditionality reflects the EU's broader strategy of externalizing migration control and making cooperation on return a prerequisite for any improvement in mobility conditions. While this approach can provide leverage in negotiations, it has also been criticized for instrumentalizing visa policy and prioritizing enforcement over genuine partnerships with third states.

VFAs are inherently asymmetrical: while they aim to facilitate travel to the EU for nationals of third countries, they do not grant reciprocal access to EU citizens, whose travel conditions are generally already largely relaxed. This imbalance can create perceptions of unequal treatment and reinforce criticisms that the EU's migration cooperation is self-serving. However, that is not to say that the third states lack any agency. The Commission itself recognised that '[t]he Russian Federation and Ukraine negotiations, for instance, only really accelerated once the EU had committed, at their demand, to negotiate visa facilitation agreements in parallel'.[67]

Despite their intended benefits, VFAs have faced criticism for their limited scope and uneven implementation. For many applicants, the practical impact remains marginal due to persistent bureaucratic barriers, lengthy processing times, and the discretionary power of consulates. Additionally, VFAs do not override Schengen visa rules, which means that facilitation remains subject to the broader framework of EU visa policy and security screening.

[65] Florian Trauner and Imke Kruse, 'EC Visa Facilitation and Readmission Agreements: A New Standard EU Foreign Policy Tool?' (2008) 10(4) European Journal of Migration and Law 411.

[66] See 'Summaries of EU Legislation: Visa Facilitation' (*EUR-Lex: Access to European Union Law*) https://eur-lex.europa.eu/legal-content/EN/TXT/?uri=legissum:4394574, accessed 7 June 2025. See, for example, Council Decision (EU) 2013/695 of 25 November 2013 on the signing, on behalf of the European Union, of the Agreement between the European Union and the Republic of Azerbaijan on the facilitation of the issuance of visas [2013] OJ L 320/7.

[67] Commission, 'Communication from the Commission to the European Parliament and the Council, Evaluation of EU Readmission Agreements' COM(2011) 76 final 6.

As a result, VFAs represent an important aspect of the EU's external migration toolkit. Their effectiveness depends on the political context, the willingness of partner countries to engage in broader cooperation, and the EU's ability to balance control with mobility.

6.6 Exploring the limitations of 'formal' law in migration

In the context of the formal aspect of EU migration policy, there has been a marked prioritization of addressing irregular migration, often positioning it as the central concern in both political discourse and operational frameworks. This is certainly in evidence in the substance of agreements with third countries. Readmission Agreements, and returns more generally, play a central role in the official discourse of EU migration law and policy. See, for example, the reference in the Global Approach to Migration and Mobility to readmission and return, which 'should be firmly embedded in the broader Global Approach'.[68] This focus has led to comparatively less emphasis on developing and promoting regular migration channels, except in cases where such pathways are strategically leveraged to support broader objectives related to the control and reduction of irregular migration. For instance, migration schemes for regular migration may be offered as incentives to third countries in exchange for their cooperation on return and Readmission Agreements.

The formal nature of these agreements, such as those under the EU's external migration partnerships or the New Pact on Migration and Asylum, requires active and sustained cooperation from third countries. These states are expected not only to engage in the negotiation and conclusion of such agreements but also to play a critical role in their operational implementation. This includes facilitating the return of their nationals, enhancing border management, and participating in joint initiatives aimed at preventing unauthorised departures. As a result, third country cooperation becomes both a legal and a practical cornerstone of the EU's external migration governance.

It is perhaps surprising therefore that there are relatively few Readmission Agreements currently in force. The Agreements have limited geographical spread beyond the European continent. They are generally with smaller states where the number of returnees can be assumed to be relatively low. Readmission Agreements concluded in Europe tend to be with states aiming to join the EU, and can thus be seen as part of the (pre-)enlargement coordination.[69]

[68] Commission, 'Communication from the Commission to the European Parliament, the Council, the European Economic and Social Committee and the Committee of the Regions: The Global Approach to Migration and Mobility' COM(2011) 743 final (GAMM).

[69] See, for instance in the case of Albania, Imke Kruse, 'EU Readmission Policy and Its Effects on Transit Countries—The Case of Albania' (2006) 8(2) European Journal of Migration and Law 115.

This apparent gap raises important questions about the effectiveness and coherence of the EU's return framework. Despite the political emphasis placed on returns as a cornerstone of migration control, the limited number of formal agreements—particularly with key countries of origin—suggests significant challenges in negotiating and implementing such arrangements. In a similar vein, the existence of a Readmission Agreement has not prevented a move to informality, as the example of the EU–Türkiye Statement demonstrates.

The drive to conclude Readmission Agreements had already stalled by 2007, after only a limited number of agreements had been successfully concluded, leading to an 'impasse'.[70] Despite the EU's perceived negotiating advantage, stemming from its economic and political influence as well as the potential incentives it can offer in the form of trade agreements, visa facilitation, or development aid, progress on readmission has been uneven and often slow. There are well-documented cases where negotiations have either stalled or failed altogether to begin, highlighting the limitations of the EU's leverage in this area. For example, negotiations with countries such as Algeria and Morocco have proven particularly difficult, despite years of engagement and the strategic importance of these countries in the EU's migration control agenda.

These challenges may include political resistance from third countries, concerns over human rights protections, or a lack of incentives for cooperation. The result is a disconnect between policy rhetoric and practical implementation, which undermines the EU's stated objectives and exposes tensions within its external migration governance.

6.6.1 The governance challenges of bilateral relationships

In several instances, third countries have demonstrated reluctance to conclude formal Readmission Agreements, citing concerns over potential domestic political repercussions, the socio-economic burden associated with the reintegration of returnees, and scepticism regarding the EU's assurances of reciprocal benefits. In other cases, negotiations have faltered due to perceptions that the EU's approach is disproportionately focused on return and border control, with insufficient emphasis on broader frameworks of cooperation, including legal migration pathways, mobility partnerships, and development assistance.[71]

These impediments underscore that Readmission Agreements are not merely technical or administrative instruments; rather, they are embedded within

[70] Annabelle Roig and Thomas Huddleston, 'EC Readmission Agreements: A Re-Evaluation of the Political Impasse' (2007) 9(3) European Journal of Migration and Law 363.

[71] Wolff, *The Mediterranean Dimension of the European Union's Internal Security* (n 27); Nora El Qadim, 'The Symbolic Meaning of International Mobility: EU–Morocco Negotiations on Visa Facilitation' (2018) 6(2) Migration Studies 279, https://doi.org/10.1093/migration/mnx048.

complex political and diplomatic contexts. The early stagnation in the EU's re-admission policy trajectory reflects not only the resistance of partner countries but also the broader challenge the EU faces in aligning its external migration governance objectives with the diverse interests, capacities, and priorities of third countries. The ability of third states to accept potentially large numbers of third country nationals who then need to be accommodated and subsequently returned to another state is a considerable challenge.[72]

As Cassarino has observed, the burden of operationalizing Readmission Agreements falls disproportionately on the third state. While the requesting (or soliciting) country may face uncertainties around the agreement's implementation, the solicited country must often undertake significant structural, institutional, and legal reforms. These reforms can disrupt domestic socio-political dynamics and strain the national economy. Additionally, the agreements may generate public backlash, both within the solicited country and among its diaspora communities abroad, especially when the perceived consequences are socially or economically harmful.[73]

The well-documented cases of Morocco and Tunisia demonstrate that the political and economic strength of the EU is not enough to persuade a key third country to conclude a Readmission Agreement. Third countries do have agency and are also subject to domestic pressures which can threaten to topple the government if there is a perception that the EU (or other actors) have succeeded in imposing their will.[74]

While the strategic geographic position of Morocco—which, it should not be forgotten, has a land border with an EU Member State[75]—would make it a priority case for a Readmission Agreement, the EU has failed over a considerable period

[72] Kruse, for example, notes that the EU–Albania Readmission Agreement included third country nationals but that Albania lacked the infrastructure or onwards agreements to return people to countries of origin: Kruse (n 69) 138.

[73] Jean-Pierre Cassarino, 'Informalising Readmission Agreements in the EU Neighbourhood' (2007) 42(2) The International Spectator 179, 183.

[74] Marguerite Bellavitis and Ariadna Servent, 'The New Pact on Migration and Asylum in a Shifting Political Context: Depoliticization and Repoliticization in EU External Migration Policy' (2025) Mediterranean Politics 1, 9.

[75] Ceuta and Melilla in Spain. See the case study in Michael Collyer, 'Migrants as Strategic Actors in the European Union's Global Approach to Migration and Mobility' (2012) 12(4) Global Networks 505; Xavier Ferrer-Gallardo and Abel Albet-Mas, 'EU-Limboscapes: Ceuta and the Proliferation of Migrant Detention Spaces across the European Union' (2013) 23(3) European Urban and Regional Studies 527; Xavier Ferrer-Gallardo and Lorenzo Gabrielli, 'The Ceuta Border Peripeteia: Tasting the Externalities of EU Border Externalization' (2022) 37(3) Journal of Borderlands Studies 645; Said Saddiki, 'Knocking at the Walls of Ceuta and Melilla: Irregular Migration and the Political-Security Nexus' (2022) Moroccan Institute for Policy Analysis, available at https://www.researchgate.net/profile/Said-Saddiki/publication/367047331_Knocking_at_the_Walls_of_Ceuta_and_Melilla_Irregular_Migration_and_the_Political-Security_Nexus/links/63bf47ee7ecd35045c3d783a/Knocking-at-the-Walls-of-Ceuta-and-Melilla-Irregular-Migration-and-the-Political-Security-Nexus.pdf, accessed 7 June 2025; Polly Pallister-Wilkins, 'The Tensions of the Ceuta and Melilla Border Fences' in Paolo Gaibazzi, Alice Bellagamba, and Stephen Dünnwald (eds), *EurAfrican Borders and Migration Management: Political Cultures, Contested Spaces, and Ordinary Lives* (Palgrave Macmillan 2017).

of time to achieve this. Negotiations on a Readmission Agreement with Morocco were suspended after their fifteenth round in 2010, whereas Tunisia never agreed even to open negotiations on this issue.[76]

Although ACP states have an obligation under the EU–ACP agreement to readmit nationals, there are no specific Readmission Agreements to facilitate returns. Therefore, the risk to Morocco and Tunisia is that they will find themselves responsible for potentially large numbers of migrants from further south in Africa in addition to their own citizens. The resistance to acting as the EU's border guard—and to the EU 'passing the buck'[77]—is significant, especially when a high-level agreement such as a Readmission Agreement may involve a large number of national veto players.[78]

In these cases, the reasons for the failure are multiple: the lack of a clear, major incentive to do so, and especially the lack of an incentive to admit the return of non-citizens who have transited through. Furthermore, as noted above, Member States continue to conclude and operate bilateral agreements (both formal and informal) with third states, which might be more attractive to the latter if there is only an obligation to readmit nationals, or if accompanied by economic or other advantages. Taken to its logical conclusion, this harms the overall approach of the Commission to increase the rate of EU-level returns. There exists a similar tension between the lack of either need or requirement for a bilateral implementing protocol for an EU Readmission Agreement and the existence of a (legally separate) bilateral agreement by a Member State.[79] It is clear that the Commission's position, as well as that of the Parliament,[80] is in favour of EU-level Readmission Agreements but unless this question of competence is resolved, Member States will continue to respond to their own domestic political pressures by avoiding the EU frame and attempting to resolve their migration issues with third counties via bilateral agreements, both formal and informal. The same can be said of the continued insistence to include third country nationals within the scope of the Readmission Agreement.[81]

[76] Mohamed Limam and Raffaella Del Sarto, 'Periphery under Pressure: Morocco, Tunisia and the European Union's Mobility Partnership on Migration' (2015) Robert Schuman Centre for Advanced Studies Research Paper No. RSCAS 2015/75, available at SSRN: https://ssrn.com/abstract=2686505 or http://dx.doi.org/10.2139/ssrn.2686505, accessed 7 June 2025.

[77] Bouteillet-Paquet, 'Passing the Buck' (n 37).

[78] Wolff, *The Mediterranean Dimension of the European Union's Internal Security* (n 27).

[79] European Parliament Briefing, 'EU Readmission Agreements: Facilitating the return of irregular migrants' (*European Parliament*, April 2015) https://www.europarl.europa.eu/RegData/etudes/BRIE/2015/554212/EPRS_BRI%282015%29554212_EN.pdf, accessed 7 June 2025.

[80] In a resolution of 12 April 2016, the European Parliament considered that 'in order to increase the efficiency of readmissions, and in order to ensure the coherence of returns at a European level, it will be necessary to adopt new EU Readmission Agreements which should take preference over bilateral agreements between Member States and third countries': European Parliament resolution of 12 April 2016 on the situation in the Mediterranean and the need for a holistic EU approach to migration (2015/2095(INI)).

[81] European Court of Auditors, 'EU Readmission Cooperation with Third Countries: Relevant Actions Yielded Limited Results' (*European Court of Auditors*, special report no 17/21, 2021), available at https://www.eca.europa.eu/Lists/ECADocuments/SR21_17/SR_Readmission-cooperation_EN.pdf, accessed 7 June 2025.

A final sticking point can be found via the EU institutions' emphasis on integrating human rights standards and procedural safeguards into Readmission Agreements. While normatively important, this has often been met with scepticism or resistance from partner countries. This insistence is sometimes perceived not as a collaborative effort to uphold international norms, but rather as a form of conditionality imposed by more powerful Western actors on smaller or less influential states. Such perceptions are particularly acute when the agreements result in the forced return of individuals to countries that may lack the capacity or infrastructure to ensure their dignified reintegration. In these contexts, the agreements can be viewed as instruments of externalized migration control that shift the burden of enforcement onto third countries, often without sufficient support or reciprocal benefits.

The European Parliament has long advocated for the inclusion of human rights protections in these agreements. A notable milestone came with the Readmission Agreement with Albania, which was mandated in 2002 and signed in 2005. This agreement was the first to explicitly reflect the Parliament's concerns about the need for stronger human rights safeguards in the readmission process.[82] Since then, the integration of such protections has become a more consistent, though still contested, feature of EU readmission policy. Herein, however, there is a twofold challenge. On the one hand, the EU institutions and Member States might (strongly) desire a Readmission Agreement with a third country, particularly one where migrants who have transited through that territory can be returned. But to conclude a formal agreement with a country that is not a signatory, or does not respect to even minimal levels the expected protections of human rights, would be expected to attract negative comment, strong opposition in the Parliament, and legal challenges due to a breach of the commitments in the Treaty. This would also be the case if the commitments to human rights were simply left out of the text. On the other hand, the partner state is unlikely to agree to become a signatory to international agreements on the basis of EU demands if it has not already done so.

With this in mind, the possibility arises that informal 'agreements' using the terminology of 'pilot projects'[83] or a 'way forward'[84] avoid some of these potential institutional blockages while retaining much of the actual content in a practical sense.[85] There is a potential practical issue with doing so, however. The Court of Auditors

[82] European Parliament Briefing, 'EU Readmission Agreements' (n 79).

[83] See, for instance, the RAPAK Project with Pakistan: Directorate-General for Migration and Home Affairs, 'The project RAPAK helps to secure Pakistan's borders' (*European Commission: Migration and Home Affairs,* 27 March 2025) https://home-affairs.ec.europa.eu/news/project-rapak-helps-secure-pakistans-borders-2025-03-27_en, accessed 7 June 2025.

[84] Afghanistan, Joint Declaration, 'Joint way forward on migration issues between Afghanistan and the EU' (2 October 2016), available at https://www.eeas.europa.eu/sites/default/files/eu_afghanistan_joint_way_forward_on_migration_issues.pdf, accessed 7 June 2025.

[85] Ramses Wessel, 'Normative Transformations in EU External Relations: The Phenomenon of "Soft" International Agreements' (2021) 44(1) West European Politics 72.

in a 2021 report on Readmission Agreements noted that 'the Commission's formal negotiating mandate does not allow it to abandon unsuccessful EURA negotiations and pursue a quicker readmission arrangement',[86] which suggests that the aims must be sufficiently differentiated to enable justification.[87]

6.6.2 Do Readmission Agreements make a difference?

Even when formal Readmission Agreements are concluded, their implementation is far from guaranteed. The existence of a legal framework does not necessarily translate into timely or effective cooperation in practice. For instance, under the Readmission Agreement with Georgia, the average response time for processing readmission requests is relatively efficient—typically six to seven days.[88] In stark contrast, the implementation of the EURA with Pakistan has proven significantly more challenging, with response times reportedly extending to more than a year in some cases. This disparity illustrates the variability in administrative capacity, political will, and institutional coordination among partner countries, all of which critically influence the operational effectiveness of Readmission Agreements.

Such inconsistencies underscore the limitations of relying solely on formal agreements to ensure cooperation on return. They also highlight the importance of sustained diplomatic engagement, capacity-building support, and mutual trust in fostering functional readmission partnerships. Without these complementary efforts, even well-negotiated agreements risk remaining largely symbolic.[89]

In terms of the numbers of individuals returned under a Readmission Agreement, there is scant evidence. The assumption is that a Readmission Agreement will lead to a higher 'return rate', or, at the very least, the presence of an agreement would be a form of implicit pressure on those who lose their legal status to depart voluntarily before being forced to do so. Stutz and Trauner's comprehensive analysis of return rates of states who have Readmission Agreements compared with those who do not reveals that these do not differ greatly. Rather, the geographical characteristics appear to weigh as more important factors:

> In general, the Western Balkans and Eastern European states are the only regions in which the EU's Readmission Agreements seem to have led to higher return rates. In fact, the increasing return rates of these Eastern and South-Eastern neighbours were a key reason why the EU managed to keep the average return rate at roughly the same level between 2008 and 2018. Many other regions in

86 European Court of Auditors, 'EU Readmission Cooperation with Third Countries: Relevant Actions Yielded Limited Results' (n 81).

87 This point is explored in more detail in the following chapter.

88 European Parliament Briefing, 'EU Readmission Agreements' (n 79) 4.

89 ibid.

> the world—most pronouncedly so in Africa—had declining return rates with the EU.[90]

The existence of an agreement is thus only one factor in the ability of the EU and its Member States to pursue returns and readmission more vigorously. But the challenges in gaining the cooperation and consent of the third country partner do not stop at the moment the agreement is signed. Third countries may choose to suspend returns, refuse to cooperate on a temporary or permanent basis, or suggest opening the borders to the EU. Much depends on the geopolitical context[91] and the health of the bilateral relationship. The EU–Türkiye relationship stands as a prime example, where the 'pull' factor of eventual EU membership has diminished sharply but where Türkiye has used both the Readmission Agreement and the 2016 statement to gain further political and economic concessions from the EU while suggesting it could 'allow the free movement of refugees into the EU . . . in the form of silencing the EU's criticisms towards massive purges and increased repression in the country'.[92]

Despite the drawbacks and challenges to negotiation and concluding formal Readmission Agreements, the New Migration Pact continues to place them at the centre of EU migration governance. The Pact talks of 'effective readmission cooperation with third countries'[93] and agreements remain the priority, noting the 'first and foremost' requirement to fully implement the existing Readmission Agreements and enhance cooperation with these third states, to complete existing negotiations and launch new ones.[94] This is premised on Readmission Agreements leading to a sustainable increase in returns, although the evidence suggests this is not necessarily the case. One initiative in place is the establishment of 'an operational coordination mechanism for the external dimension of migration' (MOCADEM),[95] the purpose of which is to operationalize 'the action plans established for eight priority countries of origin and transit, backed by concrete timelines and adequate financial support'.[96]

It is similarly difficult to understand what tools the EU might be able to deploy to further the stalled negotiations on Readmission Agreements or launch

[90] Philipp Stutz and Florian Trauner, 'The EU's "Return Rate" with Third Countries: Why EU Readmission Agreements Do Not Make Much Difference' (2022) 60(3) International Migration 154.

[91] See, for example, Tamirace Fakhoury and Zeynep Mencütek, 'The Geopolitics of Return Migration in the International System' (2023) 28(3) Geopolitics 959.

[92] Sene Aydın-Düzgit and Alper Kaliber, 'Protean Power Europe in the Southern Neighbourhood? EU in the Face of Migration and Political Crises' (2025) Comparative European Politics (early view), available at https://link.springer.com/content/pdf/10.1057/s41295-025-00421-y.pdf, accessed 7 June 2025.

[93] COM(2020) 609 final (n 14).

[94] ibid.

[95] Council Implementing Decision (EU) 2022/60 of 12 January 2022 on the Operational Coordination Mechanism for the External Dimension of Migration.

[96] ibid preamble para 3.

new ones, given that agreements are in place with the latest countries to officially apply for EU membership.[97] Rather, and explicit in the Migration Pact, is the shift towards informal or non-binding arrangements for readmission, which have yielded more results in the previous decade than the formal agreements.[98] These can be self-standing, or embedded in a wider, yet still informal, framework of a Mobility Partnership. The drive for Mobility Partnerships has had some success where formal Readmission Agreement negotiations have (so far) failed. Morocco and Tunisia signed such partnerships in 2013, indicating a successful engagement of the political will of the third countries. Mobility Partnerships are covered in more detail in the following chapters, but for this chapter the importance is that the Readmission Agreement is binding but narrowly focused, whereas the flexibility afforded by a Mobility Partnership allows for a more continuous state of bargaining and alternative patterns of cooperation on readmission[99] and can be used as a tool to support a domestic political agenda in a third country.[100] The latter can be more persuasive in support of, for instance, a Visa Facilitation Agreement which may not gain substantial support on the EU side.

6.7 Conclusion

In the external sphere, this chapter has demonstrated that agreements, in a similar way as the formal counterpart of law-making within the EU, have their limits when trying to meet the EU's stated goals in migration. While Readmission Agreements have often been positioned at the core of the EU's external migration strategy, they are not, in practice, the most decisive or effective instruments. Their significance lies less in the number concluded—still relatively small—or in the high-profile cases where negotiations have failed—such as with Morocco—and more in their broader normative and institutional influence. These agreements have served as templates and sources of technical expertise, encouraging third countries, particularly in Eastern Europe during the 1990s, to develop their own bilateral

[97] Agreement between the European Union and Georgia on the readmission of persons residing without authorisation [2011] OJ L 52/47; Agreement between the European Community and the Republic of Moldova on the readmission of persons residing without authorisation—Declarations [2007] OJ L 334/149; Agreement between the European Community and Ukraine on the readmission of persons—Annexes—Declaration—Joint Declarations [2007] OJ L 332. See, inter alia, Nadiia Koval and Milada Vachudova, 'European Union Enlargement and Geopolitical Power in the Face of War' (2024) 62 JCMS: Journal of Common Market Studies 135; Maria Giulia, Amadio Viceré, and Matteo Bonomi, 'External Differentiation as a Strategy of System Maintenance: EU Enlargement towards the Western Balkans' (2024) 48(5) West European Politics 1159.

[98] European Court of Auditors, 'EU Readmission Cooperation with Third Countries: Relevant Actions Yielded Limited Results' (n 81).

[99] Cassarino, 'Informalising Readmission Agreements in the EU Neighbourhood' (n 73) 185.

[100] Fanny Tittel-Mosser, 'Reversed Conditionality in EU External Migration Policy: The Case of Morocco' (2018) 14(4) Journal of Contemporary European Research 349.

readmission arrangements with neighbouring states. In this way, the EU's approach has contributed to the diffusion of migration governance practices beyond its immediate borders, fostering what might be described as a 'concentric circles' model of influence.[101]

Moreover, Readmission Agreements have provided the legal and procedural know-how that underpins a growing array of informal arrangements. These less visible instruments, ranging from memoranda of understanding to operational protocols, often bypass the formal Treaty-making process but are nonetheless shaped by the institutional learning and legal frameworks developed through formal agreements. Much of the operational aspect of current EU migration governance can thus be traced to informal or 'soft' mechanisms.[102] The Commission itself has acknowledged the strategic value of linking Readmission Agreements to broader migration partnerships, as reflected in its evaluations and the Council Conclusions of February 2011, which advocated for a conditionality mechanism connecting EU Readmission Agreements to Mobility Partnerships.[103]

At the same time, and bringing together the focus of this chapter and the previous one, the Treaty framework clearly envisages legislation and international agreements as foundational tools for regulating migration. Yet, despite migration's prominence on the political agendas of both EU institutions and Member States, the legislative process has frequently stalled. Proposals to recast key migration legislation, such as those introduced in 2016, have made little progress. This inertia reveals a deeper structural tension: the political salience of migration does not necessarily translate into institutional capacity for harmonized legal action. On the contrary, the heightened sensitivity of migration issues often reinforces national preferences, particularly within the Council, creating institutional deadlock. The Commission, as the initiator of legislation, finds itself constrained, while the European Parliament's role is similarly shaped by the absence of a clear legislative endgame, most notably in the protracted efforts to reform the Dublin Regulation, which continues to hinge on unresolved questions of solidarity among Member States.

These dynamics are mirrored in the EU's external migration relations. While formal agreements remain the logical starting point for engagement with third countries, they do not capture the full complexity of the EU's external migration governance. As this chapter has shown, the EU's capacity to conclude international agreements predates the Treaty of Lisbon and is the result of a long process of

[101] Theodora Kostakopoulou, 'The "Protective Union": Change and Continuity in Migration Law and Policy in Post-Amsterdam Europe' (2000) 38(3) Journal of Common Market Studies 497, 513.

[102] Frasca, 'Informal Agreements and Quasi-Legal Mechanisms in EU–Africa Cooperation on Migration' (n 28).

[103] Commission, 'Communication from the Commission to the European Parliament and the Council, Evaluation of EU Readmission Agreements' COM(2011) 76 final 6; Panizzon, 'Readmission Agreements of EU Member States' (n 42).

institutional and legal development. However, overlapping competences between the EU and its Member States have precluded a uniform approach, and this fragmentation partly explains the limited number of comprehensive agreements concluded with third countries. Even where the EU holds a stronger bargaining position, it has encountered significant obstacles in finalizing agreements—particularly on readmission—despite offering various incentives.

In some cases, even long-standing and wide-ranging agreements concluded under the relevant Treaty provisions have failed to deliver meaningful cooperation. The lack of integration in this area has created space for Member States to pursue informal, soft law instruments and policy-based arrangements, often with limited transparency or accountability.[104] Herein is wherre 'formal informality' comes to the fore.

Given this context, the relative stagnation in formal agreement-making—despite the increasing urgency of migration challenges—suggests that the real dynamism lies elsewhere. The next chapter explores how the EU's experience with formal instruments has informed the development of informal practices and flexible cooperation mechanisms. These emerging tools reflect a growing recognition that the EU's migration objectives cannot be fully realized through formal legal instruments alone.

[104] Sergio Carrera, 'Integration of Immigrants in EU Law and Policy: Challenges to the Rules of Law, Exceptions to Inclusion' in Loïc Azoulai and Karin De Vries (eds), *EU Migration Law: Legal Complexities and Political Rationales* (Oxford University Press 2014) 149.

7

Migration and EU External Relations

The Shift to 'Informality'

The launch of the Global Approach to Migration (GAM) in 2005[1] was the first attempt by the EU to place migration—in all its forms—as a strategic area of activity where the EU institutions play a leading role. The GAM opened the door to the use of tools such as Mobility Partnerships with third countries, which were not agreements in the sense of the Treaty, but which nevertheless attempted to engage third states in cooperation frameworks in migration.

By the time the GAM was repackaged and relaunched as the Global Approach to Migration and Mobility (GAMM) in 2011, the use of tools without an identifiable legal basis was explicitly recognized and expanded. The GAMM's founding document, a Commission Communication, states that 'the EU's external migration policy also builds on EU legislation and legal instruments . . . political instruments (a large number of policy dialogues, often backed up by action plans), operational support and capacity-building . . . and the wide range of programme and project support . . . The GAMM is based on this entire spectrum of tools and instruments, which should be applied in a structured and systematic way.'[2]

This strategic document therefore recognized what had already started to emerge in migration as in many other areas of EU governance, namely that regulations and decisions were not the only tools of governance in evidence. While the GAM/GAMM elaborated on some of the new tools that should be used in migration governance, these strategic documents pointed to a role for informal governance which had not previously been explicit in EU official documentation.

In the absence of an official definition of designation of informality, it is identified here as tools, instruments, measures, or initiatives that do not follow traditional established patterns of law and policymaking, whether in migration or elsewhere. Of particular interest here is the emergence of such phenomena and

[1] Council, 'Global Approach to Migration: Priority actions focusing on Africa and the Mediterranean' (Annex to Presidency Conclusions, 15744/05, 13 December 2005) https://data.consilium.europa.eu/doc/document/ST-15744-2005-INIT/en/pdf, accessed 9 June 2025.

[2] Commission, 'Communication from the Commission to the European Parliament, the Council, the European Economic and Social Committee and the Committee of the Regions: The Global Approach to Migration and Mobility' COM(2011) 743 final (GAMM).

The Governance of Migration in the European Union. Paul James Cardwell, Oxford University Press.
 DOI: 10.1093/9780191946592.003.0008

practices as an alternative to instruments that find a home in the Treaty, such as the ability of the institutions to conclude legally binding agreements with third countries. As such, the variety of names used for such phenomena (such as 'non-binding agreements', 'statements', 'pacts', 'ways forward', etc) is likely to be diverse.

As explored in Chapter 1, informal, softer, or experimental forms of governance have a long history within the context of European integration. Generally, they arise when there is a lack of consensus between the institutions and the Member States on new initiatives, or the Treaty does not (yet) have the required, specific competences, or where regulation alone is not able to meet required goals. Informality is often expressed in terms of 'soft law', though informality is the preferred term here.[3] Informality is also commonly found in international law,[4] including in migration. One prominent example is the Global Compact on Migration, which has generated increased interest in the phenomena of soft law and informality,[5] and in which the EU itself was heavily involved and influential.[6] Informality is often critiqued from the perspective of the lack of binding nature or enforcement capability, which the Global Compact has been the focus of,[7] because the risk is that states will not assume the obligations that they commit themselves to. Here, the focus on informality takes a rather different approach. The previous two chapters noted the limitations—both legal and political—experienced by the EU institutions as they

[3] See the discussion in Chapter 2.

[4] See, for example, Alan Boyle, 'Soft Law in International Law-Making' in Malcolm D. Evans (ed), *International Law* (5th edn, Oxford University Press 2018); Jaye Ellis, 'Shades of Grey: Soft Law and the Validity of Public International Law' (2012) 25 Leiden Journal of International Law 313; Joost Pauwelyn, Ramses Wessel, and Jan Wouters (eds), *Informal International Law-Making: Mapping the Action and Testing Concepts of Accountability and Effectiveness* (Oxford University Press 2012); and for a more sceptical view, Jan Klabbers, 'The Redundancy of Soft Law' (1996) 65 Nordic Journal of International Law 167.

[5] See, inter alia, Diego Badell, 'The EU, Migration and Contestation: The UN Global Compact for Migration, from Consensus to Dissensus' (2020) 6(4–5) Global Affairs 347; François Crépeau, 'Towards a Mobile and Diverse World: "Facilitating Mobility" as a Central Objective of the Global Compact on Migration' (2018) 30(4) International Journal of Refugee Law 650; Elspeth Guild and Stefanie Grant, 'Migration Governance in the UN: What Is the Global Compact and What Does It Mean?' (2017) Queen Mary School of Law Legal Studies Research Paper 252; Walter Kälin, 'The Global Compact on Migration: A Ray of Hope for Disaster-Displaced Persons' (2018) 30 (4) International Journal of Refugee Law 664; Thomas Gammeltoft-Hansen, Elspeth Guild, Violeta Moreno-Lax, Marion Panizzon, and Isobel Roele, 'What Is a Compact? Migrants' Rights and State Responsibilities Regarding the Design of the UN Global Compact for Safe, Orderly and Regular Migration' (Raoul Wallenberg Institute of Human Rights and Humanitarian Law, October 2017).

[6] It should also be noted here that despite the European Commission's role in influencing the draft of the Compact, some Member States opposed the final text. See Sylvie Sarolea, Francesco Gatta, and Eleonora Frasca, 'What Could the Global Compact on Migration Mean for Europe?' in Ellen Desmet, Toon Moonen, and Tom Ruys (eds), *Het Migratiepact: kroniek van een crisis* (Die Keure 2020); Pauline Melin, 'Two Years after the Adoption of the Global Compact for Migration: Some Thoughts on the Role Played by the EU' in W Douma and others (eds), *The Evolving Nature of EU External Relations Law* (TMC Asser 2021); Thomas Spijkerboer, 'Migration Management Clientelism: Europe's Migration Funds as a Global Political Project' (2022) 48 Journal of Ethnic and Migration Studies 2892.

[7] See, for example, Tim Höflinger, 'Non-Binding and Therefore Irrelevant? The Global Compact for Migration' (2020) 75(4) International Journal 662.

attempt to further the development of EU migration governance. Once again, the emphasis here is squarely on irregular migration.

This book takes a critical view of informality, but that is not the same as denying its usefulness or place in (effective) systems of governance. Not everything can be regulated, and institutions should—within limits—have the opportunity to meet goals via innovative means. The critical view adopted here is due to the specific case of migration, which often, though not exclusively, deals with vulnerable institutions and the difficulties they have in enforcing rights. Recalling the discussion in Chapter 2, this therefore justifies a different approach to the phenomenon of informality in governance as a legal construct.

Tracking the emergence of informality in migration faces two challenges. First, in attempting to identify informal instruments, we are dealing with an open-textured category that may or may not include initiatives that have any identifiable effects, or which can be traced either through official documentation or, for example, via budgetary spend. With the increased political salience of migration on the EU's agenda, activity in the field has become increasingly frenetic, rendering the role of the researcher in mapping out the instruments even more difficult.[8] For example, 'capacity building' may appear altruistic but often masks particular policy preferences, including the internalization of EU norms via domestic legislation in third states.[9] What follows in this chapter is not therefore a complete account of every instance of informality in migration, but rather an insight into the types of instrument—some of which have enjoyed more public prominence than others—that have emerged in EU migration governance.

As a means of narrowing the scope of enquiry, the content of this chapter focuses on the tools and instruments which bear some resemblance to the 'formal' instruments discussed in the previous chapter. The resemblance is found in the language and terminology employed and, crucially, the desired effects of the instruments. Yet, the procedural dimensions are only partly present, if at all. This is termed here 'formal informality'.[10]

[8] For mapping attempts see Paula Andrade, Iván Martín, and Sergo Mananashvili, 'EU Cooperation with Third Countries in the Field of Migration' (European Parliament: Policy Department for Citizens' Rights and Constitutional Affairs, October 2025) https://www.europarl.europa.eu/RegData/etudes/STUD/2015/536469/IPOL_STU(2015)536469_EN.pdf; Violeta Moreno-Lax, 'EU External Migration Policy and the Protection of Human Rights: In-Depth Analysis' (European Parliament: Policy Department for External Relations, 15 September 2020) https://www.europarl.europa.eu/cmsdata/226387/EU_External_Migration_Policy_and_the_Protection_of_Human_Rights.pdf; Violeta Moreno-Lax, Jennifer Allsopp, and Evangelia (Lilian) Tsourdi and Philippe De Bruycker, 'The EU Approach on Migration in the Mediterranean' (European Parliament: Policy Department for Citizens' Rights and Constitutional Affairs, 13 June 2021) https://www.europarl.europa.eu/RegData/etudes/STUD/2021/694413/IPOL_STU(2021)694413_EN.pdf, all accessed 9 June 2025.

[9] On capacity-building, see Nicholas Micinski and Philippe Bourbeau, 'Capacity Building as Intervention-Lite: Migration Management and the Global Compacts' (2024) 29(1) Geopolitics 39.

[10] Paul James Cardwell and Rachel Dickson, '"Formal Informality" in EU External Migration Governance: The Case of Mobility Partnerships' (2023) 49(12) Journal of Ethnic and Migration Studies 3121.

The justification for doing so again lies in the emphasis placed by the EU institutions themselves on all available tools and instruments and innovative practices that are capable of emerging in an advanced system of governance despite the institutional limitations already identified. The prioritization of such instruments, such as Mobility Partnerships, will be the key component of the overall relationships between the EU and third countries of origin or transit of migrants.[11] Key to understanding this approach is the way in which the EU engages with third states, via multilateral[12] or bilateral frameworks (or both). Given the informal nature of these tools, there are strong hallmarks of an 'opt-in' approach, bearing some resemblance to differentiated integration. Although bilateral agreements—both formal and informal—between individual Member States and third countries are outside the scope of enquiry here, some of the underlying logics which apply are similar and comparisons are made where appropriate.[13]

Many of the initiatives and instances of informality explored in this chapter co-exist and are often designed to straddle both irregular and regular migration, but with heavy emphasis on the former. Several third states, including Ethiopia, Tunisia, and Türkiye, feature in more than one of the categories, which are not hermetically sealed from each other. A strictly chronological exploration is not possible since some informal instruments arise concurrently. With the exception of Türkiye, most of the emphasis of informality is placed on Africa and African states. As such, the chapter begins with an overview of the multilateral EU–Africa relations, which helps us understand the basis for some of the initiatives that have subsequently arisen. The chapter then considers Mobility Partnerships, the Common Agendas on Migration and Mobility (CAMM), Migration Partnership Frameworks, non-binding arrangements on returns and readmission, the EU–Türkiye Statement, other bilateral arrangements with third states, and, finally, regular migration and Talent Partnerships.

7.1 Informality in multilateral relations with Africa

The emphasis in much of this chapter is on the bilateral relationships within individual third states that have produced informal agreements under a variety of

[11] Commission, Communication from the Commission to the European Parliament, the European Council, the Council and the European Investment Bank on establishing a new Partnership Framework with third countries under the European Agenda on Migration' COM(2016) 385 final 6.

[12] For example, Amanda Bisong, 'Trans-Regional Institutional Cooperation as Multilevel Governance: ECOWAS Migration Policy and the EU' (2019) 45(8) Journal of Ethnic and Migration Studies 1294; François Crépeau and Idil Atak, 'Global Migration Governance: Avoiding Commitments on Migration, Yet Tracing a Course for Cooperation' (2016) 34(2) Netherlands Quarterly of Human Rights 110.

[13] The Italy–Albania MOU 2023 is the prominent example here: Iole Fontana and Matilde Rosina, 'The Tools of External Migration Policy in the EU Member States: The Case of Italy' (2024) 62(6) JCMS: Journal of Common Market Studies 1448.

different names. However, much of this shift has been in part taking place under multilateral, regional approaches and dialogues. The European Neighbourhood Policy (ENP) is the most advanced of these, having built on—rather than replaced—long-term frameworks such as the Barcelona Process (since 1995) with Mediterranean states, and existing concurrently with other groupings such as the Union for the Mediterranean and the Eastern Partnership.[14] ENP was not initially focused on migration, since the background to its launch was the geographical shifting of the EU's borders eastwards. ENP also has a Treaty basis, found in Article 8(1) and the possibility of concluding specific agreements with ENP states in Article 8(2).[15]

The Euro-African Dialogue on Migration and Development (the Rabat Process), initiated in 2006, facilitates cooperation between European and African states, the EU, and the Economic Community of West African States (ECOWAS) as partners. Through joint ownership, it emphasizes a balanced approach based on four pillars: legal migration and mobility, irregular migration and trafficking, international protection and asylum, and the development–migration nexus. It has regularly adopted Action Plans, the most recent in Cadiz in 2022,[16] which balance combating irregular migration with migration 'push' factors, such as poverty and instability, by integrating development aid with migration control measures. While not a gateway to informality per se, and overlapping with some of the Treaty-based agreements—primarily the Cotonou/Samoa Agreements with ACP states—the Rabat Process nevertheless provides an informal multilateral and bilateral forum which builds the institutional relationships helpful to the operational cooperation covered below.[17]

The EU–Horn of Africa Migration Route Initiative, also known as the Khartoum Process, was launched in 2014, and brings together the EU and countries along the migration route from the Horn of Africa. Its main goal is to prevent and combat human trafficking and smuggling of migrants. Although officially a product of collaboration and joint ownership, criticism has been focused on its prioritization of

[14] Paul James Cardwell, 'EuroMed, European Neighbourhood Policy and the Union for the Mediterranean: Overlapping Policy Frames in the EU's Governance of the Mediterranean' (2011) 49(2) JCMS: Journal of Common Market Studies 219.

[15] Article 8(1): 'The Union shall develop a special relationship with neighbouring countries, aiming to establish an area of prosperity and good neighbourliness, founded on the values of the Union and characterised by close and peaceful relations based on cooperation'; Article 8(2): For the purposes of paragraph 1, the Union may conclude specific agreements with the countries concerned. These agreements may contain reciprocal rights and obligations as well as the possibility of undertaking activities jointly. Their implementation shall be the subject of periodic consultation.

[16] Rabat Process, 'Cadiz Political Declaration: 6th Ministerial Conference of the Rabat Process' (Rabat Process, 29 November 2022) https://www.rabat-process.org/en/about/cadiz-action-plan, accessed 9 June 2025.

[17] See, for example, Joint Declaration Establishing a Migration Partnership Between the Islamic Republic of Mauritania and the European Union (7 March 2024) https://home-affairs.ec.europa.eu/document/download/24425c1c-dd34-4c71-8f9e-77ecbac22305_en?filename=Déclaration-conjointe-Mauritanie-EU_en.pdf, accessed 9 June 2025.

border control over human rights protections. The Khartoum Process has, however, existed for more than a decade and adopted the Cairo Declaration and Action Plan in 2025,[18] explicitly pointing to the Valletta Declaration (below), which has proved a major catalyst for the use of informality in EU migration governance.

The Valletta Summit on Migration, held in November 2015 in Valletta, Malta, marked a key moment in the European Union's efforts to deepen cooperation with African countries on migration. The summit, with EU and African leaders from more than sixty countries, was convened in response to the 2015 migration crisis, with political attention in Europe focussed on the people, many from African states, crossing the Mediterranean into Europe. The outcome of the summit was the Valletta Declaration[19] and an accompanying Action Plan.[20] These documents outlined a political commitment to work in partnership, framed around shared responsibilities and mutual interests. The declaration reaffirmed the importance of human rights, international protection obligations, and the right to seek asylum, while emphasizing the need to combat irregular migration and human trafficking.

The Valletta Summit also launched the EU Emergency Trust Fund for Africa (EUTF), which has been instrumental in financing many of the regional migration initiatives covered in this chapter post-2015.[21] The stated aim of EUTF is to target root causes of displacement in Africa by supporting job creation, governance, and conflict prevention. The initial funds available were considerable: €1.8 billion from different European Commission financial instruments under the EU budget, including the European Development Fund (EDF), Development Cooperation Instrument (DCI), and European Neighbourhood Instrument (ENI), to be complemented by contributions from EU Member States and other donors.[22]

To support the Valletta Action Plan, the Rabat Process and Khartoum Process, as existing regional migration dialogues, were tasked with monitoring the implementation of the Valletta Action Plan, ensuring that both African and European partners had ownership of the process. This is also reflected in some of the informal arrangements with individual states, explored later in this chapter.[23]

[18] Khartoum Process, 'Cairo Ministerial Declaration and Action Plan' (Khartoum Process, 9 April 2025) https://www.khartoumprocess.net/resources/political-documents/cairo-action-plan/download, accessed 9 June 2025.

[19] Valletta Summit, 'Political Declaration' (Valletta, 11–12 November 2015) https://www.consilium.europa.eu/en/meetings/international-summit/2015/11/11-12/, accessed 9 June 2025.

[20] Valletta Summit, 'Action Plan' (Valletta, 11–12 November 2015) https://www.consilium.europa.eu/en/meetings/international-summit/2015/11/11-12/, accessed 9 June 2025.

[21] European Union, 'Agreement Establishing the European Union Emergency Trust Fund for Stability and Addressing Root Causes of Irregular Migration and Displaced Persons in Africa, and its Internal Rules' (12 November 2015) https://trust-fund-for-africa.europa.eu/document/download/4cb965d7-8ad5-4da9-9f6d-3843f4bf0e82_en?filename=Constitutive%20Agreement%20, accessed 9 June 2025.

[22] Memo, 'A European Union Emergency Trust Fund for Africa' (Valletta, 12 November 2015) https://ec.europa.eu/commission/presscorner/detail/en/memo_15_6056, accessed 9 June 2025.

[23] See, for example, Joint Declaration between the Islamic Republic of Mauritania and the European Union (n 17).

However, study of the operation of EUTF reveals that it often diverts development funds towards short-term migration control goals and contributions to the securitization of the relationship, to the detriment of both mobility and human rights, and creating an imbalanced relationship.[24] For NGOs on the ground, there is a tension between their humanitarian and developmental missions and their participation in the EU's politically charged policy of exclusion.[25] Others have noted that the possibility for cooperation on root causes of migration and a new approach to development are available under the EUTF,[26] but have been used by EU states as funding 'business as usual' in migration.[27] This means that despite the discourse around confronting the 'root causes of migration'[28] and their relationship with development, the pursuit of border externalization[29] has emerged as the strongest characteristic, with the emphasis on African countries adopting European border control norms.[30]

This was referred to explicitly by the Commission, in the following terms:

> The EU has over the past five years made significant progress on the external dimension of migration, working in a Team Europe approach to deepen comprehensive partnerships based on mutual interests. It has scaled up its work to provide a comprehensive response, building on the experience of the EU Emergency Trust Fund for Africa and addressing root causes of irregular migration and forced displacement. The EU has also accelerated efforts to help partner countries enhance their national migration governance and border management, prevent irregular arrivals and loss of lives, fight migrant smuggling and trafficking in human beings, improve return, readmission and sustainable

[24] Luca Barana, 'The EU Trust Fund for Africa and the Perils of a Securitized Migration Policy' (2021) 17 IAI (Istituto Affari Internationali) Commentaries 31.

[25] Agnese Pacciardi, 'Governing Migration through Development: The Role of NGOs in EU Border Externalisation in Libya' (2026) JCMS: Journal of Common Market Studies, early https://doi.org/10.1111/jcms.70088, accessed 30 March 2026.

[26] Gerda Heck and Elena Habersky, 'Externalising Migration Controls through Development Programs in Egypt' (2024) 30(1) Geopolitics 120.

[27] Clare Castillejo, 'The European Union Trust Fund for Africa: A Glimpse of the Future for EU Development Cooperation' (German Development Institute, Discussion Paper 22/2016, 2016) https://www.idos-research.de/uploads/media/DP__22.2016.neu.pdf, accessed 9 June 2025, 16.

[28] Natascha Zaun and Olivia Nantermoz, 'The Use of Pseudo-Causal Narratives in EU Policies: The Case of the European Union Emergency Trust Fund for Africa' (2021) 29(4) Journal of European Public Policy 510.

[29] Agnese Pacciardi, 'A European Narrative of Border Externalisation: The European Trust Fund for Africa Story' (2025) 34(1) European Security 65; François Crépeau and Idil Atak, 'Global Migration Governance: Avoiding Commitments on Human Rights, Yet Tracing a Course for Cooperation' (2017) 34(2) Netherlands Quarterly of Human Rights 113; Vincent Chetail, *International Migration Law* (Oxford University Press 2020).

[30] Eleonora Frasca, 'Informal Agreements and Quasi-Legal Mechanisms in EU–Africa Cooperation on Migration: How the EU Takes Advantage of the GCM Commitments' (2023) 5 Frontiers in Human Dynamics 1, https://doi.org/10.3389/fhumd.2023.1207628, accessed 9 June 2025; Franzisca Zanker, 'Managing or Restricting Movement? Diverging Approaches of African and European Migration Governance' (2019) 7 Comparative Migration Studies 1.

> reintegration, and further develop legal pathways, all while asserting the importance of respect for fundamental rights and international law. It launched two Team Europe Initiatives focused on the Atlantic/Western Mediterranean and the Central Mediterranean migratory routes.[31]

In this respect, the EUTF has been a powerful tool for both defining and transforming the geopolitical space as conceptualized by European actors and opening the gateway to the 'formal informality' of agreements with third countries and operationalization.[32]

The record of the EUTF has been mixed, despite the difficulties in tracking the effects of how funding is spent in often volatile geographical contexts.[33] The Court of Auditors has had two opportunities to examine the EUTF via a 'performance audit', in 2018[34] and 2024.[35] In both reports, there are challenges in relation to reporting, ensuring the sustainability of results, and safeguarding human rights. In the view of the Court, the EUTF has 'contributed to keeping migration high on the development and political agenda' but 'while it was a flexible tool, its design should have been more focused . . . at strategic level not much has changed and the support remained insufficiently focussed. The Board approved more specific priorities in 2018, but these had little impact on strategic choices or the actions to be funded.'[36] The EUTF's final implementation date is the end of 2025, but the contracting of funds for operations ended in December 2021. However, funding on migration projects will continue via the Neighbourhood, Development and International Cooperation Instrument—Global Europe (NDICI), which aims to dedicate 10 per cent of its spending to migration, with similar aims to the EUTF.[37]

[31] Commission, 'Joint Communication to the European Parliament, the Council, the European Economic and Social Committee, the Committee of the Regions and the European Investment Bank: Building Sustainable International Partnerships as a Team Europe' JOIN(2024) 25 final 6–7.

[32] Federica Zardo, 'The EU Trust Fund for Africa: Geopolitical Space Making through Migration Policy Instruments' (2022) 27(2) Geopolitics 584.

[33] Camilla Fogli, Sophia Leonie Popp, and Francesca Majorano Sarapo, 'Addressing Root Causes of Irregular Migration and Forced Displacement. What Works and What Does Not? Lessons Learned from the EUTF in HoA' (Publications Office of the European Union 2025) https://publications.jrc.ec.europa.eu/repository/handle/JRC141572, accessed 9 June 2025.

[34] European Court of Auditors, 'European Union Emergency Trust Fund for Africa: Flexible but Lacking Focus' (European Court of Auditors, Special Report no 32/2018, 2018) https://www.eca.europa.eu/Lists/ECADocuments/SR18_32/SR_EUTF_AFRICA_EN.pdf accessed 9 June 2025.

[35] European Court of Auditors, 'The EU Trust Fund for Africa—Despite new approaches, support remained unfocused' (European Court of Auditors, Special Report 17/2024, 2024) https://www.eca.europa.eu/en/publications?ref=SR-2024-17#:~:text=12%20The%20final%20date%20of,the%20end%20of%20December%202021, accessed 9 June 2025.

[36] ibid para 82.

[37] ibid para 12; European Commission, 'New Study offers insights for EU migration and development programming in the Horn of Africa' (*European Commission: Knowledge for policy,* 20 May 2025) https://knowledge4policy.ec.europa.eu/news/new-study-offers-insights-eu-migration-development-programming-horn-africa_en, accessed 9 June 2025.

7.2 Mobility Partnerships

Mobility Partnerships are the most enduring of the informal modes of governance explored in this chapter, and allow us to take a longer-term view of the shift towards informality without the lens of 'crisis'. Mobility Partnerships emerged from and in response to changes in governance and shifts in the EU's external borders in the post-enlargement period. The European Neighbourhood Policy (ENP), launched in 2004, served as both a framework and a catalyst for enhanced relations with neighbouring countries as the post-enlargement sphere has gradually taken on an increasingly migration-centric focus[38] and used conditionality, familiar to both enlargement and ENP, as a tool.[39]

The ENP built on existing frameworks for cooperation across the Mediterranean and Eastern Europe,[40] but, coinciding with the (attempted) strategic approaches to migration typified by the GAMM and European Agenda on Migration, and against the background of the Arab Spring (2011),[41] Mobility Partnerships have been brought to the fore as a means of engagement with key third countries.

One of the most notable aspects of the ENP, when set against previous (or even concurrent) frameworks for engaging with third countries, is the prioritization of the bilateral dimension over the multilateral.[42] As a result, Mobility Partnerships take a highly differentiated approach in their engagement with third countries.

The stated purpose of Mobility Partnerships is to deepen cooperation with individual third states on both regular and irregular migration, on a co-owned basis. The objectives are varied, and include facilitating circular and temporary migration, promoting cooperation on migration and development, and preventing irregular migration, smuggling, and human trafficking.[43] The incentives on offer to third states are the possibility of opening routes for regular migration, including visa facilitation, and assistance in upgrading national migration laws and reinforcing migration control.

[38] See, for example, Virginie Guiraudon, 'The 2015 Refugee Crisis Was Not a Turning Point: Explaining Policy Inertia in EU Border Control' (2018) 17 European Political Science 151.

[39] Arne Niemann and Natascha Zaun, 'Introduction: EU External Migration Policy and EU Migration Governance: Introduction' (2023) 49(12) Journal of Ethnic and Migration Studies 2965.

[40] Cardwell, 'EuroMed, European Neighbourhood Policy and the Union for the Mediterranean' (n 14).

[41] Assem Dandashly, 'The EU Response to Regime Change in the Wake of the Arab Revolt' (2015) 37(1) Journal of European Integration 37; Sergio Carrera, Joanna Parkin, and Leonhard den Hertog, 'EU Migration Policy after the Arab Spring' (CEPS Policy Paper, 2 May 2013) https://www.ceps.eu/system/files/arabspringmigration-carreradenhertogparkin-ne-jdi-feb13.pdf, accessed 9 June 2025.

[42] Foteini Asderaki, 'The EU in the Eastern Mediterranean: Multilateral and Bilateral Relations' in Aristotle Tziampiris and Foteini Asderaki (eds), *The New Eastern Mediterranean Transformed* (Springer 2021); Katharina Eisele and Anka Wiesbrock, 'Enhancing Mobility in the European Neighbourhood Policy? The Cases of Moldova and Georgia' (2011) 36(2) Review of Central and East European Law 127.

[43] See, for example, Council, 'Joint declaration establishing a Mobility Partnership between the Kingdom of Morocco and the European Union and its Member States' (6139/13, 3 June 2013) https://data.consilium.europa.eu/doc/document/ST-6139-2013-INIT/en/pdf, accessed 9 June 2025.

Mobility Partnerships are thus a key site of 'formal informality' as they occupy a central role in bilateral relations, representing more than mere statements of intent. Although they are cited by the Commission to be an 'arrangement on the basis of political declarations',[44] Mobility Partnerships effectively blur the lines between migration law and foreign policy, operating in a legal grey area with innovative and non-binding measures. The Commission describes them as 'the most complete framework for bilateral cooperation between the EU and its partners, based on mutual offers of commitments and project initiatives covering mobility, migration and asylum issues'.[45]

Mobility Partnerships are relatively concrete insofar as there is an agreed-upon, publicly available text to which both sides have committed themselves. But the partnership acts more as a gateway to cooperation rather than spelling out exactly what these are or will be. Despite lacking concrete or enforceable measures, Mobility Partnerships do have tangible effects and allow dynamic patterns of cooperation between EU Member States and partner countries. Mobility Partnerships generally cover similar ground, and it is possible to detect the reflection of EU preferences rather than tailored partner country needs. They are open-ended in the aims for cooperation. There is emphasis on support for the partner state's development and capacities, but with combating irregular migration as a central plank.

Twelve Mobility Partnerships have been successfully put in place since 2007. Although they share many of the same characteristics, the text of MPs and their relationship with formal, legal instruments, such as Readmission Agreements, has evolved and can be viewed through different phases.[46] The first MPs emerged during a 'Pilot Phase' between 2007 and 2009 with Georgia,[47] Moldova,[48] and Cabo Verde.[49] Moldova and Georgia, having signed Readmission Agreements and Visa Facilitation Agreements, focused on facilitating legal migration.

[44] Commission, 'Glossary: Mobility Partnership' (*European Commission: Migration and Home Affairs*) https://ec.europa.eu/assets/home/emn-glossary/glossary.html?letters=n&classification=2.1&detail=mobility+partnership, accessed 9 June 2025.

[45] Commission, 'Eastern Partnership: Mobility Partnerships, visa facilitation and readmission agreements' (*European Commission: Migration and Home Affairs*) https://home-affairs.ec.europa.eu/policies/international-affairs/collaboration-countries/eastern-partnership/mobility-partnerships-visa-facilitation-and-readmission-agreements_en (accessed 9 June 2025).

[46] Cardwell and Dickson, '"Formal Informality" in EU External Migration Governance' (n 10).

[47] Council, 'Joint Declaration on a Mobility Partnership between the European Union and Georgia' (16396/09 ADD1, 13 November 2009) https://data.consilium.europa.eu/doc/document/ST-16396-2009-ADD-1/en/pdf, accessed 9 June 2025.

[48] Council, 'Joint Declaration on a Mobility Partnership between the European Union and the Republic of Moldova' (9460/08 ADD 1, 21 May 2008) https://home-affairs.ec.europa.eu/document/download/c0d92bb8-c8b2-4db0-a4f3-2bdfd4584310_en?filename=mobility_partnership_republic_of_moldova_en.pdf, accessed 9 June 2025.

[49] Council, 'Joint Declaration on a Mobility Partnership between the European Union and the Republic of Cape Verde' (9460/08 ADD 2, 21 May 2008) https://data.consilium.europa.eu/doc/document/ST-9460-2008-ADD-2/en/pdf, accessed 9 June 2025.

Cabo Verde, which is not covered by the ENP, served as a test case for MP development.

Subsequent MPs with Armenia[50] and Azerbaijan,[51] both covered by the ENP, emphasized managing labour migration, including temporary and circular migration. The EU-Armenia Mobility Partnership highlighted 'concrete and effective initiatives' and information sharing for better coordination. The EU–Azerbaijan Partnership underscored international standards, human rights protection, and promotion of international protection.

The 'Next Generation' of Mobility Partnerships emerged from 2011. The content of the Mobility Partnership with Tunisia[52] shifted the focus from mobility to crisis management, emphasizing the role and responsibility of the partner in addressing problems and sharing burdens. These 'next generation' Mobility Partnerships were less oriented towards mobility to the EU and more focused on mechanisms for return and readmission. The EU–Tunisia Mobility Partnership, signed after the 2011 move towards democratization following the Arab Spring, marks a shift towards the use of Mobility Partnerships as crisis management tools, especially in the return and readmission context. This is exacerbated by the influence of the migration 'crisis', which has resulted in a decline in seeking formal agreements in the interest of finding rapid solutions which bypass lengthy, cumbersome processes and potential opposition. For example, the EU–Tunisia Mobility Partnership, while emphasizing co-ownership, has not progressed in facilitating mobility to the EU. Rather, emphasis has been placed on facilitating return and readmission as a pre-condition before the regular migration aspects. As noted in the previous chapter, the Visa Facilitation Agreement negotiations have progressed slowly due to tensions around the partners' reluctance to accept returns, particularly of third country citizens. When compared with Morocco, an EU 'privileged' partner with an EU Mobility Partnership since 2013, the relationship appears less formalized.[53] Similarly with Jordan,[54] the Mobility Partnership agreed in 2014 continues to be at

[50] Council, 'Joint Declaration on a Mobility Partnership between the European Union and Armenia' (14963/11 ADD 1, 6 October 2011) https://home-affairs.ec.europa.eu/document/download/615e4523-de26-475c-903b-c5ae35ee3bed_en?filename=mobility_partnership_armenia_en.pdf, accessed 9 June 2025.

[51] Joint Declaration on a Mobility Partnership between the Republic of Azerbaijan and the European Union and its Participating Member States (5 December 2002) https://home-affairs.ec.europa.eu/document/download/0788d79a-a8a2-43ce-9d92-649e201af7f2_en?filename=mobility_partnership_of_azerbaijan_en.pdf, accessed 9 June 2025.

[52] Joint Declaration on a Mobility Partnership between Tunisia and the European Union and its Participating Member States (3 March 2014) https://home-affairs.ec.europa.eu/document/download/dc345c7f-6d5b-478f-97f5-6b13c63ea66c_en?filename=declaration_conjointe_tunisia_eu_mobility_fr.pdf, accessed 9 June 2025.

[53] Fanny Tittel-Mosser, 'Reversed Conditionality in EU External Migration Policy: The Case of Morocco' (2018) 14(4) Journal of Contemporary European Research 349.

[54] Joint declaration establishing a Mobility Partnership between the Hashemite Kingdom of Jordan and the European Union and its participating Member States (6 July 2014) https://www.europarl.europa.eu/cmsdata/124061/20141009_joint_declaration_establishing_the_eu-jordan_mobility_partnership_en.pdf, accessed 9 June 2025.

the heart of the strategic relationship with the EU, but also on a less formal basis insofar as cooperation is concerned. The more recent EU–Jordan Joint Declaration on a Strategic and Comprehensive Partnership refers to the 'focus on an effective return policy ensuring dignified and sustainable return and repatriation that upholds international law and human rights. The EU and Jordan will also enhance cooperation with relevant EU and international agencies to address these important issues.'[55]

Scholarly opinions on Mobility Partnerships have varied. Some initial views at the outset of the process welcomed their cooperative nature and joint ownership; over time, more scepticism has crept in due to the ever-increasing emphasis on preventing irregular migration and the externalization of borders to states. The lack of clarity afforded by Mobility Partnerships as built on political declarations but with operational consequences has been at the forefront of critique.[56] MPs are viewed as striking an unequal bargain for third states, and their lack of transparency is often associated with emphasizing the securitization of migration over opportunities from regular migration.

Yet, the emphasis placed by the EU institutions on Mobility Partnerships as a key strategic tool, and the lack of more extensive use of them, suggests that they are more than merely political declarations that come without the expectation of obligations. This also explains why some third states may be reluctant to conclude them.[57] Mobility Partnerships, as informal tools, nevertheless allow for operationalization and 'to obtain cooperation from third countries, such as political and diplomatic approaches, technical support to third countries through development cooperation, as well as conditionality mechanisms'.[58] Put another way, these are the 'hard implications of soft law'.[59] As already noted, technical cooperation is important insofar as it conveys the idea of neutralizing any political or discretionary power. In fact, technical cooperation in migration, and particularly in combatting irregular migration, has the potential to do precisely the opposite.'[60] Further support for a more concrete nature of Mobility Partnerships than

[55] Joint Declaration on the 'Strategic and Comprehensive Partnership' between the Hashemite Kingdom of Jordan and the European Union, https://north-africa-middle-east-gulf.ec.europa.eu/document/download/9b466aae-7dd7-48e0-b944-7a7533e5605a_en?filename=C_2025_597_F1_ANNEX_EN_V2_P1_3897628.PDF, accessed 9 June 2025.

[56] Emanuela Roman, 'The "Burden" of Being "Safe": How Do Informal EU Migration Agreements Affect International Responsibility Sharing' in Eva Kassoti and Narin Idriz (eds), *The Informalization of the EU's External Action in the Field of Migration and Asylum* (TMC Asser Press 2022).

[57] Meng-Hsuan Chou and Marie Gibert, 'The EU–Senegal Mobility Partnership' (2012) 8(4) Journal of Contemporary European Research 408.

[58] Frasca, 'Informal Agreements and Quasi-Legal Mechanisms in EU–Africa Cooperation on Migration' (n 30).

[59] Violeta Moreno-Lax, 'The Informalization of the External Dimension of EU Asylum Policy: The Hard Implications of Soft Law' in Evangelia (Lilian) Tsourdi and Philippe De Bruycker (eds), *Research Handbook on EU Migration and Asylum Law* (Edward Elgar Publishing 2023).

[60] Frasca, 'Informal Agreements and Quasi-Legal Mechanisms in EU–Africa Cooperation on Migration' (n 30).

is indicated by their 'political declaration' basis is found in the Global Approach to Migration and Mobility, which suggests that Common Agendas on Migration and Mobility might be used as 'a viable option for partner countries and for the EU and its Member States in cases where both sides want to establish an advanced level of cooperation, but where one side or the other is not ready to enter into the full set of obligations and commitments'.[61] The reference to obligations and commitments demonstrates something more than a mere statement of intent.

The evolution of Mobility Partnerships has been marked by notable shifts in language, reflecting changes in their function over time. Initially, they were conceived as a political framework to structure bilateral relations, grounded in a general agreement and reinforced by formal readmission arrangements. However, this original purpose has gradually given way to a more ad hoc, crisis-driven approach. As a result, the formal legal dimension has diminished. This is significant because it means the EU's migration governance no longer rests on a clear legal foundation. Moreover, identifying specific instances of cooperation under the Mobility Partnership framework has become increasingly difficult, especially when such interactions occur between individual Member States and partner countries.

7.3 Common Agenda on Migration and Mobility (CAMM)

Like Mobility Partnerships, a CAMM is a strategic yet informal type of framework established by the EU to guide cooperation on migration and mobility with specific partner countries. The stated purpose of CAMMs is to put in place common agendas which aim to foster a comprehensive and balanced approach, addressing various aspects of migration, including legal migration, border management, asylum, and cooperation on addressing the root causes of migration.

According to the GAMM, 'the CAMM should set a number of common recommendations, targets and commitments for dialogue and cooperation and should include a package of specific support measures offered by the EU and interested Member States. If both parties agree, the Common Agenda could be upgraded to a Mobility Partnership at a later stage.'[62]

Therefore, CAMMs rely on a similar, informal framework to Mobility Partnerships, but with lower expectations of cooperation or potential future commitments. The GAMM goes on to state: 'The CAMM should be introduced as an alternative framework to agree common recommendations, targets and commitments within each of the four thematic pillars of the GAMM. The fundamental difference from the MP is that this framework would not necessarily require

[61] COM (2011) 743 final (n 2).
[62] ibid.

negotiating visa facilitation and Readmission Agreements. If both parties agree, the Common Agenda could be upgraded to a Mobility Partnership at a later stage.'[63]

There are two points of note here. The first is the decoupling of a partnership framework from moves towards formal agreements between the EU and partner states as represented by VFA and Readmission Agreements.[64] In contrast to Mobility Partnerships, this shift appears to exchange the 'more for more' approach, whereby cooperation on irregular migration from the third country is tied to benefits the EU is able to offer for regular migration, to a 'less for less' approach.[65]

The second, and related, point is that the Common Agenda, as established via a Joint Declaration between the EU and the third state, nevertheless goes beyond dialogue on migration due to the reference to cooperation on migration. The suggestion appears thus to be that practical cooperation between the two sides can lead to enhanced relations, but without specifying what kind of cooperation this entails or what determines the ability for a CAMM to be 'upgraded' to a Mobility Partnership. A CAMM thus appears to be a 'light' version of a Mobility Partnership.

Ethiopia is a case in point. Ethiopia concluded a CAMM with the EU in 2015.[66] As Crawley and Blitz have noted,[67] the rationale for the EU–Ethiopia CAMM as presented by Commission President Jean-Claude Juncker was the high number of refugees currently in Ethiopia and the justification for EU support.[68] And yet, documentation from the Commission notes the need from the EU side to attempt to prevent secondary movements from Ethiopia to Europe.[69]

To date, only two other CAMMs have been concluded alongside that of Ethiopia: Nigeria and India, in 2015 and 2019 respectively. References have been made to the pursuit of CAMMs with states including Ghana, Bangladesh, and the Philippines,[70] but none appear to have materialized. A Portuguese government

[63] ibid.

[64] See Chapter 6.

[65] Tineke Strik, 'The Global Approach to Migration and Mobility' (2017) 5(2) Groningen Journal of International Law 310.

[66] The text of the CAMM is no longer available on the EU Europa website, but is available here: https://download.taz.de/migcontrol/aethiopien/EU_Ethiopia_Mobility%20Partnership_2015.11.11_eng.pdf, accessed 9 June 2025.

[67] Heaven Crawley and Brad Blitz, 'Common Agenda or Europe's Agenda? International Protection, Human Rights and Migration from the Horn of Africa' (2018) 45(12) Journal of Ethnic and Migration Studies 2258.

[68] Commission, 'European Union and Ethiopia sign Common Agenda on Migration and Mobility' (Press release, 11 November 2015) https://ec.europa.eu/commission/presscorner/detail/en/ip_15_6050, accessed 2 June 2025.

[69] European Commission, 'EO Emergency Trust Fund for Africa' (*European Union External Action*, 2017) https://eeas.europa.eu/sites/eeas/files/factsheet_ec_format_eu_emergency_trust_fund_for_africa_2017.pdf, accessed 9 June 2025.

[70] As noted in the evidence presented by the Commission to the House of Lords (UK): House of Lords European Union Committee, Eighth Report: *The EU's Global Approach to Migration and Mobility (8th Report)* (2012–13, HL 91) para 141. On Ghana, see further Ilke Adam and Florian Trauner, 'Ghana and EU Migration Policy: Studying an African Response to the EU's Externalisation Agenda' in Sergio Carrera, Juan Santos Vara, and Tieneke Strik (eds), *Constitutionalising the External Dimensions of EU Migration Policies in Times of Crisis: Legality, Rule of Law and Fundamental Rights Reconsidered* (Edward Elgar Publishing 2019).

website refers to a CAMM with Brazil,[71] but it is not mentioned in any EU sources. Unlike Mobility Partnerships, the text of the CAMMs is not readily available and, somewhat curiously, the EU's official website links to copies of the CAMMs with India and Nigeria hosted by external sites.[72] The text of the CAMMs covers much of the same ground, referring to its 'open ended, flexible framework' but opening the possibility for cooperation with agencies including Frontex and annual meetings to provide overall steering. With India, the CAMM places much more emphasis on the facilitation of regular migration opportunities.

The lack of successful conclusion of CAMMs with other states can be understood in two ways. First, as with Mobility Partnerships, the EU has found it difficult to engage third states to a sufficient level to allow an agreement to be publicly announced (even if the text is not readily available). Given the strategic emphasis placed on CAMMs, this would represent a failure on the part of the EU and suggest that the decoupling from VFAs or other tangible benefit for the third state is futile. Second, despite the appearance of CAMMs in strategic documentation, it is not a necessary precursor to cooperation on migration, including operational cooperation. For instance, the Migration Partnership Facility, designed to support the operationalization of Mobility Partnerships and CAMMs, includes both the states listed above and others.[73] Furthermore, and again using Ethiopia as an example, a 'non-binding' readmission arrangement has been concluded. Therefore, if the EU's aim is to promote returns, then there appears to be little to gain, on either side, from a CAMM.

Since no CAMMs have been put in place since 2019, they might best be considered as an instrument which has outlived its usefulness. Rather, and often with the same third countries in mind, a number of other competing bilateral governance frameworks have emerged which appear to share many of the same informal characteristics. These include Migration Partnership Frameworks and Migration Compacts, to which the discussion now turns.

7.4 Migration Partnership Frameworks

The Migration Partnership Framework (MPF) was introduced in June 2016, with the aim of integrating migration into EU foreign policy. The purpose of the MPF is to mobilize the instruments, resources and influence of the EU and its Member

[71] DGES, 'EU–Brazil Common Agenda for Migration and Mobility' (*DGES: Direção-Geral do Ensino Superior*) https://www.dges.gov.pt/en/pagina/eu-brazil-common-agenda-migration-and-mobility, accessed 9 June 2025.

[72] Commission, 'International Affairs' (*European Commission: Migration and Home Affairs*) https://home-affairs.ec.europa.eu/policies/international-affairs_en, accessed 9 June 2025.

[73] Commission, 'Migration Partnership Facility (MPF)' (*European Commission, Migration and Home Affairs*) https://home-affairs.ec.europa.eu/policies/international-affairs/migration-partnership-facility-mpf_en, accessed 9 June 2025.

States to establish cooperation with partner countries to 'sustainably manage migration flows'.[74] Better cooperation on identifying, re-documenting, and readmitting nationals from these states appears as a prominent aim. As a foreign policy tool, MPFs were also referred to in the EU's Global Strategy for Foreign and Security Policy[75] and institutionally led by the European External Action Service (EEAS) under the High Representative for Foreign and Security Policy.

The agreements under the MPF were initially envisaged as 'compacts', akin to the EU–Türkiye Statement,[76] with states that were likely open to a partnership approach, and thus showing a quick 'win' for the EU in confronting the migration crisis.[77] A Commission Communication of 2016 stated that as a first stage in the process, tailor-made compacts would be launched with Niger, Nigeria, Senegal, Mali, and Ethiopia, with increased engagement with Tunisia and Libya.[78] MPFs were referred to as 'comprehensive partnerships'[79] and 'in full respect of our humanitarian and human rights obligations'. Such compacts would establish clear commitments from each partner, around which other EU policy areas could be mobilized to deliver on migration goals, including the potential for enhanced trade relations, while ensuring that migration remains in the region, as the EU–Jordan Compact has aimed for.[80]

The MPF was then described as a 'political framework for continued and operational cooperation, pulling together the different work strands in order to develop a comprehensive partnership with third countries, combining instruments, tools and leverages available to the EU and MS to deliver clear targets and joint commitments'.[81] This appears to remove any immediate benefit for partner countries, or at least ones that are publicized, since there might be benefits hidden via this demonstration of 'formal informality', particularly which suit mutual (and hidden) securitization agendas.[82] The leverages referred to point to the pressure on third

[74] Clare Castillejo, 'The EU Migration Partnership Framework: Time for a Rethink?' Deutsches Institut für Entwicklungspolitik, Discussion Paper No 28/2017 (Working Paper), https://www.econstor.eu/bitstream/10419/199518/1/die-dp-2017-28.pdf, accessed 9 June 2025.

[75] European Union, 'A Global Strategy for the European Union's Foreign And Security Policy' (European Union Global Strategy, June 2016) https://www.eeas.europa.eu/sites/default/files/eugs_review_web_0.pdf, accessed 9 June 2025, 28.

[76] Peter Seeberg and Federica Zardo, 'From Mobility Partnerships to Migration Compacts: Security Implications of EU–Jordan Relations and the Informalization of Migration Governance' (2022) 48(6) Journal of Ethnic and Migration Studies 1345.

[77] Castillejo, 'The EU Migration Partnership Framework: Time for a Rethink?' (n 74).

[78] COM(2016) 385 final (n 11).

[79] ibid 4.

[80] Marion Panizzon, 'The EU–Jordan Compact in a Trade Law Context: Preferential Access to the EU Market to Keep Refugees in the Region' in Sergio Carrera, Juan Santos Vara, and Tineke Strik (eds), *Constitutionalising the External Dimensions of EU Migration Policies in Times of Crisis* (Edward Elgar Publishing 2019).

[81] COM(2016) 385 final (n 11).

[82] Peter Seeberg, 'Mobility Partnerships and Security Subcomplexes in the Mediterranean: The Strategic Role of Migration and the EU's Foreign and Security Policies towards the MENA region' (2017) 22(1) *European Foreign Affairs Review* 91.

countries to re-admit their nationals and those of other countries who have used the third country as a transit point. Leverages might also include financial incentives, which helps to explain the need for secrecy and the reference to the MPS being a 'win–win' for the EU and the partners.[83] The lack of transparency over the financial incentives is indicated by the claim from the Commission that 'In the past, rigid rules on programming of resources have been an obstacle to responding rapidly to MS' requests, or lead to a systematic recourse to (limited) emergency funding. There are also areas where EU funding instruments could play a stronger role in the future.'[84]

The MPF makes no mention of formal agreements on visa facilitation or re-admission as a priority. Rather, the aim of facilitating 'fast and operational returns' and 'specific and measurable increases in the number and rate of return and re-admission' suggests that the use of the frameworks is revealing in terms of the emphasis placed on practical cooperation, even in the absence of formal agreements. Identification missions on returns to third countries are also cited as a priority, as is the 'involvement' of agencies including Frontex and EUROPOL in the third counties.[85] The role of individual Member States in engaging in bilateral cooperation, with the EU as a semi-detached coordinator or facilitator, appears to characterize the MPFs. The reference to funding mechanisms is also telling and offers an insight into how the participation of partner states can be secured, even as the EU and its Member States have shown themselves to be less willing to enhance regular migration opportunities.

Evaluating the MPF in its five priority states, Ethiopia, Mali, Niger, Nigeria, and Senegal, Castillejo has noted that it was a clear example of a shift towards a 'transactional, short-term and incentives-based based approach' to migration in response to the crisis. Yet, the impact of the crisis in prioritizing migration (and returns) in dialogue with third countries over other important themes such as development did not work as a strategy to engage cooperation—rather the opposite.[86] The start of negotiations for a Readmission Agreement with Nigeria[87] were a tangible outcome from the MPF, but they later stalled. The most concrete outcomes were with Niger, where the EU mobilized a number of different funding

[83] European Union External Action Service, 'Partnership on Migration One Year On: Lessons Learned, Challenges and Way Forward' (*European Union External Action)* https://www.eeas.europa.eu/sites/default/files/factsheet_partnership_framework_on_migration.pdf, accessed 9 June 2025.

[84] European Commission, 'Communication from the Commission to the European Parliament, the Council, the European Economic and Social Committee and the Committee of the Regions on the Delivery of the European Agenda on Migration' COM(2017) 558 final.

[85] European Union, 'Migration Partnership Framework: A New Approach to Better Manage Migration' (*European Union External Action)* https://www.eeas.europa.eu/sites/default/files/factsheet_ec_format_migration_partnership_framework_update_2.pdf, accessed 9 June 2025.

[86] Castillejo, 'The EU Migration Partnership Framework: Time for a Rethink?' (n 74) 37.

[87] As referred to here: European Union, 'Nigeria: Action and Progress under the Migration Partnership Framework June–December 2016' (*European Union External Action)* https://www.eeas.europa.eu/sites/default/files/factsheet-nigeria_en.pdf, accessed 9 June 2025.

mechanisms, including the EUCAP Sahel Niger[88] mission, under the Common Security and Defence Policy (CSDP) and European Trust Fund for Africa (EUTF) to engage the Nigerien authorities in cooperation on border control against migrants en route to Libya, operational training, and deployment of EU liaison officers.[89] Furthermore, this cooperation was poorly received in Niger insofar as it was perceived as becoming an external frontier of the EU, with a reduction in its own sovereignty vis-à-vis borders and free movement under the ECOWAS Treaty of West African states.[90] Reaction against this phenomena featured strongly in the overthrow of the government in July 2023 and the reversal of cooperation with the EU generally.[91]

Despite the initial flurry of activity and enthusiasm for MPFs with third states, little emphasis appears to have been placed on them since the intense 'crisis' period of 2016–18. The limited progress and uncoupling of incentives while stressing, from the EU side, the importance of returns and readmission suggests that a framework approach has not been successful. Rather, and from around the same period, greater attention has been paid to arrangements specifically for readmission. Formal agreements as per the process laid down in the Treaty were explored in the previous chapter. Here, non-binding, informal 'arrangements' occupy the same terrain but without the legal basis or framework.

7.5 Non-binding readmission 'arrangements'

The previous chapter set out the process and operation of Readmission Agreements concluded on the basis of Article 79(3) TFEU, the specific legal competence for 'agreements with third countries for the readmission to their countries of origin or provenance of third-country nationals'. The Commission's DG Migration

[88] European Union External Action, 'Common Security and Defence Policy: The EUCAP Sahel Niger Civilian Mission' (*European Union External Action*, April 2016) https://eeas.europa.eu/archives/docs/csdp/missions-and-operations/eucap-sahel-niger/pdf/factsheet_eucap_sahel_niger_en.pdf, accessed 9 June 2025.

[89] See further, Céline Bauloz, 'The EU Migration Partnership Framework: An External Solution to the Crisis?' (*Refugee Law Initiative Blog*, January 2017) https://eumigrationlawblog.eu/the-eu-migration-partnership-framework-an-external-solution-to-the-crisis/?print=print, accessed 9 June 2025; Bachirou Tinni and Abdoulaye Hamadou, 'The Outsourcing of European Migration and Asylum Policy in Niger' in Sergio Carrera Nunez, Eleni Karageorgiou, Gamze Ovacik, and Nikolas Feith Tan (eds), *Global Asylum Governance and the European Union's Role: International Perspectives on Migration*, vol 18 (Springer 2025).

[90] Abdoulaye Hamadou, 'La gestion des flux migratoires au Niger entre engagements et contraintes' (2018) 14 La Revue des Droits de l'Homme 1. See further Florence Boyer, Bachirou Tinni, and Harouna Mounkaila, 'L'externalisation des politiques migratoires au Niger. Une action publique opportuniste?' (2020) 51 Anthropologie & développement 103.

[91] See further, Amanda Bisong, 'Migration Partnership Framework and the Externalization of European Union's (EU) Migration Policy in West Africa: The Case of Mali and Niger' in Glenn Rayp, Ilse Ruyssen, and Katrin Marchand (eds), *Regional Integration and Migration Governance in the Global South* (United Nations University Series on Regionalism, vol 20 (Springer 2020).

and Home Affairs states, however, underneath the list of eighteen Readmission Agreements in force—and their legal texts—that in addition to these agreements, 'legally non-binding readmission arrangements have also been concluded with Afghanistan, Guinea, Bangladesh, Ethiopia, The Gambia and Ivory Coast'.[92] There are no associated texts with these non-binding Readmission Agreements, nor specific information on what they entail.

The language used here is significant: they are not referred to as 'agreements' but as 'arrangements'.[93] As a result of this linguistic but also legal difference, informal agreements are largely inaccessible and excepted from public access requirements.[94] The modalities of these arrangements nevertheless closely mirror those of formal Readmission Agreements. For the non-binding Readmission Agreements, there are Joint Working Groups[95] which mirror the Joint Readmission Committees for each of the third states who have concluded a (formal) Readmission Agreement on the basis of Article 79(3) TFEU.

Yet there is nothing further specifically in the Commission's 2021 paper on 'Enhancing cooperation on return and readmission as part of a fair, effective and comprehensive EU migration policy' about non-binding agreements. The question therefore is the extent to which they are operationalized or whether these non-binding agreements/arrangements are destined to be a precursor to Article 79(3) TFEU agreements, or something different to be understood on their own terms. The Commission's failure to distinguish between formal and informal, instead presenting them as merely difference in forms, blurs the distinction significantly. There is no indication as to the extent to which the desire for a common EU return system relies on this indistinguishability between the two. Rather, the Commission refers to 'the common EU return system, and pursuing deeper, comprehensive partnerships on migration with third countries, in the context of their overall relationships with them'.[96] With this in mind, the badging of an arrangement as 'non-binding' does not necessarily prevent its content being interpreted as binding, as explored in the theoretical framework on institutionalism in Chapter 2.[97] Nor does

[92] Commission, 'An effective, firm and fair EU return and readmission policy' (*European Commission Migration and Home Affairs*) https://home-affairs.ec.europa.eu/policies/migration-and-asylum/irregular-migration-and-return/return-and-readmission_en, accessed 9 June 2025.

[93] Commission, 'Communication from the Commission to the European Parliament and the Council: Enhancing cooperation on return and readmission as part of a fair, effective and comprehensive EU migration policy' COM(2021) 56 final, 6.

[94] Eleonora Frasca, 'L'instrumentalisation de la politique européenne des visas comme levier de la coopération en matière de réadmission: qui est sanctionné par ce mécanisme de conditionnalité négative?' in Claude Blumann (ed), *Annuaire de droit de l'Union européenne* (Éditions Panthéon-Assas 2022).

[95] Commission, 'Enhancing cooperation on return and readmission as part of a fair, effective and comprehensive EU migration policy' (n 93).

[96] Commission, 'Enhancing cooperation on return and readmission as part of a fair, effective and comprehensive EU migration policy' COM(2021) 56 final.

[97] Chetail, *International Migration Law* (n 29) 284.

it prevent the Member States who return migrants under an informal arrangement from escaping the (binding) terms of the Returns Directive or international and human rights law. The challenge comes when identifying when returns are taking place and how they might be challenged. [98]

A desire among Member States towards informalizing Readmission Agreements with neighbouring states was identified as long ago as 2007, via administrative arrangements, exchanges of letters, and memoranda of understanding as alternatives.[99] Certainly, the emphasis has been placed on informal Readmission Agreements since at least 2016, against a background of stalled negotiations with third countries (including Morocco, Jordan, Nigeria, and Tunisia) on formal agreements. The relatively small number of formal agreements and their geographical limitation to, predominately, countries close to the EU and often engaged in the enlargement process, or smaller countries which are not situated on the busiest migration routes, suggest that this type of instrument has reached its limit. That none of the informal agreements have been converted to formal agreements, or at the very least progressed along the negotiation route, suggests that they are not destined to be used in this way. For third countries, the interest in making non-binding agreements is that they also avoid public attention. The flexibility and lack of obligations is thus part of the mutual interest on both sides.[100]

In terms of content, thus, there appears to be little practical difference between formal and informal Readmission Agreements. The overall aim from the EU side is clear in that the purpose is to increase the rate and number of returns from the EU to the third country, including other third country nationals or stateless persons. An informal arrangement is more than something which merely, for example, observes migration flows or suggests best practices for returnees. Rather, it is about the physical return of individuals. The 'commitments' (as the informal arrangement puts it)[101] made as part of the arrangements are thus almost indistinguishable from a formal agreement, even if the words 'not intended to create legal rights or obligations under international law' are used.[102] As explored in the previous chapter, there is an open question as to whether an agreement—either formal or informal—makes a substantial difference to the return rate.[103] But evaluating

[98] Roman, 'The "Burden" of Being "Safe"' (n 56).

[99] Jean-Pierre Cassarino, 'Informalising Readmission Agreements in the EU Neighbourhood' (2007) 42(2) International Spectator 179.

[100] Peter Slominski and Florian Trauner, 'Reforming Me Softly—How Soft Law Has Changed EU Return Policy since the Migration Crisis' (2021) 44(1) West European Politics 93.

[101] See, for example, 'Joint Way Forward on migration issues between Afghanistan and the EU' (2 October 2016) https://www.eeas.europa.eu/sites/default/files/eu_afghanistan_joint_way_forward_on_migration_issues.pdf, accessed 9 June 2025.

[102] ibid.

[103] Philipp Stutz and Florian Trauner, 'The EU's "Return Rate" with Third Countries: Why EU Readmission Agreements Do Not Make Much Difference' (2022) 60(3) International Migration 154; Juan Vara and Laura Matellán, 'The Informalization of EU Return Policy: A Change of Paradigm in Migration Cooperation with Third Countries?' in Eva Kassoti and Narin Idriz (eds), *The*

whether the informal agreement is effective is more challenging given that both the agreement and the practices under it are largely hidden from view, and Member States enjoy a large amount of discretion in engaging in returns, despite the (binding) terms of EU law.[104] Furthermore, as the Court of Auditors has found, there is no specific budget line for cooperation on readmission with third states and thus an attempt to 'follow the money' to see how readmission and returns are practically operated is extremely difficult.[105]

7.6 EU–Türkiye Statement 2016

The examples above largely concern states where there is no formal Readmission Agreement in place. The EU–Türkiye Statement is a fascinating example of informality, but also one which is atypical. It is the foremost example of the very public use of an instrument designed to limit irregular migration and promote returns with a non-EU member in addition to a formal Readmission Agreement which is already in place. Its use has been praised by the Commission as ending dangerous crossings from the Turkish coast to Greece, with suggestions that it is a model to follow. It is one of the only instruments of informality which has been tested in the courts.[106]

The background to the Statement was an increase in individuals, largely from Syria, seeking to arrive on Greek islands close to the Turkish coast, primarily Lesbos. This increase in 2015–16 directly led to the characterization of the advent as a 'migration crisis' for the EU, which has dominated debates since. Greece appealed for help from other Member States in dealing with the influx of migrants and called for an EU-led response to the crisis.

A Joint Action Plan between the EU and Türkiye was concluded on 29 November 2015.[107] As part of the Action Plan, Türkiye agreed to open its labour market to Syrians under temporary protection, introduce new visa requirements for Syrians and other nationalities, step up security efforts by the Turkish coast guard, and enhance the sharing of information. The EU created a 3 billion-euro 'Facility for Refugees in Türkiye' (FRiT) for joint projects, with promises to advance visa

Informalisation of the EU's External Action in the Field of Migration and Asylum. Global Europe: Legal and Policy Issues of the EU's External Action, vol 1 (TMC Asser Press 2022).

[104] Florian Trauner and Ariadna Ripoll Servent (eds), *Policy Change in the Area of Freedom, Security and Justice* (Routledge 2015).

[105] European Court of Auditors, 'EU Migrant return policy—cooperation with third countries on readmission' (*European Court of Auditors*, July 2020) https://www.eca.europa.eu/lists/ecadocuments/ap20_07/ap_migrant_return_policy_en.pdf, 9 June 2025.

[106] Case T-192/16 *NF, NG and NM v European Council* ECLI:EU:T:2017:128.

[107] Memo, 'EU–Turkey Joint Action Plan' (*European Commission*, 15 October 2015) https://ec.europa.eu/commission/presscorner/detail/en/memo_15_5860, accessed 9 June 2025.

liberalization with Türkiye and long-standing accession talks.[108] During winter 2015–16, intense negotiations took place towards what became the EU–Türkiye Statement of 18 March 2016.

The resultant statement was the product of dialogue between the 'Members of the European Council' (i.e. the Member States) and Türkiye.[109] It was published on the Council's website as a press release[110] but use of the word 'agreement' quickly shifted to 'statement' or 'deal' when it was quickly noted out that 'agreements' with third countries are foreseen in the Treaties, and this document had not followed this procedure.

According to the Statement, all irregular migrants arriving on Greek islands from 20 March 2016 were to be returned to Türkiye 'in full accordance with EU and international law', with individual asylum applications processed by Greek authorities. For each Syrian returned to Türkiye, another Syrian was to be resettled in the EU. A mechanism, assisted by EU agencies and the UNHCR, was to oversee this process. Türkiye was to work to prevent new illegal migration routes and cooperate with neighbouring states and the EU. Once irregular crossings decreased, a voluntary humanitarian admission scheme was to be activated, with EU Member States contributing voluntarily.[111] The basis of the Statement was that Türkiye could be regarded as a 'safe third country' that migrants could therefore be returned to.

The Statement was unusual in that it was promoted heavily by the institutions as an example of EU institutions and Member States putting words into action (which has been termed as 'machine room' dynamics)[112] and stemming the flow of migrants across the sea from Türkiye to Greece. However, despite its promotion as a solution, none of the key actors and institutions appear eager to claim ownership.[113] This was apparent during the attempts to settle its legal status in EU or international law. In a debate in the European Parliament, the Statement was considered an international agreement concluded by the European Council, acting on behalf of the EU.[114] But the Legal Service of the European Parliament considered

[108] Ludger Pries and Berna Safak Zülfikar Savci, 'Between Humanitarian Assistance and Externalizing of EU Borders: The EU–Turkey Deal and Refugee Related Organizations in Turkey' (2023) 11(1) *Journal on Migration and Human Security* 57.

[109] Council, 'EU–Turkey Statement' (Press Release 144/16, 18 March 2016) https://www.consilium.europa.eu/en/press/press-releases/2016/03/18/eu-turkey-statement/pdf, accessed 9 June 2025.

[110] ibid.

[111] ibid.

[112] Sandrino Smeets and Derek Beach, 'When Success Is an Orphan: Informal Institutional Governance and the EU–Turkey Deal' (2020) 43(1) West European Politics 129.

[113] Sergio Carrera, Leonhard den Hertog, and Marco Stefan, 'It Wasn't Me! The Luxembourg Court Orders on the EU–Turkey Refugee Deal' (CEPS, 28 April 2017) https://www.ceps.eu/ceps-publications/it-wasnt-me-luxembourg-court-orders-eu-turkey-refugee-deal/, accessed 9 June 2025.

[114] Ayhan Kaya, 'Europeanization and De-Europeanization of Turkish Asylum and Migration Policies' in Ebru Turhan and Wulf Reiners (eds), *EU–Turkey Relations* (Palgrave Macmillan 2021); European Parliament, 'Minutes of the debate of Wednesday' (13 April 2016) https://www.europarl.europa.eu/doceo/document/CRE-8-2016-04-13-TOC_EN.html, accessed 9 June 2025.

it a 'simple accord politique' lacking a formal status.[115] Given that it bypassed the decision-making process set out in the Treaty, it could not be considered as an Agreement, but this still left open the question as to its validity under international law, or the possibility for challenge under EU law.[116]

The Statement was challenged in the General Court, under Article 263 TFEU, by three Afghani and Pakistani citizens who had crossed from Türkiye to Greece and claimed asylum in Greece to avoid being returned to Türkiye under the terms of the Statement. They did not intend to remain in Greece and stated that their asylum claims were made under coercion from the Greek authorities. They argued that the Statement is an act attributable to the European Council establishing an international agreement contrary to EU law, and sought its annulment.[117] By order, the General Court, using the expedited procedure, dismissed the action on the ground of the Court's lack of jurisdiction to hear and determine it.[118]

The General Court recognized, on the basis of long-standing case-law dating back to the early 1970s,[119] that measures intended to produce legal effects should be amenable to judicial review under Article 263 TFEU.[120] The form of the Statement being revealed as a press release does not, for the Court, 'preclude the possibility of finding that such a measure exists or, therefore, the jurisdiction of the European Union Courts to review the legality of such a measure'.[121] However, the Court also recognized that it has no jurisdiction to rule on the lawfulness of a measure adopted by a national authority[122] or by several Member States acting

[115] As cited by Corten and Dony: Oliver Corten and Marianne Dony, 'Accord politique ou juridique: Quelle est la nature du "machin" conclu entre l'UE et las Turquie en matière d'asile?' (*EU Immigration and Asylum Law and Policy*, 10 June 2016) https://eumigrationlawblog.eu/accord-politique-ou-juridique-quelle-est-la-nature-du-machin-conclu-entre-lue-et-la-turquie-en-matiere-dasile/#:~:text=Elle%20a%20dès%20lors%20conclu,la%20forme%20n%27importe%20pas on the basis of Nikolaj Nielsen, 'EU–Turkey deal not binding, says EP legal chief' (*euobserver*, 25 June 2025) https://euobserver.com/rule-of-law/133385, accessed 9 June 2025.

[116] See, for example, Andrea Ott, 'The EU–Turkey Statement: Legal Nature and Compatibility with EU Institutional Law' In Sergio Carrera, Juan Santos Vara, and Tineke Strik (eds), *Constitutionalising the External Dimensions of EU Migration Policies in Times of Crisis: Legality, Rule of Law and Fundamental Rights Reconsidered* (Edward Elgar Publishing 2019); Corten and Dony, 'Accord politique ou juridique?' (n 115); Maarten deen Heijer and Thomas Spijkerboer, 'Is the EU–Turkey refugee and migration deal a treaty?' (*EU Law Analysis*, 7 April 2016) https://eulawanalysis.blogspot.com/2016/04/is-eu-turkey-refugee-and-migration-deal.html, accessed 25 June 2025.

[117] Case T-192/16 (n 106).

[118] ibid.

[119] Case C-22/70 *Commission v Council* EU:C:1971:32, para 42; and Case C-114/12 *Commission v Council* EU:C:2014:2151, paras 38 and 39; see also Case C-28/12 *Commission v Council* EU:C:2015:282, paras 14 and 15.

[120] Article 263(1) TFEU: 'The Court of Justice of the European Union shall review the legality of legislative acts, of acts of the Council, of the Commission and of the European Central Bank, other than recommendations and opinions, and of acts of the European Parliament and of the European Council intended to produce legal effects vis-à-vis third parties. It shall also review the legality of acts of bodies, offices or agencies of the Union intended to produce legal effects vis-à-vis third parties.'

[121] Case T-192/16 (n 106).

[122] Case C-97/91 *Oleificio Borelli v Commission* EU:C:1992:491, para 9; and Case T-22/97 *Kesko v Commission* EU:T:1999:327, para 83.

together, even when 'physically gathered in the grounds of one of the European Union institutions'.[123] In the case of the latter, they are doing so as the governments of the Member States.[124]

The Court found that the references to the authors of the Statement was not determinative of legal actorness. In other words, the use of 'EU' in 'EU–Türkiye Statement' 'must be understood in this journalistic context as referring to the Heads of State or Government of the Member States of the European Union'[125] and the Heads of Government were meeting on the premises of the European Council building but not *as* the European Council.[126] As a result, the press release 'cannot be regarded as a measure adopted by the European Council, or, moreover, by any other institution, body, office or agency of the European Union, or as revealing the existence of such a measure that corresponds to the contested measure'.[127] Thus, the Court found that it was not an act of the EU institutions but rather one of the Member States, and therefore it had no jurisdiction.

The decision was strongly criticized for not taking the opportunity to consider the 'regrettably ambiguous terms of the EU–Turkey statement', as the Court itself termed it.[128] In light of the legal effects that were intended to be produced as a result of the Statement, much of the criticism focussed on the Court's approach to how the Statement was produced, and by whom. Given the long battles relating to institutional competence and the importance of due process and procedural regularity, and the long-held view that the Court promotes its institutional maximization, it seems surprising that the Court did not engage more fully with the contents rather than the form. Neither did the Court use existing tools of international law to dissect the Statement and assess its legal validity.[129] However, it is also notable that the Court, in explicitly stating that a press release might be the kind of format where legal effects could be produced, has less regard for the terminology employed in informal instruments than might appear. Thus, although not the case here, the Court did not give the Member States of EU institutions carte blanche to use terms such as 'statement' and automatically preclude the option for the Court to have jurisdiction.

An appeal was made to the CJEU. NF, NG, and NM sought the annulment of the orders under appeal and asked the CJEU to refer the cases back to the General Court for adjudication with a direction that it should accept jurisdiction. The

[123] Case T-192/16 (n 106), para 44.

[124] Joined Cases C-181/91 and C-248/91 *Parliament v Council and Commission* EU:C:1993:271, para 12.

[125] Case T-192/16 (n 106) para 58.

[126] ibid para 69.

[127] Case T-192/16 (n 106) para 71.

[128] ibid para 66.

[129] Eva Kassoti and Alina Carrozzini, 'One Instrument in Search of an Author: Revisiting the Authorship and Legal Nature of the EU–Turkey Statement' in Eva Kassoti and Narin Idriz (eds), *The Informalisation of the EU's External Action in the Field of Migration and Asylum* (Global Europe: Legal and Policy Issues of the EU's External Action, Vol 1, TMC Asser Press 2022).

Court of Justice was critical of the 'assertions and allegations' in the appeals,[130] referring to them as incoherent and with 'vague and confused' setting out of their pleas in law and arguments, with insufficient precision as to how the general principles of EU law have been breached.[131] The Court declined to find that the General Court erred in law by, as the appellants claimed, 'restricting its analysis to form rather than substance and failing to examine the competence of the author of the contested act'.[132] Rather, the Court found this was merely a disagreement with the conclusion of the General Court.[133] As a result, the Court dismissed the appeal as manifestly inadmissible.[134]

Part of the critique of the EU–Türkiye Statement is the extent to which it has been cited as a success by the EU institutions and Member States,[135] and thus holds the promise of forming the basis of a future template for migration governance and externalizations. The Commission has referred to the Statement as representing an 'unprecedent[ed] degree of cooperation between the EU and an external partner',[136] which led to a 'substantial decrease' in the numbers of individuals leaving Türkiye for Greece[137] and thus is 'proof of the Statement's effectiveness'.[138] The actual impact on number is disputed by Spijkerboer, who notes that arrivals had started already before the Statement was agreed,[139] and NGOs including the International Rescue Committee, referring to the high refusal rate in Greek courts to return individuals to Türkiye due to the lack of 'safe country status'.[140]

If the purpose of the Statement, and the unorthodox manner in which it was negotiated and published, was to provide a short-term solution in response to a specific situation, then it has failed to translate into a buying of time for the Member States and EU institutions to forge a more durable solution, particularly on

[130] Case C-208/17 *NF, NG, NM v European Council* ECLI:EU:C:2018:705, para 19.
[131] ibid para 16.
[132] ibid para 23.
[133] ibid paras 24, 29.
[134] ibid para 30.
[135] See, for example, comments from Council, President Tusk and German Chancellor Merkel: 'Migrant crisis: EU–Turkey deal is "working"' (*BBC News*, 24 April 2016) https://www.bbc.com/news/world-europe-36121083, accessed 9 June 2025.
[136] COM(2016) 385 final (n 11) 3.
[137] Commission, 'Communication from the Commission to the European Parliament, the European Council and the Council: First Report on the progress made in the implementation of the EU–Turkey Statement' COM(2016) 231 final.
[138] Commission, 'Communication from the Commission to the European Parliament, the European Council and the Council—Second Report on the progress made in the implementation of the EU–Turkey Statement' COM(2016) 349 final.
[139] Thomas Spijkerboer, 'Fact check: did the EU–Turkey deal bring down the number of migrants and of border deaths?' (*University of Oxford Law Blogs: Border Criminologies*, 28 September 2016) https://blogs.law.ox.ac.uk/research-subject-groups/centre-criminology/centreborder-criminologies/blog/2016/09/fact-check-did-eu, accessed 9 June 2025.
[140] International Rescue Committee, 'What Is the EU–Turkey Deal' (*International Rescue Committee: Rescue.org/EU*, 18 March 2022) https://eu.rescue.org/article/what-eu-turkey-deal, accessed 9 June 2025.

burden-sharing.[141] Rather, the informality associated with the Statement has continued, with a lack of formalized framework for adherence to rights[142] and, instead, moves towards recognizing Türkiye as a safe country for TCNs by both Member States and the EU.[143] If this were not the case, then returns would contravene the principle of *non-refoulement*.[144]

Over the longer term, the status of Türkiye as a safe third country was brought into sharp focus by an attempted coup d'etat in July 2016, the lack of progress on EU enlargement, and an increasingly strained relationship between the EU and the Turkish governments.[145] The domestic human rights situation and democratic backsliding in Türkiye has been criticized strongly by the EU, which brings into question whether the enhanced cooperation on migration should be taking place at all, and especially outside the framework of the Readmission Agreement in place.[146] Such is the domestic pressure within the EU to place migration at the heart of EU external relations, and to externalize migration by attempting to prevent migrants from reaching (and remaining) in the territory of the Member States, that the EU has thus created a dependency on third states. In the case of Türkiye, the risk of doing so is apparent in accusations of 'blackmail' levelled at Turkish President Erdoğan by EU leaders for suggesting that Türkiye would be unable to prevent migration to Europe.[147] As such, the informal basis of the Statement also means it is inherently fragile if a third state decides no longer to cooperate, and especially if the EU is unable to offer credible incentives to counteract domestic

[141] Bodo Weber, 'The EU–Turkey Refugee Deal and the Not Quite Closed Balkan Route' (Friedrich Erbet Stiftung, June 2017) https://library.fes.de/pdf-files/bueros/sarajevo/13436.pdf, accessed 9 June 2025.

[142] In June 2021 a Greek Joint Ministerial Decision (JMD) designated Turkey as a 'safe third country' for people from Afghanistan, Bangladesh, Pakistan, Somalia, and Syria: Seda Gürkan and Ramona Coman, 'The EU–Turkey Deal in the 2015 "Refugee Crisis": When Intergovernmentalism Cast a Shadow on the EU's Normative Power' (2020) 56(2) Acta Politica International Journal of Political Science 276.

[143] International Rescue Committee, 'What Is the EU–Turkey Deal' (n 140).

[144] See, inter alia, Jenny Poon, 'EU–Turkey Deal: Violation of, or Consistency with, International Law?' (2016) 1 European Papers 1195.

[145] Agustín Menéndenz, 'The Refugee Crisis: Between Human Tragedy and Symptom of the Structural Crisis of European Integration' 22(4) European Law Journal 388, 410; Ilke Toygür and Bianca Benvenuti, 'One Year On: An Assessment of the EU–Turkey Statement on Refugees' (2017) 17(14) Instituto Affari Internazionali Working Papers.

[146] Cavidan Soykan and Neva Öztürk, 'Third Anniversary of EU–Turkey Statement: A Legal Analysis' (Heinrich-Böll-Stiftung Istanbul, 19 December 2019) https://tr.boell.org/en/2019/10/03/third-anniversary-eu-turkey-statement-legal-analysis, accessed 9 June 2025.

[147] See, for example, 'Turquie: Erdogan menace d'ouvrir les frontières aux migrants vers l'Europe' (*Le Monde*, 25 November 2016); Patrick Wintor and Helena Smith, 'Erdoğan in talks with European leaders over refugee cash for Turkey' (*The Guardian*, 17 March 2020) https://www.theguardian.com/world/2020/mar/17/erdogan-in-talks-with-european-leaders-over-refugee-cash-for-turkey, accessed 9 June 2025; Nicolas Bourcier, 'EU–Turkey migration deal: Four million refugees, €9 billion in aid and a mixed record' (*Le Monde*, 25 April 2024) https://www.lemonde.fr/en/international/article/2024/04/25/eu-turkey-migration-deal-four-million-refugees-9-billion-in-aid-and-a-mixed-record_6669474_4.html, accessed 9 June 2025.

compliance costs.[148] While remaining in force, the current official status of the terms of the EU–Türkiye Statement is unclear. Financial support was provided by the EU for the reception of refugees in Türkiye, but the number of crossings has dropped considerably.[149]

Although Türkiye is in many ways a special case, due to its size, geographical proximity to the EU, and candidate status,[150] the Statement nevertheless—despite its non-binding nature—tells us a great deal about the way in which EU foreign policy and external relations has become so centrally focused on short-term solutions to migration issues.[151] Despite much of the EU's own narrative of its raison d'etre as a normative force for good, the way in which the Statement represents both a shift to informality and, at the same time, a favouring of short-term intergovernmentalism over supranationalism is instructive. In this sense, the Statement is a manifestation of an 'interest-based EU' over a 'principle-based normative EU'.[152] The specificity of the Turkish case is also evident in its candidate status, but even setting aside the other challenges in the EU–Türkiye relationship,[153] it is more in the interests of the EU for Türkiye to deal with migration outside the EU than within it.[154] In this respect, the prioritization of short-term, crisis-focused responses via informality points to bigger questions about the nature of the EU and its system of governance.[155]

The Statement became a template for the pursuit of similar deals, including with Afghanistan and Mali, that use the same type of language that evades the legal processes found in the Treaty. While the specific migration context with other third countries is likely to differ from that of the EU and Türkiye, the willingness and

[148] Ebru Turhan and Ayselin Yıldız, 'Turkey's External Differentiated Integration with the EU in the Field of Migration Governance: The Case of Border Management' in Benjamin Leruth, Stefan Gänzle, and Jarle Trondal (eds), *The Routledge Handbook of Differentiation in the European Union* (Routledge 2022).

[149] Gamze Ovacık, Meltem Ineli-Ciger, and Orçun Ulusoy, 'Taking Stock of the EU–Turkey Statement in 2024' (2024) 26(2) European Journal of Migration and Law 154.

[150] Çiğdem Yavuz, 'Analysis of the EU–Turkey Readmission Agreement: A Unique Case' (2019) 21(4) European Journal of Migration and Law 486.

[151] Nicole Koenig and Marie Franke, 'One Year On: What Lessons from the EU–Turkey "Deal"' (*Jacques Delord Institut Berlin*, 17 March 2017) https://www.delorscentre.eu/fileadmin/user_upload/20170317_EU-Turkey-deal-one-year-on-NK-MW.pdf, accessed 9 June 2025.

[152] Kaya, 'Europeanization and De-Europeanization of Turkish Asylum and Migration Policies' (n 114); Fatma Yilmaz-Elmas, 'EU's Global Actorness in Question: A Debate over the EU–Turkey Migration Deal' (2020) 17(68) Uluslararası İlişkiler/International Relations, Special Issue: Revisiting Migration in International Relations 161.

[153] See further, Fatmanur Parlak, 'Contested Norms and Shifting Boundaries: Turkey and the EU in Migration Governance' (2026) Journal of Contemporary European Studies, early view, https://doi.org/10.1080/14782804.2026.2624845, accessed 30 March 2026.

[154] Asli Aydintasbas, 'The Discreet Charm of Hypocrisy: An EU–Turkey Power Audit' (European Council on Foreign Relations, 23 March 2018) https://ecfr.eu/wp-content/uploads/EU_TURKEY_POWER_AUDIT.pdf, accessed 9 June 2025; Bianca Benvenuti, 'The Migration Paradox and EU–Turkey Relations' (2017) 17(5) Istituto Affari Internazionali Working Papers.

[155] See further, Arne Niemann and Natascha Zaun, 'EU Refugee Policies and Politics in Times of Crisis: Theoretical and Empirical Perspectives' (2017) 56(1) Journal of Common Market Studies 3.

ability to engage in returns and readmission via informality is more present as a possibility. This is the case both for the EU and for individual Member States.

7.7 More 'formal informality': bilateral engagement with third states

It is important at this juncture to note that, recalling the discussion earlier in this book, migration straddles both the internal and the external spheres of governance. For the latter, it is unsurprising that foreign relations between the EU and third states operate in some similar ways to relations between Member States. Not all international relations are conducted on the basis of legally binding Treaties, and informal or political accords are extremely commonplace. Therefore, this part of the chapter is not concerned with the numerous examples of 'soft' instruments which are either unlikely to have direct impact on individuals and their rights, or seek to replace or replicate agreements for which Treaty competences exist.

The readmission 'arrangements' between the EU and third states were considered earlier in this chapter. The extent of the shift towards informality can also be seen at the level of the Member States too, with the bilateral Italy–Libya Memorandum of Understanding,[156] signed in February 2017, and the Italy–Albania Protocol, signed in November 2023—prominent examples which have been inspired by the EU–Türkiye Statement.[157]

[156] Memorandum of understanding on cooperation in the fields of development, the fight against illegal immigration, human trafficking and fuel smuggling and on reinforcing the security of borders between the State of Libya and the Italian Republic (2 February 2017) https://eumigrationlawblog.eu/the-italy-libya-memorandum-of-understanding-the-baseline-of-a-policy-approach-aimed-at-closing-all-doors-to-europe/, accessed 9 June 2025. See also Martino Reviglio, 'Externalizing Migration Management through Soft Law: The Case of the Memorandum of Understanding between Libya and Italy' (2019) 20(1) Global Jurist 1; Anja Palm, 'The Italy–Libya Memorandum of Understanding: The Baseline of a Policy Approach Aimed at Closing All Doors to Europe?' (*EU Immigration and Asylum Law and Policy*, 2 October 2017) https://www.iai.it/it/pubblicazioni/italy-libya-memorandum-understanding-baseline-policy-approach-aimed-closing-all-doors, accessed 9 June 2025; Andrea De Guttry, Francesca Capone, and Emanuele Sommario, 'Dealing with Migrants in the Central Mediterranean Route: A Legal Analysis of Recent Bilateral Agreements Between Italy and Libya' (2018) 56(3) International Migration 44.

[157] 'Protocollo tra il Governo della Repubblica italiana e il Consiglio dei ministri della Repubblica di Albania per il rafforzamento della collaborazione in materia migratoria (Protocol between the Government of the Italian Republic and the Council of Ministers of the Albanian Republic) (13 October 1995)', https://www.esteri.it/wp-content/uploads/2023/12/PROTOCOLLO-ITALIA-ALBANIA-in-materia-migratoria.pdf and in unofficial English translation https://odysseus-network.eu/wp-content/uploads/2023/11/Protocol-between-the-Government-of-the-Italian-Republic-and-the-Council-of-Minister-of-the-Albanian-Republic-1-1.pdf, accessed 9 June 2025. See further, Andreina De Leo and Eleonora Celoria, 'The Italy–Albania Protocol: A New Model of Border-Shifting within the EU and Its Compatibility with Union Law' (2024) 31(5) Maastricht Journal of European and Comparative Law 595; Inga Broerse, 'The Italy-Albania Agreement: Externalising Asylum Procedures in Violation of Human Rights' (2024) No 26 ACMRL Migration Law Series, Amsterdam Centre for Migration and Refugee Law 1, https://doi.org/10.71881/51abe5cb-92a2-4de9-8395-9323bdc7f75c, accessed 9 June 2025; Fontana and Rosina, 'The Tools of External Migration Policy in the EU Member States' (n 13).

The EU–Türkiye Statement has, as its critics feared, provided a template for migration-focused relations with third states pursued on an informal basis. Tunisia has, to a lesser extent than Türkiye, been a testing ground for new forms of governance in migration, partly due to its geographic place on the Central Mediterranean migration route. A Mobility Partnership was put in place in 2011 and, in the aftermath of the Arab Spring, there was a great deal of emphasis on migration and other forms of cooperation.[158] Yet, building on the existence of the Migration Partnership, the most prominent example of informality in the relationship is the 'Memorandum of Understanding (MOU) on a strategic and global partnership between the European Union and Tunisia' signed in July 2023. [159] Having been foreseen by an announcement some months earlier that the EU and Tunisia had agreed to work together on a comprehensive partnership package (despite one already being in place),[160] the Memorandum of Understanding points to vague 'priorities of combating irregular migration' and 'to support the return of irregular migrants in Tunisia to their countries of origin in accordance with international law, whilst respecting their dignity'.

The MOU also contains a telling provision that 'Tunisia reiterates its position that it is not a country of settlement for irregular migrants. It also reiterates its position to control its own borders only.' This suggests that the utility of the MOU will be limited from the perspective of the EU side, since it signals a strong resistance from the Tunisian government for responsibility for accepting or dealing with migrants from states further south in Africa.

The MOU is not only focused on irregular migration—it also refers to a 'holistic approach' to migration including the creation of Talent Partnerships (discussed further below) but also green energy transition and 'people-to-people' contacts. Yet, only in migration is the language of cooperation the strongest and, on combating people smugglers and trafficking, much echoes the EU–Türkiye Statement.[161] But the language used here blurs much of what the history of EU migration governance tells us.

First, unlike the EU–Türkiye Statement, the authorship on the EU is clear—the opening paragraph tells us that the EU is represented by the European Commission. And yet, the launch of the MOU was presented as a product of 'Team Europe'.

[158] Iole Fontana, *EU Neighbourhood Policy in the Maghreb: Implementing the ENP in Tunisia and Morocco before and after the Arab Uprisings* (Routledge 2017).

[159] Commission, 'Memorandum of Understanding on a strategic and global partnership between the European Union and Tunisia' (*European Commission: Press Release*, 16 July 2023) https://ec.europa.eu/commission/presscorner/detail/en/ip_23_3887, accessed 9 June 2025.

[160] Commission, 'The European Union and Tunisia agreed to work together on a comprehensive partnership package' (*European Commission: Enlargement and Eastern Neighbourhood*, 11 June 2023) https://neighbourhood-enlargement.ec.europa.eu/news/european-union-and-tunisia-agreed-work-together-comprehensive-partnership-package-2023-06-11_en, accessed 9 June 2025.

[161] Annick Pijnenburg, 'Team Europe's deal: what's wrong with the EU–Tunisia Migration Agreement?' (*VerfBlog*, 21 August 2023) https://verfassungsblog.de/team-europes-deal/, accessed 9 June 2025.

'Team Europe' has no legal status but is referred to as an 'approach', according to the Commission website, incorporating 'the EU institutions, EU countries, and European development financial institutions clubbed together to respond, among others, to the Covid-19 crisis in a so-called Team Europe spirit' which informs its approach to international development.[162] A High Representative for Foreign Policy/Commission Communication of October 2024 refers to 'Team Europe' as an approach to migration which has made 'significant progress on the external dimension of migration . . . to deepen comprehensive partnerships based on mutual interests. It has scaled up its work to provide a comprehensive response, building on the experience of the EU Emergency Trust Fund for Africa and addressing root causes of irregular migration and forced displacement.'[163]

Second, rather than this being a mere signalling or public relations exercise to show a commitment to dealing with irregular migration from the Member States, the MOU itself refers to the role of the EU as being to 'support and facilitate the implementation of this Memorandum of Understanding also in bilateral contexts with the Member States with regard to returns and readmissions'. This appears to be a shift away from the attempts to bring returns and readmission within the EU orbit, and thus blurring under what (formal or informal) regime returns might occur. Despite the references to border management and operational cooperation, including search and rescue operations, Frontex is not mentioned in the MOU.

Third, cooperation is to be supported by financial means. The MOU states: 'The European Union shall endeavour to provide sufficient additional financial support, in particular for the provision of equipment, training and technical support necessary to further improve the management of Tunisia's borders.' Here, the use of informality meets a potential barrier with the Treaty-based competences, and particularly the budgetary role of the European Parliament. This role and the powers associated with it has long been recognized as a significant tool for Parliament's maximization of influence and for ensuring it is not side-lined in the decision-making process.[164] In a document leaked by Statewatch, the Legal Service of the

[162] Commission, 'Commission takes stock of Team Europe approach to building international partnerships' (*European Commission*, 2 October 2024) https://commission.europa.eu/news-and-media/news/commission-takes-stock-team-europe-approach-building-international-partnerships-2024-10-02_en, accessed 9 June 2025.

[163] Commission, 'Joint Communication to the European Parliament, The Council, The European Economic and Social Committee, the Committee of The Regions and the European Investment Bank, 'Building Sustainable International Partnerships as a Team Europe' JOIN(2024) 25 final 6–7.

[164] Beginning with the Treaty amending Certain Budgetary Provisions of the Treaties establishing the European Communities and of the Treaty establishing a Single Council and a Single Commission of the European Communities (22 April 1970); see, inter alia, Berthold Rittberger, 'The Creation and Empowerment of the European Parliament' (2003) 41(2) JCMS: Journal of Common Market Studies 203; Anne Vitrey de Gardebosc and Frederik Mesdag, 'The European Parliament's Contribution to the EU Budget: A Power Game' in Olivier Costa (ed), *The European Parliament in Times of EU Crisis: European Administrative Governance* (Palgrave Macmillan 2019); Giacomo Benedetto, 'The European Parliament as a Budgetary Extractor since the Lisbon Treaty' in Edoardo Bressanelli and Nicola Chelotti (eds), *The European Parliament in the Contested Union: Power and Influence Post-Lisbon* (Routledge 2020).

European Parliament has argued that 'the agreement is unable to commit the EU budget because it does not refer to specific financial contributions to be made by the EU to Tunisia, but only to future possibilities of committing the EU budget'. [165] Therefore, notwithstanding the question of whether the European Parliament would agree with the aim and content of the MOU,[166] there is a much longer-standing 'classic' EU question of interinstitutional bargaining at stake.

Finally, and in a similar vein to the EU–Türkiye Statement, the MOU has been critiqued for placing migration above all other goals, including development and democracy promotion, by ignoring the domestic situation in the partner state. As a result, the EU has been critiqued for allowing the Tunisian President to seek legitimacy for an increasing autocratic regime by leveraging EU funds into a tool for state control.[167]

Further informal agreements were concluded in similar terms with Mauritania[168] and Egypt,[169] both in March 2024. The text of the Strategic and Comprehensive Partnership with Egypt describes similar terms to that with Tunisia, although migration only appears in one paragraph, stressing the 'holistic approach' to migration and the EU providing 'necessary financial support'.

A subtle difference can be found with the Joint Declaration with Mauritania, which established a 'Migration Partnership'.[170] Unlike the states of North Africa, Mauritania is part of the ACP group of states and the Samoa Agreement. In the Joint Declaration it is stated that 'the European Union and Mauritania recall their commitments in the Samoa Agreement, *which binds them*, and will therefore strengthen their cooperation on return and readmission and ensure that the rights and dignity of individuals are fully protected and respected'.[171] This suggests that the Samoa Agreement alone is capable of being interpreted as a de facto Readmission Agreement, even though the details of how returns and readmission are to be operationalized, and the protections of human rights within them, are absent.

[165] European Parliament Legal Service, 'Legal Opinion: Legal status of the Memorandum of Understanding signed in Tunis on 16 July 2023' (European Parliament, SJ-0839/23, 19 December 2023) http://www.statewatch.org/media/4203/eu-ep-legal-service-opinion-tunisia-mou-19-12-23.pdf, accessed 9 June 2025.

[166] See the discussion in Chapter 5.

[167] Lorenzo Ghione, 'La diplomatie migratoire dans la Tunisie contemporaine, ou comment naviguer entre la légitimation interne du régime et les peurs de l'Europe' (2024) 25 La Lettre de l'IRMC: Institut de recherche sur le Maghreb contemporain 74.

[168] Joint Declaration between the Islamic Republic of Mauritania and the European Union (n 17).

[169] Commission, 'Joint Declaration on the Strategic and Comprehensive Partnership between the Arab Republic of Egypt and the European Union' (*European Commission: Enlargement and Eastern Neighbourhood*, 17 March 2024), https://neighbourhood-enlargement.ec.europa.eu/news/joint-declaration-strategic-and-comprehensive-partnership-between-arab-republic-egypt-and-european-2024-03-17_en#:~:text=The%20Arab%20Republic%20of%20Egypt%20and%20the%20European%20Union%20have,on%20mutual%20respect%20and%20trust, accessed 9 June 2025.

[170] This is distinct from a Mobility Partnership, as explored earlier in this chapter.

[171] Emphasis added.

7.8 Regular migration and 'Talent Partnerships'

Much less attention has been placed on regular migration between the EU and the third states, via either formal or informal tools. The lack of completeness of an EU competence and a legal framework for regular migration largely prevents the formal aspect from taking greater shape. Or, at the very least, only where the issues are depoliticized can the supranational element take shape via 'quiet politics'[172] to confront the 'constitutional conundrums' of this mix of EU and national competences.[173] Even where informality comes in, the limitations placed by Member States and their hesitation around discourse which might seem to promote migration and its benefits have generally not been conducive to seeking to facilitate regular migration routes. Rather, when regular migration is cited in the migration tools covered in this chapter, the discussion is of circular migration, via promoting awareness of 'legal' opportunities (which may, in fact, be limited or highly restricted).[174] The latter is also explicitly linked to a means to try to avoid would-be migrants reaching Europe via irregular means, making this the dominant policy logic.

One informal instrument that has been announced by the EU for use with third countries is the 'Talent Partnership'. This is a strategic initiative initially launched in a pilot phase under the European Agenda on Migration,[175] designed to enhance legal migration pathways while addressing labour market needs across the EU and 'balance' the emphasis on irregular migration within the context of third country partnerships. Launched by the European Commission under the New EU Pact on Migration and Asylum as a 'comprehensive EU policy framework', these partnerships are designed to be mutually beneficial frameworks between the EU and non-EU countries, particularly in North Africa, such as Egypt, Morocco, and Tunisia.[176] These partnerships are supported by EU funding instruments such as the Asylum, Migration and Integration Fund[177] and the ICMPD's Migration

[172] See, inter alia, Paula Hoffmeyer-Zlotnik, 'The Quiet Politics of Migration Supranationalization—Commission Entrepreneurship and the Intra-Corporate Transferee Directive' (2024) 46(3) Journal of European Integration 365.

[173] Tesseltje de Lange and Henri de Waele, 'The Constitutional Conundrums of Regulating Skilled Migration into the EU' (2024) 49(3) European Law Review 237.

[174] See for example, Joint Declaration between the Islamic Republic of Mauritania and the European Union (n 17), Article 3(3): 'Explore possibilities to enhance circular mobility, by improving the information available on legal migration opportunities, taking into account the respective labour market situation.'

[175] Commission, 'Communication from the Commission to the European Parliament, the Council, the European Economic and Social Committee and the Committee of the Regions: A European Agenda on Migration' COM(2015) 240 final.

[176] Commission, 'Talent Partnerships' (*European Commission: Migration and Home Affairs*) https://home-affairs.ec.europa.eu/policies/migration-and-asylum/legal-migration-and-resettlement/talent-partnerships_en, accessed 9 June 2025.

[177] Regulation (EU) 2021/1147 of the European Parliament and of the Council of 7 July 2021 establishing the Asylum, Migration and Integration Fund [2021] OJ L 251/1.

Partnership Facility. In practice, Talent Partnerships are intended to involve collaboration between governments, educational institutions, private sector actors, and civil society. This approach ensures that the skills developed align with actual labour market demand, both in the EU and in partner countries. As such, it is a prime example of the kind of new governance explored earlier in this book which has been prevalent in many areas of EU activity, but less so in migration.[178]

Nevertheless, even with a strategic outlook, Talent Partnerships are distinct from Mobility Partnerships, which—as it will be recalled—were also designed to provide a holistic framework for migration and mobility. Talent Partnerships are also distinct from the even more recent proposal for a Regulation establishing a 'Talent Pool' to plug recruitment gaps in Europe.[179]

Talent Partnerships serve multiple objectives. They facilitate the mobility of students, graduates, and skilled workers to the EU for study, training, or employment. At the same time, they support capacity building in partner countries by strengthening vocational education and training systems, improving labour market intelligence, and fostering diaspora engagement. This dual approach is intended to ensure that both the EU and its partners benefit from an exchange of skills and knowledge.

The intended launch of the Talent Partnerships was due to be in 2022, with Egypt, Morocco, and Tunisia. However, to date none have been announced. [180]

The Commission-led 'Labour Migration Platform' brings together representatives of Member States' migration and employment sectors and European Social and Economic Partners, as well as relevant stakeholders active in labour migration, to discuss regular migration in a broad sense, cooperation, and developments at the EU level. According to the minutes of the three 2024 meetings of the Platform, Talent Partnerships were mentioned only briefly as a potential future means to attract workers.[181] The role of the EU institutions in Talent Partnerships replicates that of Mobility Partnerships, that is to say performing an 'umbrella' role with Member States taking the lead.[182] Thus, the question arises as to what interest the Member States have in operating under this umbrella, since it is legally and practically possible for them to operate their own schemes, albeit mixed with the more economic and trade-focused aspects of the Treaty, suggesting that the Court

[178] See also Paul James Cardwell, 'New Modes of Governance in the External Dimension of EU Migration Policy' (2013) 51(6) International Migration 54; and Paul James Cardwell, 'Tackling Europe's Migration "Crisis" through Law and "New Governance"' (2018) (1) *Global Policy* 67.

[179] See the discussion in Chapter 6.

[180] Commission, 'Communication from the Commission to the European Parliament, the Council, the European Economic and Social Committee, and the Committee of the Regions: Attracting Skills and Talent to the European Union' COM(2022) 657 final.

[181] Commission, 'Fourth Meeting of the European Labour Migration Platform' (European Commission: Directorate-General for Migration and Home Affairs, HOME.C.2.002, 21 March) https://home-affairs.ec.europa.eu/networks/labour-migration-platform_en, accessed 9 June 2025.

[182] Frasca, 'Informal Agreements and Quasi-Legal Mechanisms in EU–Africa Cooperation on Migration' (n 30).

of Justice might be inclined to take a view if the question arises.[183] The scope of the pilot projects was limited, with few Member States involved and, as a consequence, few individuals making use of them (although the Covid-19 pandemic would have prevented greater engagement). At the same time, bilateral arrangements have already been put in place between France and India,[184] and since 2013, between Germany and a diverse group of countries including Bosnia and Herzegovina, the Philippines, Tunisia, Indonesia, and India for the recruitment of nurses under a bilateral 'triple win' scheme.[185]

Talent Partnerships, at present, thus seem to be a rather stunted attempt to balance the emphasis on irregular migration with regular migration opportunities, and an addition to the list in this chapter of repackaged attempts to overcome the lack of Member States to act collectively—or at the very least through the EU prism—when it comes to regular migration. The problem for the EU institutions is that it therefore undermines their credibility when trying to engage with third states who require something in return for cooperation on irregular migration.[186]

7.9 Conclusion

The breadth of activity in informal governance, compared to the more limited success in formal, legal means explored in the previous chapter, supports a view that informality is rapidly becoming the hallmark of EU external migration governance. At the very least, the picture of EU migration governance incorporates both the formal and informal in many similar ways that have been observed in other, internal, legal and policy spheres over a much longer period.

The evolution of EU external migration governance reveals a decisive shift toward informal mechanisms, marking a departure from traditional, formal legal instruments. This trend reflects a broader transformation in EU governance, where informality is not merely a temporary fix but increasingly a structural feature. The EU's reliance on informal arrangements, spearheaded by Mobility Partnerships, Migration Compacts, Common Agendas on Migration and Mobility, and the Valletta Action Plan, show that 'soft law' instruments, political declarations, and

[183] De Lange and De Waele, 'The Constitutional Conundrums of Regulating Skilled Migration into the EU' (n 173).

[184] 'Migration and Mobility Agreement between the Government of the Republic of India and the Government of the French Republic' (Government of India: Ministry of External Affairs, 10 March 2018) https://www.mea.gov.in/Portal/LegalTreatiesDoc/FR18B3321.pdf, accessed 9 June 2025.

[185] De Lange and De Waele, 'The Constitutional Conundrums of Regulating Skilled Migration into the EU' (n 173) 244.

[186] Jean-Baptiste Farcy and Sylvie Sarolea, 'Labour Migration in the "New Pact": Modesty or Unease in the Berlaymont?' in Daniel Thym (ed), *Reforming the Common European Asylum System* (Nomos 2022) 279.

quasi-legal mechanisms have become a defining characteristic of its external migration strategy.

This informalization is not without precedent. It mirrors patterns observed in other domains of EU policy, where formal legal integration has often been supplemented or even supplanted by informal practices. The involvement of other actors to meet EU goals, including third states and organizations such as the ICMPD, continues to play a crucial role—and one which is central to the shifts in governance to widen the scope of actors beyond EU institutions, agencies, and Member States.[187] These actors play a pivotal role in implementing EU objectives, often through mechanisms that blur the lines between development aid and migration control.

The proliferation of informal agreements and quasi-legal mechanisms has significant implications for our understanding of law. The instruments often operate in legal grey zones, producing effects that are difficult to contest or even detect.[188] The EU's migration agenda, particularly in its dealings with African states, reflects a paradigm of containment rather than facilitation. This stands in stark contrast to global frameworks like the Global Compact for Migration, which emphasize mobility and regular migration pathways.[189] There appears to be a continuous repacking and relaunching of initiatives under different names, and they often appear to fall short of their overall aims. This is especially the case when bilateral arrangements, however informal they might be, have failed to materialize in the larger number of target partner states identified by the strategic documents that have launched them.

A central concern is the erosion of legal accountability. While informal actions may still draw on traditional legal powers, they often bypass the institutional checks and balances designed to uphold EU law and fundamental rights.[190] The EU–Türkiye deal exemplifies this trend. Though not legally binding, it has had significant legal and political consequences and jettisons principles of legal certainty for those of efficiency.[191] Its informal nature has shielded it from judicial scrutiny, leaving affected individuals without an effective remedy. This raises serious questions about the legality and legitimacy of such arrangements, and also the possibility that other types of informal arrangements will have the opportunity for legal challenge in the courts, particularly the CJEU. The use of informal arrangements

[187] Julia Dessel, 'International Delegation and Agency in the Externalization Process of EU Migration and Asylum Policy: The role of the IOM and the UNHCR in Niger' (2019) 21(4) European Journal of Migration and Law 435.

[188] Smeets and Beach, 'When Success Is an Orphan' (n 112).

[189] François Crépeau, 'Towards a Mobile and Diverse World' (n 5).

[190] Bas Schotel, 'The EU–Turkey Statement and the Structure of Legal Accountability' in Eva Kassoti and Narin Idriz (eds), *The Informalization of the EU's External Action in the Field of Migration and Asylum* (TMC Asser Press 2022) 75.

[191] Martino Reviglio, 'The Shift to Soft Law at Europe Borders: Between Legal Efficiency and Legal Validity' (2023) 23(1) *Global Jurist* 23–41.

for readmission rather than the Treaty-based procedures and the scrutiny associated with them is a particular problem, and risks exemplifying a state of exception becoming the norm under the guise of 'crisis'.[192]

The EU's use of issue linkage, tying migration cooperation to incentives including visa facilitation, was designed to be strategic but has proved to be problematic. While it enables tailored, flexible responses, it also exposes the EU to political volatility in partner countries. The deterioration of EU–Türkiye relations following the 2016 coup attempt illustrates the fragility of such deals. The promised incentives have stalled, and Türkiye has threatened to withdraw from the agreement, highlighting the limitations of informal governance when mutual trust erodes. This has, potentially, a significant financial impact on the EU's budget for external relations for which the institutions are—or should be—accountable.

Institutionally, the EU's informal governance mechanisms rely on a complex web of interactions that often escape public and legal oversight. Decision-making processes are characterized by flexibility and speed, facilitated by actors moving across institutional hierarchies and bypassing formal procedures. This agility can be advantageous, but it also obscures accountability and transparency. The ability of actors to 'bridge' institutions and 'shield' decisions from scrutiny has enabled rapid deal-making, but at the cost of democratic legitimacy.

The focus on externalization and shifting migration control beyond EU borders has become the dominant paradigm. This approach prioritizes containment over mobility,[193] often under the guise of addressing root causes of migration. However, it also empowers third countries to exert 'reverse conditionality',[194] leveraging their cooperation for political or economic concessions. This dynamic complicates the EU's position and undermines its normative claims to the promotion of human rights and rule of law.

Differentiated integration and the role of the Member States in seeking to use EU migration governance as a means to upload domestic preferences of externalization further complicates the picture.[195] The AFSJ has evolved through a patchwork of formal and informal arrangements, reflecting the diverse preferences of Member States. While formal opt-outs (as seen with Ireland and Denmark) are well established, newer forms of 'flexible solidarity' have emerged.[196] These

[192] Aida Halilovic, 'Executive Migration Governance and Law-Making in the European Union: Towards a State of Exception' (2024) 9(2) European Papers 513.

[193] Catherine Costello, *The Human Rights of Migrants and Refugees in European Law* (Oxford University Press 2016).

[194] Nina Guérin and Berthold Rittberger, 'Are Third States Pulling the Strings? The Impact of Domestic Policy Change on EU–Third State Cooperation' (2020) 42(7) Journal of European Integration 991; Sandra Lavenex and Marja-Liisa Öberg, 'Third Country Influence on EU Law and Policy-Making: Setting the Scene' (2023) 61(6) JCMS: Journal of Common Market Studies 1435.

[195] Maria Vinciguerra, 'Understanding Bargaining Outcomes in Europe's Migration and Refugee Crisis: The Refugee Relocation Scheme and the EU–Turkey Statement' (PhD thesis, Apollo—University of Cambridge Repository, 2021).

[196] See, inter alia, Violeta Moreno-Lax, 'Solidarity's Reach: Meaning, Dimensions and Implications for EU (External) Asylum Policy' (2010) 24(5) Maastricht Journal of European and Comparative

intergovernmental compromises allow for variable participation but also hinder the development of a cohesive, enforceable migration policy.[197] This is particularly evidenced through the attempts to forge a coherent policy on regular migration.

Ultimately, the EU's turn towards informal governance in migration reflects both pragmatic adaptation and normative retreat. It allows for rapid, flexible responses to complex challenges but also undermines legal certainty, democratic accountability, and the EU's integration through law.[198] As informal mechanisms become entrenched, there is a risk that they will displace rather than complement formal legal structures, leading to a governance model that is effective in the short term but unsustainable in the long run.

To address these challenges, a recalibration is needed. Informal governance should not be abandoned, but it must be anchored in legal frameworks that ensure transparency, accountability, and respect for fundamental rights. The EU must also reassess its external migration agenda to align more closely with its normative commitments and international obligations. Only by restoring the balance between flexibility and legality can the EU develop a migration policy that is both effective and just.

Law 740; Nadine El-Enany, 'The Perils of Differentiated Integration in the Field of Asylum' in Bruno De Witte, Andrea Ott, and Ellen Vos (eds), *Between Flexibility and Disintegration: The Trajectory of Differentiation in EU Law* (Edward Elgar 2017) 362.

197 Deirdre Curtin and Maria Patrin, 'EU Constitutional Standards of Democracy in Differentiated Integration' (2021) EUI Working Paper RSC 2021/80, https://cadmus.eui.eu/entities/publication/795e4af9-da38-545a-8edb-9cdc58940ce2, accessed 9 June 2025.

198 Fabien Terpan and Sabine Saurugger, 'Does Soft Law Trigger Differentiation and Disintegration?' (2022) 7 European Papers 1229.

Conclusion

In July 2023, the EU launched a new migration partnership with Tunisia. As part of the blaze of publicity surrounding it, Commission President Ursula van der Leyen was accompanied by the Prime Ministers of Italy and the Netherlands, and referred to this grouping as '#TeamEurope'.[1] The use of the hashtag and the word 'Team'—while speaking directly to common usage on social media—neatly encapsulates the thrust of this book. Who is #TeamEurope; what legal capacity does it have to take decisions and make 'agreements' (in the English-language sense, rather than the legal sense) on behalf of the EU and its members? Who is responsible for the content of the statement or pact with third countries and what do those responsibilities entail? None of these questions can be answered by reference to the Treaties or other legislation, and yet the language used was that of law to show how the EU's migration goals were being met.

Far from being a technical issue of concern only to lawyers, the use of new institutional forms alongside instruments that have uncertain qualities, the rapid expansion of cooperation mechanisms with third countries, and the diversity of their content has come to the fore. It encapsulates the essence of 'formal informality' explored in this book: where something feels familiar and law-like, but has neither procedural accountability nor transparency attached.

This book has explained the EU's governance of migration through an analysis of the different types of tools being used. It has done so by highlighting how the traditional forms of law-making in both the internal and external spheres—including Regulations and Directives, and international agreements with third states—have been joined by an increasing number of tools and instruments that are best characterized as informal. A long succession of strategic documents has promoted the use of the latter as a means to fulfil various goals, of which the most vigorous work has been devoted to attempts to reduce irregular migration. 'Formal informality', whereby informal tools and instruments adopt the form and language of more familiar legal tools, is at the heart of the framework of analysis. In doing

[1] LinkedIn, 16 July 2023: https://www.linkedin.com/posts/ursula-von-der-leyen_teameurope-activity-7073629447513362432-I80t?utm_source=share&utm_medium=member_desktop&rcm=ACoAAABe8NMBBFdDL6mi9_Jenaf4akkjbovV_6Q; X, 16 July 2023: https://x.com/vonderleyen/status/1680610931829534720; Instagram, 16 July 2023: https://www.instagram.com/reel/CuxdvaPoM4Y/, accessed 7 June 2025. For comment, see Annick Pijnenburg, 'Team Europe's deal: what's wrong with the EU–Tunisia Migration Agreement?' (*VerfBlog*, 21 August 2023) https://verfassungsblog.de/team-europes-deal/, accessed 9 June 2025.

The Governance of Migration in the European Union. Paul James Cardwell, Oxford University Press.
 DOI: 10.1093/9780191946592.003.0009

so, the second contribution of the book is to use contemporary migration governance to tell us how to make sense of the EU itself and how Treaty-based EU values, including respect for human dignity, freedom, democracy, equality, the rule of law, and respect for human rights,[2] as well as commitments to accountability, transparency, and good governance, require re-examination.

The shift to informality and the use of 'formal informality' allow us to understand and make sense of the four themes identified in the introduction, namely, the place of migration in an EU at an advanced stage of governance; how EU internal and external spheres of governance interact; how challenges of EU migration policy are reflected in the slow progress and difficulties in adopting EU legislation; and how the EU not only constantly rearticulates migration as a 'crisis', but also at the same time manages that 'crisis'.

The place of migration as a latecomer to the landscape of EU governance led to a certain set of expectations about how the EU institutions would react to new competences. A plethora of splintered overlapping and interacting institutional spaces, instruments, actions, and operations have created a sense of the EU 'doing something'. This has occurred while the EU also responds to the demands of diverse actors, especially governments of Member States who experience inward migration to the EU differently but also share a commitment to a narrative of being 'tough' on migration to Europe and 'securing' or 'securitizing' the Union's external borders. Regular migration, perhaps paradoxically, appears as only a second-order priority. The involvement of Frontex in migration governance is substantially different from the many other agencies that have been created over the years, since it is directly involved in questions of international responsibility, raising both legal and ethical questions in its engagements on land or at sea.[3]

In the external sphere, agreements, as the formal counterpart of law-making within the EU, have their limits when trying to meet the EU's stated goals in migration. While Readmission Agreements have often been positioned at the core of the EU's external migration strategy, they are not, in practice, the most decisive or effective instruments. Their significance lies less in the number concluded, still relatively small, or in the high-profile cases where negotiations have failed, such as with Morocco, and more in their broader normative and institutional influence. These agreements have served as templates and sources of technical expertise, encouraging third countries, particularly in Eastern Europe during the 1990s, to develop their own bilateral readmission arrangements with neighbouring states. In

[2] Article 2 TEU.

[3] Juan Santos Vara and Soledad R Sánchez-Tabernero, 'In Deep Water: Towards a Greater Commitment for Human Rights in Sea Operations Coordinated by Frontex?' (2016) 18 European Journal of Migration and Law 65–87; Luisa Marin, 'Policing the EU's External Borders: A Challenge for the Rule of Law and Fundamental Rights in the Area of Freedom, Security and Justice? An Analysis of Frontex Joint Operations at the Southern Maritime Border' (2011) 7(4) Journal of Contemporary European Research 468; Simone Marinai, 'The Interception and Rescue at Sea of Asylum Seekers in the Light of the New EU Legal Framework' (2016) 55 Revista de Derecho Comunitario Europeo 901.

this way, the EU's approach has contributed to the diffusion of migration governance practices beyond its immediate borders, fostering what might be described as a 'concentric circles' model of influence.

As a result, migration governance is hugely complex, subject to rapid changes, and only partly explained through familiar legal instruments. All of this translates into what is a relatively stable EU approach to migration governance over time, with its own logics and patterns. These social practices, interactions, and shared understandings allow us to appreciate, as per the creation of institutional norms. These norms, as the institutional theory of law tells us, interact in a way which means that only by considering them together can we appreciate the depth of the law and governance under examination.

Law, as traditionally understood in the EU context, via Treaty-based Regulations, Directives, and the case-law of the Court of Justice, tells us only part of the story. One important role for law, so understood, is structural: it determines the way in which the institutions and Member States deal with some core issues in migration, particularly asylum. But we have not seen the depth or extent of legislation that we might expect, either based on other areas of integration where this type of law is paramount or given the political impetus behind incorporating migration into the Treaty competences at a late, or perhaps mature, state of integration. Legislation, as demonstrated in Chapters 2 and 3, was already showing its limitations in this field within a few years of the EU institutions gaining competence in migration following the Treaty of Amsterdam. The EU legislature might be formally competent, but the reality of legislative process requires *de facto* broad consensus among governments of Member States: such consensus is often missing. Other concepts, such as mutual solidarity between Member States, have pitted groups of Member States against each other on geographical or (changing) political lines.

Emphasis on legislation as a means to pursue integration, harmonization, or even coordination in migration has been eschewed in the past two decades by the emergence of a variety of tools and instruments which do not lend themselves easily to categorization. The Court of Justice has found itself in the position of gap-filling in legislation between the different levels of competences but also the variations in the application of standards in the different Member States. Yet it finds its role regarding informal tools more difficult to define. An endless release of strategic documents purporting to confront migration as a 'challenge' to the EU promises much, but they are then simply re-packaged and re-released by successive EU Commissions/administrations. Nevertheless, these documents reveal a heavy emphasis on operational cooperation with third states and externalization of migration controls, which takes their significance way beyond the level of mere discourse and into the realm of identifiable institutional norms. And while legislation appears to have been sidelined in the period following the Treaty of Lisbon, the latest iteration of migration policy via the Migration Pact (which was approved in 2024) once again appears to return legislation to a more central place in the governance of migration.

Yet it is overly simplistic to suggest that intergovernmentalism lies at the heart of contemporary migration governance. Political wrangling between the Member States explains only some of the story, as told through the repeated attempts to recast and relaunch. Migration is by no means alone in finding legislation difficult, and this is not a new phenomenon in the history of the EU and the integration process. Neither is the substantial time taken to pass core legislation enough alone to mark out migration as unique. However, a combination of these factors along with political sensitivity and public awareness, the changing roles of the institutions, and the language of 'crisis' helps to explain why there are so many attempts to reset migration law and policy and note each one as a 'fresh start' despite the policy stability of the goals. More importantly, the particular complexity of EU migration governance marks migration out as different enough to merit a renewed model for analysis and approach to understanding the EU's involvement and its meaning and significance.

The migration 'crisis' has acted as a stress test for the EU's institutional architecture, but also an opportunity for some of the institutions and agencies to maximize their potential role(s). It has revealed both the friction between institutions and the necessity of cooperation across them as actors. The role of law is central to this process, framing both the competences of institutions and the limits of their action. However, in migration governance, legal norms often collide with the political urgency to deliver fast, visible responses—generating fertile ground for institutional experimentation and contestation. While this might be (cautiously) welcomed as a general development to counter accusations that the EU and its institutions are too slow and cumbersome to act—more generally and particularly in responding to crises—the risk of sidelining of the political and legal processes designed to ensure EU values such as the rule of law, transparency, accountability, human rights, respect for human dignity, freedom, democracy, and equality becomes higher.

As a result, EU migration law represents something of a quandary. On the one hand, there is the expectation that migration as an issue, and one which has been increasingly susceptible to the language of crisis, would be the object of increased focus of legislation. Although often presented as the contrary, EU-led harmonization does not necessarily entail a loss of state power or sovereignty, but rather an opportunity to maximize it. Kostakopoulou noted in 2000 that 'Communautarization of migration and asylum policy does not imply the erosion of state power. It offers states the opportunity to expand the logic of control and law enforcement which underpinned the intergovernmental framework of cooperation, and to construct new forms of power which not only increase their regulatory capacity within a geographically contained structure, but also enable them to impose their security agenda beyond the confines of the Union.'[4] This characterization remains true today.

[4] Theodora Kostakopoulou, 'The "Protective Union": Change and Continuity in Migration Law and Policy in Post-Amsterdam Europe' (2000) 38(3) JCMS: Journal of Common Market Studies 497, 514.

A proliferation of actors and agencies reflects a broader balancing act: between national sovereignty and supranational authority, and between the need for coherence and the reality of fragmentation. Proliferation of actors and agencies has led to some institutional confusion, with overlapping mandates and unclear lines of accountability, which creates an overall lack of transparency. In turn, the emergence of new forms of governance has raised complex questions about international legal responsibility, especially where non-EU states are involved in 'pilots', 'projects' and 'hotspots' where there is no defined (international) legal regime.

At the same time, this apparent deepening of EU-level control has been accompanied by a paradoxical shift back towards intergovernmentalism. In practice, Member States and EU institutions have sought new ways to bypass scrutiny by the European Parliament, legal oversight by the Court of Justice, and even the Commission's regulatory role. A case in point is the EU–Türkiye Statement of 2016, which was politically brokered and operationalized outside of standard EU legal procedures, although with the support of the Commission. This 'reverse Lisbonisation'[5] reflects a trend toward ad hoc, informal governance mechanisms which suit both expediency and an avoidance of scrutiny.

The result is a dual movement: greater formal communautarization, but also greater intergovernmental control through informal or exceptional measures.[6] This paradox helps explain the innovation and institutional diversity observed in EU migration governance. It also reframes the role of institutions such as the Commission, which has increasingly acted as an enabler, facilitating deals and solutions even when they stretch or circumvent established legal frameworks. The rationale for doing so goes to the heart of the EU's *raison d'etre*, with institutions such as the Commission keen to demonstrate that the EU is capable of acting on and responding to crises and seeking to work with the Member States on innovative solutions and, ergo, respond to political pressures which assume that action is needed to reduce migration. The ability of the EU to respond to uncertainty and recurring migration-related crises depends critically on how its institutions interact and demonstrate their resilience. The challenge, however, in this shifting space of migration governance lies in ensuring that democratic values of accountability and transparency and the Treaty-based commitments to the protection of rights, human dignity, equality, and upholding of the rule of law—as 'red lines'[7]—are not lost.

[5] Sergio Carrera, Leonhard den Hertog, and Marco Stefan, 'The EU–Turkey Deal: Reversing Lisbonisation in EU Migration and Asylum Policies' in Sergio Carrera, Juan Santos Vara, and Tineke Strik (eds), *Constitutionalising the External Dimensions of EU Migration Policies in Times of Crisis* (Edward Elgar Publishing 2019) 155.

[6] Virginie Guirandon, '20 Years after Tampere's Agenda on "Illegal Migration": Policy Continuity in Spite of Unintended Consequences' in Sergio Carrera, Deirdre Curtin, and Andrew Geddes (eds), *20 Years Anniversary of the Tampere Programme: Europeanisation Dynamics of the EU Area of Freedom, Security and Justice* (2020) 147–56, pp 150–51, https://cadmus.eui.eu/bitstream/handle/1814/66986/MPC-Tampere-Programme-final.pdf?sequence=1&isAllowed=y#page=54, accessed 7 June 2025.

[7] Iris Goldner Lang, 'EU Values as a Shield and a Sword in EU Migration and Asylum Law' (2026) 63(1) Common Market Law Review 127–40.

Understanding the politics of the EU via new or renewed institutional formats, bargaining, and positioning is thus becoming ever more important. Tracing the ways in which such interactions shape our understandings is vital in linking the practice with the theory, and additionally the values that—as per the Treaty—are supposed to lie at the heart of all the EU does. Given the continued validity and relevance of the view that there is no singular means to understand the EU and the way it works, there is much to gain from the continued use of governance as a meeting place for law and political insights.

The detailed analysis in this book has shown that governance is the most appropriate means for the study of where law and politics meet, and where different institutions interact, creating norms—but only if we recognize that using a governance approach now applies to a more pragmatic, crisis-driven EU, one that is at least partially removed from the normative notions that have shaped its discourse in the past and the associated positive dimensions of (good) governance. Migration law scholarship benefits from not only the analysis of the text of Regulations and Directives and agreements such as Readmission Agreements with third states, but also the succession of strategic documents which help illuminate the direction of travel, the inter-institutional cooperation (or battles), and the possibilities and limitations of both formal law and informal strategy or policy. In such as a complex and fast-moving area as migration, the descriptive qualities of governance allow us to capture some of what is happening on a longer timeline and with more depth. The challenge has been to identify what is less visible as 'law', and excavate its significance.

Given this understanding of EU migration governance, what does it reveal about what the EU is, or stands for? Relevant Union values in Article 2 and so on are the respect for human dignity, freedom, democracy, equality, the rule of law, and the rights of individuals, and commitments to accountability, transparency, and good governance. The EU's commitment to international law, and particularly the principle of *non-refoulement*, are a strong focus of critiques on some of the current practices, and often those where formal informality is most prominent.

The argument in this book is *not* that informality is incompatible with either EU law or EU values. Some goals, such as promoting regular migration opportunities in third countries, cannot be met via legislation or international agreements. Rather, it is that a dividing line can be drawn when rights might be affected and where goals are pursued via formal informality.

Formal informality and its specific outworkings in EU migration governance reveal only weak commitments to these self-claimed EU values. In general in EU law, human dignity, freedom, equality, and human rights are (at least supposed to be) protected through legal accountability mechanisms where EU acts are sufficiently formal to be captured by judicial review processes. In this model, administrative actions are taken either at the national or the EU level, and constitutional accountability protections exist at each level to ensure governance in accordance with these fundamental democratic principles and protect individuals from authoritarian and uncontrolled regimes. But in many instances of EU migration governance explored in this book, that is not the case. The use of informal arrangements in place of Readmission Agreements is a stark example. For the latter, there might be opposition within the EU (from, for example, the European Parliament) to concluding an agreement with a third state, but at least there is an opportunity to engage in the process of making the agreement, challenging it and seeking information on what has occurred after it enters into force. None of this is guaranteed for informal arrangements. Consequently, transparency and good governance also suffer where informality becomes too dominant a mode of governance.

It is also worth bringing Frontex back to the argument here. Frontex embodies the broader trend of agency expansion in EU governance, but its prominence and power mark a shift in how authority is distributed within the EU framework (including the Member States) and how responsibility for its actions can be tracked when involved operationally in practices which impact directly on human dignity, human rights, equality, and the rule of law, such as screening.[8] Much of this relies on informal working arrangements. The lack of access to the courts and judicial protection by individuals who cannot assert their rights because they are unseen is a major challenge, even before we consider whether the courts are receptive to arguments about informal law having the same effects and thus allowing for scrutiny.[9] The judgments of the Court of Justice in *Hamoudi* and *WS* are, thus, welcome in terms of clarifying the legal responsibility of Frontex, particularly in 'pushbacks'.[10] Nevertheless, the institutional status is ambiguous, and the division of responsibilities between the EU and Member States remains frequently unclear.[11]

As a result, while Member State administrative bodies and/or governments can be held accountable before their own national courts and before international courts, neither of these options are available in relation to Frontex. An action for damages may be the means to close the accountability gap in the specific case of Frontex, but also more generally for informality. If it is to fulfil that role, the CJEU would have to lower the threshold for EU liability where fundamental rights are concerned.[12] Such a change would involve a significant divergence from the

[8] Silvan Pollozek and Jan-Hendrik Passoth, 'Devices of Suspicion: An Analysis of Frontex Screening Materials at the Registration and Identification Center in Moria' (2024) 50(9) Journal of Ethnic and Migration Studies 2327.

[9] Salvatore Fabio Nicolosi, 'The European Border and Coast Guard Agency (Frontex) and the Limits to Effective Judicial Protection in European Union Law' (2024) 30(1–2) European Law Journal 149.

[10] Case T-136/22 *Hamoudi v Frontex* ECLI:EU:T:2023:821, on appeal as Case C-136/24 P *Hamoudi v Frontex* ECLI:EU:C:2025:977, and Case T-600/21 *WS and Others v Frontex* EU:T:2023:492, on appeal as C-679/23 P *WS and Others v Frontex* ECLI:EU:C:2025:976.

[11] Bernard Ryan, 'The Migration Crisis and the European Union Border Regime' in Marise Cremona and Joanne Scott (eds), *EU Law beyond EU Borders: The Extraterritorial Reach of EU Law* (Oxford: Oxford Scholarship Online) https://papers.ssrn.com/sol3/Papers.cfm?abstract_id=3386143, accessed 9 June 2025.

[12] Melanie Fink, 'The Action for Damages as a Fundamental Rights Remedy: Holding Frontex Liable' (2020) 21(3) German Law Journal 532.

current legal position, demonstrating starkly the deviance from 'normal' modes of legality implicit in the EU integration process, competence division, and political settlement. This is why this book has argued that formal informality is a better way of understanding EU migration law and policy and testing where a dividing line is crossed.

More generally, the protection of fundamental rights in the European Union has been a story of a patchwork of legal provisions, intersecting with both national (constitutional) law and international law, in particular the Geneva Conventions, commitments to *non-refoulement*, and the European Convention of Human Rights (ECHR).[13] Since the EU was not created as a human rights body per se, comprehensive opportunities to consider the protection of human rights at the level of the Treaty have arisen only periodically. Some innovations, such as the Charter of Fundamental Rights, have appeared outside the process of intergovernmental conferences leading to Treaty revisions. The adoption of the Charter as a binding source of EU law was only achieved in the Treaty of Lisbon,[14] and not without attempts to dilute its effects, either real or potential. The Court of Justice has not always taken the opportunity to clarify some of the most relevant articles for the Charter relevant to migration and, in particular, asylum. The adherence of the EU as a separate party to the ECHR is a long and unsuccessful saga.

In such a changing context, there is thus the ever-present danger of a lacuna in both the protection of human dignity, equality, and human rights and the rule of law, accountability, and transparency of the actions of the EU institutions and the Member States. That is not to say that informality necessarily impacts these values negatively. Informality is to be expected in a maturing system of governance and, understood as a new mode of governance, is an integral part. For example, cooperation between the EU institutions and a third state in advertising opportunities for regular migration is unproblematic—it is not something that can be achieved via regulation, nor does it impact negatively on human rights, given that it retains respect for human dignity embedded in the autonomy and freedom it implies. Neither would such cooperation particularly need to be underpinned by a formal agreement, unless funding was to be transferred to the partner country.

On the other end of the scale, informal 'arrangements' in place of a formal agreement to *return* individuals to their country of origin, or a country they had passed through in transit, are much more problematic. Here, concluding 'arrangements' might benefit the EU and the partner state—for the former, for the purpose of returning more individuals, and for both, by avoiding potentially difficult scrutiny

[13] Emanuela Roman, 'The "Burden" of Being "Safe"—How Do Informal EU Migration Agreements Affect International Responsibility Sharing?' (2022) in Eva Kassoti and Narin Idriz (eds), *The Informalization of the EU's External Action in the Field of Migration and Asylum* (Springer and TMC Asser Press) 317.

[14] Gráinne de Búrca, 'After the EU Charter of Fundamental Rights: The Court of Justice as a Human Rights Adjudicator' (2013) 20 Maastricht Journal of European and Comparative Law 168.

by domestic actors. But bypassing the established frames for reasons of political expediency with only vague commitments to respecting human rights, including due process, is a dangerous development for the many vulnerable people whose autonomy and freedom might be removed by being covered by such an 'arrangement'. And, as this book has shown, finding out even the terms of what have been 'arranged' is challenging—the operational aspects, even more so. This type of informality is inimical to the EU's self-professed values.

Given these limitations, and assuming that the use of formal informality continues on the same trajectory, it is essential to broaden the accountability ecosystem within the EU's migration governance. Institutions such as the Court of Auditors and the European Ombudsman[15] play a crucial role in scrutinizing the performance and conduct of EU bodies. The Court of Auditors can assess whether funds are being used effectively and in accordance with EU objectives, while the Ombudsman investigates instances of maladministration and promotes transparency. The rise of AI in all aspects of decision-making, including migration, brings to the fore the urgency of doing so.[16]

National bodies, including parliaments, courts, and ombudsmen institutions, also have a role to play, particularly when EU policies are implemented at the domestic level. Civil society organizations and non-governmental organizations (NGOs) further contribute by monitoring practices on the ground, advocating for rights, and bringing attention to abuses or failures. But here again, some of the general limitations of access to courts severely restrict the opportunity for these arguments to be heard. This multi-layered approach to accountability is not only necessary but also reflective of the EU's unique governance structure. It recognizes that no single institution can provide comprehensive oversight and that accountability must be distributed across different levels and actors, including actors such as the Court of Auditors who 'follow the money' but who have not been traditionally perceived as being directly involved in ensuring the protection of human rights, respect for human dignity, equality, or rule of law values.

Ultimately, the EU must be judged not only by the number of policies it launches or the efficiency of its operations but by its adherence to the values enshrined in its founding Treaties. Article 2 of the TEU affirms the Union's commitment to respect for human dignity, freedom, democracy, equality, the rule of law, and human rights.

[15] European Ombudsman, 'Ombudsman criticises Commission failure to inform public how it assessed human rights risks in EU–Tunisia agreement' (22 October 2024) https://www.ombudsman.europa.eu/en/news-document/en/194322, accessed 9 June 2025.

[16] For exploration of AI, technology, and migration governance, see Deirdre Curtin and Tommaso Fia, 'Cracking AI Secrecy: (Beyond) EU Migration Law and Governance' (2026) European Law Open, early view, https://www.cambridge.org/core/journals/european-law-open/article/cracking-ai-secrecy-beyond-eu-migration-law-and-governance/0BDF7E96162E239A31321A000DD486F4, accessed 30 March 2026 and Chiara Graziani, 'Technosecuritization: Digital Technologies and the Securitization of EU Migration Law' (2026) 28(1) European Journal of Migration and Law 34–58

In practice, this means that even informal or operational activities must be evaluated against these standards. The externalization of border control measures must respect the rights of migrants and avoid practices such as pushbacks, which violate international law. The effectiveness of EU action should be measured not only in terms of deterrence or efficiency but also in terms of legality, transparency, and respect for fundamental rights and international law.

The EU's use of informal governance mechanisms is not inherently problematic and can, in fact, be a source of innovation and flexibility. However, the proliferation of policies that fail to meet their objectives, coupled with the limitations of traditional accountability mechanisms, underscores the need for a more robust and inclusive approach to oversight.

Most importantly, the EU must remain anchored in its Treaty-based values. These values provide the normative framework against which all EU action—formal or informal, successful or not—should be assessed. In doing so, the Union can ensure that its governance remains legitimate, effective, and true to its foundational principles. If it does not, then the purpose of the EU itself, and its narrative as a normative power distinct from the violent histories of many European states and founded on the principles of peaceful cooperation, is in jeopardy.

Index

For the benefit of digital users, indexed terms that span two pages (e.g., 52–53) may, on occasion, appear on only one of those pages.